Women in Myth

Bettina L. Knapp

State University
of
New York Press

Published by
State University of New York Press

© 1997 State University of New York

For information, address the State University of New York Press,
State University Plaza, Albany, NY 12246

Production by Bernadine Dawes • Marketing by Nancy Farrell

Library of Congress Cataloging-in-Publication Data

Knapp, Bettina Liebowitz, 1926–
 Women in myth / Bettina L. Knapp.
  p. cm.
 Includes bibliographical references and index.
 ISBN 0-7914-3163-0 (hardcover : alk. paper). — ISBN 0-7914-3164-9
(pbk. : alk. paper)
 1. Women—Mythology. 2. Women and religion. I. Title.
BL325.F4K53 1997
291.1'3'082—dc20   96-31315
                CIP

2 3 4 5 6 7 8 9 10

To my grandparents:

Fania de Pallant and

Joseph Gresser —

models of courage,

of kindness, and

of love of learning

CONTENTS

Acknowledgments • ix

Introduction • xi

1. Isis: *Harmony of Flesh/Spirit/Logos* • 1

2. Enuma Elish: *The Feminine Maligned* • 21

3. Deborah: *Judge/Prophet/Poet/Military Leader* • 45

4. Euripides' Iphigenia: *Marriage or Sacrificial Altar?* • 69

5. Herodias/Salome: *Mother/Daughter Identification* • 87

6. Virgil's Aeneid: *Let Us Sing of Arms and Women—Dido and Camilla* • 111

7. Japan's Sun Goddess: *The Divine Amaterasu* • 141

8. China's Fragmented Goddess Images • 169

9. The Ramayana: *Sita Sanctified* • 201

Conclusion • 239

Notes • 243

Bibliography • 249

Index • 261

ACKNOWLEDGMENTS

I would like to express my gratitude to the librarians at Hunter College—Norman Clarius and Suzanne Siegel. Their unstinting help in locating rare texts for me was invaluable.

INTRODUCTION

In mythical or in empirical experience, the status of women throughout the ages, with few exceptions, has not been an enviable one. Questions abound as to why women have generally been consigned—and still are in certain parts of the world—to an inferior role. Their activities circumscribed and their education virtually nonexistent, for most of human history, why were they virtually doomed, until recent times, to a life of servitude?

Women in Myth seeks to explore the role played by women in ancient societies through analysis of specific myths from nine different lands. How did august figures such as Isis, Tiamat, Dido, Camilla, Deborah, Iphigenia, Salome, Sita, Amaterasu, Nü-Kwa, Hsi Wang Mu, and others—some of whom were goddesses—fare in the world of fabulation? What were they like? What were their abilities and their outlooks? Were women the only ones capable of procreating? Or creating humankind? Were their views gender-oriented? Androgynous? Had they always been relegated to the home? Deprived of the most basic human rights? Excluded from the highest functions of religious worship? Had they done battle and led armies? Had they founded states? Ruled lands? How did they use or not use their minds? Did they experience identity crises? The probing of such questions allows the *reader* to establish parallels as well as dichotomies between the lives of ancient and of contemporary women. The reliving of specific episodes reported in the great myths may bring insight into certain relationships and perhaps shed light on events and their ramifications in today's home and workplace.

The *connections* between certain mythical protagonists, whose actions and voices are depicted and heard within the narrative structure of the epic poem or the religious text investigated in *Women in Myth*, are to be made by the individual reader. Only she or he knows what goddess, legendary figure, or power living within the writings presented is apt to arouse a psychological response. Only she or he knows—or may discover in the process of the analyses that follow—the reasons for such an occurrence. To study the deeper meanings of mythical material may help awaken readers to new perceptions and to different judgments about themselves, others, and life in general.

Myths may be understood as narrations of primordial experiences, sometimes personal but more often transcendental. They are invented sometimes for the sake of entertainment, but more often they reflect a living and burning reality that exists in the psyche and culture of a people. "Myths are original revelations of the preconscious psyche, involuntary statements about unconscious psychic happenings," C. G. Jung wrote. They are not simply allegories representative of the outer and inner lives of peoples, but *are* their psychic lives—"their living religion" (Jung and Kerényi 1969, 73). All religions are based on myths.

Every voluntary or involuntary mental construct in a myth, legend, phantasm, dream, visitation, hallucination, or apparition may be said to be *real*, or to be at least a fragment of something that occurred either consciously or unconsciously. Let us recall Herodotus's account of Artabanus's words to Xerxes after the latter had suffered a fearful dream:

> You imagine, my son, that your dream was sent by some god or other; but dreams do not come from God. I who am older than you by many years, will tell you what these visions are that float before our eyes in sleep: nearly always these drifting phantoms are the shadows of what we have been thinking about during the day; and during the days before your dream we were, you know, very much occupied with this campaign [leading the Persian army to Greece]. (Herodotus 1972, 451)

The reality factor in myths was also stressed by one of the founders of anthropology, Bronislaw Malinowski (1884–1942):

> Myth is thus a vital ingredient of human civilization; it is not an idle tale, but a hard-worked active force; it is not an intellectual explanation or an artistic imagery, but a pragmatic charter of primitive faith and moral wisdom. (Malinowski 1954, 100)

So, too, was the notion of the sacred emphasized by Mircea Eliade, whose writings focused on religion and mythology:

A myth always narrates something as having *really happened,* as an event that took place . . . —whether it deals with the creation of the World, or of the most insignificant animal or vegetable species, or of an institution. The very fact of *saying* what happened reveals *how* the thing in question was realized. . . . For the act of coming to be is, at the same time, the emergence of a reality and the disclosure of fundamental structures. When the cosmogonic myth tells us how the world was created, it is also revealing the emergence of that totality of the real which is the Cosmos, and its ontological laws: it shows in what sense the World *is.* Cosmogony is also ontophany, the plenary manifestation of Being. And since all myths participate in some sort in the cosmological type of myth—for every account of what came to pass in the holy era of the Beginning *(in illo tempore)* is but another variant of the archetypal history: how the world came to be—it follows that all mythology is ontophany. (Eliade 1960, 14)

And the ethnologist Claude Lévi-Strauss writes:

I believe that mythology, more than anything else, makes it possible to illustrate such objectified thought and to provide empirical proof of its reality. (1969, 11)

The ancients—and members of today's societies—experienced and/or understood myths according to their cultural canon: they answered a need, an inner pulsing, an aspiration, a necessity for a defensive mechanism, or a yearning, on both a personal and collective level.

A myth may be said to be both ectypal (inasmuch as it deals with the existential world) and archetypal (inasmuch as it deals with eternal experiences) (Kerényi 1963, xviii). Because *Women in Myth* may be used as a teaching text, I have included an ectypal analysis at the outset of each chapter to familiarize teacher and student with the history of the times and the place of women in the society that gave birth to the specific myth under scrutiny.

The similarities and dissimilarities among myths reveal the existence of what C. G. Jung called the collective unconscious, also referred to as the objective psyche. The collective, as distinguished from the personal, unconscious exists at the deepest level within the subliminal realm. It is "suprapersonal and non-individual" by nature and, as such, is "inaccessible to conscious awareness." According to Jung, the contents of the collective unconscious are made manifest in *archetypal images* experienced in universal motifs such as the *great mother,* the *spiritual father, transformation,* and the *Self* (Edinger n.d., 6ff.).

Archetypal images (from the Greek *archi*, beginning, and *typos*, stamp or original form in a series of variations) are implicit in dreams, visions, myths, legends, fairy tales, and cultural manifestations. The *archetype* has been compared to the instinct.

> An instinct is a pattern of behavior which is inborn and characteristic for a certain species. Instincts are discovered by observing the behavior patterns of individual organisms and, from this data, reaching the generalization that certain patterns of behavior are the common instinctual equipment of a given species. The instincts are the unknown motivating dynamisms that determine an animal's behavior on the biological level. An archetype is to the psyche what an instinct is to the body. The existence of archetypes is inferred by the same process as that by which we infer the existence of instincts. Just as instincts common to a species are postulated by observing the uniformities in biological behavior, so archetypes are inferred by observing the uniformities in psychic phenomena. Just as instincts are unknown motivating dynamisms of biological behavior, archetypes are unknown motivating dynamisms of the psyche. Archetypes are the psychic instincts of the human species. Although biological instincts and psychic archetypes have a very close connection, exactly what this connection is we do not know any more than we understand just how the mind and body are connected. (Ibid., 6)

Because archetypal images are endowed with libido (psychic energy), they arouse strong emotional reactions in the individual experiencing them; they frequently evoke the *numinosum*, a sense of the divine or transpersonal power that transcends the ego (center of consciousness). Images, symbols, and motifs will, therefore, be examined throughout *Women in Myth* in an attempt to better understand their meaning, their impact on the protagonists, and the light they shed on the cultures involved.

The *personal unconscious*, as distinguished from the collective unconscious, is derived from an individual's personal experience, and its contents are subject to awareness and may be integrated into the ego. The *ego* is that part of the psyche which "stands between the inner world and the outer world, and its task is to adapt to both" (ibid., 4). The *shadow*, those factors within the personality that the ego considers unacceptable and therefore represses, rejects, or projects, may be transformed into positive factors within the personality. If allowed to remain unconscious, however, shadow characteristics may lurk in dark and dangerous areas, and lead eventually to destructive and vicious behavioral patterns.

Jung's theory of the four functions (*thinking*, which is rational; *feeling*, which regulates values, especially in relationships; *sensation*, which promotes adaptation to reality; and *intuition*, the faculty that perceives via the unconscious) will also be explored in our probing of mythical women.

The notion of *individuation*, or the process of "psychic differentiation" that distinguishes each individual as unique and separate from the collective, is developed in terms of the personalities, actions, and events surrounding the lives of the mythical protagonists focused upon. The inner lives of these figures may then be experienced by the reader as living entities, provoking subjective and objective reflections as to her or his existential condition.

The archetypal approach to myth posited by Jung is unique in that it lifts readers out of their specific and perhaps isolated worlds, allowing them to expand their vision, to relate more easily to issues that may confront them, and to understand their own reality as part of an ongoing and cyclical reality. Awareness of the fact that people in past eras suffered from alienation, identity crises, and sexual crises—to mention but a few problems—and went through harrowing ordeals before they had a chance to know (or not to know) some semblance of fulfillment may help certain readers to face and understand their own gnawing feelings of aloneness and/or dread of disease and death.

Archetypal material impacts on today's women, writes Carol S. Rupprecht,

> because of our sense that it refers to something real in our experience—
> whether we describe that reality as a seemingly infinite variety of related
> forms, as images that are "unfathomable" and "necessary," as nodal points
> in an energy field that determine the flow of libido, or as the identifying
> mark of a transaction that is never fully resolved. The concept survives in
> these forms because it has real explanatory power. (Lauter and Rupprecht
> 1985, 13)

Because myths are relived on both ectypal and archetypal levels, they contain past, present, and future within their structure. Although generally time-related—they arose perhaps after a flood, a drought, an eclipse, an earthquake, a tidal wave, a war, an invasion, a plague, or some other cataclysmic incident or great sorrow or dissatisfaction—they also live outside of temporality. They are, therefore, not bound by the limits of eschatological, linear, or historical time. Myths flow in a cyclical, sacred, or eternal dimension; events narrated in them are perpetual. Myth time, then, is reversible.

The word *mythology* (stemming from *mythos*, "fable," and *logos*, "discourse" or "reason") signifies the relating of a fabulous event or events. In that the time factor in the myth transcends linear time, the events narrated are experienced in a kind of eternity; in that they recount a fable, they depict the *fabulous* lives of divinities, heroes, or supernatural beings. Dealing with gods and extraterrestrial figures, they are endowed with a religious quality. "Religious" here must be understood in the sense of *religio* (Latin, "linking back"). Readers who identify with certain elements of the myth are in effect sharing in the divine events. Thus integrated into the world of heroes and gods, such readers are removed from circumscribed, individual frames of reference and plunged into a collective experience. They, then, participate in the birth of a heroine/hero or a theophany.

Myths cannot, however, be understood merely on an intellectual or aesthetic level if they are to be experienced fully. Although they charm the ear with their poetry and the imagination is fired by the exploits recounted, myths also exist as *praxis* (action or practice). Descriptions of a heroine's or hero's theft, struggle, or pain endured to achieve a goal may elicit certain emotions and attitudes in the reader so that she or he identifies with the mythical individual, as well as with the society that infused life into the particular myth. The courage displayed by Isis or Deborah, for example, may arouse heroism in ourselves. In such cases, the myth answers a specific need in both the individual and the society. It plays a subtle role in the formulation of an ethos—aggressive, devouring, anguishing, loving, or otherwise. A myth may lend continuity to life and may bring order to disorder, making comprehensible that which goes beyond individual understanding and control.

Considered symbolically, myths may reveal a cultural transformation; they may also give purpose to lives considered absurd. For example, the death of Osiris and his "resurrection" by Isis gave the society that created the myth the feeling of *renovatio*—of the existence of a living God. Deborah, judge, poet, and warrior, is the prototype of the woman who not only is aware of her identity and her talents but who also acts on her own. Before her downfall, that part of the *Aeneid* which has been emphasized throughout the ages, Dido revealed her strength, adaptability, and creativity by her self-exile and acceptance of a new way of life in founding the city of Carthage.

Many cultures have myths that are adaptations of those of others. Many, therefore, have common markings: the New Year's celebration, for example, creates the illusion of beginning life anew through participation in yearly rituals. The myth of the "divine child" is also common to many cultures. Since the child—Christ for the Christians, Moses for the Jews, Dionysus-

Bacchus for the Greeks, Horus for the Egyptians, Buddha for the Buddhists—symbolizes futurity, child worship is optimistic. The human parent, or society, looks upon such a child as a deity or a messiah who will remedy all of humanity's ills. Singularly absent in this "divine child" myth is the divine infant girl; the female exists only as mother or procreating agent—as a vessel, in sum.

The popularity of certain myths at particular junctures in civilization explains the needs and deficiencies as well as the positive attributes of a given society. During periods of deep stress, one sees a resurgence of solar heroine/hero myths (Deborah, Dido, Camilla, Amaterasu) and of messianic myths (Moses, Buddha, Christ, Mohammed) from which women are notably excluded. Thus are brought into existence the unity, strength, direction, and vision that are lacking in a culture.

For the Greeks, myth functioned on one level as a form of thought *(logos),* but it also had a more comprehensive purpose, since analytical thinking and abstraction alone did not fulfill the needs of the populace, who required *thought* and *feeling* at the same time. The recounting of a myth in the theater at Epidaurus, for example, was an experience that made viewers tingle with energy. It offered them a form of language that was comprehensible on visceral and intellectual levels. By uniting "act and cult," spectators were encouraged to experience and see in new ways. The myth as an expression of heroic ideals inspired fresh attitudes and approaches to transcendental worlds.

The subtleties of societies and cultures can be better understood and explained via the ambiguities, discrepancies, contradictions, and paradoxes of the great myths. Attitudes toward humanity—women, in particular—toward nature, learning, logic, and love are projected in the mythical narratives of known or anonymous poets. The very word *projection* implies an act of thrusting or throwing forward—"a process whereby an unconscious quality or content of one's own is perceived and reacted to in an outer object" (Edinger 1978, 147–50). To project, then, is to assign to others characteristics we love or hate. While we believe the qualities we ascribe to an individual, to a group, clan, tribe, or culture belong to others, they are, in fact, our own. Because we are unaware of their existence within us, they may be said to live inchoate in our subliminal sphere. The myth at this stage, then—without conscious development—exists vibrantly and powerfully in the psyches and souls of the society to which it speaks.

The concrete happenings living unconsciously in the storyteller or writer—who begins to bring them toward the realm of consciousness by putting them into words—and in the believers who either worship the protagonists or are emotionally bound to them are conceptualized by philosophers, psychologists, historians, anthropologists, ethnologists, and others, whose explications may help clarify aspects of unredeemed, repressed, and latent contents. An understanding of the heavily charged psychic energy within a person's unconscious helps to direct it into positive and constructive channels and permits the individual to come to terms with her or his projections.

To this end, I have chosen the "ancient tradition of hermeneutics . . . Jung's . . . famous 'method of amplification'" to flesh out the ideas, tendencies, and meanings implicit in the myths under discussion. Readers may, then, interpret their messages on a personal basis, thus approaching the problematics of their own situation in a new light (Stein 1995, vii).

Frequently an individual (or a group) projecting onto a specific myth is so affectively bound by its imagery, symbology, and content that objective exploration is virtually impossible. In such cases, love or hate, admiration or denigration—such as the vilification of women—results in the individual (or collective) succumbing to the dominion of an autonomous unconscious force within the psyche. Thoughts and emotions are transformed into uncontrollable passions, divesting the ego of its independence.

The recognition of contents emerging from the unconscious is, therefore, of crucial importance for all, and especially for women, who have been victimized for so many centuries by man's projections. Particularly today, when society is changing so rapidly, a woman may have difficulty knowing what and who she is. Only by clarifying conditions and situations, and by distinguishing between subject and object, can one begin to face and deal with reality. The greater the light shed on subliminal spheres within the psyche, the better equipped we are to discriminate and understand the meaning and impact of those powers which inundate and blind us, robbing us of our psychological independence. Clarification is difficult and frequently painful. It may lead to *confrontation*, but this may encourage people to come to grips with their projections—those troublesome powers they project unknowingly onto others because they either long to possess such powers or because they are plagued and hurt by them. As Jung wrote:

> The unconscious, considered as the historical background of the human psyche, contains in concentrated form the entire succession of engrams (imprints) which from time immemorial have determined the psychic structure as it now exists. These engrams are nothing other than function-traces that typify, on the average, the most frequently and intensively used functions of the human psyche. They present themselves in the form of mythological motifs and images, appearing often in identical form and always

with striking similarity among all races; they can also be easily verified in the unconscious material of modern man. (Jung 1990, par. 281)

Jung's broad-spectrum perspective lends itself to a better assessment of humankind's behavioral patterns and of the extremes that have taken over some cultures at one time or another. As Annis Pratt writes:

Perhaps Jung's most important contribution to psychology is his recognition that a fully developed individual personality must transcend gender. His recognition of the destructive effects of excessive masculinity and femininity goes beyond the psychological to the social realm, where he attributes our century of total war to the disjunctions in the repressed personality. (Pratt 1981, 10)

Each time the reader broaches a myth—Egyptian, Sumerian, Greek, Roman, Hebrew, Christian, Hindu, Japanese, or Chinese—she or he penetrates a complex and infinitely rich realm peopled with signs, symbols, and images. To enter into a past time is to experience the myth in all of its newness and freshness, for it conveys the essence of things, both in the sensate and the ideational domains. Nature in all of its luminous beauty and monstrous ugliness comes to life in the myth. Animals, insects, minerals, vegetal matter, and humans relate and articulate their ideas and yearnings in rhythmic verbalizations and tonalities. In this archaic world, each element may interchange with another, thus modifying physical attributes and behavioral patterns. In some cases, such fluidity of form invites confusion or even chaos. Divisions separating the elements—even life and death—may also be obliterated, each entity taking on a *livingness* of its own. Forests chatter, oceans and seas make music, insects and birds speak a language of the spheres.

Great myths of the ancients may or may not hold us in their grip, may or may not work on the psyches and souls of contemporary readers, may or may not fulfill latent or unconscious needs in the reader, listener, or viewer. But aspects and thematics of ancient myths are timely today, and may answer our yearnings and help alleviate our terrors. The sorrows and joys of women faced by war or by unbridled hatreds, involved in love relationships or establishing identities of their own, are to be found in the myths under scrutiny in *Women in Myth*. In the works probed—all of which were written presumably by men—women will be seen as activators and catalysts, but also as victims of ignominious situations into which societies and religions forced them. Not even idealization enhanced the position of women: set apart—

that is, worshipped—they were denied intimate communication with others, particularly with the men who considered them so supernal. Adored, idolized, or iconicized, and thus dehumanized, they were transformed into cult objects—virtual *untouchables*.

Archetypal mothers, wives, daughters, and sisters, as humans and/or goddesses, abound in myths in all of their intricacies, enigmas, and labyrinthine behavioral patterns as they live out their credos. To explore their actions and reactions and to experience their worlds is to transcend the religious parochialism of those who are wont to look down on so-called archaic myths. Smugness and/or arrogance should cede to cognizance and feeling, for myths *experienced* openly and broad-mindedly may hold a small key to explain the behavioral problems that beset today's society.

In the opening chapter of *Women in Myth*—"Isis: Harmony of Flesh/Spirit/Logos"—we find that spirit, flesh, and logos are not antagonistic. Isis does not suffer any sense of humiliation or sinfulness with regard to the sexuality or the beauty and well-being of her body. Because spirit, flesh, and logos cohabit in harmony within her psyche, there is no need for flagellation, asceticism, or deprecation of the body. Equally significant is the fact that Isis in her power and wisdom is able to resurrect Osiris.

Chapter 2, "*Enuma Elish:* The Feminine Maligned," focuses on the Babylonian version of the Sumerian creation myth in which the events celebrated revolve around a power struggle between universal female and male principles. Tiamat, the Primordial Mother, although not depicted as a monstrous force at the outset of the myth, is referred to as a hideous dragon at its conclusion. After Marduk dismembers her, he becomes the hero/savior god.

The Deborah of chapter 3 looms unique among female biblical figures. Not only did she possess the compassion to comfort her people with wise words when they needed understanding but she had the courage and capacity to adjudicate as well. Her profound faith in the Covenant of God gave her direct communication with an infinite cosmic power that flooded her psyche with the energy she needed to function in a multifaceted capacity.

Chapter 4, "Euripides' *Iphigenia:* Marriage or Sacrificial Altar?" probes the question of marriage as sacrifice, as well as the notion of sacrifice in general. Why is sacrifice, human or animal, real or symbolic, so universal a practice in religions? How can one explain the common appeal of this ascetic, self-denying, self-violating, frequently masochistic tradition? Why is sacrifice considered an efficacious manner of washing away one's sins? Is the intent of the sacrificer strictly altruistic? or is she or he tainted with hubris?

One of the most popular myths in Western civilization, the Herodias/ Salome studied in chapter 5, is the product of the extremes of patriarchal tradition. Herodias and her daughter Salome are paradigms of the Great Mother archetype, in her avatar as castrator. Herodias is viewed by some as a sensual, destructive, heartless mother figure, while Salome, her embryonic psyche still embedded in the archaic folds of her subliminal spheres, is considered amoral. Not only is Salome divested of an identity in the original myth but her name is not even mentioned in the synoptic Gospels. How can one account for her mesmerizing power over the mind of medieval man? Why is she present in the writings of Flaubert, Huysmans, Mallarmé, Wilde; in the paintings of Titian, Ghirlandaio, Moreau, and many others; and in the music of Massenet and Richard Strauss?

In chapter 6 we explore the national epic of Augustan Rome. "Virgil's *Aeneid*: Let Us Sing of Arms and Women—Dido and Camilla" attempts to explain why society has not empathized with the beautiful, arresting, archetypal Dido, founder of Carthage and its queen. Positive in outlook, stately in bearing, kindly in manner, she was also a determined and decisive woman. Virgil, however, placed his emphasis not so much on her accomplishments as on her downfall. And what of the strong, wild, and fearless Camilla, the Amazon warrior, whose courage and authenticity earned her the admiration of young and old, male and female?

Chapter 7 deals with the Japanese sun goddess, Amaterasu. In most world religions the sun is associated with masculine power and the moon with feminine power, but the opposite is true in Japan. In chapter 7 we question the reasons why a highly repressive society with regard to women chose the female Amaterasu as its sun goddess. Not only did Amaterasu-worship become the supreme cult of the land, but this deity also became the progenitrix of the country's imperial dynasty—and, by extension, of the entire Japanese population!

In the Chinese pantheon grouped in chapter 8, we face fragmented goddess images. Because the Chinese tended, since earliest times, "to reject supernatural explanations of the universe," they humanized or euhemerized those elements that "had originally been myth into what came to be accepted as authentic history" (Bodde 1981, 79). With this in mind, we have chosen to highlight the functions of some of the principal goddesses, including Nü-Kua, creator of women and men and savior of humankind from cosmic catastrophe; Hsi Wang Mu, ruler of the Western Paradise and purveyor of the elixir of immortality; Ch'ang-O, the beautiful goddess of the moon; and Kuan Yin, goddess of compassion. The existence of such power-ful goddesses subtly indicates that what had possibly once been a quasi-ma-triarchal society was repressed in favor of a dominant patriarchate after the rise of phallocentric Confucianism.

The ninth and last chapter—"The *Ramayana*: Sita Sanctified"—is de-voted to a most extraordinary epic poem that is known and loved by the greater part of the Hindu population. Sita and Rama, the royal couple around whom the events are interwoven, although presented as flesh-and-blood human beings, are abstractions. They are ideals or prototypes that Hindus in their androcentric society were expected to emulate: Rama, the paradigm of the hero-king; Sita, the perfect wife, whose destiny was tragic, but whose self-abnegation, love, and loyalty to her husband glowed—and still do—in the minds of the readers of the *Ramayana*. My reading of this myth, how-ever, tells a completely different tale: it is not Rama but Sita who is the really heroic figure. It is she who courageously and knowingly takes a giant leap beyond the mortal realm of comprehension into the Absolute where the Multiple is One.

1 Isis:
Harmony of Flesh/Spirit/Logos

Isis, the Great Mother goddess of the Egyptians, was worshipped not only for her protective, healing, nutritive, loving, and compassionate qualities, but for her strength, initiative, independence, and rational approach to life and its vagaries. Neither passive nor all-accepting, she relied overtly on her own acumen to redress the ills and imbalances that confronted her. Consciously aware of and related to her own "center," Isis was in touch with the deepest folds of her psyche, the "source" of her instinctual sagacity. She was a woman in harmony with herself.

Mediatrix between peoples and between mortals and immortals, each of the ten thousand names awarded to Isis by her worshippers served to convey certain aspects of her multidimensional personality: "Mother of Heaven," "Queen of all Gods and Goddesses," "The Divine One," "The Light-Giver of Heaven," "Queen of Earth and Heaven," "Lady of Life," "Lady of Bread and Beer," "Lady of Joy and Abundance, "Lady of Love," "The All-Receiving," "The Female Ra," "The Female Horus." Multiple as well was the symbology used to denote Isis: among other representations she was given as the "Door," the "Coverer of the Sky," and the "Thet" (a knot or buckle, signifying life and blood). Her headdresses—a crown with a solar disk centered between a pair of horns, a small replica of a throne, a vulture, etc.—were generally associated with animals and insects, such as the cow, the scorpion, or the serpent, and each stood for a facet of her personality.

Isis's names, images, and associations, whether concrete or abstract, may be viewed as reflections of unconscious processes in the woman/deity and in the Egyptian people as well, who brought her into being and then transformed and enriched their concept of her during the course of the centuries.

1

Perhaps Isis's most unusual personality trait—for her time as for ours—was her combination of Spirit and Logos with earthiness and deep feeling, to which multitudes of worshippers responded and on to which they projected.

Ectypal Analysis

The analysis of Isis's spiritual and psychological evolution, which is my focus, is based on extracts from the *Egyptian Book of the Dead,* pyramid texts, coffin texts, hymns, and legends such as "The Conflict of Horus and Seth" and "The God and His Unknown Name of Power." Because of the lack of coherence and continuity in the extant versions of the Isis and Osiris myth, I have had recourse to the writings of authors such as Plutarch *(Isis and Osiris)* and Diodorus *(Library History).*

Within the framework of Egypt's complex metaphysics, Isis, Osiris, and their two sons, Horus the Elder and Horus the Younger, along with other immortals in the pantheon, were worshipped as individual deities. New gods were brought into being whenever a need arose among Egyptians to emphasize specific aspects of an original deity. The avatars of the original god or goddess not only were given personal names, individual physical frames, and psychological characteristics of their own but were intricately merged with one another as manifestations of the original transcendent deity.

Given the balance between spirit and matter in the society that created Isis, it is not surprising to learn that she functioned harmoniously both sexually and spiritually. No antagonism, no sense of humiliation, degradation, or sinfulness, disturbed the cohabitation of spirit and flesh. Modifications of Isis-worship in Egypt during the course of centuries—increasing emphasis on spirit while downgrading flesh—may be used as a barometer to measure the greater or lesser role played by women in that society.

Indeed, the high position women enjoyed in ancient Egypt's matrilinear society was unusual for their time and for ours as well. Until the end of the Middle Kingdom (1786 B.C.E.), women were equal with men before the law. Not only could they inherit property but they could dispose of it as they saw fit, going so far even as to disinherit their children. Since wealth descended through the female, the death of a wife saw the daughter, not the husband, become the beneficiary. It was not unusual, therefore, for a widowed Pharaoh to marry his own daughter, as had Ramses II in order to insure his power. If there were no male heirs in the ruling family, a woman could inherit the throne. Some women had ruled as queens and kings, such as Mer-Neith, Hatshepsut, Tiy, Nefertari, Nefertiti, and Cleopatra VII. Nor were religious functions denied to women: they occupied posts as priestesses, healers, magicians, and even scribes. Due to increasing Greek influence, the remarkably powerful role played by women in Egypt slowly began to erode. The downward course continued precipitously after Alexander the Great became Pharaoh in 332 B.C.E., and under the Ptolemies. Following Cleopatra's death, Egypt became a Roman province in which women were compelled to assume, with few exceptions, a subservient position.

Significant for our study of the role Isis played in Egyptian society was the authority accorded to religious centers. Divided into districts or cities (nomes), they vied for prominence, either through conquest, prestige, wealth, or by other means. Some of the districts commanding greater power were Heliopolis, Hermopolis, Memphis, and Thebes. Frequently a nome developed its own philosophical school, cosmogonic beliefs, and local deities, into which it merged those of less influential nomes.

According to the metaphysicians of Heliopolis (Sun City), the world emerged into light from dark primordial waters (Nun, a male power) when the god Atum (Totality, or Void) became manifest as a "primeval hillock." In a text dating from the Sixth Dynasty (twenty-fourth century B.C.E.), Atum, the life force, the container of all future or potential creation, "the Seed of Millions," effected the first scission when he "didst spit out what was Shu" (Air, Space, Light) and "didst sputter out what was Tefnut" (Moisture, World Order). By expelling or exhaling these cosmic elements from himself, he endowed everything with life. Spiritual in emphasis, but significant also on a feeling plane, the description continues: "Thou didst put thy arms about them as the arms of a *ka* was in them." The *ka*, an extremely complex power in Egyptian metaphysics, is defined as the vital force, essence, or spirit of a personality, and, symbolically, the source of the power that transmits "life power from gods to men" (Pritchard 1955, 1; Clark 1991, 231).

In another text in the *Book of the Dead* (Eighteenth to Twenty-first Dynasties, 1500–1000 B.C.E.), Atum evokes one of his avatars, transliterated as both Re or Ra, and splitting into masculine and feminine halves, fertilizes himself by himself.

> I am Atum when I was alone in Nun [waters of chaos, out of which life arose]; I am Re in his (first) appearances, when he began to rule that which he had made. . . .
> I am the great god who came into being by himself. . . .
> I am yesterday, while I know tomorrow. (Pritchard 1955, 4)

In keeping with the involutions of Egyptian metaphysics and the androgynous nature of their godhead, Atum's hand, instrumental in the creative act, was personified as woman (Atum's female aspect), became his consort, and was given the name of Iusas.

> Atum was creative in that he proceeded to masturbate with himself in Heliopolis; he put his penis in his hand that he might obtain the pleasure of emission thereby and there were born brother and sister—that is Shu and Tefnut. (Pyramid Utterance # 527, quoted in Clark 1991, 42)

When the first Pharaoh, Menes, united Upper and Lower Egypt (c. 3360 B.C.E.), Memphis (White Walls) became his imperial city. It was there that the ruler set down those patterns that government and religion would follow in future dynasties. The worship of the god Ptah as the First Principle, according to Memphis doctrine, was all-encompassing and lasted for three thousand years. Although a creator god who, like Atum, had brought forth the world from himself, Ptah did not have recourse to masturbation; more philosophical and abstract in concept, he gave birth to the cosmos nonanthropomorphically—through the mind ("heart," "tongue") or intelligence.

Ptah *thought* the elements of the universe with his *mind* (heart) and brought them into being by his commanding *speech* (tongue, word). Thus the Logos doctrine had been applied to Creation (see Genesis 1; John 1; Rig-Veda 1:164, 34).

> There came into being as the heart and there came into being as the tongue (something) in the form of Atum. The mighty Great One is Ptah, who transmitted [*life* to all gods] as well as (to) his *ka's*, through his heart by which Horus became Ptah, and through his tongue, by which Thoth became Ptah.
>
> (Thus) it happened that the heart and tongue gained control over [every] (other) member of the body, by teaching that he is in every body and in every mouth of all gods, all men, [all] cattle, all creeping things, and (everything) that lives, by thinking and commanding everything that he wishes.
>
> His Ennead (company of gods) is before him in (the form of) teeth and lips. That is (the equivalent of) the semen and hands of Atum. Whereas the Ennead of Atum came into being by his semen and his fingers, the Ennead (of Ptah), however, is the teeth and lips in this mouth, which pronounced the name of everything, from which Shu and Tefnut came forth and which was the fashioner of the Ennead. (Pritchard 1955, 5)

Acting through thought and conveying his will or command by prime-val speech, Ptah created Atum, and in so doing transmitted divine powers to Horus (the sun god) and to Thoth (the god of speech, wisdom, justice). As the unique creator of the world and of everything within it, Ptah was an active force throughout nature, absorbing the functions of other gods while also maintaining responsibility for ethical order.

Shu and Tefnut in turn gave birth to the sky goddess Nut, her body manifesting itself as arched over her consort, the earth god Geb, whose raised arms supported her. There followed the birth of four children—Isis/Osiris and Seth/Nephthys—the protagonists of Isis's existence in both mortal and divine spheres. Still in her mother's womb, Isis and Osiris fell in love and had intercourse, and from their union was born Horus the Elder. Upon Osiris's birth at Thebes, the following words emanated from the temple: "The Lord of all comes to light" (Hani 1976, 372).

Archetypal Analysis

Miraculous Birth and Cosmic Identification

Miracles were associated with Isis even before her birth. Her unification or marriage with Osiris in utero is an example of, and may be a partial explana-tion for, her remarkably integrated personality—a "one-in-herself" or *complete* individual.

Because of the love relationship she had experienced while still in her mother's womb, Isis was a woman connected to both masculine and femi-nine components of her psyche, each working independently and, at the same time, in harmony. Thus, it may be suggested that Isis enjoyed an an-drogynous personality. Accordingly, her psychological makeup differed from the norm: neither unconsciously nor consciously did she need to project those traits that she lacked onto a god-man—that is, onto a person with godlike authority—since these characteristics were operational within her. Unimpeded, she could draw sustenance from contents within her psyche whenever the need arose.

Nor, consequently, did Isis's comportment follow the centuries-old pat-terns devised by patriarchal societies. Strength, Logos, and self-assurance, associated with the male, as well as feeling, relatedness, and emotionality, associated with the female, were at work within her. In moments of danger or pain, for example, she had no difficulty in centering her thoughts and actions on the immediate problem, and extracting the resources necessary from within rather than relying on others. If she felt she needed further assistance, she called on the deity whose special gifts were related to the situation. Since deity, psychologically, is defined as the Self (total psyche), Isis was placing her faith in her own conscious and subliminal spheres for the solution of her problem.

Not only was the scope of her highly intuitive personality enriched by the connectedness she felt with all facets of her psyche, but the free-flowing knowledge thus placed at her disposal increased the breadth of her rational function. She was equipped, then, to assess external happenings, both concretely as well as qualitatively. As a thinking person, Isis showed equanimity, restraint, and integrity; on the emotional level, she was, as a woman who loved and was loved, able to offer warmth, compassion, and understanding.

That Isis was associated with the moon also reveals elements in her personality. The alternating rhythms, vibrations, and waves determined by the moon's force of radiation or "streams of power" impacted strongly on Isis's moods. During the first quarter or full moon, for example, she represented generative female power. During its waning phases (last quarter or new), she was disposed to sadness and tears, which, however, had positive overtones. As harbinger of dew, moisture, rain, and tides, Isis's woefulness, symbolically speaking, had a direct impact on the swelling of the Nile, crucial for the Egyptians' crops. Understandably, then, Isis became identified with fertility: "The moon, with her humid and generative light," Plutarch wrote, "is favorable to the propagation of animals and the growth of plants" (Harding 1971, 110).

Associated with the floodwaters of the Nile and with life and crops, Isis was replicated in paintings and statues as a birth and nursing goddess. She was visualized as nursing Horus, which permitted the drawing of a later parallel with the Virgin Mary. In another sculpture, she was seated on the back of a pig, her legs outstretched, awaiting the birth process to begin. That her body took the form of a triangle indicates a triad or trinity that, according to numerical symbology, suggests that the 1 *(mother)*, after coupling with the 1 *(father)*, thus forming 2, becomes 3 with manifestation *(child)*—or 1 again in that the parents exist within the offspring.

Osiris, associated for the most part with the waxing moon, became the giver of seed and was thus known as "the plant of life." Since grains like barley and other seeds sprout from beneath the black earth and are fecundated through Isis by the mud of the Nile, both deities were considered the life force in plants and the fertilizing agents in animals and humans. Osiris's power abates with the waning moon and the concomitant recession of the Nile waters. Grain dies, as does Osiris; it grows anew with his resurrection—in keeping with the moon's timed and timeless cyclicity.

As representatives of the telluric domain of swamps, rivers, and mud, Isis and Osiris together experienced the mysteries of insemination in the earth's womb and gestation in the depths of darkness—in secret.

The Earthly Sojourn

According to Plutarch and Diodorus, Isis and Osiris lived their early years on earth as monarchs of Egypt. Osiris, a divinely human and altruistic god-man, came to be known as his country's civilizing agent, teaching his people to raise crops and vines, to build cities and canals, to worship, and to devise a legal system. Out of love for humankind, he traveled to foreign lands to teach the less-fortunate classes notions of peace and productivity. During his absence, he left to Isis the government of the kingdom (Plutarch 1924, 56ff.).

Not only did Isis administer the land by adhering to its laws and customs; she also formulated new decrees, some aimed at chastising violent men for their misdeeds. In addition, she taught women the domestic arts of corn grinding, flax spinning, and bread making. In gratitude, the people offered her ears of corn—the first fruits of the harvest.

But Seth (god of evil, darkness, drought, perversity), brother of both Isis and her husband, became envious of Osiris's power and success as monarch. Moreover, he fell passionately in love with Isis. To satisfy his desires, he decided to usurp the throne of Egypt, achieve power, and take Isis for himself.

An irritating, obstructive, and negative power, Seth/Evil is an archetypal figure like other satanic powers in world religions. As a catalyst, he *is* the energy needed to pave the way for change in both the personal and collective domains. As a cosmic force, he is ever active and functions perpetually. Stepping into the lives of those who are content with their lot, he symbolizes the destroyer of the status quo, the disrupter of stasis. The test to which the integrity and wisdom of Isis and Osiris were subjected was a factor in their emotional and spiritual evolution, a kind of rite of passage. An instrument of permutation, Seth triggered the event to which the Pharaoh and his queen would respond as thinking individuals.

Planning to kill the twenty-eight-year-old Osiris upon his return to court, Seth gathered about him seventy-two conspirators, secretly ascertained his brother's measurements, and had a box/casket made to fit the size. During a banquet in honor of the monarch, on the seventeenth day of the month of Hathor (late September or early November), Seth informed the guests that the box would be awarded to the individual whose body fit into it. He persuaded Osiris to lie in the box in order to test the size; whereupon his cohorts quickly closed the cover and brought the "coffin" to the mouth of the Nile, where they set it afloat.

Upon hearing of the crime, Isis uttered lamentations that were heard throughout the land. In her grief she snipped a strand of her hair, then donned a mourning dress. Since hair (head) symbolizes one's spiritual qualities, the clipping of some strands indicates that one's vital forces will pass with the donor's properties and virtues to the receiver of the lock. Identified with the earth's tresses, or grass, hair is associated in agrarian societies like Egypt with vegetation and is thus a nurturing force. Isis's cutting of a strand of her hair may also be considered a premonitory image of Osiris's future dismemberment.

By donning a mourning dress, Isis was not only conveying her sorrow but also hiding her body within its folds—implying, psychologically, a need for introversion. Withdrawal from, or renunciation of, worldly affairs would help her come to terms with her anguish.

Isis set out on her quest for Osiris's casket. Wanderings imply both an external and inner trajectory and, in Isis's case, may be looked upon as an effort on her part to reposition *her* truth, *her* spiritual center, which had been so severely displaced by her husband's demise.[1] With the perseverance and patience so characteristic of her, Isis learned that the "coffin" had been washed ashore at Byblos (Phoenicia).

The Tree: A Desexualized Phallus

Osiris remained a fertility god—in death and in life—as attested to by Isis's discovery that his casket, lying inside the trunk of a tamarisk tree, had so stimulated nature's proliferation that the tree's bark had grown around and embraced the coffin. Moreover, the tree itself had reached such inordinate height that the king of the region had it felled to use as a supporting column of his palace (ibid., 63).

Why did a *tree*, referred to as the *djed* (stability, durability) pillar, play such a significant role in the Isis/Osiris myth? Associated in many religions with the Tree of Life or the world axis, trees, unlike other vegetation, represent duration. In contrast to inorganic stone, wood typifies organic living matter. In a semiotic humanization of the tree, outspread branches function as head and arms, and the phallic trunk as sacrum, or seat of virility. Osiris's *djed* pillar was unusual, however, in that the representation of the phallus was not in the trunk but on the top or head of the tree, implying a new understanding of a desexualized generative force. The phallus has now been awarded a "higher" and more spiritual or sublimated status. Fertilization, then, is no longer equated with lower extremities, but with the more abstract upper thinking regions (Neumann 1954, 230–33).

Horizontal and vertical symbolism also apply to the *djed* pillar: lying on the ground, it represented the physically dead or unconscious Osiris; raised, it stood for the "higher" or "head" phallus, the resurrected Lord, the "everlasting begetter." Death had divested Osiris of his telluric identification and had transformed him into an Uranian or sky entity: "I set up a ladder to Heaven among the gods," he said, "and I am a divine being among them" (ibid., 231–33). The merging of the lower phallic principle with the higher heart-soul *(ba)* permitted fusion with Osiris's *khu* (spiritual soul). His "tree birth" or resurrection into another sphere of being represented an ascension and a new spiritual orientation.[2]

A thinking and strong-willed woman, Isis immediately had recourse to her knowledge of magical art—in this case, totemism. Calling upon one of her avatars, the swallow, she assumed its attributes, suggesting a need on her part to sublimate, to hypostatize, and to induce other than rational powers.

Now a creature of the air, Isis could observe the telluric situation from above and from different vantage points, thereby distancing herself from the problem of how best to gain access to Osiris's coffin. The opening of a variety of perspectives allowed her consciousness to expand in a kind of rite of passage that tapped her intuitive, perceptive, and telepathic resources. By transcending human limitations—the prerogative of a goddess—she was able, psychologically speaking, to experience the divine within her, or the Self. From within, then, did she learn how to enact the sacred mystery that would reveal to her what course of action she must take.

Isis/swallow (soul/spirit) flew around the tree/pillar. She *saw* into matter; she saw her husband's body lying cradled within the coffin and the tree's protective bark; she drew on her powers of cognition to impose orderly thinking. First, she asked: how best could she approach the pillar? Her answer: by seeking out the queen of the land. Using her maternal qualities of warmth and tenderness to her advantage, she offered her services to the queen as nurse to her children. In this capacity, within a short time Isis felt close enough to the royal couple to reveal her secret and beg them to give her the pillar. Once her request had been granted, she removed the casket from within the tree/pillar and opened it. At the sight of Osiris's body, her grief was such that her threnodies filled the air.

Although she cognized Osiris's dead body and its physical alteration, she was not yet emotionally prepared to accept the loss of the "living phallus." She incanted her pain in the formula:

> Come to thy house, come to thy house, thou pillar! Come to thy house, beautiful bull, Lord of men, Beloved, Lord of women. (Ibid., 222)

In her role as Great Mother, she attempted to assuage her woe even while seeking to comfort Osiris during his difficult initiatory journey into the Duat (Underworld or the West).

> Thy mother has come to thee, that thou mayst not perish away the great modeler she is come, that thou mayst not perish away. She sets thy head in place for thee, she puts together thy limbs for thee; what she brings to thee is thy heart, is the body. (Ibid.)

The Dismemberment

Intent upon bringing Osiris's body, which had floated out of Egypt, back to her land, Isis again set sail. Although during the trip she opened the casket and embraced her dead husband passionately, once she reached land, she left his body hidden but unattended in a remote area. (The reasons for this are difficult to explain, because the various versions of the Osiris myth are so contradictory on this point.) During her absence, Seth, out on a hunting trip, happened upon the corpse. This time, in order to make certain that he had rid himself of his enemy, Seth cut Osiris into fourteen pieces, which he then scattered throughout Egypt.

Isis, returning and intuiting that this heinous deed had been perpetrated by the ignominious Seth, again filled the countryside with her cries. Weeping served as an outlet to help heal her mutilated psyche, but once her tears had abated, she set out once again on a long and arduous journey to gather the fragments of her dismembered husband. Wherever she found one, she had a temple, shrine, or tomb erected to honor the god-man. She found, however, only thirteen parts of Osiris's body. The fourteenth—the phallus—had been devoured by an oxyrhynchus fish.

The cult of the fish, a symbol of wisdom and fecundity, existed in dynastic times. These underwater creatures were venerated not only as animals per se but because they were also inhabitants of the abode of the living gods.

The fish is identified with subliminal pulsations and generative powers, and water with the collective unconscious. The phallus within the fish's stomach continued to assure the fertility of the nation. Whereas Osiris had formerly worked in the open, henceforth he would work in secret, thereby wielding far greater power than if he had been physically present. Religion, after all, thrives on mystery. Unwittingly, the scatterer of Osiris's body had increased his enemy's telluric stature. "Osiris, the grain" had been "threshed" by Seth, the purveyor of dissension and chaos (ibid., 223).

Seth's dismemberment of a once *whole* fertility god-king, his "breaking down of the living units" of Osiris's body, symbolizes a psychological fragmentation of this ruling archetypal power. Such sectioning is significant in that it mirrors a parallel change taking place in the Egyptian society. The mutilation of the archetype was symptomatic of the transformation of a social and religious ruling principle that no longer seemed to answer the needs of the people.

A redistribution of spiritual values had also been effected by Isis through the building of shrines to honor the places where the fragments of Osiris's body had been found. The strength of Osiris worship intensified throughout the land, the new cults serving to restructure and reevaluate the dominant religious ethos. As Osiris's role as lord of Duat increased, Ra's solar power diminished. Thus was the previous balance—or status quo—between Osiris and Ra destabilized.

Visitation and Resurrection

Still unable to accept the reality of her husband's physical demise, Isis used her own ingenuity to concretize her sexual fantasies: she made a wooden phallus to replicate the missing one. After listening to specific words pronounced by Thoth, the god of wisdom, moon god, and patron of the arts, speech, science, and hieroglyphics—or, psychologically, drawing upon her own subliminal sphere for enrichment—Isis embarked on the second step of her initiatory ritual.

She again transformed herself into a bird, or, according to some versions of the myth, a kite. No sooner had the metamorphosis been accomplished than Isis threw herself on her husband's dead body, kissing it passionately in what might be alluded to as a necrophilic act. Although erotic stimulation by corpses used to be considered a perversion limited to males only, further investigation has proven that the disorder exists in females as well.

As Isis in the form of a bird flew around the corpse, she beat her wings, sending the breath of life into Osiris. In so doing, she gained his resurrection.

> Isis by her love drew forth again the potency of the dead Osiris. Isis the magician avenged her brother. . . . She made to rise up the helpless members of him whose heart was at rest, she drew from him his essence, and made therefrom an heir. (Harding 1971, 185)

According to Plutarch and Diodorus, the Egyptians believed that Osiris was resurrected after his dismemberment. Whether he returned to life as a spirit or in physical form is unknown, although it is said that he had the power of speech and thought. Osiris, then, had not died. It was only his earthly form, which he had donned upon entering the domain of the living and had known during his rulership on earth, that had experienced death. For thousands of years the ancient Egyptians thrived on the notion of the god-man's immortality. Indeed, it was this concept to a great extent that had endowed them with their strength and power, while also inuring them to earthly disasters no matter the form they took.

The transcendental move from body to mind—or human form to bird/ spirit—had so deeply troubled Isis that her psychological disequilibrium triggered an archetypal vision which took the form of a *visitation*. Revealed to her was the future birth of Horus—the Redeemer, the hawk-headed god, whose right eye was to be the sun and the left, the moon.

The sacred eye of Atum and of Ra, one of the most complex symbols in Egyptian metaphysics, had been, according to certain nome beliefs, empowered by these deities to create the world. In Isis's visitation, the sacred eye functioned as an aspect of the great goddess herself. Psychologically, her inner sight allowed her access to certain contents of her collective unconscious, via their representations in archetypal visions, making her privy to happenings beyond the linear sphere, in a space-time continuum. It was then that she perceived Horus flying directly into the blackened sky of the Underworld, into and past Ra's domain, en route to fulfilling the destiny of his father, Osiris.

Because the *ka* (generative power) of the dead Osiris had been restored to him, Isis was able to conceive Horus while her husband continued his existence as spirit. Horus became the living and functioning son, the earthly counterpart of his father, while Osiris, who dwelled in the Duat, immobile or "at rest" for eternity, remained the abstract fertilizing or catalytic agent of all that was to be (Clark 1991, 108).

After Horus's birth, Atum spoke to him: "I salute you! May the followers of your father Osiris serve and worship you" (ibid., 215). And Isis knew the ecstasy of beatitude:

> Ah! O my son Horus, sit in this land of your father Osiris in this your name of "Falcon upon the ramparts of Him whose name is hidden. . . ."
>
> Isis approaches the "Retreated One" [Atum]. Horus is brought forward. Isis asks that he be admitted as a "distant one," among the guides of eternity.
>
> "Look at Horus, O Gods!" (Ibid., 216)

Other versions of the visitation, of Isis's resurrection of Osiris, and of Horus's conception also exist. One, for example, is based on reliefs and inscriptions garnishing the walls of the shrine of the god Sokar in the temple of King Seti I (1306–1290 B.C.E.) at Abydos. These indicate that Isis, after having discovered the body of Osiris, arrested its putrefaction and revived it. In one depiction, Osiris, held by Isis, was able to raise one arm to his head and with the other to grasp his phallus so as to arouse himself to orgasm. Isis then pressed herself onto the phallus, thus becoming impregnated (Hart 1990, 32–33).[3]

After Isis's miraculous resurrection of Osiris, the "giver of life from the beginning," he descended to the Duat, becoming not only its ruler as lord of Eternity but judge as well of the living. Because his worshippers looked upon his resurrection as a miracle offering them hope of eternal existence in Duat, he became known as the "ruler of the living." He was also a sacrificial agent who had taken upon himself "all that is hateful" or sinful in the world (ibid.), and Horus the Younger, the hawk god, God's "beloved son," was born to continue in his father's rulership (Clark 1991, 107).

Although Isis—mother, wife, sister—had been the instrument of resurrection and conception, it is surprising to learn that only Osiris, the Father (God), Horus (the Divine Son), and a third power, the *Ka-mutef* (Bull of his Mother), were consubstantial. The mystery was made manifest when Osiris changed into the Son and the Son into the Father, via the procreative or regenerative power of the *Ka-mutef*. Coming to his dead father Osiris, Horus embraced him: "By this embrace he transferred to him either his own Ka, or a portion of the power which dwelt in it; the embrace was, in fact, an act whereby something of the vital energy of the embracer was transferred to the embraced." Not only did the *Ka-mutef* (later identified with the Holy Ghost) generate the Son from the Father, but it mediated between the two as well, empowering the Son and heir to carry out his directives (Jung 1963a, par. 177).

The diminishing role that women would play in society for centuries to come is evidenced by the fact that neither Isis nor the Mary in Christianity was included in the Trinity. Although Isis appeared as the goddess Maat, one of her avatars, and was visible behind the seated Osiris in the Judgment Hall as one of the judges of the dead, she was, nevertheless, not on a par with Osiris, Horus, or the *Ka-mutef*. Despite the fact that Isis, like Mary, was a "vessel" from which flowed life and blood, both divine mothers were shunted aside in favor of the masculine principles of Osiris/Horus/*Ka-mutef* in the Egyptian pantheon, and Father/Son/Holy Ghost in Christianity (1963b, par. 261).[4]

Isis's resurrection of Osiris had both positive and negative connotations. The god of fertility's rebirth, paradoxically in a state of castration, triggered a compensatory reaction in Isis, who imagined and reproduced a wooden sexual device to replace the missing (impotent) phallus. Osiris's impotence had wrought a deep psychological change in the formerly sexually active Isis. She hypostatized, becoming a vessel for the containment of spirit. Thus, the once integrated earthly being, whose relationship with both tellurian and heavenly realms had been fluid and balanced, was transformed into a strictly celestial force. The long wooden member that had helped beget Horus may then be understood as a prefiguration of a new phase and direction in religion and in kingship. Emphasis would now be placed on the spiritual, while the physical would be downplayed.

Isis Decapitated

Fearing that Seth might try to harm the infant Horus, Thoth, god of wisdom, advised Isis to hide the baby in the papyrus marshes of the Nile delta. The child must be raised and trained, Thoth admonished, to fight his father's murderer. Isis remained ever-protective of her child: on one occasion, summoned by the gods, she found him lying on the ground "inert and helpless." Stretching out her arms to him in love and crying, "I will protect thee, I will protect thee, O my son Horus," she smelled the dying infant's breath—an approach used even today by some physicians to determine the nature and source of a disease. Concluding that Horus had been stung by a scorpion, she called upon Thoth, or, psychologically, the Self, to help her. In her remote and inaccessible depths, Isis gleaned Thoth's secret words spoken for her to hear. Thus was Horus magically and "mysteriously" restored to life.

In several tales, including "Horus and Seth" dating from the reign of Ramses V (Twentieth Dynasty, eleventh century B.C.E.), Evil was unflagging in his attempts to gain the Egyptian throne and relentless in concocting ways of destroying his young competitor. Since law and order were a highly sought goal in Egyptian society, those values existed in the divine Ennead, the supreme tribunal to which Horus appealed for help. Having accepted the case and in accordance with protocol, Thoth, "the intelligence of the gods," placed the "Holy Eye" (in this case, a symbol of authority) before Atum.

The court at times seemed to favor Horus's cause; at others, Seth's case was convincingly argued. The latter's proposal for hand-to-hand combat was, however, vetoed by Thoth, who considered it too disorderly a means of obtaining justice. Nor was a compromise offer made to Seth of two Syrian goddesses as wives deemed acceptable. Seth finally convinced the tribunal to allow the antagonists to resort to an ancient royal ritual: battling in the form of hippopotami.

Obliged to accept the council's decision, Isis was fearful ("Surely Seth will kill my son Horus?"), but in keeping with her behavioral pattern in moments of crisis, she activated her powerful thinking function. When, however, a mother interferes overtly in a child's battle, she may deprive the child of an opportunity to gain experience. Devising a weapon intended to save her son, she took a rope

> which she made into a cable. Then she took an ingot of metal and beat it into a harpoon-head. She tied the cable to it and threw it into the water where Seth and Horus had submerged. (Clark 1991, 204)

Isis assumed that she would be able to distinguish the two antagonists/hippopotami submerged in the water and would harpoon the enemy. But

> the bronze pierced the sacred body of her son Horus. Then Horus cried out loud: "Help, Mother Isis, my mother! Order your weapon to free itself from me!" (Ibid.)

Stunned when she realized she had wounded her son, Isis acted rapidly and incisively, having recourse this time to both reason and magic: she conjured the harpoon from Horus's body. Angered by her own failure to destroy Seth the first time, she hurled the weapon again, and this time made a direct hit (Hart 1990, 38).

Paralleling Horus's plea for compassion was Seth's appeal to Isis to release him from the harpoon. He astutely played on her sympathy, reminding her that they were, after all, brother and sister. Although aggressive and even ruthless in protecting her son, Isis was moved by Seth's words and conjured the harpoon from his body.

His mother had released not only his enemy but his father's murderer, and Horus's "face [became] fierce like that of a leopard." He snatched his knife and with it cut off his mother's head. (In some versions of the tale Horus cut off his mother's headdress.) Then he "took it in his arms and went up the mountain" (Lichtheim 1976, 219).

The hawk-headed Horus, the focus of his mother's existence, had suddenly felt displaced by the warmth of her response to her brother's plea. Nor, he rationalized, could he forgive her for the seeming affront to his father. Unable to cope with what he experienced as his mother's rejection of him, his reaction was drastic and instantaneous.

What was the symbolic meaning of Horus's decapitation of Isis? His act, unlike the castration of Osiris, had not been aimed against the feminine and maternal parts of her body; rather, he had shorn off her intelligence, spirituality, psyche, and mind. Was it a question only of jealousy because of his mother's interest in the well-being of her brother? Or had Horus unconsciously been so pressured by the increasing power of the patriarchate in Egypt that he could no longer accept a mother who thought for herself and acted according to her nature and principles?

Aware of the injustice of Horus's brutal act, the gods called for his punishment. Their search for him "up the mountain," however, proved futile. Seth succeeded in finding him, but kept his discovery a secret. When he came upon him, Horus was alone, dazed by his crime. This gave Seth the opportunity first to throw his opponent to the ground and then to gouge out his eyes, which he buried on the mountainside. Miraculously these eyes were transformed into two lotus flowers. Some time later, an avatar of Isis, Hathor (House of Horus) the cow goddess (milk-giver, and thus sustainer of life), came upon the blind and weeping Horus. A healer, Isis/Hathor restored his vision by rubbing his eyes with the milk of a gazelle, thus acting out the archetypal mother's compassion for her child, no matter how much pain he had inflicted on her.

Seth and Horus resumed their vicious struggle. On one occasion, Horus pulled out his enemy's testicles, while Seth his opponent's left eye. After more altercations, Thoth, the deity of order, convinced Seth and Horus to plead their case before the great council of the gods (Clark 1991, 109). In time, the conflict was settled. The Son of the Father was awarded the throne and the double crown of Upper and Lower Egypt.

Most impressive, however, was the manner in which the court handled Seth's feelings of humiliation. Although he finally withdrew his claim to the kingship, Seth was not expelled from the pantheon of gods. On the contrary, Ra took the opportunity to enlighten Egyptian worshippers with a profoundly mystical notion: "Let Seth, son of Nut, be given to me to dwell with me and be my son. And he shall thunder in the sky and be feared" (Lichtheim 1976, 222).

Evil, as the son of Ra, did not vanish, but remained a cosmic principle. Thus it is implicit in the notion of enlightenment and in the faculty of reason. Wherever the sun god appears, so, too, does the shadow force, underscoring the eternality and necessity of opposites in the manifest world—in the very life process. Never to be obliterated, antagonism plays its role, stirring deities and mortals to extend themselves beyond their limits in an effort to bring into being new ideas and fresh approaches to life.

Isis and the Power Principle

Fascinating, beautiful, and mothering, Isis was also articulate and logical. Her inquiring mind was never inactive. Indeed, there were times in her life when she, like Prometheus and Faust, yearned to acquire greater insight and power—not for herself exclusively, but to help the collective resolve its ills. Such is the thrust of the Egyptian legend, "The God and His Unknown Name of Power," written in the Nineteenth Dynasty (1350–1200 B.C.E.).

Seemingly bored with her lot on earth, Isis pondered ways of increasing her power. Might not she one day rule the earth? the stars? She is thus described by a patriarchally oriented scribe:

> Now Isis was a clever woman. Her heart was craftier than a million men; she was choicer than a million gods; she was more discerning than a million of the noble dead. There was nothing which she did not know in heaven and earth, like Re, who made the content of the earth. (Pritchard 1955, 12)

A passage in the famous *Litany of Re* (Ra) reads: "Thou [Re] art the bodies of Isis," suggesting that she, too, contains the sun's creative energy (Piankofff 1964, 19).

Isis was convinced that she could gain the power she sought by learning Ra's secret *name*. Egyptians believed that names stemmed from "primeval speech," that they originated when Atum created the Word, and that they contained the essence or godliness of a being (Pritchard 1955, 63). Within the name, then, there existed the blueprint (a kind of DNA) of a person's character, traits, and potential. Such a notion suggests an identity between *image* and *object*, as well as between "the name and the thing" (Piankoff 1964, 3). The divulgence of one's secret name (a person's reality and innermost feelings and thoughts) implies surrender of one's hiddenness. The recipient of the knowledge of one's secret name thus gains power over the revealer and is able to manipulate him or her. Ra, the sun god, although endowed with seventy-five names, possessed only one *hidden* name, which had to remain unknown in order for him to preserve his power.[5]

The Ra in our text, "The God and his Unknown Name of Power," is, however, no longer the young, vibrant, creative force he had once been. The former subduer of the monstrous serpent Apophis, the caster of spells, the hero of heroes, has grown old. The Ra who had once ruled on earth at the *beginning*, a kind of golden age known as the "First Time" when divinities and humans lived together in peace and harmony, now had the attributes and weaknesses of mortals: he is pictured as incontinent, dribbling from his mouth, and continuously calling up his glorious past in an attempt to prop up his powers.

Ra worship, as previously mentioned, was supreme in Egypt until the Fifth Dynasty, after which it began to decline as the cult of the god-man Osiris ascended. By the Sixth Dynasty, not only had the awe of Ra's worshippers diminished considerably, but his most remarkable attributes had now become identified with Osiris. The Ra–Osiris synthesis produced a *unio mystica* as a binomial God.

Did this change in religious emphasis suggest that the attributes usually identified with the sun—rational or conscious principles associated with the head—were weakening in favor of the more mysterious, darkened realm of Osiris's underworld/unconscious?

The now vulnerable Ra was subjected to humiliation as Isis applied her knowledge of magic to discover the once formidable god's secret name. Taking some of Ra's spittle that had fallen to the ground, she kneaded it for herself with her hand, together with the earth on which it was. She built it up into an august snake; she made it in the form of a sharp point. It did not stir alive before her, (but) she left it at the crossroads past which the great god used to go according to the desire of his heart throughout his Two Lands. (Pritchard 1955, 12)

No sooner did the god appear than he was bitten by the viper. As the poison slowly filtered into his bloodstream, his pain was so excoriating that he called on the children of the gods to cast their spells and apply their wisdom to cure him. Isis assured Ra that her utterances would succeed in expelling the poisons from his body. She spoke cunningly and with a perfect appreciation of her position of power:

What is it, what is it, my divine father? What—a snake *stabbed* weakness in thee? One of thy children lifted up his head against thee? Then I shall cast it down with effective magic. I shall make it retreat at the sight of thy rays. (Ibid., 13)

The holy one was, of course, delighted to benefit from Isis's curative skills. Not to be outwitted, she asked the "divine father" for his secret name. Again Ra enumerated his past achievements—including his creation of the "bull for the cow, so that sexual pleasures might come into being," and of "heaven and the mysteries of the two horizons, so that the souls of the gods might be placed therein"—but he refrained from revealing his secret name (ibid.). Undaunted, Isis persisted: "Thy name is not really among these which thou hast told me. If thou tellest it to me, the poison will come forth, for a person whose name is pronounced lives" (ibid.).

As astute dialogue continued its course, Ra grew increasingly weaker as the poison was absorbed into his blood. In agony, "[t]he great god divulged his name to Isis, the Great of Magic" (ibid.). Only now would she recite her spell to cure him who would otherwise have died.

Flow forth, scorpion poison! Come forth from Re, O Eye of Horus! Come forth from the burning god at my spell! It is I who acts; it is I who sends (the message). Come upon the ground, O mighty poison! Behold, the great god has divulged his name, and Re is living, the poison is dead...through the speech of Isis the Great, the Mistress of the gods, who knows Re (by) his own name. (Ibid., 14)

By maximizing her own thinking powers and thus depotentiating those of the god Ra, Isis enhanced the role and function of the feminine principle.

As a composite of intellect as well as the more subtle devices of ruse and cunning, she became integrated into Ra: "Thou [Re] art the bodies of Isis" (Piankoff 1964, 19).

Isis's drama—that of the inner life of woman and deity—is everywoman's. Within Isis, referred to as the Vase of Life, cohabit harmonious distillations of sun and darkness, head and body, spirit and matter. She was a woman who used reason *(logos)* to cope with the rigors of her earthly and divine experience. She drank deeply of love, sexuality, and spirituality. In some measure she may be considered the prototype of today's woman. Independent, self-reliant, and sensitive to her own needs as well as to those of others, Isis lived out the archetypal drama of a woman fulfilled!

It is no wonder that Plutarch included in his *De Iside et Osiride* the following inscription located at Saïs, one of the centers for the Isis mystery cult in ancient times. "I am all that has been and is and will be; and no mortal has ever lifted my mantle" (Plutarch 1924, 131).

2 *Enuma Elish:*
The Feminine Maligned

The Babylonian version (seventh century B.C.E.) of the original Sumerian Creation myth, *Enuma Elish* (When on high), written in the Akkadian Semitic language, takes readers into a cosmic sphere where contours fuse and non-linear time prevails. Far less sophisticated than the Egyptian creation myths, the dramatic unfoldings in *Enuma Elish* beginning in a climate of formlessness, or primordial chaos, revolve around a power struggle between universal female and male principles. Although Tiamat, the primordial mother, is not depicted as a monstrous force at the outset in the myth, she is maligned by mythologists, philosophers, critics, and literati after she assumes a confrontational position. Indeed, she is referred to as Tiamat the dragon, or Tiamat the sea monster. Marduk (Sun Child of the Gods), on the other hand, despite the bloodiness of his deeds, appears as the prototype of the handsome hero/savior, a *Deus Faber*. At the epic's conclusion, it is he who becomes the organizer and head of an ordered world; it is he who is instrumental in the creation of humankind.

Tiamat's transformation into a negative and destructive personality type during the course of the myth signals a sharp cultural and psychological shift from a quasi-matriarchal to patriarchal tendencies in Babylonia, preluding the extremes reached in the biblical Book of Revelation. Let us listen to the words of the angel who, coming down from supernal spheres, personifies the city of Babylon as woman:

> Come hither; I will shew unto thee that judgment of the great whore that sitteth upon many waters:
> With whom the kings of the earth have committed fornication, and the inhabitants of the earth have been made drunk with the wine of her fornication. . . .

21

. . . and I saw a woman sit upon a scarlet coloured beast, full of names of blasphemy, having seven heads and ten horns.

And the woman was arrayed in purple and scarlet colour, and decked with gold and precious stones and pearls, having a golden cup in her hand full of abominations and filthiness of her fornication:

And upon her forehead was a name written, MYSTERY, BABYLON THE GREAT, THE MOTHER OF HARLOTS AND ABOMINA-TIONS OF THE EARTH. (Rev. 17:1–5)[1]

Many creation myths focus on the mystery of the origin of the cosmos and, although they differ among themselves, have common denominators. These remarkable works invite readers to experience a return to the very foundation of the cosmos in a present time frame, to participate in events that both map out past cultural and religious routes as well as prophesy the future. Thus the contents of cosmogonic myths not only replicate the numinous experiences of the ancients but speak as well to contemporary societies. Their ramifications are vast, reflecting not only a particular cultural and religious tradition but also universal psychological needs in true-to-life situations. The realities portrayed are, therefore, subjective in part, depending on the author(s) of the myth and the tenor of the land that gave birth to it. Similarly, the events and personalities of great myths are frequently interpreted as reflections of the ideations and feelings within the critic's own field of consciousness. As eternal documents of the soul, creation myths, including *Enuma Elish*, dramatize the "preconscious processes" in bringing "human consciousness" to term (Franz 1972, 11).

The spellbinding *Enuma Elish* was recited aloud or sung in its entirety in Babylon on the evening of the fourth day of the New Year *akitu* (festival), which lasted from the first to the eleventh of Nisan or April, the month of the spring equinox (Oates 1986, 175). Included in the rituals were chanting, recitations of hymns, prayers, and processions. On the fifth day, the king entered the *temenos*, the most sacred of inner sanctuaries in the Esagila (the temple dedicated to Marduk). There, the priest divested the monarch of his royal insignia, after which he humiliated him by slapping his cheek and pulling his ears. The penitent then bent down before the statue of Marduk and confessed to the god that he had not sinned nor neglected his religious duties. Following an utterance by the priest and the return of the insignia to the king, he was again slapped on the cheek. If tears were visible in the monarch's eyes, it was interpreted as pleasing to Marduk. At dusk, a white bull was sacrificed. Although the concluding sections of the text have been lost, it may be inferred from other extant documents that, after the ritual purifications and prayers, the procession began, leading worshippers and the king to the Akitu, the "house outside the city." The monarch "took the hand of Marduk" and guided the deity along the "Processional Way" through the "Ishtar Gate" (ibid., 176; Kramer 1972, 77).

While permitting the king and the worshippers in general to experience the *numinosum*, the electrifying Babylonian cosmogonic myth also had deep psychological ramifications. The population was unconsciously reassured that the universe would not regress into formless chaos—to its "beginning," when Tiamat, the primordial mother, dominated the scene. By identifying the feminine with the universe's protoplasmic origins—that is, the lowest form of life—and by heaping blame on her for the "crimes" committed by Marduk and the pantheon of gods, society found the perfect scapegoat. At the conclusion of *Enuma Elish*, Marduk not only had been absolved of any criminal intent for the violence he had perpetrated to gain his end, but had been declared a savior for having regenerated society.

Ectypal Analysis

The Semitic-speaking Babylonians were heirs to the Sumerians, a non-Semitic and non-Indo-European people constituting the oldest known civilization in the Near East. The origin of these ancient peoples who settled in Mesopotamia (c. 4500 B.C.E.) still remains a mystery. Babylonia (Babylon), a generic name forged by archaeologists, refers to the Sumerians, Akkadians, Amorites, etc., who came to occupy ancient Sumer. The creators of both the city-state and a flourishing urban civilization, the Sumerians have been credited with the invention of the cylinder seal, writing (pictographs, ideographs, cuneiform), and an impressive body of literature in the form of myths, epics, hymns, and legends.

By the year 2334 B.C.E., Semitic peoples dominated northern Mesopotamia, and Semitic rulership began with the accession to the throne of Sargon the Great. He is said to have established his capital at Agade, near Kish or Babylon, whose exact locations are not known. Nor have Sargon's real name and antecedents been established by historians. It has been said that, like Moses, he had been placed in a basket and abandoned to the course of a river. Aside from his multiple administrative innovations, the creative and politically correct Sargon was also famous for the establishment at Ur of the office of high priestess of the moon god, a position lasting for five hundred years. According to legend he appointed his daughter, Enheduanna, the author of poetic hymns, to this position (Oates 1986, 38). Historians are more informed on questions of Sargon's military might: he took control of Akkad and Sumer en route to conquering nearly all of western Asia—victories that accounted in part for the slow erosion of Sumerian culture as well as its rebirth in somewhat modified form among the Amorites, a West Semitic people and founders of the First Babylonian Dynasty (1894–1595 B.C.E.).

Hammurabi (1792–1750 B.C.E.), ruler, lawgiver, and the creator of a centralized monarchy, made Babylon his capital. Jurisprudence, lexicography, grammar, mathematics, divination, medicine, and philosophy (religion) also developed under his aegis. Most memorable, however, was his code of 285 laws, engraved on a diorite cylinder, which decreed, inter alia, that he would cause justice and well-being to prevail in his kingdom. His goal would be met by annihilating the evildoers, forbidding the powerful and mighty from oppressing the weak.

Although the word *ziggurat* ("to be elevated high"; stepped tower; cosmic mountain) first appears during the reign of Hammurabi, it is thought that this structure dates back to the fourth millennium. The Sumerian literary works and religious art objects copied during the First Babylonian Dynasty fused severe Sumerian thought and sculptural forms with the tempered elegance and finesse of the Semitic peoples of the times. The integration of past and present gave birth to such incredible architectural, sculptural, literary, and engineering feats that the city of Babylon became the artistic and spiritual capital of the entire land (Saggs 1962, 47).

Although invasions by Hittites, Kassites, Mitanians, Assyrians, and other peoples reduced Babylonia to political somnolence, the energetic rule of Nebuchadnezzar I (1124–1103 B.C.E.) not only liberated his land from its enemies but renewed it culturally and aesthetically. Although Nebuchadnezzar II (604–562 B.C.E.) is portrayed as an evil despot in the Book of Daniel (he was responsible for the destruction of the Temple in Jerusalem and for forcing the Jews into captivity in Babylonia, 586–538 B.C.E.), he restored the grandeur that had been Babylon's. In keeping with plans set down by his father, the Chaldean ruler Nabopolassar (626–605 B.C.E.), he transformed Babylon into the unrivaled capital of the Near East.

It is believed that palm trees lined the banks of the Euphrates river, which ran through the commercial center of town, and that bridges and brick buildings, some probably faced with blue, yellow, and white enameled tiles adorned with animal figures in relief, added to this city's uniqueness. Herodotus mentions an immense stepped ziggurat seventy-five meters high, built in seven stages, with a base of a hundred square yards. A large stairway leading to a temple at the top of the ziggurat contained a shrine, a massive table of solid gold, and an ornate bed on which a different woman slept each night in wait for the god. About six hundred yards north of the ziggurat stood the king's palaces and their dwelling areas, with walls of yellow brick, white floors, reliefs, and an entrance guarded by huge basalt lions. Close by, supported by circular colonnades, stood one of the wonders of the ancient world: the Hanging Gardens of Babylon. Directly south of the *ziggurat*, the enormous Temple of Marduk (Esagila) had been erected. Visible within it, Herodotus wrote, was

> the great sitting figure of Marduk [Bel], all of gold on a golden throne, supported on a base of gold, with a golden table standing beside it. I was told by the Chaldaeans that to make all this more than 22 tons of gold were used. Outside the temple is a golden altar, and there is another, not of gold, but of great size . . . on the larger altar the Chaldaeans offer some two and a half tons of frankincense every year at the festival of Marduk [Bel]. (*Histories* 1.114)

Although the Babylonian Empire was conquered by Cyrus the Great in 539 B.C.E., the city of Babylon continued to live on as a religious center until the first century C.E., the cult of Marduk remaining powerfully engraved in the minds and hearts of many.

The most complete text of *Enuma Elish* was found in the seventh century B.C.E. at Nineveh, in the library of the Assyrian ruler Ashurbanipal. The oldest extant copy, however, dating from 1000 B.C.E., comes from clay tablets discovered in Ashur, an earlier Assyrian capital. Archaeologists and historians believe that the original work may have been composed as far back as 2000 B.C.E.; a more reasonable date, however, would be the twelfth century B.C.E. (Heidel 1951, 13).

That a melancholy poetic voice runs through *Enuma Elish* is not surprising, given the geographical landscape of southern Mesopotamia: a vast, flat, wind-blown alluvial plain with marshes, lagoons, and clumps of reeds. Fierce storms and north winds unleashed without warning enclosed the visible world in darkness and aroused fear in the hearts of the populations. Moods of anxiety, powerlessness, and rage are replicated in the affective psyches of *Enuma Elish*'s dramatis personae. Settling as well on the populations of southern Mesopotamia were feelings of isolation and vulnerability, inasmuch as they were forever prey to slaughter by nomadic tribes migrating from the mountainous regions of the east (Iran) and the north and northwest (Syria and

Turkey). Thus the cosmogony created by the Babylonians may be looked upon as a blueprint of their earthly preoccupations.

Archetypal Analysis

Like most great myths, *Enuma Elish* introduces readers to archetypal images experienced in a space-time continuum in a world that pursues its eternal course abstractly, unconsciously, and uninterruptedly—where anything and everything is possible.

Tiamat, the Primordial Matrix

The pantheon of gods in *Enuma Elish* includes, unlike the highly developed, conscious, thinking and feeling Isis, a primordial goddess, Tiamat, who, although referred to by later writers, critics, homileticists, and mythologists as a sea monster, serpent, or dragon, is none of these at the outset of the text. Historians, critics, and analysts, each stating the others' opinions, approach the world of myth from the patriarchal view that their cultures had inculcated for centuries and consider her a destructively negative figure from the outset. They fail to distinguish between her maternal and protective side, as manifested at the beginning of *Enuma Elish*, and her potential for evil in order to redress an injustice.

Endowed with eyes, ears, mouth, breasts, and womb, Tiamat *is*, paradoxically, the salt or bitter water of seas and oceans. Her husband, Apsu ("abyss," deep biosphere, bottomless pit), also unformed, *is* the sweet water of lakes, rivers, and springs. Sometimes, after melting snows swell the banks of the Tigris and Euphrates rivers, Apsu floods the flat lands of southern Mesopotamia. He devastates the crops but also nourishes them by depositing silt. By bringing on high tides, he helps to further trade, so crucial to a country that lacked natural resources.

Ambivalent in nature, water is both a positive power—a reservoir for potential creation—and a negative force, in its form of violent storms and great floods. That the nondescript Tiamat represents salt water and Apsu represents sweet water increases their ambiguity. When salt crystals are mixed with water, they lose their form or identity. Psychologically, this process may induce a condition of dissolution, of virtual egolessness, which permits an individual or society to exist and act unconsciously. As salt crystal, it protects against formlessness or psychological decay, but may also, in its extreme state, bring on a condition of aridity and rigidity.

Tiamat, the primordial matrix or original moist world in *Enuma Elish*, is an abstraction, an undefined potential force, viewed conceptually and metaphorically as water. Her husband, the unfathomable Apsu, or void, is equally fluid and enigmatic. Both primordial parents are, paradoxically, anthropomorphic and nonrepresentational; both live instinctually; both have been endowed with anthropoid psyches. As amoeboid substances, they veer from one extreme to another; they are either inert or, like volcanoes, suddenly erupting. Mummu, the son of Tiamat and Apsu, is also a watery, moist, vaporous divinity and is the third element in this original archetypal trinity of gods. A metaphor for the misty or cloudlike formations emanating from the bodies of his parents, he, too, remains unclear, unconscious, and undefined, sharing with his parents in a *participation mystique* or sharing an unconscious identity with the world at once subject and object, and unable as yet to separate or distinguish one from the other (Jung 1967, par. 66).

Tiamat, Apsu, and Mummu live in a floating, free, and pleasurable state of nonconsciousness. Only after future generations have come into being does the text of *Enuma Elish* define the protagonists in more detail, suggesting that a process of inner development is at work.

Primordial deities in many myths—of Greece, Japan, New Zealand, and Samoa, for example—are similarly depicted as vaguely liquid, cloudy, and contourless. Water cosmogonies are evident in religious traditions from time immemorial, such as Varuna, Prajapati, and Purusa in India; Anahita in Iran; Aphrodite in Greece; and Cybele in Phrygia (Eliade 1974b, 190, 193). Their singular importance is attributed by mythologists in part to the various powers that have been ascribed to water. A creative, curative, generative, restorative, and purifying force, it is empowered to rid individuals of past misdeeds ("I will pour upon you clean water and you shall be cleansed" [Ezek. 36:25]). It also promises eternal life ("of the doctrine of baptisms, and of laying on of hands, and of resurrection of the dead, and of eternal judgment" [Heb. 6:2]). Cults of springs and waters were popular in Neolithic, Roman, and Christian times and are still popular today (Eliade 1974b, 200).

Because of water's sustaining power, it was considered a *prima materia*: the source of life. Homer would declare the god Oceanus to be the originator of all things, even of the gods, and his wife, Tethys, the original mother. Thales, the Greek physicist and astronomer, believed the earth floated on water. And the Rig Veda states that "in the beginning. . . . all this was water"(10.129). Although undifferentiated, this rich flow contained within itself the germ or essences of possibilities.

Psychologically, water, as an inner ocean, a reservoir of archetypal images, and an infinite superpersonal sphere, has frequently been identified with the unconscious, both collective and individual. The *Enuma Elish* myth presents Tiamat as salt water and "she who gave birth to them all." This protoplasmic flowing entity may also be alluded to as a cosmic womb from which all was spawned and into which all returns.

Understandably, then, do the opening lines of *Enuma Elish* evoke an abstract, unidentifiable cosmic climate:

> When above the heaven had not (yet) been named,
> (And) below the earth had not (yet) been called by a name;
> (When) Apsu primeval, their begetter,
> Mummu (and) Tiamat, she who gave birth to them all,
> (Still) mingled their waters together,
> And no pasture land had been formed (and) not (even) a reed
>   marsh was to be seen;
> When none of the (other) gods had been brought into being,
> (When) they had not (yet) been called by (their) name(s, and
>   their) destinies had not (yet) been fixed,
> (At that time) were the gods created within them.
>
> (*E.E.* 1.1.18)[3]

Apsu and Tiamat, although undefined masses inhabiting a wet world, had the potential to create a universe. When they "mingled their waters together," the cosmogonic process began, with a sexual union of undefined opposites, as well as a cosmic fusion. Superior (celestial) atmospheric vapors and gases blended with lower waters (rivers, oceans); the bitter mixed with the sweet; the pure with the impure; and the creative with the arid. The sudden expending of energy resulted in the birth of Mummu and, later, an equally ambiguous brother-sister pair of gods—Lahmu and Lahamu (silt)—"within" the divine trinity.

In that Lahmu and Lahamu were endowed with names and thus with individual, albeit primitive, characteristics, they were removed from the world of unrealized abstractions. Even "before they [Lahmu and Lahamu] had grown up (and) become tall," they brought forth another brother-sister pair, Anshar and Kishar (the horizons separating sky and earth), progeny who "surpassed" their parents in height. After many years, a son, Anu, a sky god, was born: "the heir presumptive, the rival of his fathers" (*E.E.* 1.14.18). He begot Ea (the "all-wise"), an earth god endowed with wisdom, strength, and knowledge of magic, "who had no rival among the gods his brothers" (*E.E.* 1.20.18).

The physical and affective procreative exertions of Tiamat and Apsu left these watery gods exhausted, lethargic, and in a virtual stupor, yearning only for rest and inactivity. Although old age may have played a part in their search for slumber and repose, the desire for motionlessness and quiescence also suggests an abandonment of the life force. The yearning for an eternal Edenic realm precludes transformation or gestation, and thus is antithetical to both manifest and unmanifest worlds. Inaction leads to stagnation and therefore to a deteriorating climate within the pantheon of gods, paving the way for their eventual regression and dissolution.

Repose suggests a sinking back of libido (psychic energy) into its own depths, into the source from which it first emerged, perhaps indicating a preconscious warning of extreme introversion, which may endanger the bringing into existence of a new world or new life. Children, representatives of futurity, seek most naturally to participate actively in the world and wrench from it whatever exciting experiences they can.

The Generation Gap

The condition of inertia that Tiamat and Apsu sought to maintain ran counter to the ebullience of their descendents, who were, chemically speaking, "condensing," becoming less fluid and taking on concretion. Multiple aspects of their personalities, thought concepts, and functions were becoming increasingly distinct, and their youthful enthusiasm and energy more overt.

Understandably do immobile, peace-seeking, and slothful parents complain about their jovial progeny. The root of children's rambunctiousness lies not outside of themselves, but quite to the contrary is an expression of their need for extroverted action. Such a move out of the family compound, however, has its dangers: it may entice the inexperienced to grapple with situations for which they are yet unprepared. Their impatience, impulsiveness, and lack of worldly knowledge may lead unwittingly to confrontation. The rejection by the younger gods of their parents and grandparents sets the stage for the dramatic events in *Enuma Elish* (Jung 1969, par. 516). As the divine brothers gathered together in play,

> They disturbed Tiamat and assaulted (?) their keeper,
> Yea, they disturbed the inner parts of Tiamat,
> Moving (and) running about in the divine abode (?).

> Apsu could not diminish their clamor,
> And Tiamat was silent in regard to their [behavior].
> Yet, their doing was painful [to them].
> Their way was not good. . . .
>
> (*E.E.* 1.22.19)

Like many primordial sky divinities who, after their initial labors, neglect and finally become indifferent to the activities of their young, Tiamat and Apsu found their progeny's prancing to be a source of only annoyance and disturbance.

It is a truism that younger generations, historically, philosophically, and psychologically, have from time immemorial attempted overtly or covertly to overthrow the world of their aged parents. The fate of Tiamat and Apsu differs only little from that of such Greek divinities as Gaea and Uranus with regard to their offspring, Rhea and Cronus. Because Uranus refused to allow his children to be born, concealing them in the depths of the earth for fear they would overthrow him, his son Cronus castrated him with the sickle given him by his mother, Gaea. Once Cronus had made himself sovereign of the universe, he, too, feared dispossession. To allay his anguish, he swallowed all his children except Zeus, whom his sister-wife, Rhea, had hidden. Later, the adult Zeus forced his father to disgorge his children, after which the son reigned in his stead.

As cultures evolve, religious ideologies change: younger generations of gods take a downward path, away from the sacred to the profane. Eventually making their way down to earth, they become increasingly involved in terrestrial matters. The older and now less active gods continue to reside on high, becoming identified with changeless heavens, transcendence, and exaltation. A case in point is that of the Vedic deity Varuna. Once physically active, this celestial figure reached an age when the need for contemplation and indwelling became increasingly important to him. It was then that Varuna took on a remote and impersonal cast. Unlike Tiamat and Apsu, however, rather than regress into slumber, he resorted to magic and speculation, thereby activating the spiritual and the psychic. So did the Vedic atmospheric god Indra who, after killing the dragon Vritra and liberating the waters of life, eventually retired to an inaccessible region—the sacred Mount Meru. But the archaic Tiamat and Apsu, existing in an undifferentiated world, were not yet sufficiently developed to understand the meaning of alternate lifestyles (Eliade 1974b, 52).

Tiamat found the jostling movements of the divine children warring and/or playing their games in her belly not only emotionally draining but hurtful to her "inner parts." Rather than convey her feelings overtly, however, she interiorized them, refusing to punish her progeny; she hoped that in time reason would prevail and the shoving, pushing, and unsettling quarrels would subside. Her unwillingness to act aggressively to bring order to an evidently chaotic condition revealed either extreme understanding of the energetic needs of youth and/or a certain *passivity* or reticence on her part. In either case, it evidenced a strong protective maternal instinct—but also the beginning of her undoing. Lack of decisiveness led to increased dissatisfaction and disharmony in the cosmos. Pulsations and impulsions among the young, trying to unseat their immobile primordial parents, led to greater imbalance within the family.

Unlike the maternal and accepting/passive Tiamat, Apsu, after attempting unsuccessfully to calm the young gods, became angered by what he saw as their arrogance and bluster. How else could such a slothful figure interpret their cavorting? The affront to paternal authority had to be redressed. He whose libido was channeled almost exclusively inwardly, who clung ever more insistently to a nonconscious, peaceful, Edenic past, had reached an impasse. There could be no dialogue between Apsu and his descendents. Because he was aware of one of his shortcomings, namely his ineffective nature, he knew that he would have to rely on someone else for advice. Thus did he summon his "obedient" son Mummu, his vizier, to help quell the riotous underlings. That he also sought to discuss matters with Tiamat before undertaking any repressive measures indicated an open—fluid—relationship between the two. He spoke as follows:

> "Come, let us [go] to Tiamat!"
> They went and reposed before Tiamat;
> They took counsel about the matter concerning the gods, their
>   first-born.
> Apsu opened his mouth
> And said to Tiamat in a loud voice:
> "Their way has become painful to me,
> By day I cannot rest, by night I cannot sleep"
>
>   (E.E. 1.33.19)

After revealing his annoyance to Tiamat, Apsu's anger flares; he is prepared to sacrifice his descendents in order to gain peace:

I will destroy (them) and put an end to their way,
That silence be established, and then let us sleep!

(*E.E.* 1.39.19)

The impulses in the undeveloped anthropoid psyches of Tiamat and Apsu were unleashed without discernment. Apsu's explosive libido, involved exclusively with his own well-being, could spell only destruction. So obsessed was he with his role as genitor that the "begetter" demanded complete submission and obedience from his progeny. Tiamat, on the other hand, who loved her children in her own way, did not give primacy to her own needs. Despite the pain she endured during their violent playtime, she considered supreme her role as protector of her offspring. Apsu's rigidity in forbidding the status quo to be disrupted may have in part been due to an unconscious fear of parricide, of being dislodged or superseded in his position of authority by younger members of the pantheon of gods. His threats to destroy their children so as to avoid further disruption of the cosmos—his monomaniacal idea—touched a raw nerve in Tiamat, who reacted strongly to her husband's vociferations.

Other differences between Tiamat and Apsu now emerge. Not only is her attitude more pacific than her spouse's but her assessment of the situation reveals greater psychological insight than his. Although she understands the reasons for his one-sided decision, she is unwilling to participate in the killing of future generations. As her thinking capacity increases, she sees better into Apsu's regressive and punitive tendencies. As a protective life force, Tiamat, considered by so many mythologists, philosophers, and historians as a strictly evil and destructive force, reveals at this juncture the positive side of her personality: she is an archetypal mother approaching pacifically an untenable situation, attempting patiently to heal a breach between father and sons. Her efforts to spare her descendents from paternal wrath are, however, doomed to failure.

Mater Dolorosa

Terrorized by the thought that her offspring might be killed, Tiamat now unleashes clusters of unregenerate instincts into the atmosphere.

She was wroth and cried out to her husband;
She cried out and raged furiously, she alone.
She pondered the evil in her heart (and said):

"Why should we destroy that which we ourselves have
　　brought forth?
Their way is indeed very painful, but let us take it good-
　　naturedly!"

(E.E. 1.42.19)

Aggravating an already schismatic relationship between the parents,
Mummu bonds with his father. As catalyst, he stirs even further Apsu's criminal
intent, advising him to destroy the "disorderly way" of the young gods in order
to gain rest and sleep. Astute in matters of winning his father's favor, Mummu
used all his best ploys: he "sat on his knee, and kissed him" (E.E. 1.54.20).

The boisterous young gods were shocked when they heard of their
father's and brother's plans. Their humility and inexperience, however,
pointed them in the right direction: they took counsel with Ea, god of wisdom, patron of the arts—"of supreme understanding . . . skilful (and) wise"—
and of secret magical knowledge (E.E. 1.59.20). Ea did not rely exclusively
on his thinking principle in his adjudications. He called into play the "magical" art, or the "psychic" in contemporary terms. Ea's intuitive and perceptive proclivities (unconscious contents), "extending forward" into a space-
time continuum, enabled him to gain access to the plans of his enemies (Y.
Jacobi 1959, 61).

He made and established against it a magical circle for all.
He skilfully composed his overpowering, holy incantations.

(E.E. 1.60.20)

The psychic/magical world of spells, conjurations, charms, and sorcery
all worked together. Each suggested, psychologically, a "space connection"
or the existence of a bond between the inaccessible and the individual in
search of a solution. The magician played the role of go-between, interme-
diating among invisible transcendent powers and individuals in "sympathy"
with them. As possessor of superior wisdom that linked him to an atemporal
sphere ordered by its own organic laws, Ea was looked upon as a miracle
worker or medicine man in the pantheon of gods (Eliade 1974b, 10).

Ea's powers gave him access to the world of fantasy and allowed him to
experience irrational domains even while his wise approach to complex matters
permitted him to function in the world of contingencies, or the rational
sphere. Let us note in this regard that Babylonian medicine was practiced by
two types of doctors. The psychologically efficacious priest-doctors used

exorcism, incantations, and magic to conjure and combat the many evil spirits and demons peopling the universe and preying on humans and gods. The more scientifically inclined physicians prescribed natural medicines and salves made of chemical substances as well as of herbs and snake skin (Oates 1986, 176).

Ea belonged to the former category. The "magical circle" he drew was intended to ward off danger and prevent evil spirits from perpetrating their murderous acts. The drawing of circles—protective devices to enclose cities, palaces, sanctuaries, and temples—was routine in ancient times and in later centuries as well. Communities within the circle felt set apart from the "chaotic," unruly, external world. The inner space that they occupied represented safety, order, organization—a mystic center. During periods of crisis or epidemics, the inhabitants of towns would walk around their city wall in ritual processions, thereby reaffirming their need for the protective powers to surround them. Similar precautions are taken by doctors today who, like the exorcist, draw a circle of disinfectant around a wound, driving out tainted or contaminated matter and thus preventing the spread of infection.

Chantings of prayers, hymns, conjurations, and similar transformatory rituals stir within the celebrator a whole archaic heritage; they arouse energy from within the deepest layers of the psyche, and induce an apprehension of God. Ea's "overpowering, holy incantation" (*E.E.* 1.62.20) and the energy patterns designed by his verbal sonorities were experienced by his listeners as a *rite d'entrée*: an untying of elements that constricted and bound the other gods to their self-centered domain. The parapsychological, incantatory invocations allowed images of the collective unconscious to arise autonomously into consciousness, then constellate, paving the way for both an anabasis and a katabasis (Jung 1963b, pars. 493, 743).

Such mesmerizing devices also served to lull Apsu into deep slumber, permitting Ea to remove the primordial father's royal tiara and transfer rulership to himself. Demonstrating the hubris common to newcomers to power, Ea clothed himself in the treasure's radiance, identified with it, and became himself power and sovereignty. His new persona gave him the courage to slay Apsu and imprison—"bar . . . (the door) against"—Mummu (*E.E.* 1.70.20).

Ea, having rested after his victory over the enemy, built a large abode over the dead Apsu, who was now transformed into underground immobile waters. In this hidden biosphere or primeval abyss called Apsu[4] lay the foundations of a new cosmogony, a new center where spiritual matters would henceforth be regulated. Within the Apsu, Ea founded the "chamber of fates, the abode of destinies" (*E.E.* 1.79.21). There he and his wife, Damkina, lived in utmost "splendor." In time, Ea and Damkina "begot" Marduk, "the wisest of the gods." So handsome was his radiance and so "flashing the look of his eyes" that his father "rejoiced" and "beamed" in Marduk's presence. Because Ea "con[ferred upon him (?)] dou[ble] equality with the gods," he was exalted in every way, and even his body defied comprehension (*E.E.* 1.81–92.21).

> Four were his eyes, four were his ears.
> When his lips moved, fire blazed forth. . . .
> His members were gigantic, he was surpassing in height . . .
> Son of the sun-god, the sun-god of the go[ds]!
> He was clothed with the rays of ten gods, exceedingly power-
>   ful was he. . . .
>
> (*E.E.* 1.95.21)

Before becoming the highest of the pantheon of gods, the divine Marduk had to prove his courage and acumen.

To help him achieve his goal, his grandfather Anu, god of the skies, created four winds to act as irritants forcing the hero into action. The cosmic heavings caused by the invisible winds created disturbances in Tiamat's womb, arousing painful associations and perhaps the reenactment of her husband's slaying. Kingu, one of the older gods, visited Tiamat and convinced her to avenge her spouse's death. As the creator of "strife," Kingu used every psychological ploy, including the arousing of feelings of guilt, to win her over to the side of him and his cohorts (*E.E.* 5.23.47).

> They planned evil in their heart(s).
> They said to Tiamat, their mother:
> "When they slew Apsu, thy spouse,
> Thou didst not march at his side, but thou didst sit quietly["]
>
> (*E.E.* 1.110.22)

To cajole her into action, they spoke of retribution for the deaths of Apsu and Mummu, which left Tiamat isolated and solitary.

> Thou art [not a mother], restlessly thou runnest about.
> [. . . .] though dost not love us (anymore).
> [. . . .] our eyes are heavy.
>
> (*E.E.* 1.118.23)

Kingu was convincing. He lured the goddess into battle against the perpetrators of the patricide and fratricide. Tiamat, "who fashions all things" (*E.E.* 1.153.24), resorted to a most powerful type of warfare: she created eleven ghastly creatures—including "monster serpents," "ferocious dragons," a "great lion," a "scorpion-man," storm demons, a dragonfly, a bison, etc.—so terrifying that whoever would look upon them would surely die of fright (*E.E.* 1.133.23). The once maternal and protective Tiamat had now been transformed into Tiamat the Avenger.

The hideous forms or archetypal images rising full-blown from Tiamat's collective unconscious may be looked upon as compensatory devices designed to help her deal more effectively than earlier with the crises she faced. Personifications of rage and hatred that manifested themselves in the form of serpents, dragons, or scorpions may be looked upon as shadow forces representing the "dark, unlived side of her unconscious" (Franz 1974, 5). Like talismans, amulets, or antibodies, shadow forces frequently take shape in time of need to help the individual struggle against harm.

Since Tiamat conjured "ferocious dragons" to join her in battle against her enemies, let us consider the various meanings of this image, so frequently identified with the feminine. Dragons, believed to be in existence since the beginning of human development, are considered personifications of female power from which men have ever been trying to extricate themselves. Motifs of dragon-slayers are present in third-millennium Sumerian mythology, as well as in Greece (Heracles, Perseus), in the Judeo-Christian world (Leviathan, St. Michael, St. George, etc.), and in the Vedic religion (Indra's slaying of the serpent god Vritra) (Kramer 1972, 77–79). Fear of the dragon may also stem from this fantastic animal's inhabitation of three different spheres: the aquatic (as the maker of thunder and rain it is related to fertility or the lack of it); the terrestrial; and the chthonian. Living both on land and in caves, crevices, and underground, dragons and snakes sometimes are considered guardians of treasures, as, for example, the Golden Fleece, the golden apples of the Garden of the Hesperides, "The Pearl" in a Chinese T'ang tale, Siegfried's treasure, and so forth. Protectors endowed with enormous strength, the creatures were personified as benevolent (life-giving water, for example) or as malevolent killers and fire-spitting beasts.

Iconographically, snakes form circular images, as in the Gnostic symbol of the Ouroboros or curled-up snake biting its own tail. The image replicates a state of primordial unconsciousness, as well as eternality and rebirth (the Wheel of Samsara or Buddha's Wheel) (Y. Jacobi 1959, 146, 197).

Tiamat's other creations—the "great lion" that in battle opens its hungry maw to swallow its victims—may represent the dark subliminal spheres that engulf consciousness. The scorpion, although dangerous, was honored in Egypt in the form of the scorpion goddess Serqet. Because this venomous spider was considered sacred to Isis, it was believed that it never killed women, only men. Tiamat's creation of a "scorpion-man" lends it hermaphroditic traits. Living in darkness and having come to represent somber, anguishing, and mysterious realms, scorpions add still greater mystery to Tiamat's undifferentiated personality.

Having appointed Kingu to head her army of fantastic beasts, Tiamat also made him her spouse, exalting him beyond measure by fastening on his breast "the tablet of destinies" commanding all magical powers.

> "I have cast the spell for thee, I have made thee great in the
>   assembly of the gods.
> The dominion over all the gods I have given into thy hand.
> Mayest thou be highly exalted, thou, my unique spouse!"
>
> (*E.E.* 1.152.24)

Psychologically prepared now to battle her enemies, Tiamat was unaware that her plans had been discovered by the "wise" Ea, Marduk's father, whose approach to the situation leads the reader into the hierarchical world of the fathers—the domain in which the thinking function reigns supreme. Ea first consulted his own grandfather, Anshar, "the father of the gods," as to how he should proceed against the dangerous foe. Although pacific by nature and grieving at the thought of the slaughter to come, Anshar nevertheless encouraged Ea to fight the enemy (*E.E.* 2.92.28), enrolling his son, Marduk, in the battle. Marduk expressed surprise: "What man has brought battle against thee? . . . Tiamat, who is a woman, is coming against thee with arms!" (*E.E.* 2.111.29). Confident of his prowess, the hero assured his father that soon he would "trample upon the neck of Tiamat!" (*E.E.* 2.115.29). The strategist, Ea, seeking to protect his son from harm, advised him to use holy incantations to quiet Tiamat.

Marduk—young, energetic, and pulsating with gusto—was, like Prometheus and other religious innovators, filled with hubris. Like the Titan, Marduk was endowed with not only a fine thinking function but psychological acumen as well. Aware of the difficulty of restoring cosmic balance and understanding the extent of his bargaining position, Marduk made known his demands before agreeing to help the older generation. Fearlessly and arrogantly he demanded complete authority over all the gods: "May I through the utterance of my mouth determine the destinies, instead of you" (*E.E.* 2.127.29). Although Anshar acquiesced, the final decision to award him supreme authority over the universe rests with the assembly of divinities: they agreed to his sovereignty and to give him "kingship over everything." Following his investiture with the three royal insignias—scepter, throne, and royal robe—they encouraged him to "Go and cut off the life of Tiamat!" (*E.E.* 4.31.37).

A Virtual Quasi Matriarchy versus a Patriarchy

Having been told by the assembly of gods to assume command of the anti-Tiamat forces—"Command to destroy and to create" (*E.E.* 4.22.37)—Marduk equipped himself with bow, arrows, a quiver at his side, a club in his right hand, and "lightning [which] he set before him" (*E.E.* 4.39.38). Unlike his opponent, Tiamat, he was endowed with foresight: "He made a net [within which] to enclose Tiamat" (*E.E.* 4.41.38). His grandfather Anu, god of the skies, had given him four winds to carry the net, and Marduk added to his already significant weapons of destruction seven more furious winds of his own creation: the whirlwind, the cyclone, the hurricane, etc.

Wind is associated in Genesis with the deity's breath as it moved along the primordial waters; with the Arabic word *ruh*, signifying both wind and spirit; with the Holy Spirit's tongues of fire brought to the apostles by wind (Acts 2:4); and with Vayu, as cosmic breath and the Word (upanishad). Other examples abound in illustration of this force as an instrument of divinity. It activates, vivifies, chastises, and teaches. As the creator of winds, Marduk sought in effect to further the power of the male dominators who had appointed him their avenger. Artfully did he plan to use his "divine" powers to send storms and floods "To trouble Tiamat within" (*E.E.* 4.48.38).

> He mounted (his) irresistible, terrible storm chariot;
> He harnessed for it a team of four and yoked (them) to it,
> The Destructive, the Pitiless, the Trampler, the Flier.
> They were sharp of tooth, bearing poison;
> They knew how to destroy. . . .
>
> (*E.E.* 4.50.38)

Behold the epiphany! The blinding radiance encircling Marduk's head triggered a *mysterium tremendum* in the hearts of those gazing upon the god.

Invincible was he who drove his storm chariot against the "raging Tiamat" (*E.E.* 4.60.39), holding a talisman between his lips: a red herb designed to avert evil (*E.E.* 4.61.39).

His divine persona set Marduk apart from the other gods in the pantheon. The purveyor of special ritual secrets, he had become in body and soul the supreme spiritual leader of the collective. Let us note in this regard that societies, in need of divine figures to worship and to whom to submit, have regularly endowed them with miraculous and magical powers. "Society as a whole needs the magically effective figure" in order to compensate for and to survive the distress of earthly existence (Jung 1953, par. 237). So Marduk became *the* god for the Babylonians.

Tiamat's forces under the leadership of Kingu, dazzled and terrified at the sight of the epiphany, no longer could exercise their will and were thrown into disarray.

> Tiamat set up a roar (?) without turning her neck,
> Upholding with her li[ps] (her) meanness (?) (and) rebellion
> > (*E.E.* 4.71.30)

Enraged by the defeatism of her cohorts, Tiamat, the motivating power behind the army's maneuvers, turned to taunt and denigrate the divine Marduk. Angered by her disrespect, the mighty god raised the rain flood, then spoke to the progenitrix of all life:

> "[In arrogance (?)] thou art risen (and) hast highly exalted
>   thyself (?)
> [Thou hast caused] thy heart to plot the stirrings-up of conflict."
> > (*E.E.* 4.78.39)

A venomous and irrational onslaught against the Great Mother followed; Marduk accused her of usurping authority from Anu, of seeking evil, of inability to objectify and see into the causes of her rage and hurt. Tiamat, too, was irrational:

> She became like one in a frenzy (and) lost her reason.
> Tiamat cried out loud (and) furiously,
> To the (very) roots her two legs shook back and forth.
> She recites an incantation, repeatedly casting her spell.
> > (*E.E.* 4.88.40)

The hubristic Marduk, confident of his victory, summoned her: "Come forth (alone) and let us, me and thee, do single combat!" (*E.E.* 4.86.40). Then "Tiamat (and) Marduk, the wisest of the gods, advanced against one another" (*E.E.* 4.93.40) in mortal combat. Although frenzied and raging, Tiamat resorted to parapsychological spells to help her in battle, while Marduk, in addition to brute force and magical devices, relied on ruse and craft, setting his nets to entrap his prey.

Nets serve to ensnare enemies by immobilizing them in their webs. To be caught in a net indicates, psychologically, an inability to see clearly into a problem, to unravel the confusing tangles and snares in which one is entrapped (Ps. 116, 3; Matt. 13:48–49). In the *Tao Te Ching*, gods catch humans in their nets, attracting them toward higher purposes; and nets, although wide-meshed, are spread out in heaven to prevent escape. For the contemporary analyst, the process of a patient's search or anamnesis serves to bring *up* to consciousness the entanglements of repressed thoughts, memories, and/or feelings.

Having immobilized the primeval mother, Marduk unleashed the "evil wind" in her face. Wind, identified with divine spirit, as has been seen, was death-dealing to Tiamat. Her dragons, serpents, scorpion-man, and lions were ineffective against Marduk's weapon:

> When Tiamat opened her mouth to devour him,
> He drove in the evil wind, in order that (she should) not (be able) to close her lips.
> The raging winds filled her belly;
> Her belly became distended, and she opened wide her mouth.
> He shot off an arrow, and it tore her interior;
> It cut through her inward parts, it split (her) heart.
> When he had subdued her, he destroyed her life;
> He cast down her carcass (and) stood upon it.
>
> (*E.E.* 4.97.40)

Marduk cast Tiamat's helpers into prison, severing their connection at least temporarily with the primordial mother. Tiamat as a power principle was transformed, relegated to her most primitive form: the *prima materia* from which all life spawned. Marduk took the Tablet of Destinies ensuring undisputed power, after which he bound and killed Kingu. His victory assured Marduk—and the culture that divinized him—that the ego–consciousness had been delivered from the fatal maw of the unconscious, identified in patriarchal societies with the negative mother (Jung 1956, par. 548).

The lord trod upon the hinder part of Tiamat,
And with his unsparing club he split (her) skull.
He cut the arteries of her blood.

(*E.E.* 4.129.42)

And the "fathers" in all of their divine glory rejoiced, sent greetings and gifts to their "merciful" lord "in whose power it is to give life" (*E.E.* 7.30.55). Contemplating the body he had just killed, Marduk in his infinite wisdom "split her open like a mussel (?) into two (parts)" (*E.E.* 4.137.42), and from one half of what he might have unconsciously considered a fetus he created the sky, and from the other, the earth, establishing the triad Anu, Enlil (Lord of Wind), and Ea in their new governing posts.

Whereas creation, in Judaism, Christianity, and Islam, is ex nihilo or from a "primordial substance fashioned by God," the bringing of the world into ordered existence in Hindu and Chinese beliefs is by hierogamy and blood sacrifice—"immolation or self-immolation" (Eliade 1971, 31). The ritual dismemberment of Tiamat, associated with the notion of dividing the once unified *chaos*, preludes the rule of order in the cosmos, each section of the universe having its own reigning deity. The separation of the *whole*, psychologically speaking, fosters ideational differences that may lead to either harmony or conflict, but in any case to a sharpening and refining of the thinking process. The original *massa confusa* having been brought to a higher plane, *logos*, reflection, and discussion may take precedence over instinctual patterns of behavior.

The defeated rebel gods, commanded to do the work of the victorious deities who wished to free themselves of their arduous labors, were so dissatisfied with their lot that they pleaded with Marduk to be released from such burdensome toil. He agreed. To express their gratitude to Marduk, the formerly rebellious gods now released from their servile tasks built the city of Babylon and the temple of Esagila—an *imago mundi*—where their lord was to be worshipped forever and ever. A banquet was then enjoyed by all, after which the gods recited the fifty names of Marduk, bestowing on him forever supreme power and authority.

After consultation with Ea, and in keeping with Marduk's divine ingenuity, the new ruling divinities declared Kingu responsible for the outbreak of "the strife," inasmuch as he had encouraged Tiamat to rebel against the gods. He would be punished for his crime:

They bound him and held him before Ea;
Punishment they inflicted upon him by cutting (the arteries of)

> his blood.
> With his blood they created mankind.
>
> (*E.E.* 6.31.47)

Thus another immolation was the price paid for both the creation of humankind and for a lawful, organized, and systematized world. Humans, born from the blood of discord, had been marked from the very outset of their earthly existence with original sin. Upon the creation of man, Marduk ordered mortals to assume the functions formerly assigned to the rebellious gods—to serve and feed the gods.

That Marduk had succeeded in reorganizing the universe, as well as investing the hierarchy of gods with individual chores, suggests the birth of a new world or cosmogony. It discloses as well the slow and painful route taken by the evolving ego-consciousness of a culture to develop out of its original state of *participation mystique*. In the process, subject and object were differentiated, requiring of the Babylonians a "readjustment to reality" or the formulation of a different modus vivendi.

When Marduk took a hierodule, Sarpanit, to bed with him, he replaced the primeval Tiamat with a new ideal—a more fragile and delicate, but equally ephemeral lunar figure. Babylonian kings thereafter followed suit in a divine hierogamy, thereby revealing a different, perhaps more secure, patriarchal consciousness (Soulié 1976, 85).

The city of Babylon, whose history went back to divine origins—Tiamat and Apsu—endowed its "sacred" space not only with authority but with ancestral souls as well. The population was now able to trace its heritage back to its roots, unlike other peoples who had been cut off from their archaic past during the diasporas. The Babylonians can be compared to "the developing embryo [that] recapitulates, in a sense, [the] phylogenetic history . . . the lesson of earlier humanity." As Jung wrote:

> Knowledge of the universal origins builds the bridge between the lost and abandoned world of the past and the still largely inconceivable world of the future. How should we lay hold of the future, how should we assimilate it, unless we are in possession of the human experience which the past has bequeathed to us? Dispossessed of this, we are without root and without perspective, defenceless dupes of whatever novelties the future may bring. (Quoted in Franz 1972, 203)

The archetypal Tiamat remained *prima materia*, a nurturing but passive mother figure who was unable to evolve and to grow in *understanding*. Unlike Isis, she remained the primitive she had always been: a *giant womb*, that is, potential. Like Isis, she suffered excoriating anxiety. The Egyptian deity, however, knew how to handle herself under duress; Tiamat, motivated by an anthropoid psyche, did not.

Nevertheless, Tiamat is an eternal type, her approach to life paralleling that of many contemporary mothers. She may be recalled as a mother who suffered through the ordeals of the generation gap; a mother who put her children's well-being before her own; a mother who confronted her husband in order to protect her children against his wrath, cunning, and propensity for murder. Because her understanding of life and people remained embryonic, rage and brute force rather than wisdom superseded all else. Her destruction/ transformation and *displacement* were, therefore, inevitable, as was the emergence and dominion of a new patriarchal order that exists to this day.

3 Deborah:
Judge/Prophet/Poet/Military Leader

Deborah, featured in the Book of Judges (4, 5), looms unique among female biblical figures. Not only did she possess compassion, wisdom, and the courage and capacity to adjudicate, but her profound faith in the covenant with God put her in direct communication with the infinite cosmic power. During moments of transcendence she was endowed with prophetic gifts and became God's spokesperson.

The Book of Judges narrates in highly dramatic and lyrical terms the fearsome and joyous events experienced by the Israelites from the death of their military leader, Joshua, to the rise of the prophet Samuel. Let us recall that the Hebrews led by Moses had spent forty years in the desert following their Exodus from Egypt. Shortly before Moses' demise, he appointed Joshua chief of the twelve Israelite tribes. Organizing and directing the conquest of the Promised Land (Canaan, 1180–1100 B.C.E.), Joshua, knowledgeable in statecraft as well as in military matters, remained the leader of his people and determined to a great extent their fate for the next twenty-eight years.

Recounted as well in the Book of Judges were the dangers and oppressive measures suffered by the Israelites at the hands of the Canaanites. Their settlements were repeatedly attacked; their population was scattered and frequently decimated; their caravaners were prevented from trading; and whenever they could leave their communities with their merchandise, the unprotected villagers suffered incursions, ravages, and conflagrations (Pfeiffer 1948, 325).

God's voice commanded Deborah, who understood the severity of her people's plight, to call on Barak ("lightning"), the military leader of the Israelites, and order him to counter the Canaanite assaults and raids. Deborah was aware that passivity and nonresistance would only serve to aggravate the Israelites' precarious situation. Heeding God's words, she called on Barak, the son of Abinoam from Kedesh-Naphtali in the north, and admonished him to form a coalition of Israelite tribes to challenge the foe. Her task was analogous to that of Joan of Arc, who attempted to rally French troops to expel the English from her land during the Hundred Years' War. Fearful of his enemy's superior armaments, manpower, and military might, Barak refused to engage Sisera, the Canaanite army leader, unless Deborah accompanied him to the field. Although she acquiesced, she warned him of the humiliation he might suffer by relying on a "woman's" presence and skill in military matters. The glory of victory, she intimated, would not be his alone, but would have to be shared. As prophesied, the war was won by the Israelites thanks to Barak's fighting expertise and Deborah's presence as strategist and guiding image.

That Deborah succeeded in awakening her people was, to be sure, quite remarkable. What was truly amazing, however, was the acumen and intuition she displayed as military strategist. Her intelligence in matters of war proved to be infallible, allowing her to operate successfully in a heretofore exclusively male field. Again, she may be compared to Joan of Arc in that both women, it was believed, were saviors in their own right—instruments through which the Deity worked.

Deborah was an independent spirit. Although allegedly "the wife of Lappidoth" ("Flames," because he carried candles to the sanctuary), no husband nor father could dissuade her from the mission she had set for herself. Incomparable were the strength of her commitment to God and her people and her independence of thought and action in worldly affairs. Reason and perception, as well as a sense of her own worth, worked together in transforming what might otherwise have been merely an ordinary woman into a "deliverer judge" (Bal 1988, 37).

Many questions have arisen over the centuries about whether or not Deborah was a historical figure as claimed in the Bible and whether she had authored the famous lyrical poem, "The Song of Deborah."[1] Although mystery surrounds this unique woman, and probably always will, we are here concerned with Deborah only as she appears in the Bible: the *real/mythical* figure. Since myths and legends are the bases of world religions, and Deborah emerges prominently and in all of her numinosity in the Book of Judges, our analysis will focus only on her role as military advisor, judge, prophet, poet, and creative spirit.

Ectypal Analysis

The conquest of the Promised Land by the Israelites may be viewed as a rite of passage from the nomadism or pastoral organization of a desert people to the founding of sedentary communities and an agricultural economy.

The Bible tells us that once the Israelites had reached the Holy Land, Joshua led them across the Jordan river to victory at the heavily fortified city of Jericho (Moon City). After seven priests sounded "seven trumpets of rams' horns" and "the people shouted with a great shout," Jericho's thick double protective walls miraculously crumbled—a paradigm of divine intervention (Josh. 6:8, 20).[2]

Despite Joshua's miraculous military successes, the Canaanites' continued harassment and the lack of unity among the Israelite tribal communities fostered dangerously unstable conditions. No central power had been constituted in order to give cohesion to what was dispersed: "In those days there was no king in Israel; every man did what was right in his own eyes" (Judg. 21:25). Close contact among the various tribes was rare, save perhaps among the southern groups around Judah or those in the hill-country of Ephraim, Deborah's native area (Judg. 4, 5).

The Book of Judges also recounts changes in the alternating religious patterns of the Israelites. Periods of apostasy, when some of the population yielded to Canaanite fertility worship, were followed by intervals of punishment meted out to them by God. Divine punishment usually took the form of oppression of the Israelites by foreign tribes, after which the people, returning to his worship, were delivered from their foe (but only until they again reverted to idolatry).

Archaeologists have found many clay representations and figurines of Canaanite deities in Israel, including those of the motherly goddess Asherah, "Lady Asherah of the Sea," the chief female goddess in the pantheon, and of her husband, El, who lived in heaven. Asherah was the progenitrix of seventy gods, among them Baal ("Lord," also called Hadd, god of thunder) and his brother Mot. She also begot the fearsome Anath, "Lady of Heaven, Mistress of the Gods," goddess of war and love, and Ashtoreth (Astarte) "Queen of Heaven," whose identities were frequently confused (Patai 1967, 29–34, 61). It has been suggested that a resemblance exists between the biblical Deborah and the Canaanite Anath, "Baal's zealous and devoted [woman] warrior," and that Astarte may be identified with Jael, the second important "savior" woman in the Book of Judges (Taylor 1982, 99).

The many effigies of nude women unearthed in Israel reflects the Canaanites' veneration for the feminine principle as the guiding power of life and their customs of sacred prostitution and sexually oriented fertility rites. That some of these cult objects were supposedly used ritually by segments of the Israelite population, despite repeated warnings not to do so, might be an indication of their belief that prayer before such figurines both induces fertility and facilitates childbirth (Patai 1967, 29–34).

Antipodal to the Canaanites matriarchal, polytheistic "idol" worship was the Israelites' reverence of a patriarchal abstract God, Yahweh. Let us note that prior to the Babylonian captivity (587 B.C.E.), Judaism was less abstract and less rigidly patriarchal in concept. The Hebrew sages, after having been forcibly exiled from their land, concluded that the best way to protect their people against the growing influence of the matriarchal, "lustful" Canaanite pantheon was to go to the other extreme by establishing a spiritually oriented patriarchate. Before the sixth century, women took part in the religious affairs of their people, attended public assemblies, and participated in legal discussions (Exod. 35:1ff.; Deut. 29:11ff., 31:12–13). They involved themselves in tribal festivals (1 Sam. 2:19; 2 Kings 23:21; 2 Chron. 35), and were highly regarded as prophetesses (Judg. 4:4ff.; 2 Sam. 20:16ff.; 2 Kings 22:14ff.) and as sacred prostitutes (Gen. 38; Exod. 38:8; 1 Sam. 2:22; Hos. 4:13–14) (Archer 1983, 274). Although men were allowed several wives, both sexes were chastised equally before the law in the face of accusations of adultery or rape (Deut. 22:13–28). Judaism, in a sense, was and still is matrilineal, since descent is traced through the mother, and girls were required to be virgins, thus assuring the child's paternity. It is, however, also patriarchal.

That Judaism as well as Christianity have been patriarchal religions— their cultic rituals are rooted in misogyny, the deprecation and exclusion of women from the male sphere—is a truism. The psychological, economic, and physical origins of the prejudice are ultracomplex and will not be treated here. When, however, certain biblical texts are cast in a new light, the feminine condition may not always be as negative as formerly presumed. A case in point is the myth of Adam and Eve. Two contradictory versions of the birth of Eve may be found in Genesis. The first implies sexual equality:

> So God created man in his own image, in the image of God created he him; male and female created he them (Gen. 1:27).
> And God blessed them, and God said unto them, Be fruitful. . . . (Gen. 1:27–28)

The second suggests man's superiority:

> And the Lord God caused a deep sleep to fall upon Adam, and he slept; and he took one of his ribs, and closed up the flesh instead thereof;
> And the rib, which the Lord God had taken from man, made he a woman, and brought her unto the man. (Gen. 2:21–22)

Eve was the first to understand the "power" vested in the fruit hanging from the tree of knowledge in the Garden of Eden:

> And when the woman saw that the tree was good for food, and that it was pleasant to the eyes, and a tree to be desired to make one wise, she took of the fruit thereof, and did eat, and gave also unto her husband with her; and he did it.
> And the eyes of them both were opened, and they knew that they were naked. (Gen. 3:6–7)

Some interpreters heap blame on Eve and demean her for what has been labeled humanity's Fall—which explains why for centuries she has been identified with destructive and evil forces in society. Others, to the contrary, laud, admire, and venerate this woman for what is considered her incredibly courageous act. She intuited that the "fruit" held promise of wisdom and immeasurable inner wealth: *gnosis*. Because she was the quester of "knowledge" and the first to eat of the fruit offered by the Serpent, she absorbed within her God's *scintillae* (his "sparks of light"). Such energy charges gave thrust to her and Adam's evolution.

Eve was, so to speak, the genius of her day, just as Galileo, da Vinci, Shakespeare, and Einstein were in their own. All scientific, artistic, political, and cultural giants, ancient and/or modern, are revolutionaries, conquerors of the unknown. They reverse the status quo, and eventually become vulnerable to condemnation and chastisement by the old guard. Innovators attempting to open up the mind to the unknown work against the establishment and, therefore, have to brace themselves against society's wrath. Eve was no different.

As an *anima* figure, a soul-force, the possessor of an inquisitive mind, Eve may be regarded as a positive power, a heroine who paved the way for an increase in knowledge that impacted on future generations. Her direct violation of divinity's edict—a rejection of the patriarchal condition—suggests not evil, but rather an evolutionary step toward humanity's cultural progress.

In this new context, the Fall in Judeo–Christian doctrine may be regarded as a rite of passage from a state of unconsciousness or infantilism (Eve and Adam in the Garden of Eden) to one of relative maturity. The new condition was masked by feelings of insecurity and the anguish of choice which accompany freedom and independence. The tensions and conflicts triggered by duality became the lot of all earthly creatures. Each day finds us set at the crossroad; each day verges on the pleasurable or the harrowing. Yes, Adam and Eve did Fall—they *fell into life!*

Eve, thus viewed, becomes the harbinger of a new world spirit and a catalytic force triggering humanity's intellectual growth. It was she who lifted the passive and mindlessly obedient Adam out of blind subjection even while also instilling in him a zest for life. As a result of Eve's *heroic* act, "the eyes of them both were opened"; and thus consciousness was born, as were self-awareness and knowledge.

Other biblical women's reputations may perhaps similarly be enhanced if their earthly trajectories are reviewed from a different vantage point. Hannah's barrenness, for example, elicits great love and compassion from her husband: "Am I not better to thee than ten sons?"(1 Sam. 1:8). Her comportment reveals the "strength and forcefulness" of a "single-minded and determined woman" whose "vision transcends the immediate and the domestic" (Aschkenasy 1986, 12). Huldah, the woman prophet whom the mighty king of Judah consulted, had the courage to speak the truth to him, prognosticating the evil that would befall his people for having forsaken their Lord and having burned incense before other gods (2 Kings 22:15–18). Women such as Sarah, Miriam, Rachel, Rebeka, Naomi and Ruth, Esther, Judith, and others were instrumental in helping the Hebrews survive during periods of persecution.

Archetypal Analysis

Deborah, a charismatic personality, was inspired by God to lead the Israelite military hero, Barak, and his soldiers to a momentous military victory on the plains of Jezreel. The triumphant ode of celebration, "The Song of Deborah," which she allegedly authored and sung, is, outside of some short poems in the Pentateuch, one of the earliest extant examples of Hebrew literature. Not only is it significant because of the beauty of its lyrics but also because it represents woman as a positive and heroic force. It solemnizes Deborah not merely as wife but as an individual in her own right: judge, prophetess, poet, and spiritual leader.

The word *judge* as used in the Book of Judges does not refer merely to an adjudicator, arbitrator, or legislator. Rather, it pertains most importantly to inspired or charismatic leaders who, when their people were in dire need, rose to the occasion and were instrumental in delivering them from destruction. Unlike kingship, the power invested in judges lasted only as long as danger loomed; this dignity was therefore not granted to a single individual, but rather to various leaders who had experienced the spirit or grace of God.

The multiplicity of unfriendly neighbors surrounding the loosely cohesive Israeli tribes made a condition of vigilance and preparedness crucial: "And the children of Israel dwelt among the Canaanites, Hittites, and Amorites, and Perizzites, and Hivites, and Jebusites" (Judg. 3:5). The judges who spoke words of wisdom to the Israelites encouraged them to protect themselves from incursions by unfriendly tribes and to attempt aggressive wars.

Twelve judges took over the leadership of the tribes during periods of crisis, thus precluding lengthy authoritarian and frequently regressive reigns. The six major judges were Othniel, Ehud, Deborah, Gideon, Jephthah, and Samson; and the six minor ones were Shamgar, Tola, Jair, Ibzan, Elon, and Abdon.

What distinguishes the authority vested in them is that their "gift" is transitory, terminating with the completion of the God-directed mission. Only God's power, the Hebrews believed, was and is forever. Thus the possibility of *hubris* was avoided as was, even more crucially, the *worship of a God-man.*

Deborah's name in Hebrew signifies "bee." By association with this insect, she may be considered indefatigable, highly disciplined, and laborious. Like the bee, she, too, manufactured honey, which, as implicit in her poetic verse, "The Song of Deborah," takes on the attributes of food for the body and for the mind. The substance is transformed into a vital principle that fosters communication between the Deity and herself. Because bees are builders of hives, they assure the perennation of their species, as did Deborah by conducting the war against the Canaanites. In that the Promised Land was described as "flowing with milk and honey," she may be regarded as the dispenser of these riches in the form of the wisdom and knowledge stored within exceptional people.

Just as bees are endowed with duality—they sting as well as manufacture honey—so Deborah experienced her existence both bitterly and sweetly, and her judgments frequently impacted antithetically, as did those of Christ as judge, with whom she has been compared in this regard. Decisions arrived at

with warmth and compassion led to association with honey; but if condu-
cive to pain and sorrow, the stinging of the bee.

Deborah: Military Advisor

Upon calling Barak to arms, Deborah, the military strategist, was fully cognizant of the superiority of the Canaanite war machines as well as of the
power of their centralized, fortified city states. The Canaanite soldiers benefited from their people's expertise in iron-ore mining, which enabled them
to fashion from this metal armaments and chariots—nine hundred of them
(Judg. 4:3)—drawn by highly trained horses. In contrast to their enemy, the
Israelite tribes, living in small, sparsely settled, and isolated farming communities, were not only greatly outnumbered but poorly armed.

Why were Deborah's feelings of *certitude* in the divine word so strongly
held, convincing her to leap into a situation that on the surface looked cata-
strophic? Psychologically, we may suggest that her conviction, as she listened to the reverberations of that *inner voice* within her, resulted from a
harmonious and balanced relationship between her ego (center of consciousness) and her Self. The Self (the total psyche; in religious terms, God) has
been defined as a "latent, preexistent totality" existing within each human
being, which is "first incarnated and then assimilated through the living efforts of the individual" (Edinger 1988, 115). The highly evolved and unusually well-functioning connection between Deborah's Self and ego allowed
her to relate profoundly to both celestial (collective, universal) and terrestrial
(individual, personal) circumstances. Thus, she was in touch with and open
to aspects of existence normally closed to a less evolved and equilibrated
individual.

Unlike many of Deborah's contemporaries, whose archaic understanding of the world had remained static, her awareness enabled her both to
cognize details and transcend the particular, and thus to experience the whole
as a vibrant entity. Jung wrote:

> God wants to be born in the flame of man's [humankind's] consciousness,
> leaping ever higher. And what if this has no roots in the earth? If it is not a
> house of stone where the fire of God can dwell, but a wretched straw hut
> that flares up and vanishes? Could God then be born? One must be able to
> suffer God. That is the supreme task for the carrier of ideas. He must be the
> advocate of the earth. God will take care of himself. My inner principle is:
> Deus *et* homo. God needs man in order to become conscious, just as he

needs limitation in time and space. Let us therefore be for him limitation in time and space, an earthly tabernacle. (Jung 1963a, par. 391)

Deborah's deeply religious nature, that is, her ability to relate *(religio)* to her collective past, in addition to the fluid interconnectedness she enjoyed with regard to the various elements of her personality, invited her to experience life on both an individual and an all-encompassing level. Self-doubt, particularly with regard to the problematics of attacking the formidable Canaanite enemy, in no way lessened her confidence in the righteousness of her decision and her faith in God's *way*—the *way* that would permit her to show fortitude and exercise her intellect in the male-dominated military sphere. She commanded Barak to gather ten thousand soldiers to rout the Canaanite enemy led by Sisera.

It was said that Sisera, by the age of thirty, had "conquered the whole world." Although exaggeration always impinges on reality, his forces included "forty thousand armies, each counting a hundred thousand warriors" and enough chariots to annihilate any foe (Ginzberg 1956, 521). Legend tells us that when he bathed in a river or dove beneath its surface, "enough fish were caught in his beard to feed a multitude, and it required no less than nine hundred horses to draw the chariot in which he rode." As an archetypal figure, Sisera's image inspired terror in the hearts of his foes. Nevertheless, as a mortal, he was vulnerable.

Deborah apparently did not herself bear arms. As military advisor, however, her spirit reigned most forcefully over Barak. Because the evidently timorous—but realistic—Barak was initially unwilling to do her bidding, she had recourse to the *force* of language:

> Hath not the Lord, the God of Israel, commanded, saying, Go and draw toward mount Tabor, and take with thee ten thousand men of the children of Naphtali and of the children of Zebulun?
>
> And I will draw unto thee to the brook Kishon Sisera, the captain of Jabin's army, with his chariots and his multitude; and I will deliver him into thine hand. (Judg. 4:6, 7)

Barak responded:

> If thou wilt go with me, then I will go: but if thou wilt not go with me, I will not go.
>
> And she said, I will surely go with thee: notwithstanding the journey

that thou takest shall not be for thine honour; for the Lord will give Sisera over into the hand of a woman. (Judg. 4:8–9)

Deborah's fomenting words, together with her determination and fulgurating radiance, must surely have been instrumental in encouraging Barak to engage the enemy. Perhaps he *felt* that the presence in battle of Deborah— a living embodiment of the feminine principle and specifically of the mother figure—would inject sensations of well-being into him and his fighting men and fill them with zeal and fervor.

Understandably fearful of the enemy without Deborah at his side, Barak was nonetheless impervious to the shame that might be heaped upon him for relying on a woman. Or did he perhaps anticipate a military defeat that would leave an even deeper scar? Would not his image be less tarnished were he to share his failure with another? After all, who better than he knew the obstacles to uniting the disparate Israelite tribes? Each had its own interests at heart rather than those of the collective: Dan and Asher in the north were more interested in mercantile matters than in war; Reuben on the other side of the Jordan remained undecided; and Gilead was lazy. Barak posed his condition of Deborah's presence, perhaps hoping that it might not be met.

Deborah's warning to Barak that his need of womanly comfort during the hostilities would tarnish his image revealed how profoundly marked was her psyche by the sexist inequities rampant in the gender-oriented society of her time. On a more positive note, however, her argument, designed to point out the reality of the situation, also served to shatter the seemingly outward unity of patriarchal tradition. Equally unusual was Barak's willingness to "demean himself" by sharing with a woman his fame as a military man.

Deborah's deft and subtle reasoning, as well as her insights into human nature, were, to be sure, *extra*ordinary. Yet, might not her disputations also have had manipulatory intent? Certainly, her tendentious arguments were designed to convince Barak to do her bidding: unite the Israelite tribes against the enemy. But was it her unconscious purpose to encourage him to insist on her presence during the melee in order to prove the usefulness of women as military advisors—that is, as active participants in army matters? If so, Deborah's position would be a demonstration, as Nehama Aschkenasy has so aptly written, of "an egalitarian conception of the roles of the sexes" and "that women cannot be excluded even from the bloodshed of war, the last bastion of male domain" (Aschkenasy 1986, 167).

Once Deborah had agreed to follow Barak onto the battlefield, the military leader experienced a mood swing. He rapidly brought together and activated a coalition of six tribes and readied them to confront the enemy near Taanach and Megiddo, east of Carmel (1150 B.C.E.) (Margolis and Marx 1980, 22).[3]

Deborah, the military strategist, spoke to Barak in compelling and commanding tones. He, his ten thousand soldiers, and she would climb Mount Tabor (Judg. 4:7), from whose heights she, stalwart in her demeanor and authoritative in her pronouncements, would dictate the tactics to be followed during the early skirmishes.

Having reached the summit of Mount Tabor, they were in a position to observe the goings-on in Sisera's camp. Deborah ordered Barak in the name of God to go down the mountain:

> Up; for this is the day in which the Lord hath delivered Sisera into thy hand: is not the Lord gone out before thee? So Barak went down from mount Tabor, and ten thousand men after him. (Judg. 4:14)

Deborah took advantage of the flooding of the river Kishon to attack the foe, for a mighty storm had broken out and Sisera with his troops were attempting to cross the waterway with their horses and chariots. The huge waves of the river Kishon swept the soldiers down into the sea, and the equipment left behind became useless on the sodden ground (Ginzberg 1956, 521). Just as the Red Sea had parted, allowing the Hebrews to leave Egypt, natural forces, as ordered by the Deity, once again worked a miracle. Deborah knew intuitively that Sisera's "nine hundred chariots of iron" would not fare well in muddy waters. Again she had taken the initiative, and Barak complied. She was in control; he was being controlled.

> And the Lord discomfited Sisera, and all his chariots, and all his host, with the edge of the sword before Barak; so that Sisera lighted down off his chariot, and fled away on his feet. (Judg. 4:15)

The rational Barak needed no more proof than the sight of his foe's army at rout to realize that, without divine intervention, machinery was ineffective.

To clarify the Deity's role with regard to the military undertaking involving Deborah, Barak, and Sisera, frequently misunderstood by biblical exegetes, we offer Martin Buber's sensitive appraisal:

> JHWH [God] is not, as is frequently understood, a war-god; nor a cov-
> enant-god developed into a war-god. War-gods help their fighting peoples.
> They do not, with human and superhuman armies, wage their own wars.
> The mighty-weaponed Ashur helps Sennacherib against Phoenicians, Phi-
> listines and Hezekiah of Judah, but he does not command a war with Judah
> as JHWH with Amalek "from generation to generation" (Exodus
> 17:16). . . . The protector-god wages the war of his protégés; the *melekh*
> [king] JHWH wages His own war. (Buber 1967, 143)

When Deborah asked the reticent military hero, Barak, to take up arms
against the enemy, Buber continues, her argument was not directed to a
"devotee of a cult-numen," but rather took the form of a question posed to
"a follower of a Divine duke." Indeed, she asked Barak, "Is not the Lord
gone out before thee?" (Judg. 4: 14) It was "naive-theocratic enthusiasm,"
Buber indicates, that led the Israelites to fight the Canaanites, just as it had
empowered them to push forward during their forty-year stint in the desert
after their exodus from Egypt (Buber 1967, 143). During their wanderings
they came into contact with such "charismatic" personalities as Moses and
Joshua, who stirred their "naive-theocratic enthusiasm" to still greater pitch.

The same emotional intensity may be said to have been instrumental in
the waging of war between the Israelites and the Canaanites as described in the
Book of Judges. When Deborah took up the banner and activated energetic
pulsations in the psyches of the Israelite soldiers and their commander, the
participants *knew* that God would protect them from annihilation (ibid., 145).

Deborah: Judge

That the "Word" was and is paramount in Judaism is a truism. Let us recall
that the abstract god, Yahweh, was heard as *voice*, and his commandments as
Law. Moses said to the Hebrews:

> And the Lord spoke unto you out of the midst of the fire; ye heard the
> voice of words, but ye saw no form; only a voice. And He declared unto
> you His covenant, which He commanded you to perform, even the ten
> words; and He wrote them upon two tables of stone. And the Lord com-
> manded me at that time to teach you statues and ordinances, that ye might
> do them in the land whither ye go over to possess it. Take ye therefore
> good heed unto yourselves . . . lest ye deal corruptly, and make you a
> graven image, even the form of any figure, the likeness of male or female.
> (Deut. 4:12–15)

Since the "Word" played such a significant role in the Bible, what constituted the power of judgeship in the Hebrew tribal community? Certainly the "Word" as an ordering device and as an instrument capable of translating God's commands ruled paramount for Deborah as judge. Not surprisingly, then, does the function of judgeship entail the notion of "deliverer" of the "Word" and its message, thus assuring method and/or a return to it after an interim of chaos.

What serves to make Deborah's judgments unique was that they were directed not only by the reason and logic of her legalistic mind but by perception as well. That she was endowed with poetic talent was a distinct advantage: her words conveyed meaning, to be sure, but also a whole intuitive dimension. Thus, she was able to order difficult situations as well as, perhaps, her own tumultuous inner world; and she was able to enhance the power of her words with the fire of her inner experience.

Deborah judged, counseled, and prophesied on a hill under the palm tree which bore her name: "under the palm tree of Deborah between Ramah and Bethel in mount Ephraim; and the children of Israel came up to her for judgment" (Judg. 4:5). In that the palm tree's green leaves are universally considered symbols of victory and regeneration, their role in Deborah's world underscores the breadth and scope of her judgments. The presence of the palm tree connotes, then, not so much her routine involvement as the attainment of collective dimensions. While the palm's leaves are high above ground, its roots are embedded in the earth; thus, both are continuously fed by sun/celestial/spiritual founts as well as by shaded/earthly/ pragmatic sources.

That the palm tree was located on a hill compelled those who sought Deborah's counsel to mount to "higher" levels, to elevate or spiritualize their outlook on life. In so doing, they developed an ability to differentiate between multiple levels of understanding and rise above workaday matters. Indeed, ascensional images are not wanting in the Bible (Mount Sinai, Mount Tabor, the Mount of the Olives, and so forth). In the Noah myth, for example, the landmass that came into view as the floodwaters began to recede was also looked upon as a hill, thus becoming a paradigm for humankind's increasing ability to distinguish, discriminate, and modify the parts from the whole, or chaotic waters from stable earth forces (Judg. 8:5).

To show her people how to exercise spirit and mind in worldly affairs was one of Deborah's most significant goals. Just as she looked out from her hilltop to the plain below, broadening her perspectives yet maintaining her ideals, so the thinking patterns of the people asking counsel needed also to ascend and descend. Deborah's spirit, paradoxically liberated yet involved, remained an ideal for the populace.

Unlike the priests who had official sanctuaries or shrines for devotional practices, Deborah was a free spirit who chose the open air to pronounce her judgments. She did not rely on the decor of a fixed religious space or shrine to work her wonders. Rather was she dependent on her own personality— and the Divine Word—for her decisions.

Deborah: Prophet/Nabi

A link exists, Martin Buber suggests, between the notion of judging and the primitive "charismatic" vocation of prophecy. The great prophets of the past—highly charged personalities such as Isaiah, Ezekiel, and Jeremiah— had enjoyed a "charismatic . . . rulership." Their "peculiar gift" was that they felt themselves appointed to fulfill a "divine mission" (Buber 1967, 139). Judges, then, emerged from

> the community of those susceptible to the Spirit, uninhibitedly surren-
> dered to the Spirit, those men receiving the working of the Spirit as the
> kingly rule for the life of Israel, from the community by which they are
> supported thereafter. And they came forth by means of precisely such ex-
> periences—in such a way that these experiences brought them forth,
> snatched them forth. (Ibid., 157)

Deborah, as spokesperson in parts of the Book of Judges, was "mouth"; as one experiencing charismatic vocation as well, she was also prophet or *nabi*, having been chosen to bear God's words vertically, from heaven down-ward and from earth upward (ibid., 156). As noted by Buber, "[T]he mis-sion of the *nabi* is to let the dialogue between God and man be accomplished in his speaking," until the day when all God's people will become prophets, when the "Lord would put His spirit upon them!" (Num. 11:29) (Buber 1970, 169–70).

To be born a *nabi* was to be God's *mouth* and to be possessed by mystery. Deborah translated his "hidden, soundless utterance, God's primal word," that which is "anterior to all words." As poet, she was the interpreter, the "divulger," the one destined to put the mysterious tonalities and the veiled inaudible "speech of [her] inwardness" into the Word/Sign (ibid., 170).

The sequences of vehement phonemes ejaculating from her mouth, as well as the powerful voice or verb she used to spread Divinity's message, underscore her function as *mediatrix*: a bridge between the divine and earthly, between God and his people—a symbol of his fruitful union with the earth.

In psychological terms, during Deborah's moments of acute concentration the intensity of the energetic frequencies emanating from her subliminal spheres was such that, breaking through to consciousness, they manifested themselves in archetypal images and feelings of exaltation. Her certainty of the Divinity's presence as attested to by her visions did not, however, blind her to the overwhelming difficulties and the possible subjugation facing her people. But God, she knew, was not on the side of the enemy.

Deborah: Poet

Whatever parapsychological term we may care to use—trance, ecstasy, or self-hypnosis—to explain Deborah's prophetic voice and her poetic insights, her experience of the Godhead was immediate and, like St. Paul's vision on the road to Damascus, it established a connection between mortal and immortal worlds, immanence and transcendence (Gordis 1971, 17). The dramatic energy in her incantation of "The Song of Deborah" (sung by her either solo or antiphonally with Barak after the war) was maintained through her powerful commitment to God. Through the images, rhythms, and tonal utterances, she exhorted her compatriots to remember their spiritual heritage, their culture, and that "inner voice" which emerged in time of need from one possessed by *ruach* (spirit). Because God had touched her "mouth," she, like the other *nabi* of the Old Testament, neither "stammered" nor "babbled." Her pronouncements were dominated by "a rhythmic rigor" and "flooded with the headlong surge of the moment" (Buber 1970, 171).

"The Song of Deborah" reenacted in compelling and fearful terms the entire drama revolving around Barak's terror at the thought of attacking a formidable enemy and the lack of cohesion of Israelite forces. As the recipient of grace, Deborah's creative energy overflowed, its very dynamism empowering her to transcend the thinking function and deepen her wonderment at the Divinity's mysterious ways.

> Blessed be the Lord.
> Hear, O ye kings; give ear, O ye princes;
>   I, unto the Lord will I sing;
> I will sing praise to the Lord, the God of Israel.
>
> (Judg. 5:3–5)

The stormy atmospheric conditions and torrential rains preluding the battle announce a veritable cosmic happening. In a single compressed image from Deborah's verbal palette, the prefiguration of a theophany is clearly traced: the earth vibrates and pulsates, the flatlands and mountains quiver, while the rest of the visible world shudders in nervous animation:

> Lord, when thou didst go forth out of Seir,
> When thou didst march out of the field of Edom,
> The earth trembled, the heavens also dropped,
> Yea, the clouds dropped water.
> The mountains quaked at the presence of the Lord. . . .
>
> (Judg. 5:4–5)

These archetypal images and their daring juxtapositions, encased in lyrical yet ordered patternings and rhythmical beats, are recollections, remnants of visualizations that slumbered inchoate in Deborah's psyche. These forms, substances, and delineations existed prior to the development of consciousness, before self-reflection and understanding were born. The incandescent figurations that cascaded into her mind's eye served to broaden her mode of psychic functioning, enabling her both to assimilate and integrate what had been latent within her. The mention of past battles and the naming of former heroes, interwoven into the fabric of this epic poem, activated sequences of furious affects that streaked across her evanescent verbal canvas.

In sharp contrast are the sequences interpolating the Israelites' numerous apostasies. Then Deborah's tone is one of sadness, of poignant images including that of the "mother" whose lamentations reveal the need of a nourishing feminine principle to rectify and/or counteract an overly patriarchal condition. Deborah's role was to assume that function, thus mediating between God and humanity and paving the way for the birth of new understanding, relatedness, and love:

> Until that thou didst arise, Deborah,
> That thou didst arise a mother in Israel.
> They chose new gods;
> Then was war in the gates;
> Was there a shield or spear seen
> Among forty thousand in Israel?
>
> (Judg. 5:7–8)

As words swell in intensity, reaching crescendo tones, their very resonances become virtually unbearable. Like protracted hammer sounds, cacophonies pierce the ear. Emotions are contagious. While the intensity of battle sequences prevail, the eye travels about in boldly outlined leapings, obliterating details, giving the poetic voice precedence.

> Louder than the voice of archers,
>> by the watering-troughs!
> There shall they rehearse the righteous acts of the Lord,
>> Even the righteous acts of His rulers in Israel.
> Then the people of the Lord went down to the gates.
>
> (Judg. 5:11)

Abruptly do the tonal poundings end. Space floats in its own nebulosity. Intangible and amorphous entities seem to have taken utter possession of Deborah. As if in a trance, she sounds out her memory, explores its imagings, retrieving those of import in her mind's eye. Battles are relived, violence explodes, a strange and haunting beauty encapsulates her words as the *numinosum* prevails:

> Awake, awake, Deborah;
> Awake, awake, utter a song;
> Arise, Barak, and lead thy captivity captive, thou son of
>> Abinoam.
> Then made He a remnant to have dominion over the nobles
>> and the people;
> The Lord made me have dominion over the mighty.
>
> (Judg 5:12–13)

Orchestrated tonalities in all of their viscerality are absorbed into the landscape, accentuating the immediacy of the experience. Expert use of such figures of speech as repetitions, parallelisms, clang sonorizations, and stridently striated tones are literary strategies introduced by the poet and are designed to amplify the harrowing noises and the ruthlessness of the battle. Chaos grips the Israelites as the tribal units enter the melee.

> They fought from heaven,
> The stars in their course fought against Sisera.
>
> (Judg. 5:20)

Stars, companions to the overflowing waters of the Kishon, are welcomed into the fray, adding a fearful otherworldly dimension to an otherwise typical earthly war scene. The resulting gigantic celebration—*hieros gamos*—enhances the numinosity of the happenings and paves the way for the experience of transcendence.

According to Ugaritic texts, stars were associated with water, the two acting in consort to deliver tempestuous climatic effects. Multiple explosions occurring in the immensities of space give the impression of divine participation in mortal happenings (Craigie 1977, 33).

As earthly conflagrations in celestial spheres are intensified in "The Song of Deborah," deafening noises are accompanied by the entry of rapid, high-powered heteroclite images, thus expanding an ever more agitated battle scene. The depiction of huge waves sweeping over Sisera's perfectly mechanized chariots lends mythic resonances to an already fractured visual and tonal verbal construct:

> The brook Kishon swept them away,
> That ancient brook, the brook Kishon.
> O my soul, tread them down with strength.
> Then did the horsehoofs stamp
> By reason of the prancings, the prancings of their mighty ones.
>
> (Judg. 5:21–22)

As elemental nature triumphs over humankind's most artfully conceived contrivances and plans, landscapes expand vertically and horizontally, sweeping the listeners' gaze along. Thus does "The Song of Deborah"—like Dionysus's epiphany in Euripides' *Bacchantes*, like the parting of the Red Sea as Moses led his people out of Egypt, and like Christ's Crucifixion—maximize a series of events.

Natural cataclysms in religious texts and/or in works of art are destabilizing forces that may be viewed as projections of traumatic happenings within the psyche. Each shock to the earth's surface, or to the person's psyche, is revealed verbally, visually, or sonorously in "The Song of Deborah," thus preparing the reader for the onset of a new beginning and a fresh attitude toward life.

Energized by the Divinity, Deborah had experienced the One/Indivisible in the archetypal image of "a mother in Israel." Transcending her earthly limitations and experiencing this same expanded consciousness in the spiritual domain—as poet she, the bridge between God and humankind, transliterated ideations and feelings. Never static in their power nor encrusted in arid cerebral concepts, her stunningly original formal utterances were self-renewing, each time ascending to higher levels of inspirational rapture until *ekstasis* was reached. Never did Deborah sever herself from the Word/Sign connecting herself and her people pneumatically with the Divinity.

Jael: Heroine? or Traitor?

Jael, the wife of Heber, is the woman referred to by Deborah in her words to Barak: "the Lord will give Sisera over into the hand of a woman" (Judg. 4:9).

Heber, the chief of the seminomadic Kenite clan, had remained neutral in the Israelite/Canaanite war but was favorably inclined to Sisera (Judg. 4:17). Sisera, after having fled on foot, was followed by Barak in hot pursuit and reached the tent of the attractive, beautifully clothed, and bejeweled Jael:

> And Jael went out to meet Sisera, and said unto him, "Turn in, my lord, turn in to me; fear not." And he turned in unto her into the tent, she covered him with a rug. (Judg. 4:18)

Sisera's acceptance of her invitation proved to be a mistake in judgment on his part. He had taken for granted that because Heber had made peace with his clan or tribe, his wife, Jael, had also participated in the contract. She evidently had not concurred, which attests to the freedom women enjoyed both politically and religiously (Bal 1988, 59–60).

Nor was it out of the ordinary for Jael, a seemingly traditional home-body, to invite Sisera into her tent and offer him hospitality. Let us note that warmheartedness and cordiality in ancient cultures of the region was a cardinal rule. An invitation to a stranger or friend ensured the guest's safety; default in extending this sacred act of welcome was an offense to society at large. Did Jael lure Sisera into her tent to protect him or to harm him (ibid., 61–62)?

Sisera never questioned Jael's cordiality. Like Adam tasting the fruit of knowledge, Sisera had comported himself in a thoughtless—unconscious—manner. His lack of insight into human nature, his surrender to the world of the senses, interfered with the exercise of reasonable caution. Although highly disciplined in matters of warfare, he had little understanding of the behavior of women, perhaps considering them mainly as sex objects. Was it his undervaluation of a woman's intelligence and perception that led him to perdition?

Sisera, like Parzival as naive in the ways of the world as he was brilliant in military matters, neglected to question Jael's motivations. Rather, he allowed himself to react overtly to the warmth of her (motherly) personality and her (vampish) sensuality. Sisera had asked Jael for water to quench his thirst; she offered him milk instead—"And she opened a bottle of milk, and gave him drink, and covered him" (Judg. 4:19). Might not he have become suspicious of Jael's overly generous gesture? But how could he possibly suspect that such nutrition (milk) and protection (covering him) would cause him harm?

Some scholars have argued that since Jael gave him more than he had asked for, she not only had not complied with his wishes but had lulled him into a false sense of security, thus breaking the rules of hospitality. Nor, interestingly and perhaps for the same reason, was the milk-giving episode mentioned in the fifth chapter of Judges which features "The Song of Deborah." Other critics feel that Sisera was the aggressor in that he asked for water; and Jael, on the contrary, had been generous to a fault (Bal 1988, 62). Mention must also be made of the soothing and soporific qualities of goat milk, which caused the fatigued warrior to doze off.

Later on, however, Sisera surprisingly changed his manner toward his hostess. No longer "formal" and "respectful" as he had been upon entering the tent, he now ordered her to beware of any man that might inquire about him. In so doing, he reverted to the authoritarian position of the male military leader and assumed the dominant role in the twosome, while she, seemingly, resumed her subservient and compliant attitude (Aschkenasy 1986, 171).

> Stand in the door of the tent, and it shall be, when any man doth come and inquire of thee, and say, Is there any man here? that thou shalt say: No. (Judg. 4:20)

Suddenly and without forewarning, as if responding by reflex to Sisera's humiliation of her, and prompted by her allegiance to the Israelites

> Jael Heber's wife took a tent-pin, and took a hammer in her hand, and went softly unto him, and smote the pin into his temples, and it pierced through into the ground; for he was in a deep sleep; so he swooned and died. (Judg. 4:21)

Some critics, suggesting that Sisera's virtually immediate change of attitude was due to the fact that the two had had sexual relations in the tent, support their view by the following lines: "at her feet he bowed, he fell, he lay down: at her feet he bowed, he fell: where he bowed, there he fell down dead" before Jael who stands erect (Judg. 5:27). According to the Masoretic text:

> At her feet he sunk, he fell, he lay;
> At her feet he sunk, he fell;
> Where he sunk, there he fell down dead.
>
> (Judg. 5:27)

The metaphor "feet," implying legs, in front of which Sisera fell, is viewed as a metaphor for sexual organs.

Jael lived a semitransient existence and, according to her culture, the woman's task was to pitch the family's tent. This offers an explanation of the accessibility of the hammer and nail. Jael's manipulation of the "pin" or "tent-pin," another phallic image, indicates her power over the male, implicit in other love/death poetic motifs. The hammer, identified with brute force, as used by Jael, was the instrument par excellence that crushed and victimized: another paradigm of "sex and violence, death and seduction," and "defeat and humiliation" (Niditch 1989, 46).

The question arises whether Barak was the man to whom Sisera referred when ordering Jael to stand at the door. By using words such as "any man," did he mean a nonman? Was he mocking Barak for having accepted Deborah's aid, thus divesting himself of traditional macho qualities? Was it Deborah's intent to shame and humiliate Barak? Was she a paradigm in the intellectual sphere, as Jael was in the existential domain, of the *new woman of action* capable of bearing arms and agitating for an increase in rights in her society (Bal 1988, 90)?

Barak's humiliation reached its apex when he appeared near Jael's tent after the Israelites' victory. Again Jael went out of her tent, this time to greet Barak and invite him in:

> Jael came out to meet him, and said unto him: "Come, and I will show thee the man whom thou seekest." And he came unto her; and behold, Sisera lay dead, and the tent-pin was in his temples. (Judg. 4:22)

Twice, then, had Barak been summoned by a woman. The first time was by Deborah, who commanded him to head the Israelite forces so as to stop the foe; now by Jael, who asked him to enter her tent and view the corpse of a once gloriously fearsome, but now utterly debased enemy. Thus were Sisera and Barak, both great military leaders, revealed to be vulnerable and naive tragic heroes (D. F. Murray 1979, 173).

Were the defeat and humiliation of Barak and Sisera symptomatic of a larger battle waged between matriarchate and patriarchate? The balance of power had altered, the two warriors having been reduced to size, even while Deborah and Jael were elevated. The strength and fortitude of both the career woman (Deborah) and the homebody (Jael) had been instrumental in bringing about the victory of the Israelites. For the Israelites, Jael was a heroine. And Deborah sang:

> Blessed above women shall Jael be.
> The wife of Heber the Kenite be,
> Above women in the tent shall she be blessed.
>
> (Judg. 5:24)

Sisera's Loving Mother

Jael may be contrasted with yet another feminine figure: Sisera's loving Canaanite mother, whom we first meet in her home. Having no knowledge of the outcome of the battle, she assumed that her son had won the day against the Israelites. She did, however, wonder why he had taken so long to return home.

We find her first scanning the horizon: "through the window she looked forth, and peered . . . through the lattice," and she wept (Judg. 5: 28). Her questionings express concern for her son's well-being:

> Why is his chariot so long in coming?
> Why tarry the wheels of his chariots?
> The wisest of her princesses answer her,
> Yea, she returneth answer to herself.
>
> (Judg. 5:28–29)

Rather than accept the answers of others—the "princesses" function here as Greek choruses, that is, as the speakers of truth—the only *real* mother in the narration was persuaded that she alone could fathom the reasons for his delay. Unconsciously she assuaged her anxiety:

> Are they not finding, are they not dividing the spoil?
> A damsel, two damsels to every man;
> To Sisera a spoil of dyed garments,

A spoil of dyed garments of embroidery,
Two dyed garments of embroidery for the neck of every
    spoiler?

(Judg. 5:30)

Sisera's mother's reasoning faculties were subverted by her need for wishful thinking. Her refusal to plumb the truth was her way of shying away from reality. She indulged in fantasy, thereby denigrating woman's intellectual faculties. Prolonging her imaginings, perhaps even enjoying such an escape mechanism, her thoughts revolved around the joys her son must be experiencing as he was dividing the spoils. By the same token, she may even have been attacking the female population, suggesting that their interests revolved only around needlework, dyes, jewels, household matters, and clothes—the latter being so highly prized in those days that they were worthy of being listed as spoils of war (Bal 1988, 64). Wasn't Sisera's mother also insinuating that *other*, namely sexual, activities were also occurring in the intimacy of the tent (Judg. 5:28–30)?

The mother's emotions ranged from joy at the thought of her son's enjoyment of a profusion of riches to viciousness toward the young girls whom the Canaanite soldiers had captured: "have they not divided the prey: to every man a damsel or two . . ." (Judg. 5:30) (Aschkenasy 1986, 172). In both images, the superiority of the male and his erotic needs prevail in her mind. Psychoanalytically, her vision incorporates yet another association: a marriage between thanatos/eros, or war/love (Niditch 1989, 46).

Jael's act, undertaken in disregard of her husband's neutral position and in order to side with the Israelites, may, as we have seen, be viewed either as treacherous or admirable. The deceit that had lead to the death of the fearsome Sisera, thereby accounting for the complete victory of the Israelites, was considered heroic, yet could be understood as subversive. Whatever the interpretation, her act relieved the populace of terror and filled their hearts with a sense of liberation, at least temporarily.

Deborah's world of the mind (intellect, *logos*) as well as of the divine *(numinosum)* may be juxtaposed to Jael's world of earthliness and sensuality. Fearless, powerful, and clever, Jael's self-confidence in performing her murderous act made her victory in the battle against the patriarchal status quo that much more resounding. She was "a symbolization of self-assertion, a force of change, one who breaks free heroically from oppressive and suppressive forces" (Bal 1988, 52).

Although Deborah and Jael experienced different things, they neverthe-less acted in consort in an attempt to unseat the growing male–dominated autocracy. Both used the weapon of humiliation to despoil the two military men. Deborah, as *nabi*, heard the voice of God as it flooded her being with the creative energy to both prophesy and poetize. Jael, cognizant of the dangers she faced by murdering the military chief, proved that her sex was also capable of participating in the salvation of a people.

The melody of God's voice reverberated through the prophet Deborah's discourse. As poet, she had become a self-generating instrument catalyzing both herself and her tribe. As chanter of "The Song of Deborah," she was a *nabi*, a "pronouncer," a "bearer of the word," who used the power of speech to fill the air, thereby revealing a message from above to those on earth. Like Abraham (Gen. 20:7) and Samuel (1 Sam. 3:20), Deborah was a "mediating mouth" (Buber 1970, 152). She, like other Israelites, possessed "the genuine gift of the *Word*," which distinguished them from the Canaanites and their "wordless–ecstatic transport" after which "the tongue was loosed" (ibid.).

The importance accorded Deborah in the Bible denotes a cultural change in the understanding of the Hebrews' *imago Dei*. No longer exclusively rep-resentative of the masculine principle, God chose a woman as the harbinger of his message. It was Deborah, as his guiding principle, who brought into the Israelite tribal communities a new equilibrium equally removed from the extremes of patriarchate or matriarchate.

Unlike Joan of Arc, Deborah was not sanctified. Unlike Ezekiel, she was not "lifted up between earth and heaven" (Ezek. 8:2). She remained of this earth: sensitive, deeply perceptive, a paradigm of one whose relationship with the Deity was as open, balanced, and profound as were the segments of her personality.

4 Euripides' *Iphigenia:*
Marriage or Sacrificial Altar?

Why has sacrifice, human or animal, real or symbolic, been so universal a practice in religions? How can one explain the common lure of this ascetic, self-denying, self-violating, frequently masochistic tradition? Violence and bloodletting, either overt or covert, lie at the heart of this either laudable or unpraiseworthy practice (Burkert 1983, 1).

For what reasons was sacrifice considered, in Greek times as in ours, an efficacious way to cleanse oneself of sin? of enhancing one's image vis-à-vis friends and society? of connecting with a higher and/or supernal power? Is the intent of the sacrificer strictly altruistic? or is he or she tainted with hubris?

Is the taking of a life, human or animal, actual or symbolic, within the purview of humans? Are not mortals who immolate themselves attempting in their way to divine the Deity's thoughts and desires, thereby placing themselves on a par with this transpersonal force? Is not the very basis for sacrifice an example of hubris (Jung 1963a, par. 387)?

Agamemnon, Iphigenia's father, lived through the torment of the sacrificial experience. Although he felt obliged, ostensibly for reasons of state, to offer his young daughter for immolation, he anguished over his decision. Prophetic are his words in Euripides' *Iphigenia in Aulis* (405 B.C.E.): "No mortal knows real prosperity or happiness; never has one been born free from sorrow" (*I.* 159).[1]

Iphigenia's sacrifice hinged on a crime perpetrated by Agamemnon long before the beginning of the drama. Not only had he killed a stag sacred to Artemis but he had also boasted of his superior hunting skills. Artemis, "Mistress of the Animals," as she was called in the *Iliad* (21.470),[2] meted out an irrevocable punishment for Agamemnon's hubris. He, the mightiest of Greek princes and chief in command in the Panhellenic war against Troy, was preparing to sail with his army from the bay of Aulis to fight the enemy. But the goddess called for a calm to settle over the bay, forcing the Greek fleet to remain at anchor and thus preventing the army's departure for Troy to wage what Euripides considered a questionable war. Calchas, high priest and spokesman for the prevailing religious authority, had determined that Agamemnon could expiate his offense to the goddess only by sacrificing his daughter, Iphigenia. Once appeased, Artemis would allow the winds to blow and the ships and fighting men to sail to their destination. If Agamemnon disobeyed the priest's ruling, his judgment, reputation, and power as king and military leader would have been called into question by his soldiers, who were growing increasingly disgruntled because of their forced idleness. The war against the Trojans would have been lost and Helen, the "wanton" woman, would not have been returned to her husband Menelaus, thus restoring the sacred bond of marriage that was considered paradigmatic of an ordered society.

Ectypal Analysis

Unlike Aeschylus, who had been a soldier and had fought for his country against the Persians, and unlike Sophocles, who had held high government offices, Euripides had served neither the country nor the polis. According to traditional sources, he had spent much of his time reading and studying, seemingly fascinated by the mysteries buried within the human personality. His great tragedies, characterized as acidulous satires, contain bitter condemnations of social conditions that he considered unjust and unwarranted. In *Alcestis* (438 B.C.E.), Euripides ironized the subordinate role of women; in *Medea* (431 B.C.E.), he derided the unfair treatment of foreign women in Athenian society; in *Hippolytus* (428 B.C.E.), he took society to task for the sorry fate of illegitimate children; in *The Trojan Women* (415 B.C.E.), he decried war; and in *The Bacchantes*, he dramatized the extremes reached by religious rage/outrage in a male-dominated society that functioned by repressing the female population.

Laws, in Euripides' time, were designed to favor men: property, for example, was inherited patrilineally. Not only did the Athenian polity exclude women, as it did foreigners and slaves, but it refused even to grant them citizenship. A woman had one function: to give birth to future citizens (Vidal-Naquet 1981, 179). With this in mind, young, premenarcheal girls *(kore)* remained at home, where they were trained in household matters until the beginning of the biological change *(parthenos)*, after which they were married off as rapidly as possible. The bride *(gune)* was taken directly from her father's home to her husband's, after which she would become the mother *(meter)*, hopefully of a boy (Larrington 1992, 87). Restricted to the home, the mother spent the rest of her life directing her servants, bringing up her children, and relating to her husband only within this highly circumscribed space and context.

Because Aristotle and Xenophon, among many other philosophers, considered women's reasoning and thinking faculties far inferior to those of men, the Athenian husband rarely if ever entered into a serious discussion with his wife; nor did he experience any significant emotional rapport with her. The man's interests, feelings, and socializing remained focused on his male friends, and frequently evolved into homosexual relationships, as attested to in Plato's *Symposium*. Concubines, however, who saw to the sexual pleasures of the male, and courtesans *(hetaerae)*, like the beautiful and brilliant Aspasia (who gave Pericles a son who became the pride and joy of Athenian society) constituted exceptions to the rule.

Archetypal Analysis

Sacrifice

Euripides' irreverent and iconoclastic drama, *Iphigenia*, was perhaps an attempt on his part to overturn the highly regarded notion of voluntary human sacrifice.

Sacrifice is a mystery. A mystery is "esoteric." The word stems from the Greek *eisotheo* (I make enter), connoting the opening of a door to make accessible what has been lying hidden or buried in darkness. Sacrifice does not generally seek to teach a doctrine, but rather sets the stage for an experience to be lived. The goal of sacrifice or the playing out of a "sacred" mystery is, psychologically, "self-awareness": the gaining of increased knowledge. Thus an initiate may be invited to experience the death of the limited, profane, and temporal ego (center of consciousness) via a sacrifice, in order to be reborn in spiritual and eternal regions where the realization of the Self (total psyche) is tantamount to an encounter with the Divinity.

The practice of sacrifice, which scholars believe grew out of credence in the death and rebirth of sacred powers, may be considered a dramatic rendering or regeneration of a "force," or a repetition of a "primal creative act, which took place *ab initio.*" In most religions, the act is intended to repeat or resurrect in the sacrificer, either actually or symbolically, a first spawning, an initial energetic pulsation, that triggers new ideas and beliefs. In Judaism, Abraham sacrificed Isaac; in Christianity, Jesus sacrificed himself; in Hinduism, the primal giant Purusha was sacrificed by the gods in order to fashion the universe. In these and other examples of immolation, the act itself, by destroying a previous condition, created fresh approaches to life. Thus, broadly speaking, the sacrifice of previous ways and ideations was instrumental in creating the earth, the cosmos, and the pantheon of gods. So, too, symbolically, was grain brought forth from *sperma* (Eliade 1974b, 346).

The notion of sacrifice, then, is related to renewal both in thought and in the reality of agricultural fertility. Immolation was a way of averting the terror of crop failure and the possibility of the sun never again rising, of breaching what believers sensed to be the ever-increasing gap between gods and mortals, which grew in scope with the rise of "civilization." A yearning to return to that so-called golden age when humans ate and shared food with the gods and communicated with them with ease might also have served to foster immolation.

To sacrifice flesh and blood on altars or in sanctuaries, and then to eat and drink morsels of these substances in actuality or emblematically, was not only considered a sacred act but was also believed to insure the presence during the ritual of the god or goddess to whom the offering was being made. Sacrifice of this kind may be said to have become an alimentary ceremony, an agape, a communion in which the initiates took into themselves morsels that had been offered to the deity. Since the transpersonal power being honored was in attendance during the solemnization, the ritual could restore the original unity between mortals and immortals, thus assuaging the initial terror or feelings of isolation of the participants.

The association of the ritual of sacrifice and the regeneration of a life force or of energy also implies a renewal of time, removing it from profane (linear or eschatological) measurement and transferring it onto the sacred (mythical or eternal) plane. Thus may a historical experience become imbued with transcendental dimension (ibid., 344). Although the original historical facts related to Iphigenia's sacrifice are not and may never be known, the myth that grew out of this primordial experience lived on as a deeply meaningful document of the soul, impacting powerfully on Euripides and his contemporaries, just as it does on modern audiences.

Psychologically, sacrifice implies the need for change in an individual, a society, or a culture. Why, for example, did a condition of stasis reign in

Aulis? The stilling of the winds suggests that the Greek psyche at that time was rooted in lethargy, lacking in insight, reiterative of facile answers, and yielding to superstition and political deception. When stagnation prevails in a social order, an opposing movement frequently emerges both to halt the march of erosion and to breathe a new life force into the collective.

Change implies the death of one attitude or ideational content and the emergence of a new one. Not surprisingly, then, do transformations in a society's reigning conscious attitudes occur after the perpetration of a cruelty: a sacrificial act of blood. Just as blood flows from a woman during the birth process, so Iphigenia's would serve to end the calm, allowing the Greeks to set sail, symbolically uprooting whatever traditional structures stood in the way of what the majority considered to be progress.

The purpose of shedding blood in a religious sacrificial act or deed of "piety" in ancient times was not to take a life, but rather to perpetuate life, to create a bond between the individual and a universe that is still today seen as a terrifying transcendent force over which humanity has no power (Burkert 1983, 2).

The Artemisian Cult

What were Artemis's attributes that allowed her to wield such power over the Greeks and command Iphigenia's blood sacrifice? A maiden goddess, daughter of Zeus and Leto and sister of Apollo, Artemis, like her brother, expertly managed both lyre and bow. Just as war and hunting were tests of manhood in patriarchal societies, so, too, were war and hunting implicit in Amazonian cultures, particularly in the evolution of independent and self-sufficient personalities, such as that of Artemis.

As virgin-*parthenos*, she quested her prey freely and vigorously in raw nature. She was called "the Wild One," the unsubdued huntress, the killer of undomesticated animals. Frequently, aiming her golden shafts at humans—women in particular—she brought pain and even death.

Artemis was one of the most paradoxical feminine figures in the Greek pantheon. While "gracious to the playful cubs of fierce lions and delight[ing] in the suckling young of every wild creature that roves in the field," she was aggressive in chasing and slaying hinds and young girls, the very ones she loved (*Iliad*, bk. 21). Huntress and archer, this "Goddess of Wild Animals" also thrilled to coursing over hill and dale and into forested lands with her pack of maidens; she frolicked and danced with nymphs in open meadows; undaunted, she lived in untamed and rampantly fertile undefined spaces.

Rarely did this deer huntress enter cities, preferring to ride her chariot drawn by two stags through unmarked haunts and boundless territories, sending her golden arrows shimmering through the air in the bland light of the moon (Vernant 1991, 197).

Unlike Athena, who was also a virgin-*parthenos*, Artemis was not asexual but had her erotic side, as did her votaries. Unlike Aphrodite, she was pitiless to women (except the young and pure) who yielded to emotional love. Puzzling, too, was Artemis's role as protectress of pregnant women, of birth, and of human development, given that her arrows and ire were aimed against the gravid. Indeed, Zeus had granted her the power of life or death in childbirth as well as over animals (Jung and Kerényi 1969, 106).

Artemis's mysteriousness may be partially explained by the fact that as the moon goddess she represented a body that waxes, wanes, and disappears, only to come to life again after three moonless nights (Harding 1971, 113). Understandably she was called "the Goddess that Roves by night"; she was remote, yet a "light-bearer" (Otto 1979, 85). In contrast to her brother Apollo, a solar deity, Artemis, as moon, wandered about the land frequently shedding her shadowy and destructive substance. Vengeful for the slightest infraction, she chastised those who were disrespectful towards her (such as Actaeon), but bestowed immortality on those who adored her (such as Hippolytus). For some, her strange and fearsome wildness represented the jealous, domineering, and castrating side of the mother archetype. Others saw and admired her as an autonomous, independent woman, accountable to herself alone, acting authentically and in keeping with her values. She was lauded as well for her positive, even belligerent, attitude toward life, and for her strength and ability to indoctrinate younger generations of females into the wholehearted joys of Nature.

Identification with the hunt, Artemis's chief sport, is also paradoxical. Stabbing, puncturing, and piercing one's prey with bow and arrow, analogous to a deflowering and a catalyst for heightening sexual impulses, associates Artemis with both male and female principles as well as with fertility. "Let all the mountains be mine" are her words in a hymn by the Alexandrian poet Callimachus (310–235 B.C.E.).

Had Artemis's hunting been undirected and unbridled, she would have taken on the contours and personality of a wild animal, killing and devouring her prey in an untamed, "uncivilized" manner. But hers was "a controlled art." The very act of hunting—a sport that adheres to its own laws and regulations—requires not only great skill and practice, but also enormous self-discipline. Thus does hunting—and Artemis by extension—stand for opposition to chaos and the propagation of order.

Artemis was also the deity of girls and boys. During adolescence young people are still unsure of their sexual identities and frequently fluctuate between one sex and the other. Indeed, adolescent males and females are alike in many ways, particularly when competing with each other in various outdoor feats and games, some violent, and strengthening themselves in the process (Vernant 1991, 99).

The Brauronia, an Attic festival celebrated at the temple of Artemis at Brauron, was a mystery. The ritual, celebrated near Athens, on the southeastern coast of Attica, called for a period of seclusion during which girls ranging from seven to fourteen years of age cut a lock of their hair, and removed their girdle and their maiden garments, donning instead saffron-dyed robes to perform "the act of the bear," or *arkteuin* (the animal symbolizing the goddess's fierce and terrifying aspects). In miming the uninhibited and sometimes cruel comportment of wild bears, they were said to be going through a rite of passage, an initiation ("to go within") that took them from an undomesticated state to a tamed and domesticated condition. In this regard, the Brauronia was viewed as a preparation for marriage. The ceremony compelled young, undisciplined girls to confront obstacles and ordeals of all types and was intended to tame their unbridled instincts and ready them for entry into a social system based on what was then considered justice, harmony, and balance. It must be added that the physical strength acquired by the girls participating in the Brauronia ritual inured them to the future pains of childbirth and, most importantly, taught them to experience their body in all of its manifestations.

The symbolic intent of the Brauronia initiation ceremony was to sacrifice the uncommitted, individual virgin—*parthenos*—in preparation for her new destiny, the restricted cohabitation in marriage. The ceremony allegedly originated following an actual event. A tamed bear, brought to Brauron, had scratched a young girl during their play time. The maiden's brother became so enraged by the bear's act that he killed the animal. Other versions state that the bear had been so taunted by the young girl that it tore out her eyes. Her brother killed the animal in an act of retribution. As an aftermath of the slaughter, a plague descended on Athens, which the oracle of Apollo at Delphi proclaimed would vanish only if girls performed a ritual substitution—the "act of the bear"—by playing the role of the bear. Thus was health restored to the city (Vidal-Naquet 1981, 179).

Although, as previously mentioned, Artemis rarely entered a populated place, loving above all else wild and open spaces, she was, nevertheless, worshipped as the "Mistress of the Margins"—that is, as a "civic goddess and city founder in the sanctuaries where she [had] the young cross the boundary to adulthood, where she [lead] them from the limits to the center, from difference to similitude." Despite the fact that her haunts were mountains, meadows, and woods—free and uncultivated lands—she was considered the one who bridged the polarities between wild savage lands and civilized, defined spaces (Vernant 1991, 204). Is it any wonder, then, that young and old, leaders of state as well as humble citizens, prayed to her for courage and strength to cope with disaster prior to entering into a war? Or that city residents offered their sacrifices to her when a scourge threatened to invade their living space?

Iphigenia: Parthenos

We first meet the beautiful maiden, Iphigenia, as a happy, naive, uncommitted young girl who looks forward to her marriage to Achilles. She, the future bearer of children, has been brought to Aulis on Agamemnon's request: he plans to sacrifice her to placate Artemis, who has stilled the winds in order to prevent the Greek army from sailing to Troy.

Ironically, perhaps, are war, marriage, and sacrifice irrevocably intertwined in the Iphigenia myth. Her mock betrothal to the warrior Achilles was to be transformed into an expiatory bonding with the divine Artemis. The sexual act in marriage was, then, to be associated with a violent and brutal struggle—a kind of hunt and wounding foray that would draw blood. What Agamemnon had not foreseen, nor requested, when he invited Iphigenia to Aulis was the troubling presence of Clytemnestra on the scene. And rightly did the mother reason, maintaining that she had accompanied her daughter/ bride to help her get ready for the wedding ceremony.

Iphigenia's appearance in Aulis ushers in a mood of celebration. "Let the flute ring out in the hall, let there be the sound of dancing feet. This is a blessed day that dawns for the maid," a messenger cries out (*I*. 437). Even the Chorus, made up of girls from nearby Chalcis, has come to share in the excitement and gazes reverently at the many famous heroes and soldiers, their ships, and their weapons. No sooner does the naive Iphigenia see her father than she gleefully runs to him and speaks her heart: "I so longed to see your face. . . . Thank you, father, for bringing me to you" (*I*. 636). Despite her joy, she notices an uneasiness about Agamemnon, which he tosses off in a cavalier manner, blaming his concern on the problems confronting kings and generals. Craving for his attention, she insists, "Attend to me now. Forget your worries" (*I.* 645). Strangely, tears pour from his eyes as he assures her of the great happiness in store for her. Quick to sense her father's anxiety and his entanglement in gnawing pain, Iphigenia ascribes them to the loss of his daughter in marriage.

> Agamemnon: I must first offer a certain sacrifice here.
> Iphigenia: Yes, religion requires holy rites.
> Agamemnon: You shall see. You will stand near the lavers.
> Iphigenia: Shall we have dances round the altar, father?
>
> (*I.* 672)

Is it a marriage altar or a sacrificial altar to which Iphigenia refers? In keeping with tradition, young Greek girls were brought up to participate in expiatory rituals, such as the Brauronia mentioned above, preluding the sacrificing of their bodies given in marriage to their husbands. Betrothal, then, like sacrifice, is viewed as a surrender or renunciation of uncommitted girlhood: the death of the maiden and passage into wifehood. Iphigenia's passage from a sheltered home, where she had been the focus of her parents' attention, to her new surroundings as bride and future procreator, was a great step in her emotional development. Instrumental as well was her pledge to submit to a restrictive lifestyle in order to insure her participation in the continuity of her nation. As in the Brauronia ritual, where mothers brought their daughters in procession to Artemis, commending their prepubescent daughters to the care and protection of the "Lady of the Wild Mountains," to use Aeschylus's term, so Clytemnestra arrived in Aulis, prepared to help her daughter in the perpetuation of a tradition associated with female sexuality.

Prayer, incantation, and meditation are ways of expressing the joys of religious ecstasy, and dance also leads to transcendence. "Shall we have dances round the altar, father?" Iphigenia asks (*I.* 677). Certainly, since dance is a rhythmic and ordered way of releasing emotion and bringing new space-time relationships into being, which then fuse with the world at large. It represents energy in a perpetual state of transformation, captured or incorporated into an image, and an evolutive, active, dynamic concentration of forces. Every dance is a pantomime, a paradigm, a theurgic act. Plato considered the dance to be of divine origin: before becoming movement it was sign. Dance would play a similar role for Iphigenia in its anticipation and paralleling of the earthly and celestial events she was to experience.

Agamemnon's sorrow at the thought of sacrificing his daughter had been so acute that prior to Iphigenia's arrival he had sent a messenger with a note requesting that she not to come to Aulis. Did his change of heart symbolize a weakening of his role as military leader? a yielding to his feelings rather than a strengthening of his thinking faculty? Was he trying to defy the fate that had dictated—or genetically programmed—the events long in advance? Agamemnon's attempt to alter the outcome of what immortals have dictated may constitute an act of hubris. If so, it is not surprising that his plan to reverse events is doomed to failure: Menelaus, Agamemnon's brother and Helen's husband, happens upon the messenger on the road out of Aulis and takes the note from him.

Agamemnon's attempt to prevent Iphigenia's visit reveals both his vacillation on the subject of sacrifice and an expression of his own timorous, underhanded, and corrupt nature. Such a reversal of his original direction might also indicate a perversion of judgment on his part. Lies, masks, and duplicitous language are inherent in Agamemnon, a man possessed of a weakly structured ego. Indeed, so deeply imprisoned is he in his identification with his persona—that of a great Panhellenic leader—that he has lost sight of the righteous path.

Agamemnon tells Menelaus that he feels compelled to sacrifice his daughter for the good of the state, an urge that the latter questions.

> Menelaus: Who will force you to kill your own?
> Agamemnon: The whole assembly of the Achaean host.
>
> (*I*. 513)

The name of the seer/priest, Calchas, the oracle who had proclaimed to Agamemnon the necessity of Iphigenia's sacrifice and whom the great leader reviles, is pronounced: "The whole breed of prophets is rotten with ambition" (*I*. 520). Were Agamemnon to disobey the religious command and not sacrifice Iphigenia to Artemis, Calchas would accuse him of "playing false." In such a case, he would not only "carry the army with him" but would ask the Argives to kill Menelaus and himself and then sacrifice Iphigenia (*I*. 531).

As king and leader of his people, Agamemnon is faced with the tragic dilemma of how to comport himself as a *hero* (a collective figure) living up to his public image, and as a loving *father* (an individual). As a public figure,

Agamemnon was expected to divest himself of human emotion and to identify himself with the historical and mythical figure that he was, to be and act as a function, an image, a symbol. He was expected to stand above the "madding crowd" and assume the countenance of an inviolable paradigm. Rejection of the personal world in favor of the universal and eternal, the feminine in favor of the masculine, the real in favor of the ideal, should have been Agamemnon's choice. Instead, he vacillates, battling between his mission as leader of a people and his feelings as father. The greater the breach between the dual facets of his personality, the more emotional and unpredictable becomes his behavioral pattern.

Clytemnestra, having been told by her faithful servant that Agamemnon is planning to sacrifice Iphigenia to Artemis, convinces Achilles, who knows nothing of Agamemnon's wedding plans for him, to fight for the maiden's life. "Never shall your daughter that was spoken of as mine be slaughtered by her father," he assures her (*I.* 932). On the other hand, because this hero seeks to avoid a confrontation with Agamemnon, he counsels Clytemnestra to "beseech" the Greek leader not to kill his child (*I.* 1015). Clytemnestra angrily accuses her husband of cowardice, ascribing his determination to sacrifice his daughter to his fear of being lynched, degraded, and humiliated by the mob/army.

Has Clytemnestra correctly assessed Agamemnon's dread of the superstitious, mutinous rabble and the chaos that would ensue if he were to counter Calchas's order? Or does he tremble for his own life and his prestige? Might he not have thought it wiser to satisfy the lust for power implicit in organized religion and in military might to avert chaos?

As the Chorus steps forward, the stage space rings out with sounds and rhythmic accents of flutes, reeds, and sandals that beat the earth. Viscerality, and by extension, sexuality, associated with the deflowering of the bride by the husband, is now associated with the act of killing/sacrifice.

The attitude of the Chorus toward Iphigenia's wedding/sacrifice seems to have markedly altered. No longer does the group stand in awe of the brawn and beauty of the soldiers as at the outset. Like Iphigenia, the Chorus no longer is girlishly egocentric; it, too, has learned to see through the mask and hypocrisy of the city's political and religious leaders. The joyless Chorus foresees ominous happenings.

> But your head, Iphigenia, with its clustering tresses, the Argives shall wreathe
> like a brindled heifer, undefiled, from a rocky cave in the mountains; they

will stain a human throat with blood. Not with the shepherds' pipe were you brought up, not with the whistling of the herdsman; but you were reared by your mother's side to be one day decked as a bride for some son of Inachus. How can Shame's face or Virtue's be of avail, when Impiety is enthroned and mortals put Virtue behind them and heed her not, when Lawlessness prevails over laws and it is no longer the common problem of mortals to avoid the displeasure of the gods. (*I.* 1076)

Agamemnon cries out:

Fetch the child from the house to join her father. The lustral waters are prepared and ready, as are the meal-cakes to throw in the cleansing fire and the victims which must be slain before the marriage ceremony [victims whose dark blood must gush forth for Artemis]. (*I.* 1110)

Although Iphigenia now is aware of her father's ruse and the role she has been destined to play, she is not yet emotionally prepared to cope with the notion of sacrifice. She begs Agamemnon not to kill her. She argues her point: had she Orpheus's eloquence, she would be able to charm rocks, and even "bewitch" him.

But now my only art is tears, and those I offer; *that* I can do. Like a suppliant bough I press against your knees this body of mine which this woman [Clytemnestra] bore to you; do not destroy me before my time. It is sweet to look upon the light: do not force me to see the things below. I was the first to call you father, the first you called child; I was the first to relax my body upon your knees, to bestow loving caresses and to receive them in turn. (*I.* 1213)

Clasping Agamemnon's knees with her body, clutching him in indication of her love for and dependence on him, Iphigenia regresses into her childhood for the last time. Now, this very person who guided her first steps, to whom she had once looked up to for affection and protection, is intent upon destroying her.

Iphigenia rejects the *reason* for the sacrifice—she considers the war against the Trojans unworthy and she sees herself as being used, even maligned for an unjust cause. She is extraneous to Helen and her wanton love, she maintains. "Have mercy upon me, pity my youth. . . . A poor life is better than a grand death" (*I.* 1252).

Still Agamemnon vacillates:

It is horrible for me to do this dreadful thing, it is horrible for me not to. It is the same for me either way. You see this huge armada, this multitude of Hellene warriors—for them there can be no voyage against the towers of Ilium unless I sacrifice you as prophet Calchas says. . . . They will kill my daughter in Argos, they will kill you, and me, if I break the gods' oracles. . . . It is Hellas for whom I must, whether I wish or not, offer you as sacrifice. I cannot resist the claim of country. Free must she be, as far as you or I can make her. We are Hellenes; we must not allow our women to be violated and carried off by barbarians. (*I.* 1257)

Iphigenia's anger and resentment overflow when she is alone with her mother: "Ah the sorry day for me when I first saw Helen, evil Helen, to my cost, to my cost!" she cries out to Clytemnestra. "I am slain, I perish, foully slaughtered by a godless father" (*I.* 1316).

After some soul-searching, however, Iphigenia "suddenly" complies with her father's demands. Critics have faulted Euripides for such a rapid and implausible change of heart on Iphigenia's part: it was not in her character to veer from one extreme to another. But was the change indeed so expeditious? The discovery of her fate and her initiation into sorrow were rapid and traumatic. The chaotic aftermath of the inner upheaval kindles and reshuffles her emotions, opening her up to a new psychological understanding of life's vagaries.

Mortals are born to sorrow, ay, creatures of a day and born to sorrow; they fulfil their destiny in misery. (*I.* 1324)

Now she recognizes that her body, her "mineness" or ego, must no longer be centered on herself, but rather must be subordinated to the needs of the collective for a larger purpose, which is, psychologically, that "otherness," that Self. She becomes conscious of the profound meaning that society attaches to sacrifice: serve the needs of others instead of one's own. Rather than marry Achilles and enjoy personal happiness, she, like her father, will devote herself to a purpose superior to her own. As sacrificial victim, she sees herself as instrumental—a crucial factor—in allowing the Greeks to sail to Troy.

Iphigenia's thinking function has altered. She experiences a growing sense of her power over herself as well as a capacity to assess and even defend her father's project. Just as Agamemnon had taken into consideration his own image, she considers that shame might be heaped on her if she shuns her obligation to sacrifice her life for the well-being of her people. The slow progression from ego-centered to Self-centered existence indicates a shift from Iphigenia's earlier personal sorrows and need for well-being to concerns that reach beyond herself.

Iphigenia's Wedding/Sacrifice Ceremony

Iphigenia's wedding/sacrifice ceremony is an initiation: a descent into death or, psychologically, into Self. Such a trajectory implies a passing from one level of the subliminal sphere to another, to the deepest strata of being—the collective unconscious. Such a *katabasis* allows the initiate to reconnect with her own past and concomitantly with humanity's primordial existence. Socrates' "Know thyself" means discover the inner person—an exploration that requires a profound probing of one's being.

The object of an initiation, as has already been suggested, is an illumination; it cannot be taught, nor can it be recounted to friends or acquaintances, nor handed down from one generation to another. It can only be experienced. Because the emotions experienced by Iphigenia—or any other noviitate—during her rite of passage cannot be articulated, the entire experience is lived out hermetically.

The steps in the initiatory celebration of Iphigenia's wedding/sacrifice are outlined by Euripides as follows:

1. Bathing in lustral water.
2. Placing wreaths and garlands on Iphigenia's head and her donning of clean clothes and ornaments.
3. Dance: "Weave the dance about the temple, about the altar of Artemis, about Queen Artemis the blessed" (*I.* 1481).
4. The Chorus sings out its chants as the festival begins.
5. Iphigenia's apotheosis.

Iphigenia's marriage with death requires a purification of her body with lustral waters in order to render the gift of herself as pure as humanly possible and worthy of attendance upon Artemis. The meal-cakes to be fed to the "cleansing fire and the victims which must be slain before the marriage ceremony" heighten the intensity of the sublime moment of crossing the fine line from life to death (*I.* 1111). The incandescent image and the sensations evoked by it prelude the slaughter and the flowing blood that serve to nourish Artemis, the Earth Mother.

The holy blood—sacramental food—spilled on the altar to redeem

Agamemnon's affront, is transformed during the ritual into manna. A communal meal such as the archaic *sparagmos* (eating of the flesh), when viewed symbolically, becomes an energetic force. Iphigenia, then, will release her people from the calm or period of cultural and spiritual stagnation they had been experiencing and inject them with a new force (Harrison 1966, 154).

The once naive maiden who had first entered Aulis is now highly sophisticated in the ways of both religion and the world. Projecting on her deity, she becomes Artemis's votary, her servant, a virile power, a replica of nature's own force and, psychologically, an entity unto herself. Having transcended the limited mentality of mortals, her vision now encompasses the infinite. Death, therefore, is no longer broached in terms of a personal sacrifice, but rather as the fulfillment of a collective need—as the realization of her Self/Artemis. Indeed, Iphigenia feels she is reaching such lofty heights that she becomes transfixed by the thought of the unique role she is about to assume. Pride rather than terror and love instead of hatred swell her countenance as she plays out the role of a heroine in history and in myth—for all time. The thought of marriage with death, no longer mutually exclusive, triggers her passion and enhances her grandeur. Life and death having become synonymous, Iphigenia lived out her fantasy, experienced herself ascending to extraordinary heights, reaching directly to the Divinity. Her beatification will be earned via her sacrificial death.

Like Artemis, Iphigenia, like many contemporary young girls no matter the discipline or medium, exists as mistress of her destiny: an *anima* image symbolizing the soul of her people. Although free now from the infantile concerns that marked her at the outset of her initiatory journey, she is nonetheless considerate of her mother's feelings of woe. To Clytemnestra she explains the meaning of her sacrifice, attempting as best she can to assuage her sorrow. As "a benefactress of Hellas," she feels blessed. She bears her father no grudge or ill will. On the contrary, she feels fulfilled, deeply happy, and asks her mother not to weep for her. To do so would be cowardly. Nor must Clytemnestra cut her hair or wear a black robe as a sign of mourning, nor hate her father, whom Iphigenia no longer sees as a villain, but rather as a hero: "It was for Hellas that he destroyed me" (*I.* 1456). Because of him, both Iphigenia and her mother will become "famous"; the altar upon which the maiden is to be slain will become her memorial. She asks her mother to return home. One of her father's men will conduct her to the sacred space where the act of piety is to be enacted: "to the meadow of Artemis" where she is "to be slain" (*I.* 1464).[3]

Standing erect, Iphigenia lives out her potential—or destiny—her words ringing in jubilation:

> Let someone initiate the rites with the sacred baskets; let the fire blaze with the cakes of purification and let my father circle the altar from the left toward the right. I come to bring the Hellenes salvation and victory. (*I.* 1475)

The very effulgence of her tones has removed her from earthly spheres and catapulted her into transpersonal domains. She experiences herself as the adored virgin, who must die for her people, and the savior, ready to immolate herself for humanity.

Unlike the uncommitted bride at the outset of the drama, Iphigenia is now fully equipped to carry out her mission of wedding not the individual, but the collective; not a husband, but a nation. Strong and powerful in her vision, she may be likened to a warrior queen, iridescent, almost Amazonian in strength. As her words cascade into the atmosphere, orchestrated in a medley of sounds punctuated by cries and silences, they vibrate in the air. The atmosphere chills at the betrothal of sublimity and gore. *Ekstasis* has taken over:

> With my blood, if I must, with my sacrifice I shall wash away her oracle's bidding. Ah, revered mother, mother revered, my tears I shall not give you; at the sanctuary tears may not flow. Ho, damsels, ho! Join with me in singing the praise of Artemis who is worshipped over against Chalcas, where now in the narrow haven of Aulis by reason of me the angry spearmen are thirsting for the fight.
>
> For a light unto Hellas you nurtured me: I do not skirt death. . . .
>
> Ho, Day, the Light-bringer, ho, radiance of Zeus! Another life, another state will be mine. Farewell, beloved light. (*I.* 1483)

The priest Calchas grasps the knife to plunge it into Iphigenia's throat, when suddenly the miracle occurs:

> [T]here was a marvel to behold. Every man clearly heard the sound of the stroke, but no one saw where in the world the maiden vanished. . . . A deer was lying on the ground, gasping; she was very large and handsome to see, and the goddess' altar was thoroughly sprinkled with her blood. (*I.* 1581)

By substituting the deer for the maiden, Artemis indicated her acceptance of the offering. Carried off in a cloud to the land of the Tauri (today's Crimea), Iphigenia lives on as priestess to the goddess who has made her immortal.

Why did Artemis substitute the deer for Iphigenia? Since marriage requires the death of the *parthenos,* no wife or mother can escape the rite of passage required by the goddess. It was she who encouraged boys and girls to grow into adolescence, yielding only their childhood years to her; it was she as well who helped girls advance from prepubescence to menarche, and lads from ephebe to citizen-soldier and father. Only after clearing the hurdles between one stage of life and another, only by leaving a previously naive and undeveloped attitude to move on to what was and still is considered by many to be a more mature vision of the world did the girl or the lad earn freedom from Artemis and assume her or his life "ideally," as an independent, thoughtful and discerning individual.

Iphigenia's sacrifice—as well as that of Antigone, Alcestis and Polyxena, to mention but a few of the many women who chose martyrdom throughout history—reflects a need in the psyche of the Greek people to admire the values of the feminine principle, until then so deeply scarred and repressed. Family commitment and honor, sensitivity toward the suffering of others, strength and courage in the face of death are implicit in Iphigenia's passage from youth to maturity. Timorous comportment, looked upon as shameful, would have served to deplete the ruling moral code. Significant as well is the Greek notion that since ordinary mortals are offered no rewards for valorous actions in the afterlife—as they are in Christianity—self-sacrifice and martyrdom are, to their way of thinking, all the more meritorious (Lefkowitz 1986, 103).

Like her patron deity, Artemis, Iphigenia lives out her truth in the authenticity of her act. In need of no earthly being to guide her, she formulates her own way. As the paradigm of a profoundly moral force, her life, willingly and consciously given for the community of beings, not only nourishes and sustains them spiritually but is instrumental in their rebirth, and at the root of their ethical development.

5 Herodias/Salome: Mother/Daughter Identification

In patriarchal societies, Herodias and her daughter Salome are paradigms of the Great Mother archetype in her avatar as castrator. Herodias is viewed as a sensual, destructive, heartless mother figure, while Salome, her embryonic psyche still embedded in the archaic folds of her subliminal spheres, is considered to be amoral. A mirror image of her mother as a young girl, Salome functions as a shadow force: a performer, dancer, the instrument of her mother's will. Not only is her ego undeveloped but she has no identity; her name is not even mentioned in the synoptic Gospels. Referred to simply as "the daughter of Herodias," she is a nonperson who serves as her mother's appendage (Matt. 14:6).

The Herodias/Salome myth is, like most myths, filled with discrepancies, confusion of dates and names, contradictions, and errors that have remained uncorrected. Authors, artists, and composers expanding on the original myth have exploited and distorted the events and characters to suit their own psychological, sexual, religious, aesthetic, and literary needs.

Why was Salome's name omitted in the sacred synoptic texts yet included in the profane works of the historian Flavius Josephus (37–95 C.E.), author of *The Jewish War* and *Jewish Antiquities*? More significant is the fact that Josephus made no mention of Salome's dance; nor was it alluded to in other documents of the period. Also excluded by Josephus, but included with specific details in the synoptic texts, was Salome's request to Herod, allegedly instigated by Herodias, that John the Baptist be decapitated and his head brought in a charger to her, who in turn gave it to her mother (Dubois 1986, 55). Josephus did not specify how John died, nor did he indicate the roles played by Herodias or Salome—if any—in his demise. Nor did he point up, as had the Evangelists, Herod's seeming hesitation before the beheading.

Was Salome an innocent "damsel," a passive daughter subservient and fully obedient to her mother? Was the dance she performed—if she performed one—an iconization of a sexually awakened woman who well knew how to provoke the lust of her stepfather, Herod Antipas? Did the authors of the synoptic texts avail themselves of this nameless feminine image to warn humanity of dangerous females who lure the unsuspecting male to his doom? In keeping with the androcentric view of the Evangelists, the parameters of the Herodias/Salome myth are masculine. Mother and daughter became the prototypes of the archetypal, all-consuming, sensual female, which the ascetic John reviled as the irremediable foe of a budding Christianity. With few exceptions, the reputation of women was identified with the Salome myth and they were viewed as a destructive force. Indeed, Herodias, and her daughter by extension, became "the scapegoat of Christianity" and "representative of the oppositional force to the advent of the Divine word" (ibid., 48).

During the Crusades, for example, a John the Baptist cult was born, drawing many followers under its aegis. In the process, multiple piquant *antifeminine* details were added to the negative view of women at this period and others. Herodias and Salome were featured at times as witches riding their broomsticks and demons commanding a whole army of devils to indulge in *Walpurgisnacht* revelry. The myth aroused the interest of writers: Gustave Flaubert ("Hériodias"), Joris-Karl Huysmans *(Against the Grain)*, Heinrich Heine ("Atta Troll"), and Oscar Wilde *(Salomé)*; of painters: Bernardino Luini, Titian, Ghirlandaio, and Moreau; and of composers: Jules-Emile Massenet *(L'Hérodiade)*, and Richard Strauss *(Salome)*.

Ectypal Analysis

What are some of the historical facts surrounding the Herodias/Salome myth? And in what way may they account for its birth and popularity?

With the explosion of Hellenistic cosmopolitanism in Palestine, Egypt, and throughout the Middle East following Alexander's demise, there arose virtually continuous power plays and wars between such rulers as the Ptolemies, the Seleucid kings, and the Roman Emperors. The Ptolemies, monarchs of Egypt and Judaea (320–198 B.C.E.), were tolerant of the Jews who had been attracted to this land. Allowed to practice their religion and given their own ethnarch (hereditary head of a state), Egyptian Jews were permitted to participate in every aspect of Egyptian life. Delighted by the hellenization movement, many learned Greek, adopted Greek names, and indulged in a flurry of creativity. Not only was the translation of the Hebrew Bible into Greek (the Septuagint) begun in the third century, but the Platonist philosopher Philo Judaeus of Alexandria (25 B.C.E.–40 C.E.) wrote his *Questions and Solutions, Life of Moses,* and *An Exposition of Mosaic Law for Gentiles.* He interrelated Hellenistic philosophy and piety with the Jewish belief in revelation and Holy Scripture, and explained biblical statements allegorically, emphasizing their higher spiritual meaning.

Because the Ptolemies and Seleucids vied for dominance of Palestine, Judaea became the battleground of enemy forces until its fate was decided by Antiochus IV (175 B.C.E.) who, upon becoming king, established Seleucid rule.

In his determination to transform Jerusalem into a Greek city, Antiochus IV alienated many traditional Jews who were dismayed by the nudity of the athletes performing in the imported Greek games, as well as by the growing climate of license, luxury, and corruption. Banned by Antiochus, among other rituals, were circumcision, Sabbath observance, and the reading of the Torah. Imposed upon Jews was the transformation of their Temple into a syncretistic sanctuary honoring Zeus, who was at this time identified with the Phoenician Baal. Not only were Greek deities to be worshipped in these heretofore sacred precincts, but pigs (considered unclean by Jews and forbidden as food) were ordered to be sacrificed on the altar. So fierce was the spirit of Antiochus IV's "civilizing" innovations that many inhabitants of Jerusalem were slaughtered and/or taken into slavery as punishment for infractions. Thanks to the leadership of Judas Maccabeus, Jews united to fight the oppressive Seleucids, who finally abandoned their hellenization policy. The Temple was restored and rededicated on 14 December 164 B.C.E., an event still commemorated in the festival of lights (Cohn-Sherbok 1988, 42ff.).

The unceasing political and military strife was finally brought to a momentary halt with Julius Caesar's victory over Pompey (49 B.C.E.). Hyrcanus, a former high priest, was awarded the title of ethnarch for having allied himself with Caesar. Hyrcanus's clever minister, Antipater (one of the Idumeans, a group forcibly converted to Judaism), appointed his own three sons prefects. One of them was Herod the Great (Roth 1961, 93).

Following the assassination of Julius Caesar (44 B.C.E.), which grieved the Jews, Mark Antony formed, along with Lepidus and Octavian (later Augustus), a coalition known as the Second Triumvirate. Herod's political sagacity deeply impressed Antony who, together with Octavian, nominated him to the Roman Senate (40 B.C.E.). The Senate ironically proclaimed Herod, this non-Jew who became known as Herod the Great, king of the Jews.

Known for his cruelty, shrewdness, and cold and calculating ambition, and for his ten wives and many concubines, Herod remained Octavian's deputy for twenty-seven years. During his reign he continued the hellenization of his nation, extended its boundaries to include Hippos and Gadara, on the other side of the Jordan, and recouped much of the land Pompey had taken from Judaea (63 B.C.E.).

Herod the Great's bloodthirsty massacres of Jews and of his family (his wife Mariamme, his two sons by her, her brother, his mother-in-law, etc.) and his increasingly repressive measures created a state of virtually constant rebellion that continued even after Herod's death and ceased only after being ruthlessly put down by Roman legionnaires.

Herod Antipas (4 B.C.E.–39 C.E.), son of the deceased Herod the Great, and with whom we are concerned in the Herodias/Salome myth, received his share of his father's domain. Although appointed tetrarch (literally, "ruler of a fourth part," but applied to a subordinate prince) of Galilee and Peraea, his was a nominal title since rulership of the Jewish kingdom was decided in Rome; garrisons were stationed throughout the land to ensure a modicum of stability (ibid., 94). The situation for Jews, however, became increasingly difficult with the imposition of higher taxes; moreover, believers felt spiritually deprived because the High Priesthood had been divested of its independence as a religious body.

Nevertheless, Antipas did not go out of his way to alienate the Jews. He even sided with the Jews, at least outwardly, against the provocations and offenses of the procurator of Judaea, Pontius Pilate (26–36 C.E), who, according to Josephus, was ruthless, intransigent, and cruel (*Jewish Antiquities* 18.55–59).[1] Shortly after his arrival in Palestine, Pilate provoked the Jews by introducing Roman standards bearing likenesses of Caesar. So outraged were the devout at the sight of the graven images that "they rushed to Pilate in Caesarea, and begged him to remove the *signa* from Jerusalem and to respect their ancient customs. When Pilate refused, they fell prone all round his house and remained motionless for five days and nights. . . . Amazed at the intensity of their religious fervour, Pilate ordered the *signa* to be removed from Jerusalem" (Josephus 1959, 127).

Pilate was not so magnanimous on other occasions. When Jews rioted, protesting his spending of funds taken from the sacred treasury (*corbonas*: a religious trust) for the building of an aqueduct (ibid; Hoehner 1980, 174), he had "the Jews cudgeled, so that many died from the blows" (Josephus 1959,

127). More ignominious acts on Pilate's part are mentioned by Josephus; the Evangelists mention the Galilaeans' blood that "Pilate had mingled with their sacrifices" (Luke 13:1:1) and the Crucifixion.

Antipas's desire to defend his territory against Arabians and other neighbors encouraged him for political reasons to marry the daughter of the Nabatean (Arabian) king Aretas IV *(Jewish Antiquities* 18.109). He pursued his political courtships, stopping on one occasion en route to Rome at the home of his half-brother, Herod Philip. So mesmerized was he by his host's wife, Herodias, that he proposed marriage to her then and there. The Gospels indicate that Philip was Herodias's husband, but Josephus maintains that she was married to Herod, son of Herod the Great and Mariamme II. It has been suggested that the Herod of Josephus and the Philip of Matthew and Mark were the same person (Hoehner 1980, 130–36). His proposal having been accepted by Herodias, it was decided that after his journey to Rome he would divorce his wife, the daughter of Aretas IV, who, however, had meanwhile learned of Antipas's deceit. Escaping to her father's domain, she instigated the Nabatean royal family to invade Antipas's lands and defeat her husband (ibid., 144–45).

Although Josephus omits in his writings the dance episode that led to John's death, he does ascribe Herod's military defeat by Aretas's army to "Divine Providence"—a kind of vindication of John, since "God saw fit to inflict such a blow on Herod" *(Jewish Antiquities* 18.127).

The Herodias/Salome myth grew up around the physical, moral, and psychological depravity of the Romans, of Herod the Great, and of Antipas and his entourage of hedonists. Their perversions were anathema to orthodox dicta and ascetic practices. The austere theocracy of the Hebrews and the polytheistic Hellenistic cosmopolitanism in Palestine were on a collision course (Eliade 1980, 2:249).

Beliefs were divided in the Jewish community of Judaea. Some (John the Baptist and the Essenes), extreme in their condemnation of the pleasure principle, including sexual desire and its gratification, threatened offenders with hell, fire, and damnation; others, the Pharisees and the Sadducees, although deeply obedient to the Torah, were less intransigent. John the Baptist castigated both the Pharisees and the Sadducees, calling them a "generation of vipers" (Matt. 3:7).

The Pharisees (in Hebrew, *perash*, "to separate") were a sect, founded around 200 B.C.E., of ascetic separatists who lived according to the Old Testament ideals of the Torah as well as the Oral Law, both of which had been given by God to Moses on Mt. Sinai. They believed, among other tenets, in the resurrection of the body, in a life after death; and they tried to adapt the Torah to suit contemporary conditions. Not only did the Pharisees advocate humane treatment of slaves and criminals but they applied the much-maligned biblical rule of "an eye for an eye" to monetary compensation *only* and not to retribution for an "evil" deed. The Pharisees lived simple lives, rejected luxury, fasted, and practiced such purification rituals as frequent handwashing. Although Pharisaism fell into disuse after 135 C.E., it was influential in the development of Orthodox Judaism.

Jesus, according to Luke, had a different view of the Pharisees; he considered them self-righteous: "Woe unto you, scribes and Pharisees, hypocrites!" (Luke 11:44). According to Matthew, Jesus' words were "Woe unto you, scribes and Pharisees, hypocrites! for ye devour widows' houses, and for a pretence make long prayer: therefore ye shall receive the greater damnation" (Matt. 23:14). And again, "Woe unto you, scribes and Pharisees, hypocrites! for ye compass sea and land to make one proselyte, and when he is made, ye make him twofold more the child of hell than yourselves" (Matt. 23:15).

A priestly aristocracy formed in ca. 200 B.C.E., the sect of the Sadducees (*tzedukim*, the word stemming perhaps from King David's priest Zadok), did not embrace the Oral Law, but only Hebrew Scriptures. Nor did they believe in the immortality of the soul, resurrection, or the coming of the Messiah. The Sadducees were literalists whose world centered around the cult of the Temple; with its destruction by Titus Flaminius in 70 C.E., they ceased to exist.

The Essenes, a tightly knit sect originating in the second century B.C.E., existed until Titus's military onslaught. Their laws, more rigid than those of the Pharisees, were based to a great extent on eschatological expectations: the coming of the Messiah. Preaching repentance before Judgment Day, when sinners and the godless would perish, they were exact observers of the Written and Oral Law and had a firm faith in immortality, but not in resurrection. They lived communally, subsisting by pastoral and agricultural activities and handicrafts, and believed in the establishment of a communistic egalitarian Kingdom of Heaven on earth. Their lifestyle was characterized by no private ownership, strict observance of the Sabbath and of the dietary laws, meals taken together and in silence, extreme cleanliness (purification through baptism), and the wearing of only white garments. So firmly were the Essenes convinced of the reality of angels and demons that they considered disease to be possession by evil spirits, and used magic formulas drawn from their "secret doctrine" to exorcise ailments (Kaufmann 1976, 109).

Although Josephus, Pliny, and Philo are at variance concerning the Essenes, scholars believe that this group lived virtually monastic and celibate lives. They avoided sensual pleasures of all kinds, focusing instead on meditation, piety, abstinence, contemplation, and prayer as a means of uniting with God. Those who married did so only to procreate. In "Apology for the Jews," Philo makes known their (his) misogynist views:

> Indeed no one of the Essenes marries a wife, because the wife is a selfish creature, immoderately smitten with jealousy, and terrible at shaking to their foundations the natural habits of a man, and bringing him under power by continual beguilements. For, as she practises fair false speeches, and other kinds of hypocrisy, as it were upon the stage, when she has succeeded in alluring eyes and ears, like cheated servants, she brings cajolery to bear upon the sovereign mind. (Quoted in Fritsch 1956, 96)

The burgeoning of various cults in the Jewish community fomented political, social, and philosophical rebellion. A secessionist spirit was in the air, and these historical events served as the backdrop to the unfolding of the Herodias/Salome myth.

Archetypal Analysis

Herodias and Salome, the first couple in the quaternity of Herodias, Salome, Antipas, and John the Baptist, may be viewed as mirror images of each other, each dependent upon the other for survival.

Herodias

The granddaughter of Herod the Great by Mariamme (executed by her husband), Herodias was the daughter of Aristobulus (executed by his father) and his cousin Berenice. Orphaned at ten years of age, her grandfather married her to one of her uncles, Herod Philip. According to Josephus, their offspring was named Salome. On one of Antipas's trips to Rome, as previously mentioned, he met Herodias, was smitten with her beauty and sensuality, and proposed marriage. Independent and passionate, she accepted, thus rejecting the law of her clan in order to marry the man of her choice. Whether motivated to accept Antipas's proposal for reasons of social advancement or whether otherwise drawn to him is not known. Once their marriage concluded, she would be better poised to live out what she considered to be her great destiny.

Throughout history Herodias has been labeled as opportunistic, scheming, ambitious, aggressive, envious, debauched, and castrating. She was, nevertheless, persevering, seemingly conscious of her acts and desires, and loyal to Antipas when necessary. She even revealed traits of kindness: when her brother, Agrippa, had squandered his inheritance and found himself penniless, Herodias prevailed on Antipas to help him financially. That Antipas gave Agrippa insufficient funds and failed to continue to provide for him is another matter.

According to the Gospels, Herodias never forgave John for having condemned both her divorce from her first husband, Herod Philip, and her marriage to Antipas, his half-brother. "For John had said unto Herod, It is not lawful for thee to have thy brother's wife. Therefore Herodias had a quarrel against him, and would have killed him; but she could not" (Mark 6:18–19). John's condemnation was, however, in order. Such marriages were contrary to Jewish law (Lev. 18:16): they were considered incestuous, particularly in Herodias's case, since Herodias's rejected husband was still alive.

Usually clever and well-spoken, her grudge ("quarrel") against John might have been long-standing, dating back prior to her marriage to Antipas. It might have stemmed from the very real fear that Antipas, weak as he was, might heed the words of this strong and highly appealing man and renege on his marriage proposal. Anxiety at the thought of being dispossessed or displaced because of this ascetic may have added to her tension. Known for her subtlety and secretive nature, however, Herodias must have soon decided to bide her time until she could outmaneuver her enemy.

Unlike Herodias, Antipas apparently imprisoned John not out of anger, but out of terror at the thought of being overthrown by his multitude of followers. Who better than John, Antipas might have reasoned, *knew* how to persuade and magnetize his listeners? Whatever Antipas's motivations were for imprisoning the Baptizer, as he was called, Mark and Matthew maintain that the tetrarch acted not for himself but altruistically, for "Herodias's sake." "For Herod himself had sent forth and laid hold upon John and bound him in prison for Herodias's sake, his brother Philip's wife: for he had married her" (Mark 6:17). According to Matthew: "For Herod had laid hold on John, and bound him, and put him in prison for Herodias's sake, his brother Philip's wife" (Matt.14:3).

The Evangelists enhanced Antipas's generosity and improved his image at the expense of his wife. That Herodias received the blame for John's incarceration may in some respects parallel the excuse Adam gave for eating the fruit of the tree of knowledge: not because he wanted to, but because "the woman whom thou gavest to be with me, she gave me of the tree, and I did eat" (Gen. 3:12). As is frequently the case in androcentric societies, the woman in the Herodias/Salome myth, burdened with the responsibility for Antipas's act, took on the imprint of archetypal seducer, deceiver, instigator, and perpetrator of the future crime.

Antipas's birthday feast might have seemed to Herodias the appropriate moment for revenge. Rather than acting overtly, this subtle and disingenuous woman, as inferred from the synoptic texts, remained in the shadows. A background figure, quiet and withdrawn, she gave the impression of being a spectator and not an active force. Like a puppeteer manipulating her marionettes, she discreetly directed the events.

Why, one may ask, had Herodias remained so secreted during the celebration? Had she grown old? Was she no longer appealing to her husband? Had she become desexualized? Had her daughter become the favorite? Perhaps. Although we have no knowledge on the subject, we do know that the intuitive Herodias *knew* men: she sensed their weaknesses and understood how to manipulate them until she gained her end. In this instance, she may have encouraged her nubile daughter to dance in order to eroticize her impotent husband, psychologically, and perhaps physically.

If Salome did dance—whether she did is a moot question—her age, estimated as ranging between ten to sixteen, her naïveté, and her obedience to her mother would earn her vindication. She knew not what she did. Blame therefore was heaped on the unrepentant and depersonalized archetypal mother, Herodias, the incarnation of evil.

Josephus compounded her destructive nature by his description of her envy. Her brother, Agrippa, had been given extensive lands and the title of king by Gaius Caligula upon the latter's accession to the emperorship. "The spectacle of his royal visits in the customary regalia before the multitudes made her especially helpless to keep this unfortunate envy to herself," Josephus writes. Although she refrained from taking overt action, she "instigated her husband" into enhancing his own position. She might have mocked or maligned his lack of ambition and political astuteness. After all, she could have argued, he had been Rome's faithful servant for many years, and deserved far more than her brother (*Jewish Antiquities* 18.238, 243).

Herodias failed to kindle Antipas's ambition. He preferred to wait for what he considered to be the propitious moment. But Herodias was so insistent that he finally yielded and left for Rome to ask for power similar to that accorded her brother. They tried to discredit Agrippa with the emperor, but only brought about their own banishment. Caligula ordered that Antipas's tetrarchy and property be given to Agrippa and that the couple be condemned to perpetual exile in Lyons (Lugdunum, Gaul). Learning, however, that Herodias was Agrippa's sister, he offered to allow her to keep her personal property and not go into exile with her husband. It must be said in Herodias's favor that in this instance she not only revealed her deep commitment to Antipas but also, perhaps, acknowledged her responsibility for his downfall.

> Indeed, O emperor, these are generous words and such as befit your high office, but my loyalty to my husband is a bar to my enjoyment of your kind gift, for it is not right when I have shared in his prosperity that I should abandon him when he has been brought to this pass. (Ibid., 18.253–54)

Considering Herodias's reply to his magnanimous offer as arrogant, Caligula ordered her to share her husband's exile and to give all of her property to Agrippa. "And so God visited this punishment on Herodias for her envy of her brother and on Herod for listening to a woman's frivolous chatter" (ibid., 18.255).

Given the patriarchal society of the time, it is not surprising that the synoptic texts identify Herodias with the *vagina dentata* type: a terrifying, lurid, unmodifiable, and immutable maw ready at every moment to devour her male prey. Androcentric assumptions assign her the role of evildoer.

Salome

Unlike Herodias, Salome is virtually a nonperson. Even her name, as previously mentioned, was omitted in the synoptic Gospels. We know nothing about her, not even whether she was married to her uncle, the tetrarch Herod Philip II, at the time of or following the alleged performance of her dance. Historians, however, confirm the fact that upon the death of her first husband, she wedded the Armenian king, Aristobulus (d. 34 C.E.).

The unnamed Salome is featured as a dancer and an obedient daughter: a *persona*, mask, masquerade. Did she reveal her personal disposition as she moved about on stage? Did Matthew, Mark, and Luke, by omitting her name, paradoxically indicate her presence by her absence? Was she a willing participant in such subterfuge, dissimulating her identity behind her persona? Or was she simply devoid of personality, as she was of a name? *Was* she the *Other:* her performance, her dance, her mask, her sign?

The Evangelists reacted negatively to Salome's *seemingly* seductive dance. Questions arise, however, as to the very *actuality* of her performance. That a princess in Judaea should have danced before an audience at a banquet to which illustrious dignitaries had been invited was well nigh impossible in her day (Psichari 1915, 138).

But if she did dance, did she uplift the onlookers with a sacred performance or did she regale them with a sensual belly dance? That women have danced since biblical times is a truism. When Miriam leaped for joy following the crossing of the Red Sea, she conveyed her feelings of religious *ekstasis* physically (Exod. 15:20–21). After the building of the Temple by King Solomon (tenth century B.C.E.), maidens also expressed their pleasure in life and in God by dancing in the vineyards. Forbidden by the rabbis, however, were solitary erotic dances (Isa. 23:16). For the orthodox Hebrews of the time—Pharisees, Sadducees, Essenes—the titillating dance Salome was purported to have performed was immoral and degrading. Young princesses did not make it a practice to dance before male strangers. Rather they remained discreetly concealed in some closed-off space. Had the princess Salome been trained to dance before audiences that included illustrious dignitaries and high officials? Like the accomplished courtesan or the sacred dancer, in her performance she neither feared nor faltered. Her dignity and restraint may have served even to increase her sensual allure. Had she been taught that covert rather than overt ways frequently enhance the mysteries of form? Was Salome, then, an artist trained in the dance? Or was she a "sexually perverse" and "degenerate" woman?

Salome's dance may also have been used by the authors of the synoptic Gospels as an infallible argument to downgrade women, in keeping with patriarchal standards. Salome's lascivious body movements rendered Antipas virtually mad, to the point that he offered her everything and anything. Significant as well is the thought that her performance may have been designed by her mother, or by Salome herself in keeping with her role as Herodias's appendage, for the express sadomasochistic purpose of obtaining sexual stimuli from the Baptizer's powerful moral condemnation. Perverse provocation by mother and daughter nicely illustrated to the people the thrust of the Evangelists' narrative: Salome was to evil just what Eve was to evil.

John, as has been noted, condemned the *pleasure principle* because it detracted from complete immersion in the worship of God. In that Herodias felt no conflict between spirit and body, but rather appreciated the latter for its beauty, sensuality, and elegance, she may have relished the thought of using its power to arouse man's appetite. So, too, must Salome, as her mother's mirror image, have pleasured beneath the gaze of her audience. The center of attention, she lured and allured, triggering that *je ne sais quoi*—that inner energy—which mesmerized Antipas.

The rhythmified forms interwoven in three-dimensional space, which came into being only to vanish moments later, so aroused Antipas that he lost contact with the temporal world, becoming virtually absorbed by his phantasms. His ego/identity departed as in a dream; he was transformed into a mighty ruler and felt it incumbent upon himself to offer the performer "whatsoever she would ask" (Matt. 14:7), even "half of [his] kingdom" (Mark 6:23). The archetypal vision of the dancing Salome must have en*tranced* him. It triggered his libido (psychic energy) so powerfully as to endow the primal image before him with an inner life of its own, which then encapsulated him entirely.

As an archetypal figure Salome may, however, be understood as one who used her body not only to arouse Antipas sexually but also to satirize the weakness of this flesh-dominated man and downgrade *male* power.

> And when the daughter of the said Herodias came in, and danced, and pleased Herod and them that sat with him, the king said unto the damsel, Ask of me whatsoever thou wilt, and I will give it thee. (Mark 6:22)

One may read the synoptic texts as an enhancement of the stature of woman: Salome was the one who directed "man's" downfall.

Could a tetrarch such as Antipas have been so easily destabilized? Could a simple vision of a dancing figure affect him so completely? Or was he drawn, consciously or unconsciously, to his stepdaughter in the hope of making her his mistress? "And he sware unto her, Whatsoever thou shalt ask of me, I will give it thee, unto the half of my kingdom" (Mark 6:23).

Matthew wrote that the mother had told the daughter to ask for John's head prior to her dance: "And she, being before instructed by her mother, said, Give me here John Baptist's head in a charger" (14: 8). Mark claims that Salome asked for her mother's counsel after her performance: "'What shall I ask?' And she said, the head of John the Baptist" (Mark 6:24).

Both agree that Antipas regretted his decision (Matt. 14:9; Mark 6:26). Having given his pledge before so many important people, he could not lose face by withdrawing it. That the severed head was brought to Herodias gave the mother proof of her enemy's demise and marked her victory over the forces of extreme patriarchal asceticism.

Was it an irony of fate that John the Evangelist's mother was said to have been called Salome (Mark 15:40, 16:1), the very name of the one who had requested John the Baptist's head?

Mother/Daughter Identity

From the male perspective, Herodias was considered irritating, destructive, castrating; her daughter, a younger version of the older figure. Other mother/ daughter archetypes have also been conflated: Jezebel/Athaliah (Kings 1 and 2), Clytemnestra/Electra, Demeter/Persephone. As mirror images of each other, they are timeless collective beings involved in a battle of the sexes.

The evidently close bond between mother and daughter, or the symbiotic relationship they enjoyed, could be penetrated by no man. Herodias, that sexually desirable woman who swept Antipas off his feet the minute he saw her, was the vamp or femme fatale; Salome, the *puella*. Mother and daughter in this regard were two versions of the same person.

As *puella,* Salome was a tabula rasa. Like Adam and Eve, she lived unconsciously, as does a child, unaware of right or wrong. Her identification with her mother seemed to prolong her undeveloped adolescence, in an overpowering relationship typified by the biblical twosome of Jezebel and Athaliah. Salome may be said to have lived in her mother's shadow: unable to grow as an individual (in the light of consciousness), her ego remained stunted, amputated from the very outset. The fruit of her mother's creation, she was a recipient of Herodias's attitudes and needs. By yielding to her mother's desires, she erroneously believed herself to be reaching out to her, thereby expressing harmony between them. Instead, she was possessed by her driving, compelling, and powerful mother.

Salome's *unformed, empty, identityless,* and *unlived* ego had unwittingly transformed her into Herodias's weapon: the *dancer* or *actress,* whose gestures and role called for the mutilation and dismemberment of the enemy—John. As Herodias's daughter, there existed in Salome the energy of the Terrible Mother, albeit in mitigated form. Her tragedy stemmed from her lack of awareness, her identitylessness, her inability to understand that she was being manipulated by her mother—and her stepfather as well.

The Salome in myth and in history may be viewed as the archetypal *puella:* the nonperson who lives through another and yields to "any" authority figure, for better or for worse. Her unformed characteristics, which the ego did not recognize, remained dormant until provoked into action by the authority figure. Salome's lack of lucidity enabled her to roam in comfort in her own darkened and limited realm. Without worry or anxiety, she enjoyed a state of psychological myopia. No conflict eroded her world because differentiation was nonexistent. The rotating energy of her disorienting and dizzying dance achieved complete obliteration of perspective and an opening up to *ekstasis*.

Devoid of any sense of herself, save as a performer, she was at a loss to accept Antipas's offer on her own. Antipas twice, according to Mark (6:22, 23), once according to Matthew (14:7), asked Salome what she would like as a recompense. Matthew wrote that she, "being before instructed by her mother," answered him immediately (14:7–8). Mark said she turned to her mother for advice after her dance (Mark 6:24–25).

The obedient Salome carried out her mother's will. By functioning as Herodias's chthonic power, she took on the attributes of a killer force, and thus participated in the destruction of the adversary, becoming the foe of patriarchal Christianity's rising hero, John.

Antipas/John Polarity

Unlike Herodias and Salome who felt no moral conflict, Antipas, according to the synoptic Gospels, suffered great inner torment. Although he outwardly rejected John's approach to life, fearing it would lead to his overthrow, Antipas was seemingly haunted by its powerful message. Perhaps John's ultrapuritanical and emotionally deprived patriarchal credo gave rise to the conflict described by the Evangelists. Or was Antipas's anxiety inspired by guilt and fear of damnation in the next world?

To John, the so-called indigenous matriarchal and animistic way of life was anathema. Women were looked upon as vessels, as child-bearers, whose main function was to perpetuate the human race. Antipas also downgraded women as objects of pleasure serving to entertain the male. But unlike John, who had cut himself off from the feminine on both a spiritual and physical level, Antipas was dominated—enslaved—by women.

The androcentric extremes that both men reached not only caused them to devalue the role of women in society, but revealed their own unconscious discomfort with the female sex. The male felt distressed with the unconscious feminine side of his own psyche. Remaining unintegrated in his personality, the feminine principle was treated as an outcast, as that "other," and was feared like an enemy. An individual's or a society's initial reaction to danger is to seek the annihilation of what is perceived as the threatening force. Thus may we explain to some extent the reason why the majority of women were legally and socially deprived at that time. The ever increasing hellenization of the Middle East and the birth and spread of patriarchal Christianity served to accentuate their plight.

Antipas

Antipas had neither the strength, the vision, nor the astuteness of his father. As the prototype of the antihero, he was revealed as ineffectual, shallow, irresolute, indolent, and pusillanimous. His decisions were, for the most part, made for him or arrived at through persuasion or emotionally explosive encounters. Deep injury to his self-image pervaded his psyche.

According to Josephus, Antipas, having been encouraged by his sister to go to Rome to claim his father's throne, experienced so visceral an affective reaction to Herodias that he felt propelled, as if driven by some inner force, "brazenly" to broach the subject of marriage to her. Acceptance of his proposal rested on the requirement that he divorce his first wife, the daughter of Aretas. Although Antipas was legally allowed several wives, Herodias refused such a lifestyle. Her argument may have been that, as a Hasmonean, she was unwilling to share a house with an Arab, her people's traditional enemy. On a more personal level, she knew from her own mother's experience that a wife could be displaced and/or replaced indiscriminately, and she sought to avoid such a fate for herself. Antipas yielded to her terms without thinking of their political ramifications.

Although the marriage of Antipas and Aretas's daughter had seemingly been one of convenience, his wife's pride was hurt by his proposal to Herodias. Cut to the quick and refusing entrapment, she used her wiles to find a safe haven for herself. Assuming the role of an unsuspecting and naive wife, she "who had discovered everything, asked him [Antipas] to send her away to Machaerus, which was on the boundary between the territory of Aretas and that of Herod" (*Jewish Antiquities* 18.111). So filled with his newfound love was Antipas that he failed to see anything out of the ordinary in his wife's request. Nor did she give any hint as to her plans. Her desire to remain for a time in the fortress town bordering the Nabatean kingdom seemed perfectly logical (Hoehner 1980, 147).

Antipas allowed Aretas's daughter to make the trip, having "no notion that the poor woman saw what was afoot" (*Jewish Antiquities* 18.111). Instead of remaining at Machaerus, however, she went directly to her father, king of the Nabateans—"the Arabians of Arabia Petraea," as Josephus referred to the tribe that was so hostile to the Judaeans. Antipas's reason for having married Aretas's daughter was to bring peace to the area, or at least to create a modus vivendi between the two groups. For nearly thirty years, his intentions were realized. When, however, Aretas's daughter fled to Machaerus (according to Josephus, she fled by prearrangement via Petra, a rich Greco-Roman city), to inform her father of Antipas's marriage plans, the Nabatean king was angry. Peace that had existed between the two kingdoms had now come to an end.

Antipas's relationship with John also demonstrated his lack of integrity and leadership as well as his cowardice. What makes Antipas's complex attitude toward this ascetic most fascinating, however, was his deep-seated projection onto him. The word *projection* implies an act of thrusting or throwing forward of ideas or impulses that belong to some extent to the subject. It is a "process whereby an unconscious quality or content of one's own is perceived and reacted to in an outer object" (Edinger 1978, 147ff.). To project is to attribute or assign characteristics that the subject loves or hates in him or herself onto a specific object. The transfer process is subjective.

Unaware of his own void—his undeveloped potential—Antipas was unconsciously drawn to his opposite. John's strength, his spiritual and moral fiber, mirrored the tetrarch's own failings and low opinion of himself. His objective assessment of John was the fruit of his subjective reactions. Antipas both yearned for and feared those qualities he attributed to John.

Antipas's projection onto John masked his own weak-willed, effete, sybaritic, and passive side, even while endowing him with John's strength. He may even have excluded problematic questions from his consciousness by focusing on material and sexual matters. By momentarily obliterating his seeming discomfort with his unconscious perception of himself, he might have viewed himself as on a par with the Baptizer: he, the powerful tetrarch; John, the powerful zealot.

Although, according to the synoptic texts, Antipas was taken aback by John's disapproving remarks concerning his marriage with Herodias, his attitude toward him was not negative. It was ambivalent, as are most love-hate relationships. According to Mark, he considered him "a just man and an holy, and observed him; and when he heard him, he did many things, and heard him gladly" (Mark 6:20). Nevertheless, when he "observed him," that is, scrutinized his message, although attracted to its strength and power, he also felt threatened by John's enormous will and determination to impose his doctrine. The reality of his own helplessness, antipodal to the dominion this rigorous man enjoyed over himself as well as over the people who joined his cause, may have served to humiliate Antipas. His very sense of disgrace perhaps forced his own emotional insecurity to surface, thereby actuating the libido necessary to act overtly. The only way he knew how to cope with his deteriorating self-image and the fear it triggered in him was, indeed, to order John's imprisonment.

Josephus tells us that Antipas's incarceration of John was politically motivated. At the sight of ever greater crowds "aroused to the highest degree by his sermons, Herod became alarmed." "And when he would have put him to death, he feared the multitude, because they counted him as a prophet" (Matt. 14:5). Because he feared John's "eloquence" would lead to "sedition," he decided "to strike first and be rid of him before his work led to an uprising, than to wait for an upheaval, get involved in a difficult situation and see his mistake" (*Jewish Antiquities* 18.118–19).

Thus, affectivity once again dominated Antipas's weakly structured ego. Or had he listened to Herodias's powerful arguments in favor of John's incarceration? Perhaps both factors encouraged the tetrarch to have the Baptizer "brought in chains to Machaerus" (Josephus 1959, 396).

During the formal celebration of his birthday banquet, Antipas's partially repressed aggressivity toward John took a turn for the dramatic. That John was decollated on Antipas's birthday suggests a symbolic link between the two men: asceticism, a concept born of the head (decapitated), versus a culture that favored license (the body). Antipas invited Roman dignitaries—"high captains, and chief estates of Galilee" (Mark 6: 21)—to the festivities, at which Salome's dance was the high point (Matt. 14:6–11; Mark 6: 22–28). So mesmerized was Antipas by what he *saw*—body, gestures, and the aura of sexuality exuding from Salome—that he promised "with an oath to give her whatsoever she would ask" (Matt. 14:7). Although some critics maintain that her dance was in no way sensual but rather pure and maidenly, it is difficult to believe that ethereal gestures alone would elicit such immoderate promises from the tetrarch.

Antipas was a voyeur type, inordinately aroused by what might have appeared to him as scabrous gestures. A victim of scopophilia (voyeurism), his sexual pleasure was derived from his contemplation of the erogenous zones of the object of his gaze. Focusing on Salome's eroticized body must have stimulated his fantasy to extremes, driving him into the same behavioral pattern as when he "brazenly" proposed to Herodias at first *sight*. In both instances he had allowed his visceral reactions to overwhelm him and direct his actions irrationally.

Viewed from a patriarchal standpoint, Salome was a paradigm of danger for Antipas and for any male. But the *cause* of his heightened sexual excitement, to the contrary, lay not in the object of his gaze, but in what it triggered in his psyche: a phantasm common to the imagination of many men, revolving around the *mystery* they associate with women. That the female's sexual organ is concealed within her body, whereas the male's is exposed, excites their libido. The vagina's hiddenness, viewed as a cavernous region, is associated with a fertile terrain—that dark, moist earth in which seeds are implanted and germinate. Sexual excitation and gratification are generated with each ritual opening of the "other's" realm—that foreign erogenous zone.

In such a context, the woman may be viewed as a prop for performances in men's fantasy world: a kind of foreplay to the sexual act. As penetrators, males see themselves as strong, virile conquerors—hunters able to manipulate their prey as they wish. In their world of illusion, they are featured as enforcers of their power over the so-called weaker sex, when, in fact, the female in this instance lords it over the male since she is the instigator of his fixation. It is he who is ensnared, he who becomes her captive audience. Imagining himself as that youthful, strong, virile inseminator he had been when young, like Faust, Antipas felt reborn and rejuvenated. His libidinal drive, aroused by Salome's dance, preempted all measure of rationality and this, according to the synoptic Gospels, underscored the magnitude of the female's responsibility and blame for the *evils of sex*.

As previously suggested, Salome, the *puella*, may have represented for Antipas the once young Herodias. The conflation of mother and daughter not only increased his attraction to her but served also to confuse the two in his mind. Hadn't he tried to please his bride prior to his marriage by divorcing his first wife, by giving Herodias "whatsoever" she asked? He fell into a similar behavioral pattern with his offer to Salome, in order to demonstrate what he erroneously believed to be his power over this nubile girl.

The need in the synoptic texts for the degradation or vilification of women, save those who performed the role of vessel, was perfectly filled by the unnamed nonperson, Salome. Ironically, however, the requisite works both ways. As the provocative dancer was an object and not a subject for the tetrarch, so he was an object and not a subject for her. Like the prostitute who degrades herself by selling her services, so Antipas, although unaware of it, also humiliated himself by paying for the seductive image with which she provided him. The interlude of scopophilia serviced by Salome's dance obliterated his own sense of deficiency or sexual impotence. Although Antipas may have had no personal feeling for Salome, he must surely have drooled as he observed her, his voyeuristic tendency unleashing a full-bodied orgy in his psyche. Quite literally we may say that he was "beside" himself, divested of lucidity, imagining himself to be the great monarch and the great lover he was not.

Salome's words—"Give me here John Baptist's head in a charger"—wrenched Antipas out of his reverie (Matt. 14:8). By rescinding his promise, he would have broken his pledge to Salome, which he was not strong enough to do before his august guests. Perhaps he cleverly took advantage of this opportunity to rid himself of a potentially dangerous man. Or could the very thought of transgressing against one whose moral values were so rigid, so high and mighty, have titillated him sexually?

Strangely enough, Josephus makes no mention of John's beheading. He merely writes that "there [in Machaerus, he was] put to death" (*Jewish Antiquities* 18.119). Was such an omission due to the pervasiveness of this form of punishment? According to Plutarch and Suetonius, the beheading of slaves and/or prisoners was considered a form of entertainment during Roman feasts. Plutarch reports an incident in which Titus Flaminius's brother, Lucius, had a prisoner decapitated at a banquet to please his boy lover. And Caligula, according to Suetonius, thrilled to order this amusement for his guests during the course of his orgiastic feasts (Plutarch, *Lives of Illustrious Men* 1:420; Suetonius, *Twelve Caesars* 32.20). Josephus mentions Alexander Jannaeus, who had invited his concubines, among others, to a banquet and to amuse the guests ordered eight hundred rebels to be crucified as their wives and children looked on (*Jewish Antiquities* 18.380).

Without the instrumentality of Antipas, John's execution would not have been transformed into an apotheosis; nor would the sacrifice of his life have preluded Christ's on the cross. They had to die, according to the Scriptures, for Christianity to come into being. Antipas was to John what Judas had been to Jesus.

John the Baptist

Josephus, the thrust of whose writings was political and economic, considered John's murder as one of the many excoriating crimes perpetrated by the Herodian, Roman, and other monarchs of the time. Hadn't Herod the Great put to death, among others, his Hasmonean wife, Mariamme, along with three of their children (Antipater, Aristobulus, and Alexander)? Nor is it necessary to mention the deeds of the Caesars, as described by Suetonius.

An archetypal figure, John stood apart from others; his values were antipodal to those practiced by the majority and most conspicuously by the
rulers. Josephus had called him "a good man" who "exhorted the Jews to
lead righteous lives, to practise justice towards their fellows and piety towards God, and so doing to join in baptism" (*Jewish Antiquities* 18.117).
John's approach to religion was polemical. Performing his ministry in the
wilderness of Judaea not far from the Dead Sea (Matt. 3:1), he arrogated to
himself the position of supreme arbiter, considering himself God's missionary. He called upon his listeners to repent, saying "the kingdom of heaven is
at hand," convinced as he was of the imminence of judgment and the manifestation of the "Coming One" (Matt. 3:1). He used both concrete and
abstract reasoning to persuade his followers to earn redemption by treading
the ascetic path during their earthly trajectory. Mark wrote of John:

> The voice of one crying in the wilderness, Prepare ye the way of the Lord,
> make his paths straight.
>   John did baptize in the wilderness, and preach the baptism of repen-
> tance for the remission of sins. (Mark 1:3-4)[2]

Sinners had to prepare themselves *now* for the Last Judgment. John's message
spelled doom for the unrepentant, for they would suffer damnation and the
eternal flames of hell. His passionate conviction that evildoers would be
destroyed and the good redeemed reinforced his intransigence. Nor did John
shy away from menacing the recalcitrant.

> Whose fan is in his hand, and he will thoroughly purge his floor, and
> gather his wheat into the garner; but he will burn up the chaff with un-
> quenchable fire. (Matt. 3:12)

A religious activist, John predicted that God's reforms would occur in
the near future and would include the most brutal destruction of the wicked.

> And now also the ax is laid unto the root of the trees: therefore every tree
> which bringeth not forth good fruit is hewn down, and cast into the fire.
> (Matt. 3:10)

His prophecies of the early onset of the Kingdom of God may have instilled
"acute apocalyptic expectations and human involvement in the attainment
of these eschatological goals" (Flusser 1988, 142).

Eating "locusts and wild honey," "clothed with camel's hair, and with a girdle of a skin about his loins" (Mark 1:6), John partook neither of "bread" nor of "wine" (Luke 7:33). Because eating meant taking in the dirt of the earth and thereby binding one to dross, religious ascetics ate only enough food to keep alive. By not filling their stomachs they were convinced they could maintain a condition of lightness, a state that facilitated the performance of acts of levitation, and thus rise to supernal spheres. Was the accomplishment of such a feat marked with hubris? Were they trying to rise *above* others? Yet hadn't Elijah, carried in the fiery chariot to heaven, performed such a miracle (2 Kings 2:11)? And Christ, in his transfiguration, ascending into heaven (Matt. 17:2; Mark 9:2)?

John, the committed zealot, was consumed by his ideology in which there was *no* mention of love. He repressed entirely *feeling* and *love* to the point of virtually annihilating them. The emphasis he placed on self-deprivation, suffering, atonement of sin, sacrifice, and psychological discipline underscored a nonexistential view of the life experience. Some suggest his was an escape mechanism; others, a discovery of the transcendental sphere. In both cases it led to the annihilation of the ego. In that most of the instinctive demands of the body were rigorously denied by him, he remained the model for such holy individuals as St. Anthony, the father of Christian monasticism, and such groups as the order of penitents and the brotherhood of flagellants in the Middle Ages.

The rigorous extremes preached by John as well as by other ascetics suggested a rational defense on their part against a deep-seated fear of life and of sexuality. Patristic ideology, banishing sexuality from its ethic, erroneously conceives the male to be safe from ideas and impulses that the ego (center of consciousness) judges to be incompatible with it. John's intemperate attitude, however, disclosed something quite different: an unconscious fear of the female. Because the values *she* represented (sexuality and the pleasures of this earth) seemed threatening, his response was to build up even harsher defenses against their possible encroachment into his body/heart complex. By reviling Herodias and Salome—mother/daughter figures viewed as great destroyers—John was ostensibly protecting society, and by extension himself, from the embodiments of "evil."

The denial, banishment, or rejection of women by men have, however, had a boomerang effect on both sexes. The promulgation of harsher laws against women, and/or the repression of *feelings* to the extreme, may build up to an increasingly disruptive and explosive condition in the psyche. Anger, rage, and discontent are catalyzed; insecurity and chaos set in. Thus does the vicious cycle take on momentum, concluding in one extreme or the other—asceticism or hedonism—with a resultant increase or lessening of regulatory measures by the subject/enemy or object/enemy.

Extremes, whether with respect to faith or to gender, may lead to a *dehumanizing process*. Psychiatrists have labeled intransigent comportment as masochistic, and thus "a disease"; religion, on the other hand, regards it "as a cure" (Cowan 1982, 19). In either case, the human dimension is downgraded: it is considered negative and unworthy of too much attention, or as the sole focus in life, centering exclusively on the here and now and the pleasures-of-the-flesh principle. Such dehumanization compels people to look exclusively outside of themselves, toward *otherworldly* spheres or *toward others*.

The spiritual and physical disciplines advocated by John sought to detach him and his followers from their earthly condition by rechanneling their instinctual desires toward heaven or toward hell. These two paths—transcendental and existential—which have been offered humankind since the beginning of time, answer not only specific needs within a personality but reflect a cultural climate as well. They represent a means of alleviating to some degree humanity's metaphysical anguish and assuaging its longing for immortality.[3]

John's intransigence, his holiness, his rigorous attitudes, and what must have been his magnetic personality judging from his great number of followers, were antipodal to Antipas's characteristics. Yet, some factor linked the two in one way or another. Why, otherwise, would both Matthew and Mark have tried to excuse Antipas for ordering the execution? Matthew attributed the deed to Antipas's fear of the multitude, while also mentioning the tetrarch's emotional discomfort: the "king was sorry" (14:5, 9). Mark noted even greater inner conflict in the ruler: "And the king was exceeding sorry; yet for his oath's sake, and for their sakes which sat with him, he would not reject her" (6:26).

Nevertheless, had Antipas experienced such acute distress as the synoptic texts would have us believe, he might not have sent for the executioner "immediately" (Mark 6:27) but would have perhaps weighed the possible consequences of his act. In Mark, Antipas sent for "an executioner, and commanded his [John's] head to be brought"; any mention of the time factor is omitted (6: 27). Was Antipas's acute distress provoked in part by the fear of transforming John into a martyr? Or was it guilt? The tetrarch's disturbed mental condition may be attested to in his confusion between John and Jesus.[4] After having heard of the latter's miracles, Antipas was "perplexed, because that it was said of some, that John was risen from the dead"

(Luke 9:7). Luke wrote: "And Herod said, John have I beheaded: but who is this, of whom I hear such things?" (9:9).

Antipas's conflation of John and Jesus is not, however, unfounded. Biblical scholars have pointed to parallels between the two: John was Christ's age, he possessed prophetic gifts, he baptized Jesus, the disciples of both men were known to each other, and so forth. Miracles had been associated also with the Baptist: despite the advanced age of John's mother, his birth was announced by the angel Gabriel to his aged father, Zacharias, in a vision (Luke 1:11–24). As for John's beheading, it was considered by the devout to be a prelude to Christ's Passion. What remains puzzling (or unknowable), however, was that an event of the magnitude of John's martyrdom, alluded to by Luke, is reported only by Matthew and Mark, and not even mentioned by John.

When the *head*, the seat of reason, seeks exclusive dominion over the body and *asceticism* minimizes to the extreme the world of *instinct*, their opposite seeks its share or place. Heraclitus described the oppositional relationship as a condition of *enantiodromia*. When "one side of a pair of opposites becomes excessively predominant in the personality, it is likely to turn into its contrary" (Edinger n.d., 2).

To codify morality is to ossify it, to transform it into an absolute. Morality, looked upon as an end unto itself, may become an evil. The search for perfection indicates a repression of one aspect of the personality. In some cases, dissociation between a conscious set of moral precepts and an unconscious rejection of them brings about a dissociation of the psyche. Only by reconciling and accepting the good and evil within the human being, rather than repressing one or the other, may an individual come to terms with both. If one has a *reservatio mentalis* and refuses to confront the rejected part of oneself—in this case, the body—one comes under its dominion. Nietzsche wrote in *Thus Spake Zarathustra*: "Man is a rope stretched between the animal and the Superman—a rope over an abyss" (Nietzsche 1937, 29).

Broad disharmony within the human psyche of the collective is implicit in Plato's *Phaedrus*. Rational consciousness, which he identified with the "divine part of man," was at odds with what he considered humankind's decidedly lower emotional, feeling, and instinctual functions. Humankind's head/reason, or the Apollonian, associated with "light," was awarded the highest value; while the body/Dionysian, that is, the so-called animal side, associated with darkness, was considered the lowest denominator. A. N. Whitehead has noted: "Twenty-five hundred years of Western philosophy is but a series of footnotes to Plato" (Barrett 1962, 79). Irremediable antagonism between these polarities created top-heavy people in Western cultures.

Were the *head*, as *spirit*, as John preached, to have complete autonomy over the body, the metaphor of decapitation was in order.

To adore light and attempt to eradicate darkness leads to internecine warfare between the two sides of a personality. The advent of Christianity and its hold through the centuries brought havoc to the psyche and to culture. Just as light complements darkness, so the head needs the body in order that each may flourish side by side, be nourished by and interpenetrated by the other. As William Barrett has written: "In Plato's myth first appears that cleavage between reason and the irrational that it has been the long burden of the West to carry, until the dualism makes itself felt in most violent form within modern culture" (ibid., 83).

Extremes, be they philosophical, religious, social, or other, usually call the scapegoat factor into being with the goal of assuaging personal and/or collective feelings of impotence, inadequacy, and incompetence. Rather than projecting one's (society's) problem on someone else, thus losing any means of healing the scarred psyche that triggered the imbalance in the first place, intransigent attitudes have ways of accentuating it. No common denominator existed between Salome/Herodias and the ascetics making deep inroads in the society of the day. Nor did mother or daughter ever know *wholeness*. Each was a fragment of the other. Salome, the still-unformed nonperson, however, ran the greatest risk of psychological dissolution. The decadent society that gave birth to these archetypal figures sent Herodias into exile with her husband, her daughter's fate remaining a mystery in the deepest sense of the word. Hidden within the folds of the psyche is where Salome remains, to reappear in all of her luster, beauty, and sensuality as an explosive force in yet other faction-ridden societies.

6 Virgil's *Aeneid:*
Let Us Sing of Arms and
Women—Dido and Camilla

"I sing of arms and the man," Virgil (70 B.C.E.–19 C.E.) wrote in the opening line of the *Aeneid*, the national epic of Augustan Rome.[1] Let us instead sing of arms and the women—of Dido and Camilla—two archetypal protagonists who sprung full-blown from the poet's mind and psyche.

Since the *Aeneid* was written at the request of the emperor Augustus, Virgil pridefully underscored his country's accomplishments and glorified its self-image. His hero, Aeneas, the son of the goddess Venus, fled his native Troy after this city's destruction by the Greeks. With him he took his young son (Ascanius), his aged father (Anchises), whom he carried on his shoulders, and a group of followers, but in the confusion of leaving the burning city his wife disappeared. Aeneas was *fated* to found the Italian nation. His divinely inspired mission, which took him to many lands over a period of years, included a memorable love affair with Dido, as well as long and ferocious wars, one of which led to the demise of the female warrior Camilla.

The beautiful and arresting Dido, whose behavioral patterns were transhuman as well as down-to-earth, founded Carthage and then became its queen.[2] Positive in outlook, stately in bearing, kindly in manner, she was also a determined and decisive woman. Virgil, however, placed his emphasis not so much on her accomplishments as on her downfall. Her memorable curse—war between Carthage and Rome—became a literary strategy and political necessity for the author to explain the cause of the hatred between the Carthaginians and Romans. It also served as a justification for the three Punic Wars: the first in 264–241 B.C.E., the second in 218–201 B.C.E., and the third in 149–146 B.C.E. Roman victory and the razing of Carthage, instrumental in the creation of his country's world empire, allowed Virgil to honor his patron and the golden age of Augustus.

111

The tragic life of the highly romantic heroine Dido—abandonment by her lover Aeneas, grief, and suicide—inspired artistic works in later centuries. Among these are a tragedy, *Dido, Queen of Carthage* (1593), by Nash and Marlowe, and an opera, Purcell's *Dido and Aeneas* (1689).

The strong, wild, and fearless Camilla was an Amazon warrior devoted to Diana. Her courage and authenticity earned her the admiration of young and old, male and female. Her love for and expertise in warfare encouraged her to excel in military matters, putting her on a par with other great army leaders. Usually concentrated during dangerous armed undertakings, on one single occasion she allowed her fantasies to alight on a colorful insignia she desired for herself. A split second was time enough for her enemy's spear to penetrate her body and kill her.

Ectypal Analysis

Julius Caesar, tracing his lineage to Iulus Ascanius, the son of Aeneas, benefited from an added cachet—descent from Venus. He had a magnificent temple built in the Forum (46 B.C.E.) to honor her as *Genetrix*, mother of the Roman people. Who else but a partially divine mortal, his people must have believed, could rule with firmness and wisdom one of the greatest empires of all time?

Brutus and Cassius, both republicans, convinced they were putting kingship to an end, planned and carried out Caesar's assassination (44 B.C.E.). Their crime, however, was not to go unpunished. Antony, who had been close to Caesar, allied himself with Octavian (the future emperor Augustus) and Lepidus, and together they formed the Second Triumvirate. Although Octavian, Caesar's nephew and heir (he had been officially adopted by him) was destined to rule the empire, he had to prove his mettle. He did so by defeating Antony and Cleopatra at Actium (31 B.C.E.) and annexing Egypt. As sole ruler of Rome, Octavian was awarded the title of *Augustus* by the Senate and life tribuneship from the people. He was made *imperator* (commander), *princeps* (leader), and *pontifex maximus* (high priest); and the month of August was named in his honor. Augustus is regarded as the first Roman Emperor.

Although the long years of war and neglect prior to Augustan rule had seen the breakdown of administrative and social systems, the reformer Augustus took things in hand. He rid the Senate of many of its unworthy and dissolute members; to stimulate economic growth he began a system of public works that increased employment and encouraged production and investments. Following Augustus's restoration of order and reformation, living standards rose, as did real-estate values; crime diminished; laws were relatively well administrated, and taxes became more equitable.

The mood of optimism, stability, and celebration that pervaded the atmosphere ushered in what has come to be known as the golden age of Latin literature. Maecenas (69–68 B.C.E.), advisor and friend of Augustus and a most generous patron of letters, protected such writers as Virgil, Horace, and Propertius.

Although the *Aeneid* was written during Augustus's rule and at the direct suggestion of the emperor, Virgil chose to live a quiet and meditative life mainly outside of Rome, perhaps because of his poor health. It was in the Campania region that he wrote his epic celebrating the birth of Rome and its rebirth under Augustus.

After having worked on the *Aeneid* for eleven years, Virgil planned to perfect his manuscript during and following a three-year trip to Greece and surrounding areas. He could not have predicted that he would develop a fever in Greece and die at Brundisium, en route back to his native land. Just prior to his death, he asked that his unfinished manuscript be burned. Augustus, however, refused to carry out the poet's wishes. Instead, he had Varius and Tucca, friends of the author, edit the *Aeneid*, but without making any additions.

Status of Women

The depictions of female protagonists in the *Aeneid* have led some critics to label Virgil a misogynist. He was also a man living out his zeitgeist. A familiarity with the status of women prior to and during the Augustan era will hopefully lead to a better understanding of Dido and Camilla and to the roles they played in the patriarchal organization of their day.

Despite the fact that Roman women in antiquity exercised no political rights, they enjoyed far greater freedom than their Grecian sisters. That they never voted, nor functioned administratively in any capacity, nor held public office did not prevent some women from standing firm in state matters. A notable example is that of the traitor Coriolanus, who was intent upon attacking Rome (491 B.C.E.), but was persuaded to desist by the pleadings of his mother and wife. Women also played important roles behind the scenes, influencing their husbands—as did Augustus' wife, Livia—or manipulating events and people for political purposes (as did Fulvia, Marc Antony's wife) (Pomeroy 1975, 185).

Although a patriarchal society was surely in place in Rome and the paterfamilias ruled outright over the life and death of his daughters, the situation of women in antiquity was both complex and confusing (Fau 1978, 26). While the austerity of patriarchal custom was scarcely relaxed up to the third century B.C.E., by the second century the status of women had improved and in many ways they were juridically and socially emancipated. In aristocratic and wealthy families, marriages were arranged frequently without transfer of power from father to husband, so that in case of divorce or the death of the husband, the woman became in fact free to manage her property as she pleased. In the society of the late Republic, women moved with complete freedom, sometimes choosing their own husbands and lovers, the goal being to enhance family income or acquire useful political connections. Although the minimum legal age for marriage was twelve, prepubescent girls were encouraged for political and economic reasons to take up residence in the groom's home prior to that age, and at times the union was consummated before the legal age (Pomeroy 1975, 164). Wives practiced abortion, contraception, and exposure of newborns (not to be confused with infanticide) (Corbier 1991, 178). Both husband and wife had the right to seek divorce, with the proviso that the husband was required to make full restitution of his wife's dowry to his father-in-law, if the latter was still alive, and if not, to his wife. Understandably, husbands were often reluctant to bring their wives to court for adultery, alcoholism, or any other reason. If a will had been made, children could inherit property from their mother (ibid., 187). By the end of the Republic, women could marry with separation of wealth, the wife remaining in complete control of her finances. If she lent money to her husband, as Cicero's wife had done, she could charge him a commission. Nor were Roman women cloistered in their home. They could go to theaters, spectacles, and the public baths (open until Hadrian's time to both sexes), alone, with friends, or with their husbands.

Although girls, unlike boys, were taught at home, many women of the aristocracy were well educated. In the middle of the second century B.C.E., Cornelia, daughter of Scipio Africanus, held a salon for Rome's intellectual elite. Sempronia (Brutus's mother) had not only been taught foreign languages but also played the kithara and danced. Caesar's daughter, Julia, was well versed in literature, music, and geometry. Women rode horseback, hunted, played ball, and engaged in combat sports—armed, to be sure, with protective headpieces and shin guards, which Ovid in his *Art of Love* (bk. 3) declared to be unbecoming (Fau 1978, 12, 15).

Augustus attempted to put an end to what he considered the excessive liberation of the female. With the passage of the "Julian Laws" (ca. 18 B.C.E.), he was convinced he was restoring the virtues that he identified with the ancient Romans: a simple lifestyle, and a high regard for morals, chastity, and fidelity in marriage and parentage. Because the institution of marriage offered the state stability, insured procreation, and continued family life and tradition, marriage was obligatory for all males under sixty and women under fifty.

Flagrant flaunting of the "Julian Laws" was proof of their failure. Ironically, the very consuls who had structured the laws were celibate and hence childless. As for the great "puritan" Augustus, he had but one child and carried on liaisons with numerous married women, including the wife of his friend Maecenas. His passion for Livia, who was not only married at the time he met her but also pregnant with her second child, was such that he took her to bed with him and forced her to divorce her husband and submit to marrying him. The love affairs of Julia, Augustus's daughter, were so numerous as to warrant her condemnation to exile (ibid., 69, 85). The same fate awaited her own daughter. It could be said that adultery, villainy, and immorality of all types flourished under the "Julian Laws," which had been designed in an attempt to protect the dignity of marriage.

Archetypal Analysis

Because religion generally plays such a significant role in the *Aeneid* and particularly for Dido and Camilla, who call upon their patron deities—Juno, Venus, Diana—in times of need and of thanksgiving, the interplay between the mortal and the immortal will be briefly examined here.

That divinities both commingled and copulated with mortals is implicit in ancient epics and religious tracts. Proximity between gods and humans is attested to in the visitations, visions, apparitions, hallucinations, premonitory dreams, and parapsychological experiences narrated in the *Aeneid*. Nor was it unusual for humans to be deified: Livia and Julia, respectively wife and daughter of Augustus, were both worshipped as goddesses outside of Rome.

For the protagonists in the *Aeneid* and for Romans in general, the gods were viewed as realities and existed as physical entities. They were endopsychic factors, that is, they belonged to the individual's personal as well as her or his collective unconscious; thus gods may also be understood, as they will be here, as components of the human psyche, each representing an affect, a tendency, an unreflected or unconscious need in the worshipper. They come into being both as projections of the individual believer and of the culture. As psychic powers, they are archetypal in nature—"innately formed concepts or imprints in the human soul." In this regard, they are comparable to DNA: scientifically programmed but also partaking in a cosmic mystery (Franz 1980, 36, 34, 39).

The Romans worshipped and heeded the advice not only of their deities but also of those attendant powers embodied in the *genius* (etymologically associated with *gignere*, "beget" or "engender"). In time, the genii became the representatives of patriarchal powers and their productive energies were handed down from father to son, the genius of the *paterfamilias* being worshipped within the Roman family structure. If duly honored, genii such as *lares*, *penates*, and *vesta* guaranteed the safety and well-being of the home. Impersonal until the third century B.C.E., their characteristics became increasingly individualized. Becoming guardian spirits, they may be likened to some extent to the personal *daimon* of the Greeks (ibid., 147).

The goddess Juno, individualized, became a female guardian angel. As every man had his *genius*, every woman had her *juno* to whom she sacrificed. A *genius* had the power to dictate that individual's fortune—*fate*—during his or her earthly existence.

The two most important genii/divinities in our study are Juno and Venus. The first, queen of the Roman pantheon of gods and wife of its sovereign, Jupiter, despised Aeneas and his Trojans for reasons dating back to their war with the Greeks. Intent upon retribution, Juno did everything possible to prevent Aeneas from reaching his destination, Italy, and achieving his goal—the founding of a nation. It was to her, *Iuno Caelestis*, that Dido prayed and sacrificed. Following the Third Punic War, this guardian deity of Carthage was taken from Carthage to Rome.

Venus, Aeneas's mother and supporter of the Trojan cause, helped her son in her own way and protected him from Juno's wrath. As divine mother, covering her son and his companions as they made their way to Carthage "in a cape of cloud so thick" as to make them invisible, she believed she was shielding Aeneas from danger (*Aeneid* 1.587). But having planned the love affair between Dido and Aeneas, she was responsible for having stirred a deadly passion in her worshippers/victims. Had Aeneas lingered in Carthage, forgetful of his destiny, his wanderings would have ceased and he would have allayed Venus's maternal fears for his safety. Fate, however, decreed otherwise.

Dido

The legendary Tyrian princess Dido (Elissa, in Phoenician), having founded Carthage (Qart Hadasht, "New City") between c. 824 and 813 B.C.E., became its queen. She was a woman of determination, willpower, and courage, and was possessed as well of intelligence and organizational talent. Her physical attributes of beauty, grace, and stature were equally impressive.

What prompted Dido to depart from her native Tyre in Phoenicia? The extraordinarily beautiful, luxurious, commercially successful and politically powerful city was described by Isaiah as "the crowning city, whose merchants are princes, whose traffickers are the honorable of the earth" (Isa. 23:8). Its artists, craftsman, and architects were among the most renowned in the ancient world. The Phoenicians were the inventors of an alphabet, upon which European writing is based, as well as of a unique dye made of murex shells, referred to by Greeks and Romans as "royal Tyrian purple" (Soren, Khader, and Slim 1990, 39).

Jealousies within a family sometimes precipitate murderous acts. As long as Dido's father, Belus, was king of Tyre, her life, at least outwardly, ran a smooth course. Her husband, Sychaeus, whom she "loved with much passion," became "the wealthiest landowner in Phoenicia" (*Aeneid* 1.484, 488). After Belus's demise, however, her power-hungry brother, Pygmalion, "a monster in crime" and driven by greed, murdered Sychaeus. That she did not know the identity of the criminal who had killed her husband increased Dido's suffering, depleting the vibrant energy that had been hers during Sychaeus's lifetime. Perhaps as an unconscious device to insure self-preservation, she avoided commerce with others, remaining withdrawn and silent, lest she antagonize the culprit, who surely must have been in her entourage. That her libido (psychic energy) during this interim period had been driven inward indicated a need for deep introversion. The charged subliminal currents repressed during her period of mourning had, however, preserved their potency to the point of imperiously forcing her husband's image to emerge in a premonitory dream. Nor is such an occurrence rare. In periods of such desperation and deep crisis as Dido's, the unconscious comes to the aid of the sufferer in the form of a dream, compensating and thus alleviating to some extent the tragedy that is being experienced.

In Dido's dream image, Sychaeus "lifted his pallid face . . . and laid bare to his wife . . . his breast impaled upon the blade." In so doing, he revealed the identity of the criminal to her (*Aeneid* 1.503). Her loving husband "urge[d] her to speed her flight, to leave her homeland," warning her that her life was now in danger. Not only did he reveal the criminal's identity, but he also advised her how to go about planning her flight by disclosing an "ancient treasure in the earth, a hoard of gold and silver known to none" but to him (*Aeneid* 1.506).

Gold, the most precious and perfect of metals, is used in ancient and modern times in paintings and sculptures to honor religious figures. It symbolizes incorruptibility, indestructibility, and immortality. Identified with sun and fire, it is endowed with the power to clarify what formerly was cloudy or murky, thus paving the way for *gnosis*. Its brilliance, equated with the *yang* or energetic force, inspires activity. As is true of everything in the manifest world, gold is a double-edged sword: it represents the highest spheres of being, but also serves to pervert individuals and societies. It is, therefore, a paradigm that shows the pure becoming impure: Dido's brother, who had become possessed by gold, gave in to his murderous instincts. Royalty stooped to covetousness, corrupting and degrading life's highest values.

By revealing the treasure's secret hiding place to Dido, Sychaeus helped her not only pragmatically but psychologically, encouraging her to penetrate a higher dimension within her being. Her search for that inner gold led her to discover her own untried abilities. Henceforth she would depend on herself to carve out her future. Her quest would yield further knowledge about her own talents and inspire her with greater self-confidence. Sychaeus's appearance in her dream to the listless Dido showed her the way and motivated her to act overtly.

Because treasures in myths and legends are not gratuitous gifts to humankind, the very energy needed for their discovery and extraction *is* to be viewed as the treasure itself. Once the "hoard of gold and silver" was discovered, it was loaded onto the waiting ships—a feat in itself, requiring not only enormous organizational effort on Dido's part but also astuteness and subtlety. Tending to every detail relating to her departure, she revealed her intrinsic but until now unused inner strength, determination, and willpower. The enlightenment or inner gold she gleaned from the interaction between subliminal and rational spheres had served to expand her consciousness and provide her with both the insight and inner drive necessary to combat her enemies. To assure the success of her venture, she chose highly motivated companions to take along on her journey: "those who felt fierce hatred for the tyrant / and those who felt harsh fear" (*Aeneid* 1.512). Acting in consort with one another, they carried "the wealth of covetous Pygmalion overseas" (*Aeneid* 1.515). It may be said that necessity had transformed Sychaeus into Dido's psychopomp: guide, mentor, and inspiration.

Dido, it may also be suggested, underwent a personality change after her dream. When Sychaeus was alive, he played the role of worker, organizer, business manager, and head of the family, while Dido basked in the joy of loving and being loved, spending her days as a satisfied and fulfilled wife. The warmth, solicitude, and caring he had demonstrated toward her during their marriage had disclosed her *feeling* world in which her judgmental faculties encouraged relationships and strengthened a natural bent for kindness. Following Sychaeus's death, her life was lived in a vacuum; hers was now a condition of depression and directionlessness. The activation of the deepest unconscious, or sympathetic nervous system, by means of the dream was due paradoxically to Sychaeus's ever living presence within her.

The impact of Dido's healing dream on her psyche prevented a dissolution of consciousness, or what may be referred to as a nervous breakdown. Were such a helpful relationship between subliminal and rational spheres prolonged indefinitely, however, Dido's increasing reliance on her unconscious for direction (or increasing introversion) would have disturbed her equilibrium still further. Because her husband had encouraged her to act overtly by pointing out a new course to her, Dido was saved from taking refuge in a dead past and becoming a prey to self-indulgence. Her newly renewed activity fomented both a living present and a future mode of existence.

"A woman leads," Virgil wrote insightfully, as the ships set out from the Tyrian harbor onto the high seas (*Aeneid* 1.516). Assuming the power ordinarily allotted to a man, Dido, no longer the happy and fulfilled wife, had been transformed into a leader of people and director of their course. Once the ships had docked on Libyan shores, Dido "bought the land called Byrsa" (*Aeneid* 1.519) owned by King Iarbas, the son of a nymph and of the god Hammon or Jupiter (*Aeneid* 4.262). Although accepting Dido's monetary offer, Iarbas stipulated that she could have only the land that the hide of a bull could enclose. Because such an infinitesimal amount could not serve her purpose, she stirred her innate but heretofore slumbering adroitness: cleverly cutting the bull's hide into strips, she stretched them around the Byrsa hill so that they enclosed a much larger tract of land, which would become the "extremely rich" city of Carthage (*Aeneid* 1.22).

Soon after setting foot on land, Dido and her companions "dug up an omen that Queen Juno had pointed out: the head of a fierce stallion" (*Aeneid* 1.629). Overjoyed at having safely arrived on North African shores, Dido interpreted the image of the magnificent animal in its positive, energy-giving, nourishing aspects, neglecting to assess its chthonian and tenebrous sides. Like the utterances of the ancient sibylline oracles, omens, verbal or concrete, are complex in meaning, their interpretation depending on the human factors projected onto them.

Instinctual as well as insightful, stallions and horses in general were considered the harbingers of both death and life, of destruction and triumph.[3] Like the humans who mount them, they assume different roles depending on the circumstances. By day, the rider guides the animal's direction as it gallops blindly ahead, but in the darkness of the night leaves it to its intuitiveness, sometimes leading to death. The one-sidedness of Dido's interpretation of the omen rendered her vulnerable to her own impetuous and affective nature, which had blocked out other reasonable explanations. Impulses enclothed in darkness may be used effectively when energized and guided by the thinking function. If, however, these same affects are abducted by some frenetic power within the psyche, the devouring of the ego by such a passion—love or hate—may lead to volcanic inner upheavals, divesting the individual of consciousness, harmony, and stability.

Aeneas's arrival on North African shores, following his departure from his native and now-destroyed Troy and seven years of wandering, may be regarded symbolically as another step toward the completion of his destined mission. Having weathered hardships and treacherous storms instigated by Juno's relentless and formidable hatred for him (due to the choice of the Trojan prince, Paris, of Venus over her as the most beautiful goddess of them all), he finally landed in what he hoped would be safe surroundings. Making his way through a wooded area, he happened to come upon an impressively tall woman wearing the disguise of Diana, the huntress. Only moments after being advised by her to proceed to Carthage, where he was to be welcomed by its queen, did Aeneas recognize her as his mother Venus.

If Venus, as divine mother, is experienced by Aeneas as an archetypal figure, her behavioral patterns may be interpreted as projections of aspects of his own personality traits. Indeed, Venus's cautiousness may be construed as paradigmatic of concealment and secrecy—certainly wise defensive measures for any stranger entering the unknown, but also symptomatic of Aeneas's future deceptive and/or covert ways.

From a hilltop overlooking the city of Carthage Aeneas and his companions "marveled" at the sight of the citadel's high walls, towers, enormous buildings, and paved streets.

Dido was the generator of such intense industry in the newly founded Carthage. Combining a rational approach and innate enthusiasm, she inspired constructive activity on the part of a people. Her sense of the esthetic and her vision as "chief" added to her roster of heretofore unused and thus unexpected talents. Like the finest of kings, this queen was responsible for appointing the architects, city planners, and engineers, who in turn chose their subordinate functionaries to realize her ideas.

A deeply religious woman, Dido did not forget Juno, her patron genius/ deity. Because she believed that the stallion omen augured greatness for Carthage—"the nation's easy wealth and fame in war throughout the ages"— she had a "stupendous shrine" erected in Juno's honor (*Aeneid* 1.633).

Dido's one-sided assessment of Juno, like that of the stallion omen, predisposed her to danger. Her view of Juno as only all-giving was simplistic. She overlooked the deity's darker side and ignored the complicating factors of the jealousy and vengefulness of a woman scorned.

The temple Dido erected to Juno was so extraordinary that it surely could have been declared one of the wonders of the world. It was also to be the *fated* meeting place of Dido and Aeneas. The Trojan prince, still enclosed in a cloud, walked up to the dazzling monument, and marveled at every detail of the enormous sanctuary. Arresting for him were its richly decorated panels depicting the harrowing events of the Trojan War. The past intruding into the present, Aeneas was overcome by the bloodbath inflicted on his family and people by the Greeks.

His pain was suddenly dispelled by the appearance of "the lovely-bodied" Dido accompanied by groups of young people. The sense of power, strength, and self-possession conveyed by her expression of triumph caught his attention: "in her joy, she [Dido] moved among the throng as she urged on the work of her coming kingdom" (*Aeneid* 1.711).

Mounting her throne under the temple's central dome, Dido, the achiever, demonstrated still more latent qualities: rectitude and nobility in her capacity as lawgiver and judge.

> Dido was dealing judgments to her people
> and giving laws, apportioning the work
> of each with fairness or by drawing lots. . . .

> (*Aeneid* 1.715)

Dido assures the Trojans that they will be received by her with "kindliness," but also justifies the savagery of her guards, explaining, almost prophetically, that she and her people, having encountered harrowing problems after leaving Tyre, needed to closely protect her frontiers. As a "veteran of hardships" Dido understands only too well the meaning of wretchedness, but without bitterness she greets the visitors to her shores with generosity and warmth: "I can now learn to help the miserable" (1.882). Hearing that Dido has offered the wanderers equality with her people, the reassured Venus lifts the cloud that had hidden her son.

In official welcome of her guests, a magnificent banquet is organized in their honor in Dido's gleaming royally furnished palace.

Like Aeneas, Dido takes pride in her lineage, details of which are depicted in the gold engravings about the hall:

> the sturdy deeds of Dido's ancestors,
> a long, long line of happenings and heroes
> traced from the first beginnings of her race.
>
> (*Aeneid* 1.895)

At the banquet Aeneas presents Dido with gifts of material but also of symbolic value: the diadem, sceptre, and necklace worn by Priam's eldest daughter, and the mantle and gown that had once adorned Helen's beautiful body. If associated with the motif of the wooden horse that had brought disaster to the Trojans at the hands of the Greeks, these exquisite objects interject an ominous note into the scene.

Because Dido is unaware of Venus's plans—to "inflame the queen to madness and insinuate a fire in Dido's very bones. . . . to girdle Dido with a flame so that no god can turn her back"—she is vulnerable, the target of love (*Aeneid* 1.922, 943). That her defenses against emotional upheavals have been dropped leaves her unprepared to stem the tide of love for Aeneas.

Venus pierces Dido's soul/psyche deeply and circuitously via her son Cupid disguised as Aeneas's progeny, Ascanius. The effects of the poison without antidote, as potent as any sent to Phaedra, Medea, or Agave, are unleashed instantaneously. Overwhelmed by the trauma of passion, the victimized Dido is incapable of subduing or rationalizing her emotion. The march of fate as dictated by the gods has been mandated.

Radiant in her unawareness and jubilant in her naïveté, Dido, "already settled on her couch of gold beneath resplendent awnings, at the center," glows with a sense of well-being that envelops hostess and guests (*Aeneid*

1.975). Aeneas and his Trojans "recline on purple covers" as hundreds of servants "pour out water for their hands . . . bring towels smooth in texture . . . offer bread" (*Aeneid* 1.978). Food and wine are plentiful in an agape that unfolds in a swell of increasing ebullience.

Dido fills her goblet with wine, and then utters her prayer to Jupiter for happiness for both Tyrians and Trojans. While Dido occupies center stage, she is also the center of Venus's attention and is thus already "doomed to face catastrophe" (*Aeneid* 1.994). An expert psychiatrist, the goddess of love had orchestrated her strategy with deftness and precision. The atrophy of Dido's emotional existence after Sychaeus's death, which deprived her of love and sex, was compounded by the excessive use of her thinking function in order to follow the directives in her dream. Prolonged and intent use of her rational sphere superseded all else, the building of her new city having entailed a concentrated effort to synthesize, categorize, and conceptualize. Clusters of energetic charges existing inchoate in her subliminal world had been systematically channeled toward reaching her desired pragmatic goal. She had become a driven personality and the power drive had been efficacious as a means of self-preservation, but her instinctual and emotional sides had been forced underground. Lying inchoate in her unconscious, these unredeemed and undernourished subliminal factors hungered for attention. The possibility of maintaining a cohesive and harmonious relationship between the polarities within her personality had considerably diminished. Her rational attitude, so workable when it came to city planning, no longer answered the growing and nagging need within her. As her thinking function floundered, its opposite—the instinctual—came to the fore. The increasingly overt and demanding upheavals or rumblings emerging from Dido's unconscious brought about *un abaissement du niveau mental*. It was only a matter of time until they would catapult forth and the love/sex drive would take over her life.

Dido perfectly fits Heraclitus's definition of the condition of *enantiodromia* or play of opposites within the personality. Unable to find her ground bed— a safety zone that would inspire her with a sense of security—the vulnerable Dido begins to shift from her disciplined, ordered, and authoritarian course toward the other extreme of uncontrolled instinctuality.

Her condition of relative stability having been upset, Dido suffers ceaselessly from "love's pain," which flays body and psyche and eats away at flesh and soul. It "strips her limbs of calm and rest," cloaks her world in darkness, and imposes on her a fearful restlessness that prevents her from finding a space of her own (*Aeneid* 4.1). Gone is her imperiousness, her self-assurance, her joyous productivity. Now doomed to live out an exclusionary existence, her increasingly distorted vision of reality transforms former friends into fearsome enemies. Guilt corrodes her psyche. Her wretchedness, she contends, is due to her desire to violate the oath of celibacy she had sworn after her husband's death. Anna, her sister, is the single person whom Dido considers trustworthy and to whom she confides her agony. Hoping to relieve her sister of her excoriating sense of remorse, Anna appeals to Dido both emotionally and concretely. Why should she bury herself in loneliness? she asks. Why should she never taste the joys of love, marriage, and motherhood? Not only would happiness in marriage to Aeneas be hers, but the alliance, she points out, would also have political advantages: "[W]hat a kingdom [would the two create], sister, you will see" (*Aeneid* 4.64). So blind or undifferentiated has Dido's ego become, contaminated as it is by the tempestuous flow of her undirected instincts, that she can no longer control the irrational stirrings within her. With the breakdown of reason, unconsciousness prevails. Will-less, as she had been prior to her first dream, Dido again becomes prone to suggestion, but her sister shows neither insight into people nor an empirical approach to life. Anna's seemingly logical but actually faulty arguments dissimulate reality and feed Dido's psychopathological state. Her marriage to Aeneas, Dido now erroneously reasons, would fill her with happiness and security, banish all doubts about his love for her, and thus free her from the guilt and shame she had harbored vis-à-vis Sychaeus.

With the depotentiation of the thinking function, Dido's mood swings become flagrant and indiscriminate. Despite her offerings to Juno, among other deities, she enjoys neither rest, nor calm, nor inner peace, having become prey to sudden and uncalled-for reactions each time Aeneas leaves her presence. No longer part of an ordered world, Dido has entered into those uncharted domains where dark and dangerously uninhibited impulses pullulate. It may be said that she has already emotionally abdicated her queenly sovereign power.

A "marriage" between Aeneas and Dido would serve Juno's purpose, we learn: it would distract him from his mission to found a nation. Similarly, the love alliance between Dido and Aeneas would foster Venus's goal of keeping her son in safety in Carthage. The two divinities, formerly at odds, now work together, at least outwardly, to encourage a union between Dido and Aeneas.

A hunting party is organized. Although the hunt implies hard work, perseverance, and wakefulness, its goal of killing animals may also be identified with violence and cruelty. The royal sport takes on religious and spiritual values—as it did for Romans—when the hunted animals are used for sacrificial purposes.

Dido must have sensed the danger involved in hunting down, killing, maiming or, symbolically, destabilizing her status as queen of men and women, by entering into a marriage. She hesitates, lingering in her room. When she does emerge, evidently reassured that an alliance with Aeneas will pave the way for her future happiness, the gatherers enjoy a breathtaking vision.

> Her splendid stallion,
> in gold and purple, prances, proudly champing
> his foaming bit. At last the queen appears
> among the mighty crowd; upon her shoulders
> she wears a robe of Sidon with embroidered
> borders. Her quiver is of gold, her hair
> has knots and ties of gold, a golden clasp
> holds fast her purple cloak.
>
> (*Aeneid* 4.179)

By riding a "stallion"—evocative of the image/omen she had discovered upon her arrival on Libyan shores—Dido symbolically is attempting to dominate her mount. The stallion represents her heretofore contained volcanic inner pulsations.

The hunting party in the forest is scattered by a heavy storm prearranged by Juno. Dismounting, Dido and Aeneas take shelter in a spacious, isolated cavern, where they consummate their love.

> That day was her first day of death and ruin.
> For neither how things seem nor how they are deemed
> moves Dido now, and she no longer thinks
> of furtive love. For Dido calls it marriage,
> and with this name she covers up her fault.
>
> (*Aeneid* 4.224)

The withdrawal of the lovers into the cavern may be viewed symbolically as a *regressus ad uterum*—a descent into the collective unconscious. Such a penetration into their own dark inner worlds, into the profoundest recesses of their psyches, allows them to partake of the nourishing waters of the archetypal maternal uterus. Such a descent, reminiscent of an Eleusinian death and rebirth initiation mystery, renews what had been dead in both of them: repressed feelings and sexual activity.

The cavern experience allowed Dido and Aeneas to reinvigorate sensations that had lain fallow and taste sexual rapture again after the hiatus caused by the loss of their respective spouses. Once the floodgates are opened, however, a tidal wave of needs for love, affection, and physicality rushes in, obliterating realistic thinking in favor of exclusionary *ekstasis*.

Dido's intense jubilation not only masks whatever feelings of mortification she might have had but invites her to fantasize. Blind to everything but Aeneas, she views her relationship with him as a marriage, despite the fact that no marriage formula has been pronounced.

Oblivious to the necessities of the empirical world, the couple are now involved solely with each other "in lust, forgetful of their kingdom," and taking "long pleasure" (*Aeneid* 4.254). The pleasure principle, anathema to the early Romans and during the Augustan period as well, finds expression in Dido's and Aeneas's withdrawal into the bedchamber. Their self-indulgence invites individual and collective effeteness, and paves the way for the decline of a nation. Unable to function in a social setting, they damage their own reputations and bring about the deterioration of the very city Dido had built with such fervor.

The situation having reached an impasse, Jupiter sends Mercury to remind the Trojan prince of his divine mission: the founding of a nation. Mercury, observing Aeneas's sword "starred with tawny jasper," and his cloak "blazed with Tyrian purple" that had been "a gift that wealthy Dido wove for him," resorts to shock tactics to force Aeneas out of his fantasy world. Aeneas, Mercury points out, is "servant to a woman" (*Aeneid* 4.349, 355).

Mercury's reference to his sword to downgrade Aeneas is significant. Considered by some to be a phallic object ready to penetrate its victim, this cutting instrument also serves, symbolically, to reduce virtually insurmountable problems to their component parts, permitting examination from different perspectives. Sword symbolism, as it appears in many myths such as *Parzival* and *The Song of Roland*, invests the bearer of the sword with greater vision, allowing him to cut up, examine, scrutinize, and weigh smaller segments of problematic situations. The shedding of light on smaller portions of the whole reveals new angles of approach or attack.

Not by chance, then, does Mercury disdainfully comment on Aeneas's sword, implying that both he and the object are symptomatic of effeteness, impulsiveness, and extreme lust, and that his comportment lacks royal virtues.

Are you
now laying the foundation of high Carthage,
as servant to a woman, building her
a splendid city here?

(*Aeneid* 4.353)

Mercury may be considered a manifestation of aspects of Aeneas's unconscious contents, and his words serve to provoke the Trojan's irritation. The very idea that he is "servant to a woman" implies the dominion of matriarchal consciousness in his psyche. Such a thought shatters the incipient hero's world of bliss and stirs him into activity, as had Dido's dream of Sychaeus. So stunned is Aeneas by the remote possibility of female domination that instead of reassessing his life in order to equalize the polarities within him, he, like Dido, veers to the opposite extreme. "He burns to flee from Carthage" (*Aeneid* 4.375). Let us note that his haste to abandon Dido was, in Virgil's time, symptomatic of heroic virtue. Mercury has brought to the surface, then, what has been subordinated in Aeneas's psyche during the Dido interlude: the paterfamilias, or Anchises, principle.

Interestingly enough, the very traits that Mercury lauds and identifies with masculinity—energy, perseverance, activity, vision, self-control—were Dido's own prior to her love affair. Had she been able to integrate the male and female polarities within her psyche, she might have lived out what is termed a psychologically androgynous condition. Dido's psyche is not *one* or *whole*—as in the archetypal image of the androgyne. Like Aeneas, she swung from one intemperate or radical attitude to its opposite (Singer 1976, 20).

Humiliated and destabilized, Aeneas understands the necessity of renouncing his comfortable and happy existence in order to fulfill his destiny. His retreat from temptation—the darkness of the cavern experience—sets the stage for his so-called "enlightenment," but some element of fear still impinges on his hastily made decision. "With what words dare he face the frenzied queen?" (*Aeneid* 4.378) Rather than reflect on this problem, he takes the easier path and hurries to order his men to ready the ships to sail *in secret*. The cloud Venus had sent to protect Aeneas when first he reached Carthage has now been transformed into a character trait—or propensity. The weakly structured hero, fearing outright confrontation, resorts to secrecy and/or deception.

The intuitive Dido, however, has sensed Aeneas's guile. Challenging her former lover, now turned antagonist, she gives vent to her hurt and humiliation:

Do you flee me? By tears, by your right hand—
this sorry self is left with nothing else—
by wedding, by the marriage we began,
if I did anything deserving of you
or anything of mine was sweet to you,
take pity on a fallen house, put off
your plan, I pray—if there is still place for prayers.

(*Aeneid* 4.422)

Adamant in his decision to fulfill his higher destiny, Aeneas, his emotions under strict control, is objective in the arguments he presents to Dido. Or, one wonders, has he simply wearied of Dido and decided it is time to leave for other lands? He admits she rescued him at a time of need, that her generosity was beyond reproach, but he rejects her interpretation of their relationship.

I have never held
the wedding torches as a husband; I
have never entered into such agreements.

(*Aeneid* 4.457)

No longer experiencing life on an individual and personal level with love reigning supreme, the semidivine Aeneas has become a collective being: the representative of the future Roman nation. His so-called male characteristics—power, ambition, struggle, and conflict—are now in the ascendant. Willingly, therefore, does he submit to the directives of Providence; joyfully does he assume his responsibility as builder of an empire. On a human level, he has conveniently forgotten or repressed whatever feelings he had entertained for Dido. Yearning for excitement, he yields to the lure of fame and adventure.

Aeneas's imminent departure provokes Dido's anguish and uncontrollable rage, reminiscent of Medea's and Phaedra's in their moments of agony. The hatred that she now nourishes identifies her increasingly with her patron goddess Juno, the wife of Jupiter, whose continuous infidelities had transformed her into the woman scorned.

In a breach of royal self-control, Dido, enslaved by the extremes that have polarized her psyche, displays her volatility and instinctuality. The submersion of her ego has left her prey to the undifferentiated chaotic pulsations in her being. More and more does she resort to threats—"I shall hunt you down with blackened firebrands" (*Aeneid* 4.527)—only to regret her imprecations moments later.

Again Dido calls on Anna to plead her cause with Aeneas: she begs for time to cure her love-disease. Gripped by madness, Dido's speech becomes disjointed and argumentative, and her thoughts wander. Sychaeus, the psychopomp, fails to point the way, to stabilize her at this juncture. Nor do prayers and sacrifices offered to the gods dissipate the pain of Dido's searing love. Undone by her failure to retain her lover and unable to cope with his departure, the mentally dysfunctional Dido seeks to destroy herself. Having turned virtually completely inward, away from the objective world, her libido encourages her to bury herself in her subjective obsession. That she proceeds rationally, courageously, and forcefully in the planning of her suicide is not unusual for those who are preoccupied exclusively with themselves and cling for survival to the goals about which they fantasize.

The funeral pile that Dido orders to be built in the courtyard of her palace is tended to with exactitude and method. Most important are Aeneas's mementos to be placed on it for burning: this "cursed man's" cloak, sword, portrait, and the "bridal bed" that she believed had led to her ruin (*Aeneid* 4.486). The destruction of material objects associated with her former lover is Dido's first step toward severing her earthly ties.

However rational her method may be in planning her suicide, each time the image of Aeneas's departure intrudes in her mind's eye she becomes victimized by affects: derangement, madness, invocations, and sacrifices. Excoriating dreams haunt her nights. The same scorn and humiliation that had fed the emotionally maimed Juno and triggered her unquenchable hatred nourish Dido's loathing and feed the fires of her hysteria.

Dido unsheathes the sword given to her by Aeneas as a token of his love and admiration, then plunges it into her flesh before the people. As if to vindicate her earthly existence, she sums up her achievements and failures in a strikingly orderly fashion.

> I have built a handsome city,
> have seen my walls rise up, avenged a husband,
> won satisfaction from a hostile brother. . . .
> I shall die unavenged, but I shall die.
>
> (*Aeneid* 4.903)

Imperious and self-willed, this passionate ruler of men and women soon is no more. When her people realize their queen is dead, a "clamor rises to the high rooftop" and "lamentations, keening, shrieks of women sound through the houses" (*Aeneid* 4.918). Carthage becomes a city in mourning.

Even Juno takes pity on the queen. She sends to earth Iris, the rainbow, to free Dido's soul and take it to the afterworld.

Aeneas and his men, sailing toward their destiny, turn to look back at Carthage. Seeing flames rising to the sky, Aeneas considers for a moment that Dido's unquenchable passion might have driven her to suicide, but no feelings of remorse or of longing for the once majestic queen can interfere with the goal he—Destiny—has set for himself. To make his mark on earth and invite eternal praise from mortals and immortals is more important to him than ephemeral love. The gods (the Self or total psyche) had succeeded in awakening Aeneas's slumbering reason, now transformed into *pneuma*, a creative force within his psyche. The obligations of a collective figure—standards set by Cato the Elder (234–149 B.C.E.)—direct him to build a new and firmer connection between his ego and the Self, the finite and the infinite, the mortal and the immortal—and forge ahead. Had Aeneas remained possessed by his love, he would not have been able consciously to realize the Self as *spiritus rector* and he, like Dido, would have been lost to the world.

Dido and Aeneas will meet one last time in Hades. As he crosses the threshold from life to death or, symbolically, passes through a dark birth passage or cavern, he descends into the underworld, which may be identified with the collective unconscious. Unlike his first cavern experience—withdrawal from the world to enjoy love—Aeneas here will not know *ekstasis*.

The sight of Dido's shadowy form vaguely outlined by the rays of the moon confirms the suicide that he had only suspected when sailing away from Carthage. He recognizes this cold, stonelike countenance only dimly, as well he might, since he has banished from consciousness the feminine powers she represented within him and assumed instead a new personality identified with the paterfamilias. A shade or *shadow* force, Dido now symbolizes those factors existing in his own psyche that his ego now considers negative and unacceptable.

That Dido's image *(eidolon)* as a shade is barely discernible to Aeneas ("who either sees or thinks he sees among the cloud banks, when the month is young, the moon rising") (*Aeneid* 6.597) suggests that in death she reveals herself as a *persona*, a visible mask or ancestral spirit living on eternally in the eye of the beholder as a genius. Let us note in this connection that the Roman word Genius, although first understood as "the mortal essence of being or of the identity of the individual," after undergoing Graeco-Egyptian influence was defined "as the entity which survives death" (Franz 1986, 124).

Upon first seeing Dido as a shade, Aeneas feels the loss of *his* happiness, not hers; of *his* youth and the idyllic months of pleasurable abandon he had enjoyed with her. Although begging her forgiveness, weeping some tears, and pitying her somewhat, he declares rather unvirtuously (*vir*, manliness) that he takes no personal responsibility for his departure from Carthage. He left at God's command. Nor is he answerable for her suicide: "I could not believe that with my going I should bring too great a grief as this" (*Aeneid* 6.610).

That Dido comports herself with dignity as she slowly moves away from her former lover reveals her acceptance of her loss of love and life. If we consider her death in psychological terms, as a descent into the collective unconscious, one may affirm that she has grown during the process. Her detachment from the world of contingencies gives her a new and enlarged vantage point: she now understands that life and death are two facets of a *whole*. Aware of what had been *beyond* her ken in the heat of passion, she now accepts Aeneas's timorous nature and her powerlessness to alter his course. Just as he had been "destined" to found a great nation, so she has been "fated" to love a weakly structured man.

Aeneas asks her not to withdraw from his presence, attempting in this way to "soothe the burning fierce-eyed Shade." Dido, no longer subject to her passion, refrains from speech (*Aeneid*, 6.616). Recoiling from her "enemy," she enters "the forest of shadows" where her husband, Sychaeus, the positive, guiding, and saving force in her life, gives "her love for love" (*Aeneid* 6.624). As she returns to her *domus aeterna* or grave in the Beyond, Aeneas peers at her body-spirit as it vanishes into the distance.

Just as Anchises, and such male deities as Jupiter and his messenger Mercury, transfers the values of the *father* to the *son*, thus establishing continuity of purpose and tradition, so Sychaeus (or what she projects onto him) appeases Dido's pain in that he accepts her in her every role: wife, former queen of Carthage, and as a scorned and rejected woman.

Dido's animated corpse, which Aeneas sees or thinks he has seen, may be understood parapsychologically, as C. G. Jung suggested, as an image of light:

> [P]sychic reality might lie on a supraluminous level of frequency, that is, it could exceed the speed of light. "Light," would appropriately enough be the last transitional phenomenon of the process of becoming unobservable, before the psyche fully "irrealizes" the body . . . and its first appearance after it incarnates itself in the space-time continuum by shifting its energy to a lower gear. (Franz 1986, 146)

Thus has Dido been transfigured into a type of "window into eternity," or the materialization of what she represents in him and in the society of which she is a part: the woman weakened by love, obeying her emotions rather than her reason. Earthly raiment once shed, she lives on as a pitiful memory.

Camilla, the Amazon

The Amazons are believed to have lived on the Anatolian plain prior to the colonization of Greece by the Ionians. Although archaeologists have discovered artifacts in the area of Catal Huyuk (Turkey) and elsewhere depicting women driving chariots, using swords in warfare, and bows and arrows in the hunt, the existence of the Amazons has not yet been established with certainty. Nevertheless, mythology is studded with Amazon types: Queen Hypsipyle, Myrine, Atalanta, Harpalyke, Kyrene, Britomartis, and so forth.

Customs in the Amazonian societies were strictly enforced: only women were allowed to bear military arms either in the defense of their country or in raiding neighboring lands. Men, if not entirely excluded from their society, were tolerated simply for procreative purposes and were allotted inferior positions: they performed the same daily household tasks that women did in patriarchal lands. Some men were even taken into slavery.

Diana, the divine Roman huntress honored by the Amazons, did everything possible to avoid being ruled by a man. That she was a virgin (*parthenos*, unmarried) did not mean that she was chaste, the word chastity becoming later identified with and defined by Christian morals. Because Diana valued neither marriage, nor men, nor even sons, the Amazons generally refused to relate to or be dependent upon a man, seeking to remain their own person and as objective as possible in their activities and relationships (Neumann 1954, 52).

The Amazon sought to develop both physical and emotional strength, attributes identified throughout the centuries with male power. Her association with men was based for the most part on their respect for her accomplishments and understanding of her needs. Adamant and confident, she was awarded by some men the equality she sought and deserved.

"Decus Italiae Virgo"

Let us take up our story following Aeneas's visit to Hades. Returning to earth, he fought many battles, lived through clusters of harrowing adventures, and finally reached Latium, south of Rome, where he was well received by its ruler, King Latinus, a descendent of Saturn and the ancestor of the historical Romans. Latinus's only daughter, Lavinia, although courted by many young men, loved and was loved by the mighty warrior, Turnus. His rival, Aeneas, however, was fated to marry her.

Turnus had appointed to lead his cavalry Camilla, a warrior-maiden to whom he referred as "decus Italiae virgo" (O Virgin, you pride of Italy) (*Aeneid* 9.668)—a perfect appellation for one who was courageous, committed, wild at times, and dedicated to human affairs as well as to war. Her favorite habitat was the woods; her favorite sport, hunting, like her patron deity, Diana.

Psychologically, Amazon types usually identify with their fathers. Aeschylus's Athena, in the *Eumenides*, asserts,

> For me no mother bore within her womb,
> And, save for wedlock evermore eschewed,
> I vouch myself the champion of the man . . .
> In heart, as birth, a father's child alone. . . .
>
> (L. 735)[4]

Camilla was no exception. Her mother, Casmilla, after whom she had been named, died when she was but an infant, depriving the child of a role model. Camilla's father, Metabus, king of the Volscians, was a single parent. His daughter, understandably, was his uppermost concern.

Obliged to flee from the ire of his people who considered him a tyrant, Metabus had taken his beloved infant into exile.

> And he carried her
> clutched to his breast while traveling across
> long ridges, through the solitary forest;
> on all sides savage lances pressed against him;
> far-ranging Volscian soldiers hemmed him in.
>
> (*Aeneid* 11.714)

Fearing for her life—perhaps a premonitory image of the dangers Camilla was to face later on—Metabus resorted to ruse to save her from his onrushing enemies. Because he had to cross a rain-swollen river to escape certain death, his first impulse was to swim to safety with his infant in his arms. He realized that the power of the treacherous currents was so great that she would be swept from him. He resolved the impasse by his sudden realization that he was carrying in his hand a "giant lance . . . well-knotted, tough of seasoned-oak." He bound Camilla "in cork-tree bark" and then fastened "her neatly around the middle of the shaft" (*Aeneid* 11.726). After offering fervent prayer to Diana, he cast the spear with all his might across the river. He then dove into the torrential waters and swam to the other side, where he picked up his treasure safely ensconced on the opposite bank.

That Metabus succeeded in saving his daughter with a spear, a weapon used mainly for armed hostile conflict, suggests an association between love and war. The energy and drive expended in war may be interpreted as both a manifestation of the libido linked with love and a substitute and/or sublimation for it. Camilla, identifying with her father in infancy, childhood, and adolescence, would consider war and the performing of heroic feats—on foot or astride a horse—sheer rapture, a love feast.

Metabus, as widower and exile, had but one focus—his love for Camilla. Rather than raise her in a city, he decided to bring her up in wild and isolated mountainous areas. He nursed and fed "her wild milk from a brood mare's teats"; to make certain she was nourished "into her tender lips he squeezed the udder" (*Aeneid* 11.753). No sooner had she begun to walk than he

> placed a pointed
> lance head within her hand, and from that little
> girl's shoulder he made bow and quiver hang.
>
> (*Aeneid* 9.756)

Instead of regal clothes and "golden hairbands and long robes," Metabus dressed her in tiger skins (*Aeneid* 11.759). Camilla's early years were lived out not as a woman in a patriarchal society, but rather as a man, among shepherds and beasts.

Although she bore feminine features, her internal spirit of martial frenzy inclined her toward behavioral patterns that are traditionally identified with the male.

As the carrier of the father image, she did not invite her repressed feminine side to develop to its fullest. Thus, she was unable or unwilling to heal the breach between the polarities within her. Nor was there any need to do so, since she lived compatibly with a brilliantly developed masculine aspect and a virtually nonexistent feminine side. No rejecting of the paternal image was required on her part—a struggle most adolescents must experience if they are to pass into maturity. Indeed, as the saying goes, like father like daughter: Camilla had become his prototype, carrying out his will and ideations.

While the home—an enclosed area shared by both parents and their progeny—usually represents a place of shelter and protection for a child, the opposite was true in Camilla's case. Open spaces and thickly forested areas were her habitat. There she learned endurance and the ability to fend off or befriend wild animals. Because Camilla was able to project her own raw instinctual propensities onto Mother Nature in all of her manifestations, she familiarized herself with her own powerful needs and learned to cope with and channel her drives. She lived openly—neither ignoring nor repressing her innate pulsations.

In that her father and Mother Nature played the most important roles during Camilla's impressionable years, both acted as control forces for the young girl. Metabus indoctrinated her into his military ethos; Mother Nature, into her love for the ferocious struggle needed to survive in the wild. The fact that Camilla enjoyed a close bond with both personal and impersonal parents suggests that she represented one side of a composite figure.

In addition to a personal father, Camilla had yet another active factor contributing to her psychological makeup: a divine archetypal father, Mars (in Greek, Ares). Although the brutal, violent, and aggressive god of war did not play a significant part in Greek culture, his love of carnage and battle appealed to the militaristically oriented Romans. Not surprisingly, then, did Camilla and Metabus hold what Mars represented in high esteem.

She was drawn as if magnetically toward

> war and prodded by an inner urge to lead
> on her band of horsemen, squadrons bright
> with brazen armor. She is a warrior;
> her woman's hands have never grown accustomed to
> distaffs or the baskets of Minerva;
> a virgin, she was trained to face hard battle
> and to outrace the wind with speeding feet.
>
> (*Aeneid* 7.1055)

Camilla's background did not encourage psychological wholeness, but rather singleness of purpose. Like her patron Diana, she belonged to herself; she was in harmony with her lifestyle, and free from any inner conflict. Nor did she suffer an identity crisis. She was aware that she *knew* who she was and *knew* what she wanted to do. Nevertheless, her life consisted mainly in physical activity and armed conflict. Strength, honor, and vigilance in her undertakings and relationships were constants in her world.

Unmarried, independent, self-contained, her own person, in Camilla fighting and sexuality were seemingly equated, the one nourishing the other. Like her patron deity Diana, she remained unmarried despite the fact that mothers sought her out for marriage to their sons.

Inasmuch as Camilla's Amazon characteristics existed preconsciously and formed the structural dominant of her psyche, one might say that, like Dido and Aeneas, she was an archetypal figure. Within her there existed "a living system of reactions and aptitudes" that determined her behavioral patterns. But unlike Dido and Aeneas, who during their love interlude were concerned with themselves alone, Camilla's motivations were collective, hinging on matters that altered geographical boundaries and political powers (Y. Jacobi 1959, 36).

Camilla gave herself over both mentally and viscerally to what she loved best in life. Because of her great dexterity, agility, and strength, as well as her rationality in matters of strategy, she considered herself the equal of any man. In a patriarchally oriented society, she may have been considered hard and unfeeling but, on the contrary, she shared not only a sense of camaraderie with her band of maidens but friendships with men as well. Turnus, because he was himself self-confident and secure in his reputation as a military leader, could accept her as a power in her own right. He neither had to save face by denigrating her nor did he feel compelled to resort to tactics of self-defense to prove himself. Her presence was not seen as a threat to his sterling reputation. On the contrary, rather than tarnish his valor as soldier, she enhanced it by helping him dazzle his enemies. As the antithesis of Mercury, who convinced Aeneas to leave Carthage by telling him he was serving a woman, thus humiliating him, Turnus admired people who excelled—be they men or women.

Confident of her prowess, Camilla offered her services as warrior to Turnus. And he responded with "O virgin, you, pride of Italy," sending her with troops of his own to meet the Tuscan horsemen head-on (*Aeneid* 11.669). In his mind there was little or no difference in battle between male and female. Camilla's courage, fearlessness, and genuine talent for leadership put her on a par with any warrior. Indeed, she was Turnus's female counterpart, his double. Both were authentic in their behavior, both endowed with understanding and devotion toward friend and ferocity toward foe. Not surprisingly did Turnus share his leadership of the Latins with Camilla, for no other man or woman merited his confidence or possessed her abilities: "[S]ince you are above all praise or prize, then share the trial with me" (*Aeneid* 11.669).

An analogy may be drawn between Camilla and Penthesilea, daughter of Ares and queen of the Amazons, whom Virgil looks upon as a paradigm of male virility (*Aeneid* 1.490). The mettle of Penthesilea, who had come to the aid of King Priam, ruler of Troy, after the demise of his son, Hector, put the Greeks to shame. Having been mortally wounded by Achilles, she aroused love in her killer because of her extreme beauty and courage.

Camilla was pitiless in her relentless pursuit of the enemy. A presumptuous adversary having duped her into dismounting during their combat, on foot she overtook rider and horse and tore her prey to pieces in one of the *Aeneid's* many gory sequences.

Camilla was fully prepared to direct an attack against Aeneas and his men. Fearless of the physicality involved in combat, she was equally unmoved by the thought of death—hers or that of others. But a lapse of attention during a battle was her undoing. The superb golden armor of Chloreus, a Phrygian priest of Cybele, caught her eye. She longed to have it.

> The virgin singled him out in battle;
> and whether she had wanted to hang up
> the Trojan arms of Chloreus in the temple
> or just to dress herself in captive gold,
> she hurried after him, blind to all else,
> a huntress. Fearless, with a female's love
> of plunder and of spoils, she raged through all
> the army.
>
> (*Aeneid* 11.1033)

Meanwhile, Arruns, an Etruscan fighting on Aeneas's side, saw her rushing toward the coveted armor, oblivious to danger. Stalking her every move, he bided his time before striking, his lance digging deep into her flesh. Camilla paid no heed. Was it her trancelike state—her attraction to this dazzling insignia—that inured her to pain? "All Volscians turned anxious eyes and minds upon the queen" (*Aeneid* 11.1063). She mustered the strength to fight on "until the shaft drove in below her breast, held fast and drank deep of her virgin blood" (*Aeneid* 11.1066).

Temptation led to Camilla's downfall. Her desire for gold, based on greed rather than on the higher values of purity of intent and spirit, was transformed into an agent of destruction. Just as gold had aroused acquisitiveness in Pygmalion, Dido's brother who killed Sychaeus, the gleaming glorious trophy incited Camilla's pride and a desire for the spoil—albeit to offer to her deity. Because preoccupation with material things was not in Camilla's character, her lust had blinded her to the dangers of battle and had deafened her to the warning sounds of her enemy's pursuit.

Her companions, shocked at the sight of Camilla struck down by a spear, ran to her side.

> Camilla tries to tug the lance out with
> her hand; but its steel head holds fast her bones
> within the ribs in that deep wound. She falls, bloodless; her
> eyes are faltering, chill in death;
> her color, once so bright, has left her face.
>
> (*Aeneid* 11.1082)

Aware that her death is imminent and unwilling to leave her troops without a leader, she instructed her sister, Acca, to advise Turnus to "take [her] place and drive the Trojans from the city gates" (*Aeneid* 11.1094).

A profound sense of loss gripped those who had loved Camilla. Upon hearing of the death of his ally, Turnus raged, then quit "his ambush on the hills" (*Aeneid* 11.1193). "She who [was] more dear to me than any other" was mourned by the nymph Opis, one of the "holy band" of Camilla (*Aeneid* 11.702, 704). The bereaved Latin "mothers on watchtowers raise[d] laments," then, inspired by Camilla's powerful love for country, emulated their heroine by fighting the enemy, each to her own capacity (*Aeneid* 11.1162).

Turnus fought on until he, too, was destroyed by "fate"—forces superior to his own. The victorious Aeneas married Lavinia, founded Italy, and thereby completed his destiny.

Unlike the more complex Dido and Aeneas, Camilla and Turnus were psychologically undifferentiated. Neither knew soul-searching or soul-searching conflict. Their choices were guided by military strategy, command performances, and leadership in battle. Both were made for the deadly sport of war; both bore arms superbly. Fearless in their approach and confrontation of the enemy, it may be said that the greater the challenge the more ecstatic were their feelings of elation and power. Like the mythological "berserkers" depicted in the *Volsunga Saga* and generally identified with ancient Germanic tribes, Turnus and Camilla were protected by what may be referred to as their condition of "trancelike" *ekstasis* (Eliade 1958, 81). Unlike the "berserkers," who did not wear shields but were invulnerable because they fought with "trancelike" fury, Camilla and Turnus both perished in the melee.

Nevertheless, their martial ideals and capacity to survive harrowing ordeals transformed them into *superbeings* worthy of adulation for their courage and will to succeed, and honor for their intransigence and authenticity.

The popularity of the Amazon archetype expands usually during culturally turbulent times when sexual identity is undergoing change. The rejection of the feminine aspect of woman and the opting for the all-dominance of what she perceives to be as her male side creates an explosive situation in the environment, forcing society to take stock of itself, its rules, its regulations and ideals. Virgil, ensconced in his patriarchal society, feared female independence as exemplified in the equality Camilla demanded as female warrior or in the person of Dido, queen and builder of a city (Neumann 1963, 267).

Camilla was no more psychologically androgynous than Dido had been. She did not combine the softness and relational qualities that patriarchal societies associated—and still associate for the most part—with the woman, and the warlike, aggressive, and at times ferociously cruel characteristics identified in Roman times with the male. But her upbringing allowed her to resist the patriarchal authority of the time. Even today a determined stance and conviction of one's own strength may serve as a means for women to cope with oppression and male encroachment—a condition so powerfully ingrained in both Camilla's and our own culture.

Both Dido and Camilla had, each in her own way, attempted to find a disposition that would answer her needs and help her gain independence and fulfillment. Only Camilla, the psychologically undifferentiated woman, succeeded in her endeavor.

7 Japan's Sun Goddess: The Divine Amaterasu

Unlike many world religions in which the Sun is associated with masculine powers and the Moon with the feminine, the opposite is true in Japan. The glowing daylight celestial body is a Shinto goddess: Amaterasu no ô Kami (Heaven-Shining-Great-August-Deity).

> The resplendent luster of this child shone throughout all the six quarters [North, South, East, West, Above, Below].
>
> Therefore the two Deities [her parents] rejoiced, saying: "We have had many children, but none of them have been equal to this wondrous infant. (*Nihongi* 1.18)[1]

Not only did Amaterasu-worship become the supreme cult of Japan, but this deity also became the progenitrix of the country's imperial line—by extension, of the entire race! Amaterasu's grandson descended from heaven, and his grandson in turn became the first emperor of Japan, ascending the throne in 660 B.C.E. Her cult embraced ancestor worship and nature worship: veneration for parents and grandparents as well as awe in the presence of every element of the earth. Because Amaterasu taught humankind how to grow food, how to make clothing, and how to build homes, she was looked upon as the great provider. Her understanding, warmth, and rectitude heralded her as the goddess of peace.

Poets throughout the centuries sang their adoration, respect, and love for Amaterasu, at times without mentioning her sacred name but simply alluding to her as Sun. In *The Diary of Sarashina* (eleventh century) the author projects her feelings onto this constellation whose presence inspires her with joy and whose withdrawal fills her with sorrow:

> The setting sun that hung above the mountain's edge
> Has now sunk out of sight.
> How sad it was to see you go!
>
> (Morris 1971, 59)

For the author of *The Confessions of Lady Nijo* (fourteenth century), Amaterasu is her confidante. Not only does she share her sorrow with a humanized Amaterasu, but by alluding to the Grand Shrine at Ise, constructed in her honor, she asks her for direction.

> O god of Ise, guide me
> Through the span of life
> Allotted to me still
> In this world of grief.
>
> (Brazell 1973, 218)

In the twentieth century, Fumiko Enchi, in her remarkable novel *Masks* (1958), refers to Amaterasu obliquely in such images as that of a white chrysanthemum. An emblem of the Japanese imperial house, its petals, disposed in a circular pattern, represent the earthly counterpart of the Sun's rays—Amaterasu in all of her burgeoning purity, power, and eternality.

Awesome yet friendly, Amaterasu welcomes those who seek to be warmed by her glowing rays and illumined by her numinosity. She becomes a mediating force between the universal and the personal, the cosmic and earthly, light and shadow, the cyclical and the perennial. Nevertheless, despite the intensity of Amaterasu-worship, the lot of women in Japan worsened progressively from the eighth century to the twentieth century. Not only were women deprecated and virtually enslaved in the increasingly patriarchal state, but they were associated with evil: they appeared as the devil, monsters, and ghosts, as angry spirits returning to extract their due vengeance on the male. Were these characterizations an expression of the male's subliminal fear of women?

How could a society have so drastically veered away from its beginnings, from a time when, it was thought, the existing social organization enjoyed equality between the sexes, to the extremes of a patriarchal system? What was the genesis of events that led to the virtual incarceration of women—at least those of the higher classes, whose lives were spent hidden in the home, and even within this limited area behind screens and sliding doors?

Ectypal Analysis

The unusual aspects of the religious scene in Japan may shed some light on the above questions. Cohabiting with Shinto ("The Way of the Gods," i.e., of the Kami [gods, "unseen powers"], a word coined in the sixth century C.E.),[2] were Buddhism and Confucianism. Shinto was favorably disposed to women; Buddhism and Confucianism were not. Although the statements to follow certainly do not do these three great religious philosophies justice, a brief description of each will facilitate the reading of this chapter on Amaterasu.

In Shinto, Amaterasu, as previously mentioned, was the main deity of nature as well as of ancestor worship. An animistic religion, Shinto is an earth-centered theology with highly complex rituals, scriptures, and code of ethics. Shintoists, we might say, believe that a life force exists in all things, animate or inanimate, and everything in the world of phenomena is endowed with a spirit. Worship is based on the simple feeling of "awe" for all things in nature: a waterfall, a flower, a stone, an insect, a mountain, snow, an ancestor, a hero, the emperor, the sun, the moon. Such numinous forces are called Kami, which is translated in either the plural or singular, as "god," "superior," or "above." It is not, however, the Kami per se that is worshipped, but rather the *spirit (mitama)* inhabiting it (Herbert 1967, 16). Human beings approach Kami in reverence and in friendship, and without fear. Before doing so, however, they must purify themselves by washing their hands and mouths, and taking part in devotions, such as standing within a sacred enclosure (a shrine within a quiet grove) or before a particular stone or mountain.

Buddhism, founded by the Indian Siddhartha Gautama (566–438 B.C.E.), preaches the doctrine of Buddha, the Enlightened One. Happiness and salvation result from inwardness and are not dependent upon transitory exterior phenomena; life on earth is the product of imperfection and sorrow; the annihilation of desire leads to salvation and "perpetual enlightenment" (Nirvana). After Buddhism was introduced into Japan in 552 C.E, it was modified by the Japanese and divested of most of its theology. It became a philosophy.

Prior to the writing of the *Pure Land Sutra* (100 B.C.E. to 100 C.E.), one of the most popular of philosophical texts, Buddhism considered woman to be an obstacle to man's spiritual evolution. Her sexual energy led to bondage *(samsara)*, pain, suffering, and desire, culminating in cycles of rebirths. Because it was believed that women represented a threat to the stability of the monastic communities and the disciplines practiced therein, female chastity was emphasized. The thirty-fourth vow of the *Pure Land Sutra,* however, partially rectified the injustice toward women by allowing the worthy ones to "progress in the Bodhisattva vehicle" (Paul 1985, 5).

> O Bhagavan [lord], if after I have obtained Bodhi [enlightenment], women in immeasurable, innumerable, inconceivable, incomparable, immense Buddha countries on all sides, after having heard my name, should allow carelessness to arise, should not turn their thoughts toward Bodhi, should, when they are free from birth, not despise their female nature; and if they, being born again should assume a second female nature, then may I not obtain the highest perfect knowledge. (*The Larger Sukhavativyuha,* 19, trans. Max Müller, quoted in ibid., 169)

The great hope for these worthy women was to be reborn as men in the next life, thus enabling them to realize their spiritual potential.

Confucianism, along with Buddhism, played a significant role in the growing patriarchate that Japan was to become. Confucius (551–479 B.C.E.) preached a family-style morality based on the ethical wisdom of "superior men." Emphasis was on character building, learning, virtue, filial piety and ancestral piety; it gave virtually no importance to women. For Confucius, "filial duty and fraternal duty" were "fundamental to Manhood-at-its-best." Because only the wisest and most honorable men were capable of governing society, moral integrity was stressed. It was incumbent, then, upon a "gentleman" to elevate those he ruled by serving as an example rather than by exercising autocratic control. Civilization's continuity depended upon the moral fiber and rules of conduct of the central authority.

Shinto, Buddhism, and Confucianism advocated reverence for ancestors, and all three were based on purity of soul and ethical action. Only the latter two, however, preached asceticism and intellectuality and minimized, if not denigrated, women, accounting to a great extent for the inferior position of the female in post-eighth-century Japan. As a result, women's social and political dominance vanished; they became the "handmaids," so to speak, of the masculine-oriented Buddhism and Confucianism. Although in the centuries to come some women struggled valiantly and at the cost of deep sacrifice to earn their independence, few reached the sought-for goal. Only after World War II, with the promulgation of the 1947 constitution, did the condition of women in Japan alter (Reischauer 1979, 211).

Let us look back in time and explore the historical and cultural conditions which gave birth to Amaterasu, saw to her ascension into Heaven, and to the implementation of her worship throughout Japan.

Japan's beginnings are bathed in mystery. The first recorded date for the founding of the Japanese empire—660 B.C.E.—appears in the *Chronicles of Japan* (*Nihongi*, 720 C.E.). According to the punctilious records kept by the Chinese, however, Japan was referred to for the first time in 57 C.E. This later date calls attention to Japan not in terms of a unified land but in terms of one made up of some hundred tribal communities (de Bary 1964, 1).

Although the inhabitants of Japan in Neolithic times were the ancestors of the partly proto-Caucasoid Ainu, later groups, originating perhaps in the steppes of northeastern Asia, were possessed of distinctly Mongoloid features. Some invaders came from Korea to northern Kyushu and western Honshu. Partly nomadic, they were horse-riding, warlike people. Working in iron, stone, and bronze, it was they who brought to Japan the long straight iron sword, the curved stone in the shape of a large comma, and the round bronze mirror. One of the invading clans gained dominance over the others and, settling in the Yamato Plain, won power over central and western Japan, and sections of southern Korea (Reischauer 1946, 11–12).

What arrests our attention at this juncture of Japan's history is the political and religious substructure of its tribal units. Each was ruled by a chieftain—either a female priestess or a male priest. Documents refer to the "queen's country," indicating her leadership over the other clans. Such references not only are in keeping with Shinto cosmogony but also shed light on the subject of female/male relationship.

Emperor Sujin (97-30 B.C.E.), having built a sanctuary for the solar emblems (stone, mirror, sword) consigned, according to Shinto belief, by Amaterasu to her divine son, appointed his daughter to oversee their worship. Emperor Suinin (29 B.C.E.–70 C.E.) ordered his daughter, Yamato-hime no Mikoto, to find an appropriate site for Amaterasu's glorification. Accordingly, a sanctuary was built in Ise province in keeping with the dictates of the oracle, through whose voices she heard the great goddess's commands.

Credible documentation, drawn from official Chinese sources such as the *History of the Kingdom of Wei (Wei Chih)* (297 C.E.), refers to Japan (known then as Wa) as a society characterized by equality between the sexes. "In their meetings and in their deportment, there is no distinction between father and son or between man and woman." Still, it was noted that men in the upper echelons of the hierarchy had four or five wives, while those on lower tiers had only two or three (de Bary 1964, 5).

Even more astonishing for our purposes is the fact that this same *History of the Kingdom of Wei* mentions the fact that the country of Wa, once ruled by men, had undergone so many upheavals that the people decided they wanted to be governed by Pimiko, a woman. She was depicted as a kind of shaman:

> She occupied herself with magic and sorcery, bewitching the people. Though mature in age, she remained unmarried. She had a younger brother who assisted her in ruling the country. After she became the ruler there were few who saw her. She had one thousand women as attendants, but only one man. He served her food and drink and acted as a medium of communication. She resided in a palace surrounded by towers and stockades, with armed guards in a state of constant vigilance. . . . (De Bary 1964, 6)

It is further recorded that Pimiko or the Queen of Wa sent an emissary to Tai-fang in China 238 C.E., requesting permission to pay tribute to the emperor at his court. That she had official stature and was much admired is evident from the emperor's proclamation to the queen of Wa, which reads:

> Herein we address Pimiko, queen of Wa, whom we now officially call a friend of Wei. The Governor of Taifang, Liu Hsia, has sent a messenger to accompany your vassal, Nashonmi, and his lieutenant, Tsushbi Gori. They have arrived here with your tribute consisting of four male slaves and six female slaves, together with two pieces of cloth with designs, each twenty feet in length. You live very far away across the sea; yet you have sent an embassy with tribute. Your loyalty and filial piety we appreciate exceedingly. We confer upon you, therefore, the title "Queen of Wa Friendly to Wei," together with the decoration of the gold seal with purple ribbon. The latter, properly encased, is to be sent to you through the Governor. We expect you, O Queen, to rule your people in peace and to endeavor to be devoted and obedient. (Ibid.)

After Pimiko's demise, a mound over a hundred paces in diameter was raised and more than a hundred male and female attendants were buried with her.

No sooner had a king been placed on the throne of Wa than the people manifested their dissatisfaction by murdering and assassinating over a thousand people. Seemingly, the inhabitants of Wa wanted to be ruled by a woman. When the thirteen-year-old Oyo, a relative of Pimiko, was chosen to be queen, bloodshed ceased (ibid.).

Women are again mentioned during the reign of Emperor Temmu (672–

86) who, for political reasons, appointed a committee to set down in writing his country's old traditions. One of his female attendants (some say he was male), Hieda-no-Are, endowed with an extraordinary memory, was ordered to memorize the ancient legends surrounding the Age of the Gods and the founding of the Japanese Imperial dynasty. In 711, Empress Gemmio (707–15) had Yasumaro Futo no Ason commit to writing the tales told to him by Hieda-no-Are. His selection became the *Records of Ancient Matters* (*Kojiki*, 712 C.E.), a collection of myths, legends, songs, poems, clan genealogies, and some historical accounts beginning with the Creation—the separation of Heaven and Earth—and concluding with the death of Empress Suiko (592–628) (Herbert 1967, 36). Mention is made of other women rulers: Kogyoku Tenno (642–45); Jito Tenno (686–97); Genmei (707–15); Gensho (715–24); and so forth.

Further details concerning the pantheon of gods are also to be found in the previously mentioned pseudonational history, the *Nihongi*. In the Commentary *(Konin Shiki)* on the *Nihongi* (810–24), it states that after the completion of the *Nihongi*, it was "laid before the Empress Gemmio in A.D. 720 by Prince Toneri and Yasumaro Futo no Ason," the compilers of the work (Aston 1984a, xiii).

Other sources indicate that the information concerning the origin of the gods and ancestors included in the *Nihongi* was compiled from the statements made by a hereditary group of *kataribe* (reciters), whose role was to recite "ancient words." Their recitations at great Shinto festivals, on important state occasions, and at banquets at the imperial court or palace for highly placed families were frequently accompanied by music. Whether or not Yasumaro's informant was a member of the group is unknown, but he was, seemingly, conversant with the myths and legends recited by the *kataribe* (Aston 1977, 20).

Contact with China increased considerably in the early centuries, and the cultural interchange enriched Japan both scientifically and religiously. The continental civilization whetted the Japanese appetite for learning, expansion, and creativity. It was also responsible for the introduction of Buddhism to the Ya-mato clan in 552 C.E. Understandably, Buddhism was considered a threat to the authority of the Kami from which the Japanese descended. But the Soga family, a branch of the Yamato clan, fighting for the establishment of Buddhism in Japan, defeated the Shintoist Manonobe, who opposed the importation of the new religion. The dominant Soga rulers arranged for the assassination of the Yamato chief, after which they proclaimed his niece, Suiko, Empress (Hall 1970, 42).

Extraordinary changes took place in the Yamato court under the reign of Empress Suiko. According to the *Nihongi*, she was both unusually beautiful and intellectually competent.

> Her appearance was beautiful, and her conduct was marked by propriety. At the age of eighteen, she was appointed empress-consort of the Emperor Nunakura futo-damashiki. When she was thirty-four years of age . . . the Emperor was murdered by the Great Imperial Chieftain Mumako no Suskine, and the succession of the Dignity being vacant, the Ministers besought the Empress-consort . . . to ascend the throne. (De Bary 1964, 43)

Twice she declined the great honor, as was the custom, and accepted only upon the third request. Under her rule, the Inner Doctrine (Buddhism) was promoted, as were the building of Buddhist temples, the constructing of statues of Buddhas, one of which was sixteen feet in height, the collecting of relics, and the establishment of priestly orders and nunneries (ibid., 45).

Empress Suiko's nephew, Prince Shotoku, was appointed "regent." Emulating the much-admired Chinese civilization, he imposed the adoption of the Chinese calendar, the erection of Buddhist temples, and the reorganization of the government, with the court becoming the central authority. An official embassy was sent to China in 607. A devout Buddhist, Prince Shotoku recommended that young scholars specializing in literature, philosophy, history, Buddhist theology and ritual, and artistic skills be sent to China to study. Upon their return to the Yamato court, they were given positions that enabled them to impart their learning to the Japanese.

Archetypal Analysis

That Amaterasu was identified with the Sun is in itself unusual. Some ancient religions embodied such associations. The tribal Arabian Shamshu, a sun goddess, may be regarded as one. The right eye of the Egyptian Hathor, goddess of the sky, became the sun, and her left, the moon. Hathor was also considered both mother and daughter of the sun god, Ra. In the Sumerian, Babylonian, and Assyrian pantheons, both the moon (Sin, Nanna) and the sun (Utu, Shamash) were male. The sun was worshipped as female by the Celts (Sulis), by the Germans (Sunna), and by the Norwegians (Sol).

Shinto beliefs with regard to Amaterasu cast an extraordinary light on our story. Nevertheless, there remain the problems and confusion connected with myths in general—not only in terms of the events recorded but also in their chronology. Because we are unable to include the hundreds of pages of recorded material, we choose to base our discussions on the significant deeds highlighted in important sources as translated by renowned scholars in the field.

We are told in the *Nihongi* that in the beginning "Heaven and Earth were not yet separated, and the *In* and *Yo* not yet divided." (The *In* and *Yo* have been compared to the yang and yin of the Chinese Taoist cosmogony.) In time, the *In* (male) and the *Yo* (female) principles "formed a chaotic mass like an egg which was of obscurely defined limits and contained germs" (*Nihongi* 1.1.1). When the egg took on life, its purer and clearer part was drawn to and formed Heaven, the domain of the Kami, which was looked upon with reverence; its heavier element became earth.

First heaven was produced, and then earth.

> Hence it was said that when the world began to be created, the soil of which lands were composed floated about in a manner which might be compared to the floating of a fish sporting on the surface of the water. (*Nihongi* 1.1.2)

A form resembling a reed-shoot suddenly manifested itself between Heaven and Earth, and became a Kami: Kuni-toko-tachi no Mi-koto (Land-eternal-strand-of-august-thing). Seven generations of Kami were then born; the last couple, with whom we are concerned, were Izanagi (Male-who-invites) and Izanami (Female-who-invites). It is from them that humankind, land, and more Kami descended.

When Izanagi and Izanami were ordered by the Kami to stabilize and fertilize the mobile Earth, analogized to "floating oil," they did so. While standing on the "Floating Bridge of Heaven," according to one version, they used "a heavenly jewelled spear" given them by the gods to stir the mighty waters beneath them.[3] Once coagulation had begun, they withdrew the lance, and the drop that fell from its tip formed the island of Onokoro (Naturally Coagulated). Descending onto the island that had just come into being, "they saw to the erection of a heavenly august pillar, they saw to the erection of a hall" (*Kojiki* 1.4.20).[4] Izanagi and Izanami were now prepared to beget countries.

The image of the "Floating Bridge" that links heavenly to earthly spheres indicates the coming into being of a new relationship or covenant between the celestial and the terrestrial. Some scholars believe the "jewelled spear" represented the solstitial axis. In that it was used by Izanagi and Izanami for Creation purposes, it was also identified with the phallus: a metaphor for power, force, and the energy capable of piercing and stirring the watery mass below, until it self-congealed or self-curdled. Still others, including the scholar Atsutane Hirata, considered the spear to have esoteric meaning: he associated the Japanese word *tama* not only with jewel but also with soul. Thus was it reminiscent for him of the Judeo-Christian God, who breathed a soul into *adamah* or clay—Adam.

The ocean—water being the *fons et origo* of everything—has been identified with proto-matter (Herbert 1967, 254–55). "Coagulation" suggests a progressive hardening, fixing, or solidifying of a previously unformed liquid. The happening as a whole, we may suggest, replicates the fact that ideologies were in the process of congealing, and a realistic point of view or ruling principle was becoming more broadly based.

The erection of the "heavenly august pillar" has been associated with the world axis as well as with the phallus. Let us note that the stout pillar erected in the center of traditional Japanese homes had religious significance: it represented the head (male) of the family. The hall separated from the home was considered as a "parturition-house," where future begetting would take place (ibid., 258).

In keeping with the proscribed ritual, Izanagi, turning to the left, began walking around the pillar; while Izanami, turning right, did likewise. When the two met, Izanami spoke first: "How delightful! I have met with a lovely youth." Izanagi was angered.

> I am a man and by that right should have spoken first. How is it that on the contrary thou, a woman, shouldst have been the first to speak? This was unlucky. (*Nihongi* 1.6.13)

Izanami had violated tradition by addressing her husband before he had spoken to her. Such a breach of etiquette merited punishment. Thus, the fruit of Izanami's first impregnation was imperfect: an ugly, abnormal "leech-child" was born to her. So distraught was the couple by the birth of this malformed infant that they disowned their leech-child and set it adrift on a raft. In this manner did the island of Awa come into being. Upon returning to heaven to seek counsel from the gods, they received confirmation that their abnormal offspring was the direct result of the female's crucial *error*—having spoken before the male. The onus was placed on the woman, which seems symptomatic, as we will see, of the future relationship between this primal pair.

Izanagi and Izanami were then ordered to repeat out the ritual around the pillar respecting the correct procedure between husband and wife. When again they met, the male deity spoke: "How delightful I have met a lovely maiden." He asked: "In thy body is there aught formed?" Izanami replied: "In my body there is a place which is the source of femininity." Izanami said: "In my body again there is a place which is the source of masculinity. I wish to unite this source-place of my body to the source-place of thy body" (*Nihongi* 1.6.12–13).

The ritual of walking around the pillar could suggest a coming to consciousness on the couple's part of each other's basic sexual anatomy. Only after this discovery could lands, islands, and other Kami be born.

Among the Kami emerging into life was the almighty sun goddess, Amaterasu, whose resplendence reached throughout the universe. So beautiful was she that Izanagi and Izanami declared: "She ought not to be kept long in this land, but we ought of our own accord to send her at once to Heaven, and entrust to her the affairs of Heaven" (*Nihongi* 1.2.18).

After sending Amaterasu up on the Ladder of Heaven, the parents produced the moon god, Tsuki-yomi-no-mikoto. Although his light was dimmer because he became the consort of the sun goddess and was to share in her government, he, too, was sent to heaven. The next god to be born, Susano-wo-no-mikoto, a troublesome child, had "a fierce temper and was given to cruel acts" (*Nihongi* 1.2.19). Along with him were created the gods of the wind, trees, mountains, fire, etc. Izanami was badly burned while giving birth to the last named, Kagu-tsuchi-no-kami, causing her not only intense suffering but even leading to her death (*Nihongi* 1.14.21).[5]

So disconsolate was Izanagi that he cut off the child's head, and then, like Orpheus in search of his Eurydice, went down to the Land of Yomi (Dead) to retrieve Izanami. Upon their meeting, Izanami said:

> My Lord and husband, why is thy coming so late? I have already eaten of the cooking-furnace of Yomi. Nevertheless, I am about to lie down to rest (in a house). I pray thee do not look at me. (*Nihongi* 1.18.24)

Once again, like Orpheus who was forbidden to look back at Eurydice during their return journey to earth, Izanagi, overwhelmed with curiosity, disregarded his wife's wishes. He proceeded to break off a prong of the "many-toothed comb" stuck in his hair and then torched it in order to dispel the utter blackness reigning in Yomi. What he saw was traumatic. Izanami's once beautiful body was now rotted and filled with maggots. Izanagi fled, aghast at the sight of his hideously "polluted" wife, as Izanami angrily screamed out, "You have humiliated me!"

The couple's love was destroyed because the husband lacked confidence in his wife. For lack of respect for her privacy, for wanting to uncover that which she willed to keep secret, as was her prerogative since it belonged exclusively to her, Izanagi sought to usurp what was not rightfully his. Such had been Psyche's crime when she lit a candle in her attempt to look at her husband, Cupid, and Raimondin Lusignan's breach when he betrayed his oath not to look at his wife, Mélusine, in her nudity.

If we identify the Land of Yomi with subliminal spheres, one might suggest that Izanami's physical decay was a manifestation of her unconscious feelings of her own inner ugliness. Had she sought to secrete this aspect of herself because she anticipated her husband's complete disregard of her needs and his infamous betrayal? The revenge she ordered—his pursuit and attack by the "Eight Ugly Females of Yomi"—leads us to respond affirmatively to the question. The Ugly Females, then, could be viewed as projections—like the Greek Erinyes or goddesses of revenge—of the "ugly" and "angry" feelings she harbored since those earliest moments when he was enraged at her having spoken first. Thanks to his knowledge of magic, or to his superior intelligence, Izanagi was able to defend himself against the Ugly Females as well as the Eight Thunder Gods and the Soldiers of the Underworld sent to destroy him. Upon reaching the upper slope of Yomi, Izanagi assured his freedom by blocking the entrance to this polluted world with a huge boulder. Henceforth, the two worlds were separated: life from death, consciousness from unconsciousness. Having reached safety, "he pronounced the formula of divorce." His wife's reply was menacing: "My dear Lord and husband, if thou sayest so, I will strangle to death the people of the country which thou dost govern, a thousand in one day" (*Nihongi* 1.18.25).

To resort to threats indicates not only Izanami's hurt but also her sense of failure at being unable to rekindle any kind of relationship with her husband. Her relegation to Yomi indicates the eclipse of her functions—as mother and wife on Earth or in the visible world. Her condition may have been paradigmatic of a change in society's judgments concerning the equality of the sexes: Izanami, the woman of independent thought and feeling who had taken the initiative by speaking before her husband, had all but vanished from earth. Forced into exclusion/inaction, she was sent to the underworld/subliminal spheres, where she remained to rot, albeit temporarily. What becomes evident thus far, at least with respect to the primal pair's marital relationship, is the ongoing conflict for supremacy between the male and female. It may also be considered an unconscious attempt on the part of patriarchal forces in Japan's earliest days to control and even to overrule the autochthonous tendencies toward matriarchy.

Izanagi is next to be found on the plain of Ahagi at Tachi-bana. Feelings of contamination and pollution carried over from his sojourn in Yomi prompted him to perform purification rituals. In a contradictory version of the myth, we learn that Izanagi—and not the couple as previously related—was the sole parent of future Kami. During the course of his ablutions, Izanagi washed his left eye, after which he gave birth to the great sun goddess, Amaterasu; upon washing his right eye, the god of the moon, Tsuki-yomi-no-mikoto, was born; and following the cleansing of his nose, the god Susano-wo-no-mikoto came into being and was put in charge of governing the plain of the ocean (*Nihongi* 1.26.32).[6]

In contradistinction to western ideology, which considers the left side (Lat. *sinistra*) of a human being to be somewhat "sinister" in that it is associated with the emotions, impulses, and unpredictability of the heart, such distinctions are not evident in Japanese or Chinese belief. Indeed, the reverse is true. For the latter, the left is identified with nobility and is representative of celestial or yang power.

Amaterasu and Tsuki-yomi, who were born from the eye—and the eye in most religions representing perception and intelligence—endowed Izanagi's progeny with these qualities and established a hierarchy of social values for society. The left side, identified with the active and dynamic Sun/Amaterasu, was awarded characteristics most ideologies normally link to the male: wisdom, spirituality, consciousness, and insight, but instinct as well. The right eye, which gave birth to the male moon god, Tsuki-yomi, was associated with what was traditionally considered the passivity and quixotic nature of the female: water, tides, biological rhythms, and the passage of time. Because the moon's silvery body was visible at night and only via the reflection of the sun's rays, he came to represent indirect reasoning—reflected or past happenings living inchoate in subliminal spheres.

Amaterasu versus Susano-Wo: Sibling Rivalry

As sun goddess, Amaterasu had a many-sided and multidimensional personality. Beautiful, delightful, perceptive, spiritually oriented, warm, and sunny when appropriate, she also revealed a shadowy and mysterious cast, dimming the earth's radiance by veiling her feelings behind clouds, mist, rain, or snow. Anger could cause her to withdraw her light entirely, thus enveloping the world in darkness. When called upon to defend herself, to protect others, or to feed the hungry in her capacity as mother, she was capable of tenderness, understanding, and generosity, but when situations warranted a strong attitude, Amaterasu assumed a warrior-like stance. Most frequently, however, her actions were direct and not duplicitous, fruitful and engendering rather than devouring and death-dealing.

A sense of rivalry arose from the very outset between Amaterasu and her brother Susano-wo. Continuously dissatisfied with his lot, he was given to whining and lamenting. Unable to deal with what he might have considered his father's unjust division of power, or what he believed to be his own sense of inadequacy, Susano-wo indulged in a variety of brutal acts, especially toward his sister. Rather than rule the Earth, as his father had charged, he neglected it, preferring to expel his feelings of inferiority by indulging in bouts of fierce jealousy. He left the Earth unattended, revealing his lack of commitment and his disregard for his father's wishes; his departure also had the destructive effect of desolating the mountains and drying up the bodies of water, thus sowing death.

Yet Susano-wo plays a significant role in Shinto's pantheon. In that he was born from Izanagi's nose, he was endowed with a sense of smell—hence heightening his discernment and aptitude. Let us not omit the fact that this organ for inhalation and exhalation allows life and spirit to exist. To increase the ambiguity of nose symbolism, the Japanese connect the nose with the *tengu:* "a long-nosed, red-faced monster who abducts young women, kidnaps little children and does all sorts of other mischief, but can also on occasion 'chastise the rascals'"(Herbert 1967, 177). Such a type, although frequently defying explanation, may be looked upon as a trickster or devilish creature whose pranks, although seemingly negative and visceral, are not without purpose nor without spiritual intent.

Questioned by Izanagi as to his unwillingness to tend to terrestrial matters, Susano-wo, attempting perhaps to cover up his weakly structured ego (center of consciousness) and to hide his long-term wish of usurping his sister's power, duplicitously told his father that he wanted "to depart to [his] deceased mother's land, to the Nether Distant Land" (*Kojiki* 1.13.51). Angered by what he considered to be his son's puerile response and complete disregard of responsibility, Izanagi summarily banished him from Heaven and sent him to the Land of Yomi. Prior to his descent, however, Su-sano-wo begged to be allowed to see his sister again.

I will now obey thy instructions and proceed to the Nether-Land (Yomi). Therefore I wish for a short time to go to the Plain of High Heaven and meet with my elder sister, after which I will go away for ever." (*Nihongi* 1.28.33)

Permission was granted for him to see Amaterasu face to face.

Upon hearing of her brother's visit, Amaterasu called into play her perception and rationality:

Is my younger brother coming with good intentions? I think it must be his purpose to rob me of my kingdom. By the charge which our parents gave to their children, each of us has his own allotted limits. Why, therefore, does he reject the kingdom to which he should proceed, and make bold to come spying here? (*Nihongi* 1.29.34)

Knowing him to be belligerent, underhanded, unpredictable, deceitful, and given to murderous urges during his abrupt mood swings, Amaterasu grew suspicious of his motivations. Wisely did she consider the best defense to be offense. To this end, she prepared herself for Susano-wo's possible aggressivity. In one version of the myth, she went so far as to ponder her own behavioral mode: "Though I am a woman, why should I shrink?" She aptly decided to put on martial garb—transforming herself into a combination of the Greek Artemis and the Germanic Brunhild—as she readied for battle (*Nihongi* 1.40.51).

So she bound up her hair into knots [in male fashion] and tied up her skirts into the form of trousers. Then she took an august string of five hundred Yasaka jewels, which she entwined around her hair and wrists. Moreover, on her back she slung a thousand-arrow quiver and a five-hundred arrow quiver. On her lower arm she drew a dread loud-sounding elbow-pad! Brandishing her bow end upwards, she firmly grasped her sword-hilt, and stamping on the hard earth of the courtyard, sank her thighs into it as if it had been foam-snow, and kicked in all directions. Having thus put forth dread manly valour, she uttered a mighty cry of defiance, and questioned him in a straightforward manner. (*Nihongi* 1.30.35)

In the *Kojiki* we see an Amaterasu endowed with the energy and the force of a stallion:

[S]he stamped her feet into the hard ground up to her opposing thighs, kicking away [the earth] like rotten snow, and stood valiantly like unto a mighty man, and waiting, asked: "Wherefore ascendest thou hither?" (*Kojiki* 1.13.53)

In keeping with Susano-wo's dark, hidden, and deceptive behavioral patterns, this quixotic youth did not confront her with his usual bravura and brashness. Rather, he humbled himself, attempting in this way to win his sister's confidence and pity. "I have no evil intents," he said, simulating utmost sincerity. In another version, he informed her of his effort and perseverance to reach her domain: he had to traverse clouds and mists. His feelings toward her, he intimated, were so profound that he wanted to see her once again before descending to Yomi. "It is therefore solely with the thought of taking leave of thee and departing that I have ascended hither" (*Nihongi* 1.13.52).

Still unconvinced of his candor, Amaterasu asked for proof of his change of manner: "If that be so, whereby shall I know the sincerity of thy intentions?" (*Nihongi* 1.13). To prove himself, Susano-wo says: "Let each of us swear, and produce children" (*Nihongi* 1.13.53). Evident in his reply is a dichotomy between his stated meaning and the reality of his feelings. Since his behavioral patterns had been childish and duplicitous until now, the oath that would bind him to his word was valueless.

Susano-wo continued:

> If the children which I produce are females then it may be taken that I have an impure heart. But if the children are males, then it must be considered that my heart is pure." (*Nihongi* 1.31.35)

In another version, it was Amaterasu who, in a gesture of forgiveness, established a covenant with her brother, saying:

> If thou has not a traitorous heart, the children which thou wilt produce will surely be males, and if they are males, I shall consider them my children, and will cause them to govern the Plain of Heaven. (*Nihongi* 1.36.39)

After agreeing to her brother's plan, Amaterasu asked him for his ten-span sword, which she then broke into three pieces and rinsed in the "true-well of Heaven." Upon chewing them with a crunching noise, she then blew them away, and gods were born (three daughters) "from the true-mist of her breath" (*Nihongi* 1.31.35). Following her performance, Susano asked his sister for the

> august string of 500 Yasaka jewels which was entwined in her hair and round her wrists, and rinsed it in the true-well of Heaven. Then chewing it with a crunching noise, he blew it away, and from the true-mist of his breath there were Gods produced [five males]. (*Nihongi* 1.31.35)

Amaterasu would now prove her astuteness: since the seed of the five males born from the Yasaka jewels entwined around her hair had been hers, so the children were hers as well. The sword that had allowed her to procreate had been her brother's, and the three female deities were his (*Nihongi* 1.32.36).

Emphasis in her argument was placed on the fact that both female and male participated in virtually the same manner in the birth process. The product of her seed (elements she had given to him) made her the mother of males; and the product of his seed (elements he had given to her) made him the father of females. Amaterasu continued:

> As for the seed of the five male Deities born last, their birth was from things of mine; so undoubtedly they are my children. As for the seed of the three female Deities born first, their birth was from a thing of thine; so doubtless they are thy children. (*Kojiki*, 1.14.58)

In other versions, Susano-wo voiced disagreement with his sister's reasoning. He claimed as his own the children of the ornaments he had chewed (males), whereas those crunched by Amaterasu (females) were to be hers.

Since myths are the offspring of the cultures creating them, that Amaterasu chose the male Kami to govern the Plain of Heaven, while sending the females down to Earth, indicated a decided preference on her part for the patriarchate, perhaps, because she—a mother figure—had been awarded a supreme position by her father in a male-directed pantheon. Amaterasu's edict, however, did not become law without a struggle with Susano-wo, indicating that antagonism between the two still existed.

What also fascinates in this chapter of the Japanese Creation myth is the manner in which the couple's progeny came into being. The "jewels" wrapped around Amaterasu's head and wrists and which she had given to her brother may symbolize the treasure and mystery involved in the procreation process. The fact that the jewels had been wrapped around the hair on her head associate them with the mind or inner knowledge. Whereas such esoteric wealth (primordial energy) had been hers alone at the outset, her copulation with her brother (their exchange of jewels and sword), and the birth of the children, caused her to yield some of her attributes to Susano-wo while she, in turn, absorbed some of his.

The entire ritual, as depicted in the *Kojiki* and *Nihongi*, has been summed up as follows: "The ordinary male and female functions are reversed in establishing the genetic relationship, which gives priority to the Sun Goddess but suggests the absorption of Susano-wo's power into the imperial line" (de

Bary 1964, 15). By sharing to some extent what had been solely the other's prerogatives, the two deities became somewhat androgynous.

Amaterasu broke Susano-wo's sword into three fragments and chewed them, thereby indicating her assimilation of the phallus—that is, some of her brother's personality traits. Similarly, by ingesting her jewels, Susano-wo had been awarded some of her power. The chewing process per se may be considered an aggressive act in that it involves the taking into the body of something outside of it, then crushing and consuming it. The content of this exchange was, following gestation, exhaled in breath, thus altering the normal sexual route for procreation. Rather than the vagina acting as the birth canal, another orifice, the mouth, had taken on this function. As the organ of speech (in Latin, word, *verbum;* in Greek, thought, *logos*) and the opening through which breath is exhaled and inhaled (in Latin, spirit, *spiritus;* in Greek, soul, *pneuma;* in Hebrew, soul, *ruach*), the mouth/head rather than the sexual organ/lower body was responsible for the birth process.

The fact that she was the source of light suggests an ability on her part to cognize and see clearly into murky situations. Thus she was the one to divide, partition, section, compartmentalize, organize, and thereby clarify what remained obscure or problematic. She decreed the separation of the sexes. Similarly, Izanagi, after giving birth to his offspring—Amaterasu (light, consciousness), Tsuki-yomi (darkness, unconsciousness), and Susano-wo (rebellion, destruction)—also programmed or divided his progeny's functions. An infraction of Izanagi's rule by any of the progeny was considered a transgression of the limitations imposed upon them by their creator.

Although sister and brother may have sought balance in their converging acts, peace between them did not ensue. Susano-wo's increasing dissatisfaction with his position as subaltern served to strain their relationship even further, and the more violent and base would become the underling's actions.

Amaterasu: Fructifier

Amaterasu, regarded in Japan as a bearer of fruit, was honored in ceremonies and festivals in sacred precincts and shrines during the spring season at rice plantings and in the fall at harvest time.[7]

According to the *Nihongi*, Amaterasu's association with fertility rituals took root when the goddess Ame-kuma-bito brought her the millet, rice, wheat, and beans that she had found on the dead food goddess, Uke-mochi-no-kami. Rejoicing at the sight of this food, Amaterasu said: "These are the things which the race of visible men will eat and live." Accordingly, the seeds were planted and by autumn "drooping ears bent down, eight span long, and were exceedingly pleasant to look on." Not only was the harvest plentiful; Amaterasu also took "silk worms in her mouth, and succeeded in reeling thread from them." Thus the silk-worm industry supposedly originated (*Nihongi* 1.28.33).

Amaterasu's "august rice-fields of Heavenly narrow rice-fields and Heavenly long rice-fields," upon which her countenance shone, suffered neither drought nor flood (*Nihongi* 1.28.33). On the other hand, Susano-wo's rice fields were virtually barren, the soil being swept away or parched by too much rain or dryness. His jealousy of his sister's power and his dependence on her will for his seeds—identified with Earth—to fructify without the participation of her heavenly sunlight took on obsessional force.

To remedy the injustice, Susano-wo broke down the divisions between his and her fields during the spring season. With the coming of autumn and the forming of the grain, he filled the ditches separating the two plots of land, thus making it impossible to distinguish between them. He assumed for himself, naturally, the fertile land. Even worse, upon learning that his sister was about to celebrate "the feast of first-fruits," he voided excrement under her seat in the New Palace (*Nihongi* 1.43.47). Having seated herself, Amaterasu became "sickened," then enraged (*Nihongi* 1.43.47; *Kojiki* 1.15.61).

But she compassionately turned her anger into patience; she "upbraided him not." Indeed, she went as far as to excuse him:

> What looks like excrements must be something that His Augustness mine elder brother has vomited through drunkenness. Again, as to his breaking down the divisions of the rice-fields and filling up the ditches, it must be because he grudges the land [they occupy] that His Augustness mine elder brother acts thus. (*Kojiki* 1.15.61)

Amaterasu, the peacemaker, seeking to retain cosmic harmony, may have sensed her brother's deep-seated need, which perhaps explains her attempts to find ways of excusing his seemingly puerile antics. She blamed his irrational behavior on drunkenness. Wine, the new element introduced, is identified with the blood of life and with immortality, and may be considered a way of rejecting the status quo dictated by Susano-wo's father. Reprehensible and rudimentary, as was Peer Gynt, he was seemingly dominated by his impulsive antics.

Why had Susano-wo chosen to void excrement under his sister's seat? Considered by some to be repugnant, dirty, and unimportant, excrement, for others, takes high value. As fertilizer, body waste not only has vitalizing power but has been likened to gold, the purest of metals, and hence is associated with the most spiritual of values. In certain societies and in certain coprophagic rituals in Mali, Cameroun, and the Congo, feces are considered sacred biological substances. They are burned and their ashes are cast into a river, which then restores to the world this purified and regenerated power in the form of earth-nourishing rain. In more esoteric traditions, fecal matter is seen as the fusion of the eater and that which is eaten—as were the jewels and the sword crunched by Amaterasu and Susano-wo for conception purposes. The same valuations may be awarded to decomposition and rot, as in Izanami's case. Izanagi, instead of understanding the richness of his wife's new state, ran away, fearing contamination from such "pollution."

The symbology in Susano-wo's prank may indicate a cosmic need for a better understanding between the extremes of the heavenly, earthly, and death spheres. The first, represented by Amaterasu as sun goddess, symbolizes extreme purity, theological abstractionism, and remoteness from everything that might "pollute" or "contaminate" the pristine incandescence of celestial spheres. Susano-wo, intent upon breaching the gap between polarities, tried to persuade her, via his antics, to be more conciliatory toward Earth—the material world, dirt, concretion. To this end, he tore down the barriers in the rice-field incident, separating an ideal condition from a real one. The same reason may be given for his desire to visit his mother in the Land of Yomi: to lessen the disparity between one form of matter and its denser other aspect—life and death. Prior to Izanagi's and Izanami's descent from celestial spheres on to the "Floating Bridge," prior to the congelation and creation of land and Kami, prior to the birth of Amaterasu, Tsuki-yomi, and Susano-wo, all was fluid, interchangeable. No hierarchies, no values, no separation, no thought existed, merely the *In* and the *Yo* or the void—that is, potential. Might not Susano-wo perhaps have wanted to return to the Beginning before Creation—the Westerners' Eden—a condition without worry or care, but also one devoid of consciousness, sought by the *puer aeternus* type?

Amaterasu's attempt to penetrate Susano-wo's motivations and perhaps understand his fears and insecurities suggests not blindness but motherly and parenting qualities. Amaterasu knew that the illogical Susano-wo, subject to tantrums, was a rebellious adolescent who refused to accept the fact that the Earth's wealth—the material world—depended on Heaven's munificence. Because he was forever attempting to reverse the distribution of power established by his father, it may be said that he was the instigator of cosmic chaos. Such provocation could have positive effects, as in the case of Prometheus, who stole fire from Zeus to give to mankind. The question is whether there was a higher purpose to Susano-wo's seemingly unthinking, spiteful, and jealous acts. Was he trying to better the lot of those existing in the material or earthly domain? Or were his acts self-serving?

Seeking first to procreate with his sister might be interpreted as an attempt on Susano-wo's part to diminish the distance separating Heaven (abstract) from Earth (material, physical), thereby bringing about a working relationship between the all-powerful Kami and those who must endure the vagaries of terrestrial existence. Indeed, his desire to renew contact with his mother in the Land of Yomi suggests a yearning to bridge the gap between the three worlds, the heavenly, the earthly, and death.

Amaterasu as Weaver

Susano-wo's rivalry with his sister became highly dramatic when he learned that she and her sun priestesses were busy weaving ceremonial garments for the Kami in the Great Weaving Hall.

Traditional feminine arts, weaving, sewing, and embroidering were and are looked upon as creative activities. They refine and shape what is considered crude, unaesthetic, and unserviceable. As such, they may also be viewed as transformation rituals—like the birth process—and are not without physico-erotic ramifications. The latter is implied by the piercing action of the phallic needle and by the touching and feeling processes involved in the fashioning of the garment.

Because purification rituals played and still play a crucial role in Shinto, cleanliness, both ideological and physical, is applied not only to food but also to clothing. The process of cloth making and garment fashioning had to be carried on in keeping with strict rules.

Unable perhaps to stand the exclusive nature of the creative work performed by his sister and her weavers, Susano-wo decided to disrupt the pleasurable and harmonious mood the women were enjoying. Not only might he have intended to torment the ladies in their work/pleasure, but he may also have unconsciously sought to intrude in the closed society of women by performing what could be construed as an oblique sexual act of violence.

As the Heaven-Shining-Great-August-Deity sat in her awful [sacred] weaving-hall [garment-house] seeing to the weaving of the august garments of the Deities, he broke a hole in the top of the weaving hall, and through it let fall a heavenly piebald horse which he had flayed with a backward flaying. . . . (*Kojiki* 1.15.62)

Amaterasu was so shocked by the intrusion of the horse that she pricked herself with her shuttle (*Nihongi* 1.41.45). Another version tells us that some weavers were so alarmed that they fell from their looms and "stuck their shuttles into their private parts and died" (*Kojiki* 1.15.62).

This time Amaterasu was not so forgiving. Not only had Susano-wo been the perpetrator of pain and death, but he had flayed a piebald colt backwards—an act considered criminal in ancient times. "Thou hast still evil intentions. I do not wish to see thee face to face," she cried (*Nihongi* 1.41.45). Rather than act overtly, Amaterasu withdrew into the Rock-Cave of Heaven, fastened the door, and refused to come out. Thus was the world bathed in eternal darkness.[8]

Eighty (some sources say countless) gods met to attempt to remedy the catastrophe. Birds were called to sing their celestial melodies, musical instruments were fashioned, divinations and liturgies were uttered, tools, bellows, and forges were constructed. On the upper branches of the five-hundred branch sacred "True Sakaki" tree were hung "an august five-hundred string of [curved] Yasaka jewels" and, on the middle branches, the eight-hand sacred mirror (*Nihongi* 1.41.43). But neither the sounds resonating throughout the universe nor the supplications of the Kami could persuade Amaterasu to emerge from within the cave.

The goddess Ama-no-Uzume no Mikoto (Her Augustness-Heavenly-Alarming Female) produced a novel idea: she took the True Sakaki tree and made it into a headdress; she transformed some club moss into shoulder straps and some leaves of bamboo-grass into a posy for her hands; then she kindled some fires and spoke some incredible utterances. Bedecked in her strange attire she mounted a tub that had been turned upside down at the entrance of the cave, stamping on it to make noises that reverberated throughout the cosmos. Then she began what has gone down in myth and in history as a virtually unique mimed erotic dance

as if possessed by a Deity, and pulling out the nipples of her breasts, pushing down her skirt-string *usque ad privates partes* [exposing her genitals]. Then the Plain of High Heaven shook, and the eight hundred myriad Deities laughed together. (*Kojiki* 1.16.64)

Because Amaterasu could not be persuaded to leave her cave, Ama-no-Uzume no Mikoto had to resort to another method to save the world from eternal darkness. So antithetical was nudity in a culture where bodies were completely clothed and nakedness unheard of that the dancer's revelation of her sexual parts created shock waves—as intended—all around. The sight of the performer's antics triggered such a sense of discomfort, embarrassment, and nervousness in the onlookers that their inhibitions were released in laughter. Indeed, humor is the perfect recipe for the altering of moods. Let us note in this connection that the meaning of the bawdy gestures made by the goddess during her dance was other than erotic: by pointing to her breasts and nipples, she identified them as nourishing agents; and to her genitals, as procreative powers. How did Uzume's antics affect Amaterasu? Understandably, she was amazed at the laughter and merriment outside the cave.

> Methought that owing to my retirement the Plain of Heaven would be dark, and likewise the Central Land of Reed-Plains would all be dark: how then is it that the Heavenly-Alarming-Female (Uzume) makes merry, and that likewise the eight hundred myriad Deities all laugh? (*Kojiki* 1.16.65)

Her curiosity thus sparked, Amaterasu's mood changed. She also grew somewhat tense, wondering whether or not another deity had usurped her popularity? Upon looking out at the mirror that had been purposefully placed on the tree outside the cave, she became, according to some versions, fascinated by the beauty and brightness of her own reflection. "She opened for a narrow space the Rock-door and peeped out," whereupon Ama no Tajikara-wo no Kami "forthwith took Amaterasu by the hand, and led her out." Other Kami "then drew a limit by means of a bottom-tied [straw] rope . . . and begged her not to return again (into the cave) (*Nihongi* 1.40.45).[9] No sooner had she emerged from the cave than the sun goddess's radiance "filled the universe" (*Nihongi* 1.46.49). Like Persephone's return to Earth from underground regions, so Amaterasu's emergence into light ended spiritual and terrestrial barrenness.

Because humor had invited a breakdown of constraints and inhibitions, it may be considered, psychologically, an opening up process as opposed to rage—a walling in or incarcerating development. Amaterasu, having been released from her state of physical/psychological withdrawal in the cave (subliminal regions), allowed the dynamism of light (consciousness) to flow forward and fill the world.

Although Susano-wo was summarily expelled and ordered to consolidate

and improve Earthly conditions (*Kojiki* 1.18.71), his efforts to create a working relationship between the three cosmic spheres—Heaven, Earth, and
Yomi—had been effective.

Amaterasu and Earth Matters

Amaterasu's newly acquired expansiveness and power, now that her brother
was no longer attempting to usurp her authority, encouraged her to devote
more energy to Earth matters. With this in mind, she gave her precious
mirror to her to son, Ame no Oshi-ho-mi-mi, and said:

> My child, when thou lookest upon this mirror, let it be as if thou were
> looking at me. Let it be with thee on thy couch and in thy hall, and let it be
> to thee a holy mirror. (*Nihongi* 2.23.83)

Mirrors play a significant role, as we know, in Shinto. The surfaces of
metal ones, usually convex and their backs embossed with complex images
of flowers, birds, or nature scenes, created an intriguing phenomenon:
"[S]unlight reflected from their *face* displays a luminous image of the design
on their *back*!" For some, therefore, the mirror was considered a source of
magic.

Amaterasu's divine octagonal mirror, the one into which she gazed prior
to her emergence from the cave, reflected for worshippers the Sun's light or
celestial intelligence throughout the world. Because it also reflected its viewer's
face, it was believed to contain the gazer's soul. Understandably, it was placed
in Amaterasu's sacred shrine at Ise as well as in other sanctuaries devoted to
her worship (Davis 1989, 190).

To her son she gave not only her eight-hand mirror but the rice-ears of
the sacred garden intended for the festival of first-fruits and planted according to the strict ceremonial rules of purity (*Nihongi* 2.23.83). The wife that
Amaterasu then bestowed on her son soon gave birth to a boy child, Ama-
tsu-hiko-ho-ho-ninigi no Mikoto. So taken was the sun goddess with Prince
Nini-gi, alluded to as the "August Grandson," that she not only nurtured
him, but covered him with special affection and appointed him to rule over
the earthly realm (*Nihongi* 2.23.83).

Amaterasu was aware of the fact that Earth had its share of rebellious and
violent deities. As would any concerned parent, she sought to subdue and
even annihilate them, before allowing Nini-gi, lord of the central land of
reed plains, to descend. In one version of the myth, she gave Ame-waka-

hiko, a Kami known for his valor, a heavenly deer-bow and heavenly true-deer-arrows, ordering him to either expel or humble the evil earthly deities. Instead of accomplishing his mission, however, he married a number of earthly daughters. After eight years had elapsed without news, Amaterasu questioned Omohi-kane (the Thought-Combiner) about Ame-waka-hiko's failed mission. After reflection, the Thought-Combiner suggested that Amaterasu send a pheasant to spy on the miscreant. Perched on a cassia tree to better observe the events, the pheasant was summarily killed by one of the evil Kamis that Amaterasu had hoped to defeat, but in time the malignant ones were put to death (*Nihongi* 2.3–4.65).

Amaterasu's August Grandson, Nini-gi, stepped from the Floating Bridge of Heaven onto a sand bank and then onto earth (*Kojiki* 2.10.70). With him he carried the three treasures given him by the sun goddess: the "curved jewel of Yasaka gem, the eight-hand mirror [into which Amaterasu had gazed from her cave], and the sword Kusanagi" (which Susano had found in the mouth of an eight-headed snake [dragon] he had killed) (*Nihongi* 2.15.76). These sacred objects then became the Three Imperial Regalia, which were and are emblems of power in Japan.

To the August Grandson, Amaterasu commanded:

> This Reed-plain-1500-autumns-fair-rice-ear Land is the region which my descendants shall be lords of. Do thou, my August grandchild, proceed thither and govern it. Go! and may prosperity attend thy dynasty, and may it, like Heaven and Earth, endure forever. (*Nihongi* 2.16.77)

The August Grandson's great-grandson, Emperor Kami Yamato Iharebiko, known in history as Jimmu Tenno, founded the imperial line of Japan in 660 B.C.E. It was at this point that Japan's "official" history began and, with it, the establishment of the cult of Amaterasu, the progenitrix of the imperial family.

Amaterasu: The Grand Shrine of Ise

Emperor Sujin, as previously mentioned, built a sanctuary for Amaterasu's sacred mirror and designated his daughter, Yamato-hime no Mikoto, to attend to its proper worship. After years of constant displacement of the mirror, Emperor Suinin ordered his daughter to find an appropriate site for it, where Amaterasu would be sanctified. Accordingly, a sanctuary was built in Ise.

> The province of Ise—of the divine wind—is the land whither repair the
> waves from the eternal world, the successive waves. It is a secluded and
> pleasant land. In this land I wish to dwell. (*Nihongi* 6.16.176)

Architecturally, shrines were usually simple, and the one at Ise was no
exception. Made of wood, with whole tree trunks used for beams, it consisted of a single partitioned room, raised from the ground with steps in the
front or side giving access. Around the Grand Shrine in Ise, which was re-
built every twenty years, and its fourteen subsidiary shrines founded about
260 C.E., solemnity and tranquility could be experienced. Further divine
instructions led to the building of an Abstinence Palace at Kaha-kami in
Isuzu, commemorating the spot where Amaterasu had first descended from
Heaven (de Bary 1964, 23).

The decision was made that when an Emperor acceded to the throne,
an unmarried Princess of the Imperial House would be appointed to serve at
the Shrine of Ise. If there were no unmarried Princesses at the time, then
another Princess was selected by divination. She was to reside in the Wor-
ship-Palace for the duration of her tenure (*Nihongi* 6.16.176, n. 4).

The sanctuary's sacred octagonal mirror, *shintai* (the object through which
the goddess's spirit enters), enabled Amaterasu not only to listen to the prayers
of the faithful but also to be present during the ceremonies. Cocks, considered sacred to Amaterasu since they greet the dawn, were also in the vicin-
ity. Because Amaterasu was the weaver of divine garments and because, as
previously mentioned, she officiated in Heaven at ceremonies for the harvest, festivals honoring her were celebrated in April and September at the Ise
shrine. As the Sun rose between "the Wedded rocks" on the seashore of
Futami, pilgrims piously saluted her ascension by clapping their hands.

An inspiration to ancients and moderns, prayers of great beauty have
been addressed to Amaterasu. The following is an excerpt from a prayer for
a plentiful harvest:

> More especially do I humbly declare in the mighty presence of the Great-
> Heaven-Shining Deity who dwells in Ise. Because the Great Deity has
> bestowed on him [the sovereign] the lands of the four quarters over which
> her glance extends as far as where the walls of heaven rise, as far as where
> the bounds of Earth stand up, as far as the blue sky extends, as far as where
> the white clouds settle down; by the blue sea-plain, as far as the prows of
> ships can reach without letting dry their poles and oars; by land, as far as the
> hoofs of horses can go, with tightened baggage-cords, treading their way
> among rock, beds and tree-roots where the long roads extend, continu-

ously widening the narrow regions and making the steep regions level, in drawing together, as it were, the distant regions by throwing over them [a net of] many ropes—therefore let the first-fruits for the Sovran Deity be piled up in her mighty presence like a range of hills, leaving the remainder for him [the sovereign] tranquilly to partake of.

Moreover, whereas you bless the Sovran Grandchild's reign as a long reign, firm and enduring, and render it a happy and prosperous reign, I plunged down my neck cormorant-wise in reverence to you as our Sovran's dear, divine ancestress, and fulfill your praise by making these plenteous offerings on his behalf. (De Bary 1964, 23)

The Grand Shrine in Ise is today one of the holiest spots in Japan for the Amaterasu cult and is visited by over five million pilgrims yearly. Nor must the cult of Susano-wo be underestimated, since it was he who through Amaterasu compelled heavenly Kami to heed the matters of Earth.

Amaterasu was the central figure of the Sun cult. As nature's most important deity as well, she was revered for her powers over fertility, her understanding and kindness of heart, and her munificent beatitude in protecting the nation's good fortune.

For Amaterasu worshippers, nature's colors, values, and rhythms were carriers of her energy and magic. For painters, poets, and composers, lakes became mirrors replete with crystal markings; their endless reflections, a measure of infinite presences. Mountains, with their geological folds, were sacred bearers of mystery. Even when veiled by mist, cloud cover, or snow, the awe-inspiring Sun, though fugitive in its cyclicity, was always there to light the way. As transcendence, she was enigma, silence, and revery, as well as erotic aspiration. Amaterasu always inhered in the continuously unfolding and evolving scapes of mind, body, and psyche.

Shinto's animistic approach to Earth and Heaven and its reverence for their infinite wonders through Amaterasu not only suggests the acceptance of the feminine principle; it also implies its importance for Japan's well-being.

8 China's Fragmented
Goddess Images

Whereas Western myths are wholly recorded by poets such as Homer, Aeschylus, Euripides, Sophocles, Ovid, and Virgil, Chinese religious texts are fragmented, episodic, contradictory, and obscure. Cosmogonic, creation, stellar, and flood myths, as well as tales of divine and/or virgin births, visitations, and apparitions overlap and reoccur, forever altering the emphases and philosophical impact of the particular passage involved. Allusions and brief statements about miraculous or monstrous deeds of divinities, as well as incredible feats of heroines and heroes, are generally diffused in bodies of ancient esoteric astrological, scientific, historical, and geographic works.

Because the Chinese have tended, since earliest times, "to reject supernatural explanations for the universe," they have chosen to humanize or take a euhemeristic approach to what "had originally been myth" and made it come "to be accepted as authentic history." This may offer partial explanation of why myths were not recorded "in their pristine mythological form" (Bodde 1981, 79).

Due to a lack of narrative continuity and coherence in the written records, the present approach to the study of Chinese myth will differ from that of preceding chapters. Little attempt at analysis will be offered. Instead, sections of myths drawn from specific ancient sources will be presented. In that the feminine principle is to be highlighted, focus will be placed on the accomplishments of goddesses such as Nü-Kua (or Nü Wa or Nu Gua), creatrix of women and men and savior of humankind from cosmic catastrophe; Hsi Wang Mu (or the Queen Mother of the West), ruler of the Western Paradise and purveyor of the elixir of immortality; Ch'ang-O (or Heng-O), the beautiful goddess of the moon; Pi-hia yüan-kün (or the Holy Mother), the protectress of childbirth; and Kuan shih yin tzu tsai (or Kuan Yin), goddess

of compassion. It has been suggested that the honor accorded to such goddesses as Nü Kua and Hsi Wang Mu indicates the prior existence of a less
intransigent patriarchal society than the one that came into being with the
rise of phallocentric Confucianism that repressed women (Kuo Mo-jo, quoted
in Loewe 1979, 58).

The underlying philosophical and religious principles, as well as the climate that nurtured Chinese mythology, are contained in Taoism, Confucianism, and Buddhism, whose precepts provide obvious but also subtle insights into the manner in which mythical women—by extension earthly
females—were perceived and treated in China. Unfortunately only a brief
purview will be given of these religious concepts, but it will be sufficient,
hopefully, to familiarize the reader with their broad concepts.

Intuitive, ambiguous, and mystical in essence, the Taoist approach to
life is conceptually bipolar. Nature's cyclical processes (seasonal changes,
growth and decline, night and day, etc.) indicate two factors at work in the
universe: yang (viewed empirically as masculine) and yin (viewed empirically as feminine). Both life principles form a *whole*, each containing its opposite. Woman, as "the *mother* of all things" participated and participates
fully in cosmic functioning; she, as yin, plays as significant a role as the male,
albeit different, in maintaining a balance in the bipolar universe. We read in
Lao Tzu's *Tao Te Ching* (*The Way and its Power*, c. sixth century B.C.E.):

> The Tao [Way] that can be told of
> Is not the eternal Tao;
> The name that can be named
> Is not the eternal name.
> Nameless, it is the origin of Heaven and earth;
> Namable, it is the mother of all things.
>   (Quoted in de Bary 1960, 51)

The notion of the Great Mother, which suggests the existence of a lim-
itless supply of energy or life force, is continuously feeding the limited if not
weak capacities of the male. Interesting as well is the fact that Taoism praises
inactivity rather than activity, holding weakness above strength.

Paradoxes, ambiguities, and symbols prevail in the mysterious timed/
timeless worlds of the nonmanifest/manifest.

> Always nonexistent,
>   That we may apprehend its inner secret;
> Always existent,

That we may discern its outer manifestations.
These two are the same;
Only as they manifest themselves they receive different names.

(Ibid.)

Images and abstractions are gender-oriented.

That they are the same is the mystery.
Mystery of all mysteries!
The door of all subtleties! . . .

.   .   .   .

The Tao is empty [like a bowl],
It is used, though perhaps never full.
It is fathomless, possibly the progenitor of all things. . . .

(Ibid.)

In the above quotations, we note that words such as "door," "fathomless," and "progenitor" suggest the yin principle. The same applies to the following images:

The spirit of the valley never dies.
This is called the mysterious female.
The gateway of the mysterious female
Is called the root of heaven and earth.
Dimly visible, it seems as if it were there,
Yet use will never drain it.

(*Tao Te Ching* 6.62)[1]

Confucius (Master K'ung; c. 551–479) preaches character building, learning, virtue, filial and ancestral piety, and a family-style morality based on the ethical wisdom of "cultivated" or "superior men." For Confucius, "filial duty and fraternal duty" were "fundamental to Manhood-at-its best." In the *Canon of Filiality* (or the *Hsiao ching*, third century B.C.E.), a collection of pronouncements allegedly made by Confucius, we read: "Filiality is the root of virtue, and that from which civilization derives" (Thompson 1969, 39).

Because only the wisest and most honorable men were capable of governing society, moral integrity was stressed. No one but a "gentleman" was capable of ruling China, and it was incumbent upon him to elevate those he governed by serving as an example rather than by exercising autocratic control.

Women, virtually spurned, were barely mentioned in Confucius's writings; when they were, it was negatively. In the master's opinion, women were clearly inferior to men.

> The Master said, "In one's household, it is the women and the small men that are difficult to deal with. If you let them get too close, they become insolent. If you keep them at a distance, they complain." (*Analects* 17.25)[2]

By separating the sexes male purity could be maintained; thus, women lived in the inner rooms of the house, while the men occupied outer ones. The existence and function of women as individuals were reduced to procreation and adherence to the prevailing societal regulations.

Buddhism, up to the time of the writing of the *Pure Land Sutra* (100 B.C.E. to 100 C.E.), one of the most popular of philosophical writings, considered woman to be an obstacle to man's spiritual evolution. Her sexual energy led to desire, bondage *(samsara),* pain, and suffering, culminating in cycles of rebirths (Paul 1985, 5). Because women represented a threat to the stability of the monastic communities and the discipline practiced therein, male chastity was emphasized. The following is an exchange between the Buddha and Ananda, his favorite disciple:

> [Ananda:] "How are we to conduct ourselves, Lord, with regard to womankind?"
> [The Buddha:] "As not seeing them, Ananda."
> [Ananda:] "But if we should see them, what are we to do?"
> [The Buddha:] "Not talking, Ananda."
> [Ananda:] "But if they should speak to us, Lord, what are we to do?"
> [The Buddha"] "Keep wide awake, Ananda." (Quoted in ibid., 7)

According to the *Pure Land Sutra,* any and every worshipper who invokes Amida Buddha's name will be released from the pain of this world. Pictorially, Amida Buddha has been depicted seated on a lotus throne in his Western Paradise next to his attendant bodhisattva Avalokitesvara, the androgynous Kuan Yin, "Goddess [God] of Compassion," savior/savioress. To men who come for solace, Kuan Yin appears as a male; to females who are anguished, she manifests herself most frequently as a beautiful and gracious woman with a child in her arms (*Kuan Yin* 1944, 4).

Whereas Confucianism and Buddhism considered the feminine as fearsome and destructive, although necessary in the procreating process, Taoism alone accepted women as a power implicit in nature's cyclical process and as part of the ordering principle of eternally interacting and continuously transforming elements making up Tao.

Ectypal Analysis

Turning back the centuries to China's uncertain beginnings, we find its origins, as in many a land, bathed in mystery. The latest archaeological digs in China suggest that, as in India, Japan and other nations, ancient China enjoyed, if not a matrilineal culture, at least a far less stringent form of a patriarchate. A mother or earth goddess was worshipped in Paleolithic, Neolithic, and early historical periods. Among some small statues unearthed by archaeologists are the head of a female (c. 3000 B.C.E.), and a pregnant goddess figure encircled with birds, tortoises, and dragons of jade.

Nevertheless, China's legendary culture heroes are, as to be expected, male: Fu Hsi invented writing, music, and domestication of animals; Shen Nung introduced agriculture, commerce, and pharmacopoeia to humankind; Ch'ih Yu brought metallurgy and metal weapons to the land; the Yellow Emperor taught the potter's art and shipbuilding, as well as the use of armor and wheeled vehicles; Ti K'u invented music; and Hou Chi taught how to sow grain. Three virtuous demigod rulers—Yao, Shun, and Yü—revealed the meaning of wisdom, courage, and integrity. Yü the Great, allegedly born miraculously from a rock, "pacified" a terrible flood by digging channels into which the excess water flowed, thus saving humanity.

According to Ssu-ma Ch'ien (145–c. 90 B.C.E.), one of the most renowned Chinese historians and the author of the *Shi chi (Records of the Historian)* and the *Shu Ching* (Book of history or Book of documents), Yü labored thirteen years to control the flood. It was Yü as well who established hereditary rule and founded the Hsia dynasty (2205–1766 B.C.E.). Despite numerous archaeological digs, however, there is no incontestable proof of the existence of the Hsia civilization. But since it is believed so fervently, it may be considered a reality.

The Shang (Yin) dynasty (1766–1122 B.C.E.) introduced bronze and bronze-casting techniques, thus affecting both Chinese technology and culture. Magnificent bronze weaponry, decorated vessels, vases, buckets, and artifacts of all types yielded by excavations bear witness to the complexity and creativity of this period during which arts and crafts flourished. Jade, which for the Chinese had and still has religious significance, served both as ornamentation and as a means of sealing the various orifices of entombed bodies, thus insuring their regeneration. Exquisitely carved jade plaques, chimes, and ritual objects were also unearthed.

Ancestral cults characterized Shang worship; human sacrifices were offered to deceased rulers and their mothers on fixed dates, the belief being that the dead were intermediaries between the gods and humankind. The most venerated deity, Shang ti, was considered the Son of Heaven and emperor on earth. (He might also have been a deified ancestor.) Heaven *(t'ien)* was identified with the power that ruled over all creation—that is, a cosmic moral order (de Bary 1960, 5). A oneness existed between Heavenly spheres and the Earth as, for example, in the falling of rain to fertilize the land, from which sprung new life.

In order to secure smooth transitions of power and wealth in a logical and orderly world, the systems of succession and marriage grew increasingly complex during the Shang dynasty, Chou dynasty, Warring States Period (403–221 B.C.E.), Ch'in dynasty (221–207 B.C.E.), and succeeding feudal dynasties. Although primogeniture was firmly rooted, little is known concerning the rights of the offspring of primary and secondary wives. It is believed that a moiety system regulated the selection process of the main wives. Suggestions have been made that a matrilinear system existed in the lower echelons of Shang society. In the Chou dynasty and thereafter, however, the oldest son by the primary wife inherited the fief and/or kingdom; and it was he who represented the family in ceremonies devoted to ancestor worship. Daughters did not inherit land. They were awarded to their husbands for a bride price: the husband had to pay the family for the cost of the girl's upbringing, from birth to the moment of her marriage (Eberhard 1987, 51).

There were exceptions. Ssu-ma Ch'ien reported that King Ho-lu of Wu was so impressed with Sun Wu's work on military theory that he asked him to teach the art of warfare to some of his palace concubines. Most frequently, however, the position of women was servile.

Li Chi (The book of rites), supposedly edited and compiled by Confucius, sets down the rules of conduct for daily life. In this treatise, seven-year-old girls of the upper class are separated from all males except for their closest relatives; at ten, they are forbidden to leave the women's quarters and its gardens. Daughters of farmers, artisans, and merchants are accorded greater liberty, since it is incumbent upon them to help in the fields and in the shops. For the female progeny of imperial bureaucrats, traveling is possible only in closely curtained sedan-chairs or carts. Their visits are limited to relatives or temples (Rexroth and Chung 1972, 139).

Although the literate woman's lot was difficult and writing was frowned upon, she somehow managed to convey her feelings in poetry. Lady Ho (c. 300 B.C.E.), the wife of Han P'in, a retainer for Duke Yüan of Sung, was a case in point. The enamored duke, having had Lady Ho's husband arrested, forced her to marry him. So distraught did she become that after composing "The Song of Magpies," she hanged herself.

Nor did the suffering of women diminish during the militaristic Ch'in dynasty. The most famous of the ancient rulers, Ch'in Shih Huang-ti (August Sovereign), was responsible for the unification of his land, the promulgation of harsh laws, and the founding of the first autocratic empire.

With the creation of a gentry class during the Han dynasty (200 B.C.E.– 220 C.E.), "political marriages" were favored, thus slightly improving the lot of women. Marriage into one of the powerful and wealthy families required that a man be courteous and well-behaved toward his wife, and her role in society could be relatively important. Significant as well was the fact that a widow had the right to remarry. She could also take part in official ceremonies and maintain semi-official positions (Eberhard 1987, 71).

Although most women were both powerless and passive, there were some exceptions. After Empress Lü became chief of state (195–179 B.C.E.) following the death of her husband, Kao Tsu, founder of the Han dynasty, she attempted to have members of her husband's family killed in order to install her own relatives in positions of power. Resistance ran high and anger rose at the thought that, rather than a "Son of Heaven," a woman had become ruler. That a widow had tried to do away with members of her husband's family ran counter to the principle of legitimacy and patriarchal dicta. Upon Empress Lü's demise, her husband's relatives had each and every member of her family put to death (ibid., 75).

Chinese historians did not treat Empress Lü kindly. Indeed, they sullied her reputation (as they had that of other strong women), blaming her for the many misfortunes that had struck their land. In Pan Ku's *Han Shu* (History of the former Han dynasty, third century C.E.), we read that as Empress Lü was returning after performing a temple sacrifice,

> something that looked like a blue dog appeared and bit her in the arm pit, and then suddenly disappeared. Divination proved it to be the evil spirit of the King of Hao, Ju-i. She grew ill of the wound in her side and shortly after died. Earlier Empress Lü had poisoned Ju-i and cut off the hands and feet of his mother, Lady Ch'i, put out her eyes and made her into what she called a "human pig." (De Bary 1960, 172)

Under certain circumstances, a woman might even benefit from the Confucian concept of filial piety, one of the cornerstones of Chinese morality. When, for example, a ruler was enthroned after the death of his father, he owed service and honor to his mother. These obligations were assumed with utmost gravity, and any failure on the part of the ruler to fulfill his obligations was considered a serious affront. Understandably, many of the Han empress dowagers increased their demands to the utmost, and their emperor-sons, increasingly Confucian in their point of view, sought to demonstrate their filial piety by bestowing gifts of land and government posts on their mother's male relatives (ibid., 169).

More commonly, however, women were subjugated and looked upon as objects for man's pleasure. Whenever a powerful man desired a damsel, he simply had her kidnapped. T'sai Yen (162?–239? C.E.), who is considered the earliest great Chinese woman poet, is a case in point. The daughter of Ts'ai Yung, an illustrious writer, she was widowed at an early age, captured by Hunnish horsemen, and brought north, where she became one of the chieftain's concubines. After living at his court for twelve years and bearing him two sons, a friend of her father's, a warlord of the Three Kingdoms, ransomed her and gave her in marriage to one of his officers. Upon her return to China she composed two poems recalling in highly moving terms the tragic events of her life after her capture.

Of utmost interest, and running counter to the concepts of sin and guilt rampant in Western cultures, is the Chinese notion that "sexual activity was the most natural thing in the world" (Needham 1983, 184). Despite patriarchal Confucianist and Buddhist assaults on Taoism for its emphasis on sexuality, the Chinese believed that a connection existed between sex, health, longevity, and immortality (ibid.). "The mutual benefit of sexual union, analogised with that of Yin and Yang, heaven and earth, was essential and undeniable; celibacy was dangerous and inadmissible" (ibid., 185).

In the Western world, spirit and matter are opposed and it is assumed that the individual's unique soul is attached to the material body; in Chinese thought, they are not dualized. Because the Chinese looked upon the "world as a continuum which passes without interruption from void to material things, the soul did not take on this role as invisible and spiritual counterpart to the visible and material body." In that the soul was neither spiritual nor material, no separation existed between spirit and matter. Indeed, for the Chinese, "the body [was] unique." The immortality for which the Taoists searched was not conceived "as a spiritual immortality but as a material immortality of the body itself" (Maspero 1981, 266).

Archetypal Analysis

The stratified and hierarchized celestial organization of China's deities may be understood in part as a mirror image of this culture's rigid, ultrapatriarchal society. In psychological terms, we may view these dominant powers as the governing archetypal or primordial figures on which Chinese beliefs rested. Just as all in heaven was structured, regulated, and ordered, each deity having clearly defined powers, so each government administrator, minister, or head of a family reported to his immediate superior, who, in turn, reported to his. Directives were issued to inferiors, censuring or praising them as the case warranted; they were always in keeping with the formalities required by the administrative code of ethics. The sovereign deity in China's spiritual construct, Shang-ti (Lord-on-High, *ti* meaning supreme ruler of human society), was not considered a creator god, as in Judeo-Christian belief, but only the originator of the mandate from which the ruling dynasties obtained their ordination.

Creation Myth: Egg/Chaos

According to Chuang-tzu, Creation from a Taoist point of view implied the reduction of chaos to order.

> The emperor of the South Sea was called Shu [Brief], the emperor of the North Sea was called Hu [Sudden], and the emperor of the central region was called Hun-tun [conceived as a Cosmic Egg, gourd, or primordial *Oneness*, which then split, or transformed into Heaven and Earth, thus setting off the process of separation and multiplicity: Chaos]. Shu and Hu from time to time came together for a meeting in the territory of Hun-tun, and Hun-tun treated them very generously. Shu and Hu discussed how they could repay his kindness. "All men," they said, "have seven openings so they can see, hear, eat, and breathe. But Hun-tun alone doesn't have any. Let's try boring him some!"
> Every day they bored another hole, and on the seventh day Hun-tun died. (Chuang Tzu 1964, 95)

The parable suggests that only after the end of primordial unity (a nonconscious state)—or innocence—that comes with Hun-tun's demise, do the onset of multiplicity and the possibility of civilization or of order come into being.

The Progenitor: Pan Gu

In earliest times, it was believed that the progenitor of the universe was a giant, Pan Gu, who gestated for more than eighteen thousand years in the cosmic egg from which he finally emerged. The heavy elements of the Egg formed the Earth (yin); the light ones, the sky (yang). Fearing heaven and earth would come together again, Pan Gu stood between them like an immense pillar, his head supporting heaven, and his feet implanted on earth. After his death, his breath turned into the winds and clouds; his voice was heard as thunder; his left eye became the sun, and his right, the moon; his body formed the cardinal points and the five great mountains; his blood and bodily fluids made the rivers and seas.

Taoism's "The Mother of All Things"

Unlike the Confucianist hierarchical patriarchal view of deity and its social uniformity and regularity, Taoism approached life, as previously mentioned, in terms of a bipolar concept. Nature's cyclical processes (night/day, seasonal changes, growth and decline, etc.) indicate two factors at work in the universe: yin and yang. Each contains its opposite: within yang there is a dot of yin, and within yin, a dot of yang. One polarity, however, is not necessarily at war with the other; rather, it is viewed as complementary to its opposite. Yang and yin, frequently alluded to as ordering principles, interact eternally and constitute the only certainty in life—the continuously transforming elements in Tao.

While yang was identified with ethereality, light, spirituality, and the highest values, yin was equated with earth, moisture, darkness, and gross matter. It must be stressed that moral judgments are not to be assigned to these cosmic forces. As transpersonal powers, yang or yin, translated into empirical terms, both have their destructive and constructive sides. Aridity and sterility may mark a society that overvalues the yang, or rational function; but if yang is properly diffused, illumination results, the thinking function becomes productive, and cosmos replaces chaos. So, too, may yin be deadly when used immoderately, or nutritive, warm, and healing when applied to situations and individuals in a moderate manner. When Tao is violated and either the yang or yin principle becomes overpowering, one of the polarities is seen as sinning against the other. Then a reconciliation of opposites is in order.

Tao, viewed as a life principle (breath or life) that circulates throughout the cosmos as yang or yin, was compared by Lao-tzu to a perpetually flowing force, like water. It was the source of energy that vitalized nature and was considered "the mother of all things."

As an operative force meandering about the universe, Tao, as psychic energy, one of its infinite forms, flowed from patriarchal (yang) to matriarchal (yin) spheres. Since it was universal and eternal, activator and determinator of individuals' and societies' paths, it may be said to be archetypal.

Since Tao was continuous interaction and perpetual renewal, life and death became part of a cosmic—or organic—process of eternal transformation. Death, then, was to be looked upon not as something to be feared, but as a natural occurrence implicit in the evolutionary nature of Tao. When the Taoist philosopher Chuang-tzu (396?–286? B.C.E.) sought to depict the image of death, he did so analogically. He spoke as follows to a family in mourning: "Go, hush, get out of the day. Do not disturb the natural evolution. . . . Great is Nature! What will she make of you? Will she make you into a liver or a rat? Will she make you into the arm of an insect?" (Thompson 1969, 11).

The Virgin Birth

One of the poems in *Shih ching* (The book of odes), an anthology of poems from the Chou dynasty (1115–403 B.C.E.), allegedly selected and edited by Confucius, relates the virgin birth of Hou Ch'i (The Abandoned), who became both the founder of the Chou people and the grain or millet deity (patron of agriculture).

In the prose narration of the Hou Ch'i myth, it is said that his mother, Chiang Yuan, had had a seemingly erotic relationship with the deity Ti K'u in a field, and conceived after having been barren for years. The fertility motif—as exemplified by a line in the poem, "she trod on the big toe of God's footprint"—is evident in the sudden bodily joy she experienced in the fields. That she knew she would be spared both pain and the tearing process of birth underscored the miraculous nature of her conception. (Women's feet, however, were to become a sexual fetish for men in tenth-century China, which lends added interest to the sexual identification Chiang Yuan made with the foot image.) After giving birth to a male infant, she believed him to be unlucky and abandoned him, thus accounting for his name, "The Abandoned." The infant was, however, protected from danger by divine intervention and miraculously survived three different attempts on his life. Thenceforth Chiang Yuan thought of her son as a god, took him back, and raised him.

She who in the beginning gave birth to the people,
This was Chiang Yuan.
How did she give birth to the people?
Well she sacrificed and prayed
That she might no longer be childless.
She trod on the big toe of God's footprint,
Was accepted and got what she desired.
Then in reverence, then in awe
She gave birth, she nurtured;
And this was Hou Chi.

Indeed, she had fulfilled her months,
And her first-born came like a lamb
With no bursting or rending,
With no hurt or harm.
To make manifest His magic power
God on high gave her ease.
So blessed were her sacrifice and prayer
That easily she bore her child. . . .

(Waley 1960, 241)

In another version of the myth, Chiang Yuan stepped on "a giant's tracks"—a usage later found in certain parts of England, for example, where women who sought to conceive would sit on "pre-historic figures of big men traced on chalky hills," or in other lands where women trod on giant footprints of deities (ibid., 338).

Significant as well in the Chiang Yuan myth is the gender ambiguity in the translation of the name Hou Ch'i: it means at once lord of grain or millet, or empress or goddess of grain or millet (Birrell 1994, 55). Since certain parts of China were subject to droughts, floods, epidemics, diseases, and famines, as well as invasions of locusts which decimated entire regions, the popularity of a myth concerning the miraculous virgin birth of Hou Ch'i, the grain god (goddess), is easily explainable. Prior to the deity's manifestation, terror was rampant and remained unredeemed.

The god Ti K'u was responsible for not just one virgin birth, but two of them. His wife, or concubine, Chien Ti, gave birth to Ch'i (or Hsieh), who became the founder of the Shang people (*The Shih chi,* quoted in ibid., 116).

Other kings, such as Liu Chi, known as Kao-tsu (Exalted Ancestor; 202–195 B.C.E.), the founder of the Han dynasty, was also said to have been born miraculously.

Before he was born, Dame Liu [Kao-tsu's mother] was one day resting on the bank of a large pond when she dreamed that she had encountered a god. At this time the sky grew dark and was filled with thunder and lightning. When Kao-tsu's father went to look for her, he saw a scaly dragon over the place where she was lying. After this she became pregnant and gave birth to Kao-tsu.

Kao-tsu had a prominent nose and a dragonlike face, with beautiful whiskers on his chin and cheeks; on his left thigh he had seventy-two black moles. He was kind and affectionate with others, liked to help people, and was very understanding. (Ssu-ma Ch'ien 1969, 105)

Miraculous and virgin births abound in Chinese, Japanese, Hindu, and Occidental pantheons. They probably answer a deep-seated need in people throughout the world and in all periods for some kind of answer to unfathomable questions.

Nü Kwa: Creator/Savior

Nü Kwa (the prefix Nü means woman), the "Goddess of Go-betweens" or "Arranger of Marriages," was said to have existed originally as both an empress and a female spirit. Her sexual ambiguity persisted, however, until the first century C.E., when she was definitively identified as a female (Bodde 1981, 62).

Born three months after her brother, Fu Hsi (2953–2838 B.C.E.), one of the ancient culture heroes, Nü Kwa duly became his wife. Thus did she come to be known as the inventor of the institution of marriage. In Han times, the brother and sister relationship symbolized feminine and masculine principles or the yin and yang system. The relationship was looked upon as a hierogamy, and each gender was endowed with some attributes of the other.

Nü Kwa and Fu Hsi were said to have been provided with human bodies and intertwining dragon tails. In other versions of the myth, Nü Kwa was described as having "a long head with two fleshy horns" and the body of a snake; or as formed with "the body of a serpent and [the] head of an ox." Elsewhere she is rendered as an icon with a human head (Lieh-tze 1990, 54)

According to the *Shan Hai Ching*, Nü Kwa not only was endowed with a woman's face and the body of a snake, but she had the power to alter her appearance seventy times a day (16.239).

There are ten spirits here called Nü Kua Chih Ch'ang (Nü Kua's bowels [intestines]). They changed to spirits [from her intestines after her death]

and dwell in Li Kuang (chestnut wide) wilderness where they block the
roads. (*Shan Hai Ching* 16.233)[3]

That Nü Kwa could transform herself at will was a fact of life for the Chinese. It was not unusual for foxes, tigers, dragons, and other animals to assume human shapes—a skill interpreted as manifestations of creative ability
and capacity for self-renewal.

During Nü Kwa's early years, she considered earthly existence pleasurable, but in time her loneliness saddened her. To allay her melancholy, she
grasped a handful of yellow earth and kneaded and fashioned it into human
likenesses. In another version of the myth, we read:

> It is popularly said that when Heaven and Earth had opened forth, but
> before there were human beings, Nü Kua created men by patting yellow
> earth together. But the work tasked her strength and left her no free time,
> so that she then dragged a string through mud, thus heaping it up so as to
> make it into men. Therefore the rich and the noble are those men of yellow
> earth, whereas the poor and the lowly—all ordinary people—are those
> cord-made men. (Ying Shao, *Feng-su t'ung-yi*, quoted in Bodde 1981, 64)

A T'ang dynasty (ninth century) version of the Nü Kwa legend presents
her incestuous relationship with her brother, and the very notion of sexual
intercourse in general, as a factor that introduces into the world the notion
of "shame and guilt" (as in the case of Adam and Eve).

> Long ago, when the world first began, there were two people, Nü Kwa
> and her older brother. They lived on Mount K'un-lun. And there were
> not yet any ordinary people in the world. They talked about becoming
> husband and wife, but they felt ashamed. So the brother at once went with
> his sister up Mount K'un-lun and made this prayer:
>
>> Oh Heaven, if Thou wouldst send us two forth as man and wife,
>> then make all the misty vapor gather.
>> If not, then make all the misty vapor disperse.
>
> At this, the misty vapor immediately gathered. When the sister became
> intimate with her brother, they plaited some grass to make a fan to screen
> their faces. Even today, when a man takes a wife, they hold a fan, which is
> a symbol of what happened. (*Tu yi chih,* quoted in Birrell 1994, 35)

The Taoist *Huai-nan Tzu* (compiled by Liu An, c. 139 B.C.E.) introduced other elements into the Nü Kwa myth. A primeval god, Kung-kung (euhemerized as a human "rebel" in Chou writings, but depicted "as a horned monster with serpent's body" in the late Han period), functioned as the administrator of punishment. On one occasion, he battled against the monstrous god Chuan-hsü (legendary ruler in the twenty-fifth century B.C.E.) for the godheadship (Bodde 1981, 63). In so doing, Kung-kung knocked down Pu-Chou Mountain, one of the four supporting pillars on which Heaven rested (Birrell 1994, 97). In another section of the *Huai-nan Tzu*, it was said that not one but "four poles collapsed," after which the sky fell (ibid., 69). The absence of sky subsequently caused the displacement of astral bodies, accounting to a great extent for the earth's disequilibrium and for the onset of terrestrial floods. Because the sun's rays were unable to reach the earth (due to the tear in the sky), the power of the flaming dragon who had meanwhile taken over the space increased in intensity, causing fires to rage on earth.

> In very ancient times, the four pillars [at the compass points] were broken down, the nine provinces [of the habitable world] were split apart, Heaven did not wholly cover [Earth], and Earth did not completely support [Heaven]. Fires flamed without being extinguished, waters inundated without being stopped, fierce beasts ate the people, and birds of prey seized the old and weak in their claws. Thereupon Nü Kwa fused together stones of the five colors with which she patched together azure Heaven. She cut off the feet of a turtle with which she set up the four pillars. She slaughtered the Black Dragon in order to save the province of Chi [the present Ho-pei and Shansi provinces in North China]. She collected the ashes of reeds with which to check the wild waters. (Bodde 1981, 62)

Thanks to Nü Kwa's knowledge of the science of metallurgy, she repaired the fault in the sky. Thus did she—virtually single-handedly—avert the deadly cosmic disaster. On a human level, the torn sky and the ensuing cataclysmic events that had given rise to a break in communication between heaven and earth had now been mended by Nü Kwa.

Nü Kwa's understanding of engineering—in this instance, dam building—saved the world from devastating floods. Following her great achievement, as detailed in the *Huai-nan Tzu*, not only was harmony between beasts and humans restored, but cosmic and seasonal order was ushered in.

> Ever since then, there have been no birds or beasts, no insects or reptiles, that do not sheathe their claws and fangs and conceal their poisonous venom, and they no longer have rapacious hearts. When one considers her achievement,

it knows only the bounds of Ninth Heaven above and the limits of Yellow Clod below. She is acclaimed by later generations, and her brilliant glory sweetly suffuses the whole world. She rides in a thunder-carriage driving shaft-steeds of winged dragons and an outer pair of green hornless dragons. She bears the emblem of the Fortune of Life and Death. Her seat is the Visionary Chart. Her steeds' halter is of yellow cloud; in the front is a white calf-dragon, in the rear a rushing snake. Floating, drifting, free and easy, she guides ghostly spirits as she ascends to Ninth Heaven. She has audience with god inside the holy gates. Silently, solemnly, she comes to rest below the High Ancestor. Then, without displaying her achievements, without spreading her fame, she holds the secret of the Way of the True Person and follows the eternal nature of Heaven and earth. (*Huai-nan Tzu,* quoted in Birrell 1994, 71)

Nü Kwa's character traits, intellectual capabilities and sense of responsibility, as distinguished from those of her brother, are depicted semiotically in the legend. Because Fu Hsi had been given a carpenter's square, an instrument designed to measure and trace quadrangular forms, he was identified with the earth. Nü Kwa, on the other hand, was provided with a compass, which served to trace circles, thus connecting her with heaven.

An instrument associated with the precision of mathematics and exact sciences, the compass was believed to represent also rectitude and imagination. In that it was used by the Chinese as an important astrological symbol, it served as a link between heavenly and earthly spheres. Understandably, then, did Nü Kwa function, as we have seen, as the restorer of order and the maintainer of cosmic equilibrium (Christie 1985, 88).

Although Nü Kwa's power and achievements were great, the Chinese had problems rationalizing her creative abilities. For example, since she had been provided with a body prior to her own creation of humankind, questions as to who had endowed her with form were posed in the *Tian Wen* (Questions of heaven, from the *Ch'u-tz'u,* third century B.C.E.).

> Nü Kwa had a serpent tail.
> By what standard was her body formed?
>
> (Field 1986, 98)

No answer was put forward. Not only did the question remain unanswered; others arose. As the primordial creator of both women and men, from what prototype did she fashion them?

A dichotomy existed between the Nü Kwa worshipped in ancient times and the depotentiated deity of later centuries. Her early attributes identified her as creatrix of humankind and mender of the cataclysmic cosmic fault, and thus the savior of the universe. Moreover, her repairs had been accomplished with such expertise and such profound knowledge in a variety of disciplines, namely engineering and the sciences, that she succeeded in both balancing and steadying the earth's extremities. With an increase in patriarchal power in post-Han times, however, Nü Kwa was no longer considered a model of perfection. Divested to a great extent of her miraculous powers, she was no longer worshipped as humanity's redeemer and rescuer. With her demotion, there followed a concomitant diminution of feminine power in the new and evolving Chinese pantheon. Scholars have come to believe, therefore, that the ancient myth of Nü Kwa was what remained of China's early less intransigent phallocentric culture.

Other Female Deities

Hsi Wang Mu (Queen of the West)

Hsi Wang Mu (Queen Mother) was not a primeval deity—she dates to late Chou and early Han times—but archaeologists have noted that her name is visible on sacrificial Shang oracle bones that date to the thirteenth century B.C.E. (Birrell 1994, 171). When Chuang-tzu referred to the Tao as having its "reality and its signs" but as being "without action or form," he also stated that among the deities to have attained the Tao was "The Queen Mother of the West [who] got it and took her seat on Shao-kuang—nobody knows her beginning, nobody knows her end" (Chuang Tzu 1964, 77–78).

Nevertheless, Hsi Wang Mu, like other Chinese deities, also went through some metamorphoses. In early times, for example, she was depicted as a wild deity, endowed with a leopard's tail and tiger's teeth, and having a terrible snarl.

> 350 *li* [leagues] west is Yü (jade) Mountain where Hsi Wang Mu . . . resides. Hsi Wang Mu resembles a human, with the tail of a leopard and teeth of a tiger, and is good at screaming. In her dishevelled hair is a jade hair pin. *Li* (calamity) and *wu ts'an* (five destructions, execution) are managed by Hsi Wang Mu. There is an animal here that resembles a dog, with markings of a leopard and horns of a cow, called the *chiao* (cunning). It makes a sound like a dog's bark. If someone sees one, then that nation will have a bountiful harvest. (*Shan Hai Ching* 2.32)

Scholars have variously interpreted the words *li* and *wu ts'an*, which describe Hsi Wang Mu as the harbinger of calamities and the punisher for five types of crimes, suggesting that she had been designated to oversee humankind's moral behavior. The jade hair pin or tiara she wore is thought to have referred to either a headdress or a crown placed over her disheveled hair. The staff she carried has been identified with a scepter lending her regal status.

Described elsewhere as the "Goddess of Epidemics," Hsi Wang Mu became the ruler of malignant spirits, thus linking her with astronomical and cosmic forces. Despite her reputedly savage, wild, and vengeful nature, and her attribute as harbinger of disease and death, Hsi Wang Mu also had a curative, kindly, and peaceful side. Known as healer of the sick and stayer of epidemics, within her cohabited a complex of opposites: both cause and effect.

Hsi Wang Mu's negative side could erupt in outbreaks of anger which, if powerful enough, fomented cosmic cataclysms, as occurred when learning that the moon goddess, Ch'ang-O, had stolen the brew of immortality that she alone had the power to distribute.

> The Old [Mother] of the West broke her *sheng* [crown] hair ornament, and the Yellow Thearch moaned. The wings of flying birds were injured, and four-footed animals became lame. Mountains were denuded of trees, and the flatlands were devoid of fresh water. Foxes and racoons headed for their dens, horses and oxen escaped and wandered away. Fields were bare of growing grain, and roadsides of sedges and reeds. Gold bars were chipped at their edges, and jade discs had their surface decorations worn away. Shells of tortoises were pierced until they no longer yielded responses; divining-stalks were cast repeatedly. (*The Huainanzi*, 6, quoted in Major 1993, 201)

But in another description of Hsi Wang Mu, she assumes a noble attitude and a regal posture:

> Hsi Wang Mu leans on a small table and wears a headdress. To the south are three green birds that bring food to Hsi Wang Mu. This is north of K'un Lun Mountain. (*Shan Hai Ching* 12.195)

K'un Lun, the most notable of the several mountain ranges in China, was Hsi Wang Mu's abode. Situated in high, snowy, and misty regions between Heaven and Earth, its numinosity inspired mystery and awe. Closer to the celestial vault than any other area, the K'un Lun mountain range was considered the *axis mundi*, separating yet connecting heaven and earth. This beautiful, magical, and sacred realm—a virtually paradisiac space—was also the abode of the Taoist Immortals, those once mortal men and women who had been granted the gift of eternal life. In the *Tian Wen*, K'un Lun is depicted in ethereal and idyllic terms:

> What Hanging Garden of Kunlun,
> What does it rest upon?
>
> (Field 1986, 40)

> Terraced walls of nine layers,
> How many miles tall?
>
> (Ibid., 41)

> Gates of the Four Directions,
> Who passes through them?
>
> (Ibid., 42)

The "Hanging Garden," which reached as far as the first level of heaven, refers to the highest peak in the K'un Lun range. As such, it extends far into the clouds, as if cut off from the earth and floating mysteriously in the sky above. When Hsi Wang Mu sought to travel from one area of the sacred mountain to another, her mode of travel was equally spectacular: she was depicted iconographically as sitting on the back of a crane or of a phoenix.

A painful and melancholy note is implicit in Ssu-ma Hsiang-ju's work, *Ta-jen fu*, which he presented to the throne in c. 130 B.C.E. In it, he alludes to the Queen Mother's habitat as a "grotto," implying a state of joylessness in deathlessness.

> I perceive Hsi Wang Mu today with my eyes. On her brilliantly white hair she wears a jewel but she lives in a grotto; happily does the three legged raven serve her as messenger. If one has to live such a life and never die, to survive ten thousand generations will not be a source of joy. (Loewe 1979, 94)

Hsi Wang Mu was in later times transformed into an awesome and regal deity as well as a very beautiful and cultured one. Indeed, she was known to have been a seducer of emperors!

Not only ruler of her kingdom of the Western Paradise, Hsi Wang Mu had also been granted the most formidable power of all: that of bestowing immortality upon humans. Let us again note that the Taoists understood immortality or long life "not as a spiritual immortality but as a material immortality of the body itself" (Maspero 1981, 266).

How did the Queen Mother herself acquire immortality? In Chung Ho Tzu's work, *Yü Fang Pi Chüeh* (fourth century C.E), we read:

> It is not only the Yang that can be nourished, the Yin can also be. Hsi Wang Mu was a woman who obtained the Tao (of immortality) by nourishing the Yin (within her). Whenever she had intercourse with a man he would immediately fall ill, yet she herself was fair of colour and form, glowing with beauty and needing no rouge or fard. Feeding on nothing but milk, she played the five-stringed lute, so that her heart was always harmonious, her thoughts composed, and no other desires plagued her. Having no husband, she liked to couple with young men and boys. But such secrets must not be spread abroad, lest other women copy the methods of Hsi Wang Mu. (Needham 1983, 194)

The secret of life prolongation was contained in Hsi Wang Mu's balanced existence and the special victuals she absorbed: life by means of yin and yang.

As the purveyor of the elixir of life, Hsi Wang Mu was not only known for her great wisdom but was also referred to as an abstract transpersonal power: "the Original Breath of the Great Yin" (Maspero 1981, 326). Her very being and/or reality in the minds of the Chinese was a manifestation of the Taoist concept of interconnectedness between the individual and the cosmos (Needham 1969, 146). Whatever attempts were made by deities (or humans) to cut off or to impede Nature's continuous rhythms—the eternal flow from yin to yang—were rejected by Taoists.

For many Chinese, the Queen Mother enjoyed a fulfilled existence. She lived not in a "grotto," as was claimed by Ssu-ma Hsiang-ju, but in a magnificent jade palace enclosed within a golden wall, and she adhered to a hierarchy of values based on the certain colors—red, blue, black, violet, yellow, green, and nature's colors—used in the vestments worn by the Immortals.[4]

A fountain constructed of rare gems was located at the spot where Hsi Wang Mu hosted her famous banquet—the Feast of Peaches. The sacred peaches used for the celebration were grown from a giant cosmic tree in her imperial orchard. Not only did its trunk measure three thousand *li* (three thousand miles) around, but its fruit endowed the eater with immortality. Serving as well as a sky-ladder, this miraculous tree enabled deities to ascend and descend as they wished from K'un Lun up to heavenly spheres.

Hsi Wang Mu officiated over her birthday banquet held on Jasper Lake.

The menu, although consisting to a great extent of the Peaches of Immortality, which ripened once every three thousand years, also included delicately prepared meats with bears' paws, monkeys' lips, dragons' livers, and phoenix marrow (Werner 1961, 164).

The Queen Mother's meeting with Han Wu ti (who reigned from 141 to 87 B.C.E.), was minutely described in the *Po-wu-chih* (*The Treatise on Research into Nature*, ascribed to Chang Hua, third century C.E.). Whether aware or not of the King's obsessive desire to acquire the elixir of immortality, the Queen Mother played coy:

> Han Wu ti loved the ways of the immortal beings and he used to worship famous mountains and great lakes so as to seek the ways of those holy ones. Once upon a time the Queen Mother of the West sent her messenger riding upon a white stag to tell the emperor that she was coming; so he furnished the Hall of the Nine Flowery Delights with curtains to await her visit. On the seventh day of the seventh month, at the seventh division of the clock, the Queen Mother arrived at the west side of the hall, riding in her carriage of purple clouds. Being on the south [*sic*] side she faced east; on her head she carried the seven-fold energies of new growth, pulsating like clouds. Three green birds, as large as crows, waited in attendance at her side; and at the given moment the lamp of nine lights was set up.
>
> The emperor was on the east side, facing west. The Queen Mother produced seven peaches, the size of pellets; five she gave to the emperor, two she ate herself. When the emperor had eaten his fruit he straightway laid the pips in front of his knees. "What shall you do with the peach stones you have taken?" asked the Queen. "The peaches are so sweet and excellent that I should like to plant them," replied the emperor. With a smile the Queen Mother told him that the peach trees would bear fruit only once in every 3,000 years. (Loewe 1979, 116)

Another narrative referring to the apparition of the Queen Mother of the West to Han Wu ti is included in the *Han Wu ku-shih* (The old fable of [Emperor] Wu of the Han; third century; attributed to Pan Ku).

> The Queen Mother sent her messenger to tell the emperor that she would be visiting him on the seventh day of the seventh month. When the appointed day came, the emperor swept the inner parts of the palace and lit the lamp of the nine decorated branches. On the seventh day of the seventh month he kept vigil in the hall of the Reception of Flowery Delights. At the exact hour of midday he suddenly saw that there were green birds arriving from the west and roosting in front of the hall.

That night, at the seventh division of the clock, there was not a cloud in the sky; it was dark, as if one might hear the sound of thunder, and stretching to the edge of the heavens there was a purple glow. By and by the Queen Mother arrived. She rode in a purple carriage, with the daughters of jade riding on each side; she wore the seven-fold crown upon her head; the sandals on her feet were black and glistening, embellished with the design of a phoenix; and the energies of new growth were like a cloud. There were two green birds, like crows, attending on either side of the Mother. When she alighted from her carriage the emperor greeted her and bowed down, and invited her to be seated. He asked for the drug of deathlessness, and the Queen said, "Of the drugs of long, long ago, there were those such as the Purple Honey of the Blossoms of the center, the Scarlet honey of the Mountains of the clouds, or the Golden juice of the fluid jade. . . . But the emperor harbours his desires and will not let them go, and there are many things for which his heart still yearns; he may not yet attain the drug of deathlessness."

Then the Queen drew out seven peaches; two she ate herself and five she gave to the emperor. . . . She stayed with him until the fifth watch, and although she discussed matters of this world, she was not willing to talk of ghosts or spirits; and with a rustle she disappeared. . . .

Once she had gone the emperor was saddened for a long time. (Loewe 1979, 117)

The Queen Mother of the West makes her appearance in *The Book of Lieh-Tzu* in the narration of the tale of King Mu of Chou (1001–947 B.C.E.). An inveterate hedonist, King Mu traveled to upper cosmic stratas, to the palace of a magician he idolized. In this dazzlingly perfect aerated realm with its continously flowing cloud formations, King Mu experienced joy in all of its forms. When, however, the magician attempted to lead him to still higher climes, he grew frightened and asked to be returned to his earthly habitat. Acceding to his desires, the magician gently propelled him through space. Only upon awakening and finding himself seated in his palace, surrounded by attendants awaiting his word, did the king realize that time seemed to have stopped—that he had been dreaming. "Your Majesty has only been sitting here absorbed in something," his courtiers told him. The king was so disturbed by the answers of his courtiers that he became virtually nonfunctional. Once again he had recourse to the magician's favors. He spoke as follows:

Your Majesty has been with me on a journey of the spirit. Why should your body have moved? Why should the place where you lived be different from your own palace, or the place of our excursion different from your own park? Your Majesty feels at home with the permanent, is suspicious of the sudden and temporary. But can one always measure how far and how fast a scene may alter and turn into something else?" (Lieh-tzu 1990, 63)

The king was so pleased by the entire experience and especially by the explanation given to him that he gave up working on state affairs. Although the magician had taken King Mu to higher spheres, hoping such a trajectory would develop a sense of nobility, rectitude, and balance in the monarch, it had no such effect. He remained amoral and hedonistic. Without deepening his understanding of life's course in keeping with Taoist doctrine, he persisted in his self-indulgence, lasciviousness, and egotistical desires. Moved to take another trip—this time to K'un Lun Mountain—King Mu reached the realm of abundance, where cares no longer exist and where oblivion is experienced. At his audience with the Queen Mother, she sang her wisdom to him in song.

> Then he was the guest of the Western Queen Mother who gave a banquet for him on Jasper Lake. The Western Queen Mother sang for the King, who sang in answer; but the words of his song were melancholy. He looked Westward at Mount Yen, where the sun goes down after its daily journey of ten thousand miles. Then he sighed and said: "Alas!, I who am King, have neglected virtue for pleasure. Will not future generations look back and blame me for my errors?" (Ibid., 64)

Because King Mu did not cognize nor take advantage of the lessons revealed to him in his dreams, nor understand the words of Hsi Wang Mu's song, he never developed the wisdom necessary to become an Immortal.

As the incarnation of the purified essence of Western Air, the Queen Mother, representing yin, attempted to work in consort with King Mu, symbolizing yang force. By using the primitive vapor with which she had been endowed each time she uttered her celestial melodies and verbalizations, she attempted to accustom him to a more rarefied existence. But King Mu failed to benefit from the knowledge imparted to him during his visits to higher climes. Detachment, sagacity, and balance were, therefore, beyond his ken. If the lessons the magician had attempted to inculcate in him remained unabsorbed, those taught him via Hsi Wang Mu's tonal modulations and aspirate verbalizations in supernal spheres compelled him to accept the reality of his own mortality.

The cult of the Queen Mother of the West grew to frenzied proportions during the soteriological movement that took place in China in 3 B.C.E. (from February to March). The predictions made at the time of a terrible drought about a future epidemic struck terror into the hearts of the populace. Charms, identified with Hsi Wang Mu, were placed on the doors of the homes of her worshippers. Only with her help, it was believed, could death be avoided. The outbreak of religious fervor and furor was described as follows:

> There was a severe drought. . . . In the area east of the passes, the people were exchanging tokens in preparation for the advent of the Queen Mother of the West. They passed through the commanderies and kingdoms, moving west to within the passes and reaching the capital city. In addition persons were assembling to worship the Queen Mother of the West, sometimes carrying fire to the roof-tops by night, beating drums, shouting and frightening one another. (*The Han-shu*, quoted in Loewe 1979, 98)

In keeping with the mood of religious hysteria was the unusual cosmic phenomenon that occurred in the heavens as on earth.

> [A]t the fourth hour (March 4, 6 B.C.E.) a white emanation filled the skies. It was as broad as a bolt of fabric and over 100 feet long, moving in a southwesterly direction with a roar like thunder, and remaining for about one division of time. It was named Hound of Heaven, and it was repeatedly said that failure to obey its commands would result in an outbreak of [hydrophobia?] and the outburst of songs of anger.
>
> In the first, second and third months of the fourth year of that period (Feb. to May, 3 B.C.E.) the people were in a state of high excitement, frightening one another with a clamour and an uproar. People were running around hither and thither, exchanging tokens, preparing for the royal advent and worshipping the Queen Mother of the West. In addition it was said that the straight-eyed folk were due to come. (Ibid., 99)

The cult of Hsi Wang Mu enjoyed great favor with the people. Featured in reliefs paying homage to the Queen Mother of the West were humans and animals as well, the implication being that it was she—the woman—who determined the life span of all living creatures. It was she, therefore, who *knew* the secret use of magical herbs. Considered the paragon of judgment and prescience, she had been the one to inspire admiration, veneration, and awe in her worshippers. In some iconographical representations, she was featured enthroned or striding along with a peacock, or simply surrounded by her ladies-in-waiting, as worshippers bent before her in adoration.

Ch'ang-O: The Moon Goddess

The moon goddess, Ch'ang-O (or Heng-O), referred to as "the essence of the moon," was known for her beauty. Indeed, her name was used by poets and novelists throughout the centuries in such expressions as "beautiful, as if Ch'ang-O had come down from the Moon" (Birrell 1994, 144).

The moon cult for women and children (men were excluded) celebrated Ch'ang-O's coming during the full moon of the autumn equinox at an annual festival which took place on the fifteenth day of the eighth month. During holiday observances, women offered fruits and sweet cakes to Ch'ang-O. They also bought and sold miniature effigies of white rabbits or helmeted soldiers resembling a hare, an animal reputedly identified with the drug of immortality.

Ch'ang-O was married to Yi the Divine Archer, slayer of fierce monsters and of nine of the ten suns (one for each of the ten days in the Chinese week). Due to a cosmic aberration during the reign of Yao (2357–2256 B.C.E.), instead of ten Suns appearing on successive days, they all emerged together on a single day. Inevitably, death and destruction, scorched earth, boiling seas, and famine ensued. Commanded by the god Ti Chün, who gave him a divine vermilion bow and plain arrows, Yi saved humankind by destroying the excess blazing celestial fireballs. The single remaining sun then moved on its regular course through the sky. As a reward for his heroic deed, Hsi Wang Mu bestowed on Yi the elixir of immortality.

The people were relieved and joyful after the solar hero's death-dealing deed. Nevertheless, tensions grew. Although it was Ti Chün who, according to one version of this myth, had ordered Yi to rid the world of the excess suns, he was unhappy about the outcome, the nine suns having been his children. Yi and his wife, Ch'ang-O, were summarily banished to earth.

Once on earth, Yi spent his time hunting. Ch'ang-O, on the other hand, dissatisfied with her lot and faced for the first time with the notion of her own mortality, must have brooded. In another version of the myth we learn that Yi, sympathetic to his wife's fears, decided to visit the Queen Mother of the West on K'un Lun Mountain to ask her for the elixir of immortality. To accomplish his mission, however, like most solar heroes he had to overcome great obstacles. Having done so, he obtained an audience with the Queen Mother. Sympathetic to his plight, she awarded him a sufficient quantity of her magic brew to immortalize both husband and wife, warning, however, that the swallowing of the entire dose by a single person would result in his or her direct propulsion to heaven. Once the allotted quantity of potion had been consumed, no more would be available.

Upon Yi's return to earth, he decided he would wait for the propitious moment to give the magic brew to Ch'ang-O. But Ch'ang-O—like Pandora, perhaps—grew impatient. After searching for and finding the brew, she took a draft of it but was surprised by Yi's sudden and unexpected return. Fearing his anger, she literally took flight, her body growing lighter and her feet lifting from the ground. Floating through space, she gazed at the beautiful night enveloping her and at the stars shining so brilliantly from the vault of heaven. She was thrilled by the sight, but wondered where she would alight. Not having imbibed a sufficient quantity of elixir, she could not reach Heaven. Instead, Ch'ang-O landed on the moon (Loewe 1979, 54).

Once on the barren sphere of the Moon, a body formed from the accumulation of cold yin effluvia, Ch'ang-O felt cut off, isolated, exiled from divine life. Nevertheless, the moon was far from being a dead body. Nor, much to her surprise, was Ch'ang-O alone. A hare, a toad, and a cassia tree had also made their abode on the moon (Mathieu 1989, 43, 54). Despite the presence of the hare and the toad, which might have been instrumental in dissipating her loneliness, Ch'ang-O's powerlessness to leave her habitat left her dispirited.

The hare is a fascinating feature of the myth. This animal's prolificacy may be due (although the people of the time were unaware of its scientific implications) to "its peculiar and probably unique capacity for superfoetation, i.e. the 'fertilization of an already pregnant female which causes the simultaneous development of eggs of two different ovarian cycles within the ovarian tract.'" Thus, the hare was associated with birth, death, and rebirth—or immortality. Iconographically, the animal is linked to both the moon and the Queen Mother of the West, particularly when the hare is featured pounding the drug of immortality at the foot of a cassia tree (Loewe 1979, 133, 132).

The three-legged toad was also an inhabiter of the moon. Like the satellite whose power accounts for alterations in tides and rainfall, the toad was also associated with water or yin. In that this animal was believed to live many years—ten thousand years—it was associated with longevity. It also had the power to endow others with immortality: "Horns grow on the toad's head, consumption of which brings 1,000 years of life and ability to feed on the Essence of the Mountains" (*The Hsüan-chung-chi,* quoted in ibid., 54). In another version of the myth, we find that Ch'ang-O, after having fled to the moon, was transformed into a toad—an identification of the animal that sheds its skin as it renews itself virtually perpetually with the moon, whose forms also alter upon passing from one phase to another in its seemingly endless cycles. In both versions of the myth, emphasis was placed on the notion of rebirth and the eternal return.

In some renditions of the moon myth, Yi, too, obtained immortality. He paid his monthly visits to his wife on the moon, and spent the rest of his time in his Palace of the Sun or Palace of the Lonely Park. It was during his visits to the Moon that Yi was said to have built Ch'ang-O a palace out of cinnamon trees.

An interesting comparison is made in the *Huai-nan-tzu* between Ch'ang-O's theft of the elixir of immortality and Yi's request for the miracle drug.

> We may compare I's [Yi's] request for the drug of deathlessness from the Queen Mother of the West and Heng O's [Ch'ang-O's] theft and flight with it to the moon. He was saddened by the loss, having no means of replacing the drug. Why so? Because he did not understand whence the drug of deathlessness originated. (Ibid., 94)

Ch'ang-O's forced residence on the moon—a virtual incarceration for her—was, according to some scholars, her punishment for her impulsive and thoughtless theft of a brew which she had not the wisdom to handle. If, however, she had stolen this "power" for altruistic purposes—as had the demigod Kun who, to save the world from flooding had stolen the Divinity's magic soil to dam the waters—she would have been pardoned. The fact that she stole for egotistical purposes sealed her fate: she was doomed to solitude, isolation, and coldness, and came to be associated with the iciness, remoteness, and detachment so frequently ascribed to yin. Yi, who had acted selflessly with the thought of helping humanity, represented the warmth, glow, and energy of yang. In that the moon is dependent on the sun's reflection for light, Ch'ang-O was considered to be passive and receptive.

Because the moon's configurations follow biological rhythms and patterns, Ch'ang-O represented the notion of becoming: dying for three days each month, yet forever eluding death through rebirth. Ironically, she was imprisoned by the eternality and variability of her course. As ruler or controller of water, rain, vegetation, and fertility, Ch'ang-O assumed an awesome stance, accepting her fate and living on eternally in the Palace of Great Cold.

Kuan Yin (Kuan-shih-yin)

One of the most popular and most beloved goddesses of the Chinese pantheon was Kuan Yin (or Kuan-shih-yin). Tao–hsüan, a seventh-century monk,
linked the name of Kuan Yin with that of Miao-shan, the third daughter of
King Miao-Chuang Wang (696–681 B.C.E.), ruler of Hsing-ling, situated
between India and Siam (Thailand) (Maspero 1981, 169).

The Kuan Yin myth relates how, after the still-childless, fifty-year-old
Miao-Chuang Wang sacrificed for eight days to the God of the Western
Peak (Hua-shan), his wife bore him three girls. Upon reaching marriageable
age, Miao-Chuang chose, as was the custom, an appropriate bridegroom for
each of his daughters. The oldest wed a scholar, and the next in age a general, but the youngest, Miao-shan, rejecting marriage, was determined to
enter a convent. Neither threats, nor orders, nor any amount of cajoling
could change the young girl's mind. Finally, her father yielded to her request
and allowed her to enter the Monastery of the White Sparrow. In order to
make her life as unpleasant as possible and in the hope she would renounce
her religious vocation, he ordered the nuns to assign to her all the cooking
and washing duties for the five hundred nuns in the convent. Predictably,
the mother of the Great Bear deity, Tou-mu, helped her accomplish her
tasks: a dragon was sent to dig a well to provide sufficient water; a tiger, to
bring wood for the fire; birds, to gather vegetables; and the God of the
Hearth to cook them. Upon being apprised of the miracles, the king was so
infuriated that he had the convent set ablaze. The nuns would have perished
had it not been for Miao-shan, who, thanks to another miracle, extinguished
the fire. Enraged, the frustrated Miao-Chuang Wang ordered his daughter's
strangulation. After her soul had left her body it went to hell, where Miao-
shan undertook to recite sacred texts. Almost immediately the anguish and
pain of hell were replaced by a climate of paradisiac joy and goodness. The
ruler of the underworld, Yama, thwarted because he could no longer punish
the "wicked" victims inhabiting his realm, dispatched Miao-shan to Earth.
More trials followed. Finally, the Buddha appeared to her in a vision and
gave her a Peach of Immortality to eat, after which he led her to the Isle of
P'u–t'o (Potalaka; some scholars have identified it with Potala) near Chekiang.
There, Miao-shan took it upon herself to save sailors from shipwreck. Upon
a visit from Ti-tsang, a Brahman who had been converted to Buddhism, she
was enthroned as a bodhisattva in an unforgettable ceremony featuring king-
dragons, the Gods of Five Peaks, the ten kings of hells, eight immortals, and

others. Shang-ti, outraged by Miao-Chuang Wang's unrelenting attacks on his daughter, ordered the God of Epidemics to afflict him with an incurable disease. Doctors were consulted. Not one could heal him. Only with the hands and eyes of a living person could a proper brew be made to cure the king. Upon learning of her father's sad plight, Miao-shan went to him immediately, plucked out her eyes and cut off her hands, and transformed these into a medicine that cured her father. In gratitude, he ordered that a statue be sculpted in honor of his daughter "with completely formed arms and eyes." His orders were misunderstood, however, and a statue was erected featuring a woman with a thousand eyes and a thousand arms. Miraculously, Miao-shan's eyes and hands were subsequently restored to her (ibid., 170). Henceforth, she was worshipped as Ch'ien shou ch'ien yen ta tz'u ta pei Kuan Yin ("the Bodhisattva Kuan Yin who has a thousand arms and a thousand eyes, great in mercy and great in compassion" (Werner 1961, 226).

After the advent of Buddhism in China, Kuan Yin was looked upon as an incarnation of a male bodhisattva ("a Buddha to be"; a being seeking enlightenment), Avalokitesvara (or Padmapani), one of Amida Buddha's two assistants. Having been a female originally, Kuan Yin was considered androgynous. Therefore, to men who came to her for solace, Kuan Yin appeared as a male; to females who were anguished, she manifested herself most frequently as a beautiful and gracious woman with a child in her arms. She was transformed by the masses into a compassionate, loving, and kind mother figure, and worship of her as the "Lady who Brings Children" into the world, who cares for them and heals them, increased with the passage of time. By the eighth century, the androgynous goddess—known as "Kuan-yin Clad-in-White"—was featured iconographically draped in a white veil and seated on a lotus flower holding a child in her arms (Maspero 1963, 354). In her capacity as goddess of fertility, she advocated sexual/spiritual love. Because she was also empowered to heal the ill, her image was and is the object of worship both at home and on pilgrimages.

As goddess [god] of mercy and savioress/savior, Kuan Yin came to be known under the name of Kuan shih yin tzu tsai, translated as "the sovereign who looks on the sounds of prayers." This name was awarded to her, according to legend, because as she was about to enter heaven, she heard a wail emanating from the world. She hesitated for a moment, "looking on, or heeding, the sound," instead of proceeding immediately toward her destination (Werner 1961, 225).

The continuous and progressive elevation of Kuan Yin in society through-out the centuries suggests an unconscious need on the part of the collective psyche of the Chinese people to rectify the sharp imbalance existing between yin and yang forces. She, who exuded tenderness, compassion, love, and eros, filled the void that had been created by the rigid and austere patriarchal consciousness that dominated the culture.

Sheng Mu: Holy Mother, The Princess of Motley Clouds

Associated with Kuan Yin in her capacity as "Giver of Children," Sheng Mu, also referred to as Holy Mother and the Princess of Motley Clouds (or Pi-hia-yüan-chun), was a protectress of women and children. Present at child-birth, healer of the diseased, and nourisher of the needy, she fulfilled the characteristics implicit in the helpful mother archetype. Iconographically, she was frequently featured wearing a headdress made of three birds with outspread wings, one facing the front, the other two facing out from both sides of the head.

Sheng Mu was at times accompanied by two helpers and six minor deities, each a specialist in childhood diseases and problems revolving around the growing process. Although these goddesses were not separate and dis-tinct, each transformed herself into a kind and gentle being able to answer the specific needs of the sick (Maspero 1963, 352–53).

The Princess of Motley Clouds is identified with a legend focusing on King Wu of Chou. Her strikingly beautiful image appeared to King Wu one night in a dream. He saw her on a road—weeping. She told him she was married to the son of the Spirit of the Western Sea, but was prevented from visiting her husband because to do so, she would have to cross through the principality of Chiang T'ai-kung. Since her retinue—wind and rain—al-ways accompanied her, she hesitated to inflict gale winds and storms on the land ruled by Prince Chiang T'ai-kung, which was known for its harmony. Indeed, so peaceful was his principality that not even the slightest wind blew within its precincts. Upon awakening from his dream, King Wu summoned Chiang T'ai-kung. Shortly after his arrival, a powerful wind began to blow, followed by a heavy rain. King Wu knew, then, that the goddess had been able to cross the principality and join her husband. Another version of the myth is less romantic: seemingly, Sheng Mu's husband, Mao Ying, who had attained immortality, ruled a land so distant from his wife that he had all but forgotten her (ibid., 350).

A Kingdom Peopled by Women

Of deep interest is the ancient myth revolving around kingdoms peopled by women. One of these kingdoms was situated in the middle of the sea; another, in Western lands. The women have been referred to as Oriental Amazons, and scholars believe there is some connection between the kingdom of women and the system of polyandry practiced in certain parts of Tibet (Mathieu 1989, 163). In *Shan Hai Ching*, we read:

> Nü Tzu (girl) Land is north of Wu Hsien. Two girls live here, surrounded by water. Some say they live in one gate [the same village]. (7.156)

Descriptions of kingdoms populated by women are to be found in the *Bowu zhi* (chap. 2) and *Liangshu* (chap. 54). It is reported that if the natives leave their seaward island to return to China, they refuse food and die. Nor is verbal communication possible between these female islanders and the Chinese, as witnessed by the Amazon who, according to the myth, had been captured alive.

These women were seemingly attractive, with their pale skin and their long hair reaching to the ground. Their bodies, however, were covered with hair. They conceived miraculously after bathing in sacred pools for two or three months, and gave birth in their sixth or seventh month (Mathieu 1989, 163). Female babies survived in the kingdom of women, whereas male infants were abandoned and died (Birrell 1994, 113). Although these Amazon women had no breasts, a white juice that flowed from the white roots of the hair that grew on the nape of their necks was used to nurse their newborns. At the end of a hundred days, a child was capable of walking. At the age of three or four, the progeny behaved like adults.

So fearful were these women of men that they fled at the sight of them. Their food was that of the animals of the region: a kind of very salty algae, a plant whose leaves resembled a kind of meadow saxifrage or hartwort (Mathieu 1989, 163).

Mention must also be made of a country of men, where males gave birth to male infants through the "center of their body" (Birrell 1994, 113). Births by males only are notable in such Chinese myths as the birth of the Great Yü, the hero who saved humankind from the flood. No female, not even an egg, was involved in the event. Strictly phallocentric in motif, the Great Yü was born from the corpse of Kun, his father, who had been executed for having stolen the deity's "self-renewing soil," which he used to dam up the flood waters (ibid., 121).

Although more questions than answers remain, we may suggest that Chinese goddesses and gods are in essence deified humans. Not immutable in the Western sense, they may be replaced by new deities in accordance with altering needs. Because of the interconnectedness of heavenly and earthly spheres, if disorder reigned on earth, a similar condition would exist in heaven, thereby placing the entire universe in danger. Understandably, emphasis was placed on the maintenance of strict regulations in the human domain.

When the pendulum swung toward Confucianism and neo-Confucianism, ultramasculine forces prevailed on earth as in heaven. When Buddhism's ascetic and otherworldly thrust was added to the already phallocentric way of life, imbalance between yin and yang increased. Only when Tao was heard in pre-Han eras did Nü Kwa with her compass and wisdom, Hsi Wang Mu with her brew of Immortality, Kuan Yin with her compassion, and Chang-O with her forever altering luminosities adjust and rectify a painfully one-sided condition.

And what of the lot of women in post-Han times? What of the "Mysterious Female" mentioned in the *Tao Te Ching*? She—the prototype of all women—had her place in society, expressed her yearnings and sang her chants and lamentations, which were so frequently repressed, suppressed, and even obliterated. Yet, they have sounded almost continuously throughout the centuries—vibrantly, stridently, subtly, in their infinitely nuanced tonalities—in protracted unheard, yet audible, silences!

> There was something nebulous yet complete,
>   Born before Heaven and earth.
> Silent, empty.
>   Self-sufficient and unchanging,
>   Revolving without cease and without fail,
>   It acts as the mother of the world.
>   (Quoted in de Bary 1960, 56)

9 The *Ramayana:*
Sita Sanctified

Valmiki's epic poem, the *Ramayana*, known and loved by the greater part of the Hindu population, was allegedly written between the eighth and the third centuries B.C.E. Sita and Rama, the royal couple around whom the events are interwoven, although presented as flesh-and-blood human beings, are abstractions. They are ideals or prototypes that Hindus were expected to emulate: Rama, the paradigm of the hero-king; Sita, of the perfect wife whose destiny is tragic but whose self-abnegation, self-discipline, love, and loyalty to her husband glow in the minds and hearts of the readers of the *Ramayana*.

Like most women of Valmiki's time, Sita was the product of an androcentric society. She was not, therefore, looked upon as an individual in her own right, but rather as her husband's consort and appendage. Nevertheless, she was somewhat of an anomaly in that she made *her* will known and stood *her* ground in times of crisis. Her determination to act in keeping with *her* hierarchy of values reflected a courageous nature. It is she who acted authentically, dauntlessly, and great-heartedly, becoming for this reader the *real* hero/heroine of the *Ramayana*. Not Rama. Although Sita's conduct in certain instances may be said to have deviated from the norm, and though she may have overstepped the closely defined parameters of her times, her adamantine essence radiates throughout the entire epic.

The interpretations of the dramatic unfoldings in the *Ramayana*, which places such emphasis on philosophical speculation, are innumerable. Hidden behind each event, each action, and each characterization are metaphysical and psychological explanations that determine not only the future of the

201

protagonists but, by extension, of humankind as well. The depth of the reader's projection onto the happenings may be considered as a barometer of his or her emotional and spiritual involvement.

That the protagonists are neither exclusively gods nor humans but rather a blend of both is crucial to the multiple readings of the *Ramayana*. According to Hindu theology, Sita and Rama, having no recollection of their previous identities, were destined to experience the same limitations and impediments as other earthly creatures. Rama, as an avatar of the good and merciful Lord Vishnu (preserver of the universe), and Sita (in Sanskrit, furrow), as daughter of the Mother Earth goddess and avatar of the goddess Lakshmi (consort of Vishnu, harbinger of fortune, prosperity, success, and happiness, and their opposites) cannot, however, be evaluated in terms of human behavioral patterns alone. Also to be considered is their stature as personifications of ideologies implicit in the great Vedic and Hindu texts. Readers' difficulties are increased by having to deal with cosmic and mortal powers, but the resulting expansion of their consciousness affords them even greater enlightenment.

Ectypal Analysis

Important for our study of the *Ramayana* is the light it sheds on the quality of life awarded women during the five-century time span of the epic's composition. Myths in general—and the *Ramayana* is no exception—reveal the problematics and inner tensions of society as the protagonists thread their uneasy passage through this world. A brief depiction of the historical, religious, and cultural happenings in India is therefore in order. Hopefully it will help us to understand the underlying problems and inequities existing in the Indian patriarchal society and their impact on the semidivine beings in Valmiki's sacred text.

Extensive archaeological digs have brought to light artifacts of the Zhob Valley and have led to the discovery of Kulli (Baluchistan) peasant cultures in isolated mountain communities west of the Indus Valley. Although little factual knowledge is available, the crude female figurines unearthed in folk-art tradition supposedly dating back to the second or third millennium B.C.E. point to the existence of a matriarchal culture. Were the exhumed objects iconizations of the Great Mother goddess responsible for Nature's bounties? "If these figurines represent goddesses, their religion, whatever it might have been, was more open to the divine or the sacred as revealed through women than through men. . . ." (Kinsley 1988, 214).

The artifacts unearthed in the main urban centers of the Indus Valley—Mohenjo-Daro and Harappa (Punjab)—include primitive terra-cotta figures, highly sophisticated bronze female forms, such as the well-known "dancing girl," some male, and some androgynous effigies. Revealing are the small and delicately carved steatite seals and amulets featuring female nudes: a woman, legs spread, with a tree emerging from her womb; one with an animal head and feet, and so forth (ibid., 216). Molded on other seals were fantastic images: horned male deities believed to be the prototype of Shiva, lord of beasts, to mention only one of his attributes; and horned females, considered early fertility symbols.

Although the stable Indus Valley culture was seemingly male-oriented, some archaeologists have suggested that "it was dominated by a cult of the Great Mother," like those existing in Asia Minor and the Mediterranean lands (ibid.). That she was the progenitrix of humans and animals may account for the fact that she was frequently featured surrounded by beasts, snakes, birds, and fish, as well as vegetative growth. Other researchers see her as the precursor of today's goddesses Kali (Sleep, Night, and Death) and Sakti (female cosmic energy), the embodiments of divine dynamic power as distinguished from its passive male aspect.

After flourishing for nearly a thousand years, the Indus Valley civilization began suffering the signs of disintegration that are the fate of cultures in general as they move from unity of purpose—usually evident in their building stages—toward a decline marked by internal dissension. The white-skinned Aryans, one of many Indo-European tribes, took advantage of their superior military power to cross the mountain passes of the northwest and to make their way to the Indus Valley (1500 B.C.E.). They soon imposed their hierarchical social structures on the declining civilization, absorbing some of the tenets and practices of the indigenous Mother Earth cults into their doctrines.

The nomadic Aryans brought with them a highly developed Brahmanic culture, as attested to by the hymns of the Vedas (in Sanskrit, knowledge). The *Rig Veda, Sama Veda, Yajur Veda,* and *Atharva Veda* are the product of remarkable philosophical speculations compiled over a period of five hundred years. Complex in nature, their thematics revolve around notions such as the transmigration of souls, rituals based on the fire sacrifice personified by the fire god Agni, and a belief in the concept of primeval sacrifice. The latter, gradually increasing in intricacy, focused on the image of the cosmic male, Purusha, who offered himself as an oblation in order to allow Creation to come into existence. Thus did he become the primordial agency which brought everything into being (de Bary 1958, 13).

The first reference to the four social orders establishing the caste system appeared in a hymn in the *Rig Veda* (10.90), thus underscoring their magico-ritualistic beginnings. The four castes, fundaments of Hindu culture, are the Brahmans (intelligentsia of priests, thinkers, lawgivers, judges, ministers of state); the Kshatriyas (rulers, feudal nobility, kings, and warriors); the Vaishyas (land-owners, merchants, money-lenders); and the Sudras (workers, artisans, and serfs).

The Hindu *Upanishads* (c. 700 B.C.E.), speculative treatises focusing on esoteric knowledge and interpretation of the Vedic rituals, imparted to the initiate a secret understanding of various philosophical doctrines (Vedanta, Yoga, the *way* of the ascetic) and cults, such as those of Vishnu and Shiva. Extreme creativity in spiritual and intellectual matters marked Indian culture between the seventh and fifth centuries B.C.E., paralleling the trend in Palestine (the Hebrew prophets), in Persia (Zarathustra), in China (Lao Tzu and Confucius), and in Greece (Socrates and Plato) (de Bary 1958, 35).

Adding to the ferment of the times was the advent of Buddhism, founded by Siddhartha Gautama, called the Buddha (Enlightened or Awakened, c. 563–c. 483 B.C.E.), and of Jainism, traditionally established by Parshvanatha (b. 817 B.C.E.) but historically founded by Vardhamana Mahavira (The Great Hero; d. 486 B.C.E.), who established a celibate order of itinerant monks practicing nonviolence and extreme asceticism.

These philosophical doctrines entrenched themselves during the reign of Chandragupta (317–293 B.C.E.), the founder of the Mauryan dynasty. It was he who brought relative unity to the then separate and frequently conflicting Indian kingdoms. To his credit as well was his expulsion of Alexander the Great following the latter's invasion of Gandhara province in northwest India, once part of the Persian empire. In his later years, Chandragupta became a patron of Jainism and a monk as well, joining other naked ascetics on their way to the Deccan region to practice devotional theism. Chandragupta's grandson, Asoka (c. 273–232 B.C.E.), after his military victory in the region of Kalinga (Bay of Bengal), further unified the various segments of the Indian population. Hitherto having lived a life of luxury and pleasure, Asoka suddenly experienced pangs of remorse. His ensuing missionary zeal encouraged him to send forth his son and daughter, among others, even as far as Sri Lanka, to convert the populations to nonviolent Buddhism.

The Place of Women in Society

Let us glance at the lot of women prior to and during the patriarchal Vedic period (1500–500 B.C.E.). Before the composition of the *Rig Veda* (c. 1200 B.C.E.), a female deity played a significant role in religious rituals among some indigenous peoples. Identified with the moon and mares, as well as with other natural phenomena, she not only chose "a royal human consort" but also endowed him with temporary powers. In her negative aspects, she lived on in the *Rig Veda* as Urvasi, Saranyu, and Yami (O'Flaherty 1980, 79).

Although goddesses were included in Vedic texts, they were not considered on a par with gods. Aditi, for example, mentioned almost eighty times in the *Rig Veda* as the primordial mother, is characterless and "virtually featureless physically" (Kinsley 1988, 9). Her function determines her identity:

> In the first age of the gods, existence was born from non-existence. After this the quarters of the sky were born from her who crouched with legs spread. (*R.V.* 10.72)[1]

Female principles—such as Dawn (referred to as Usas at *R.V.* 1.92), Night (as Urmya at *R.V.* 10.127), Waters (*R.V.* 10.9, 7.49), Forest (as Aranyani at *R.V.* 10.146), Destruction (as Nirrti at *R.V.* 7.104, 10.108)—were frequently reified. Vac, goddess of speech, made it possible to communicate sacred knowledge to mortals through the mystery of language. "The whole universe exists through the undying syllable that flows from her" (*R.V.* 1.164). Immortals such as Yami, daughter of Yama, ruler and judge of the dead (*R.V.* 10.10); Urvasi, a nymph who married a king (*R.V.* 10.95); and Surya, daughter of the sun god and bride of Soma (*R.V.* 10.85), also played their minor roles in divine and human matters.

Nor did most of the female divinities enjoy a positive reputation: from a man's perspective, they were frequently considered destructive, seductive forces "who wilfully make the good man bad" (*R.V.* 7.104). A husband alluded at times to his wife as "dangerous woman" (*R.V.* 10.95). A case in point was Lopamudra (eroticism), married to the sage Agastya (asceticism), who sought to lure her husband away from his vow of chastity in order to beget a child. Although he resisted—"We two must always strive against each other"—he finally yielded to her entreaties:

> Desire has come upon me for the bull who roars and is held back, desire
> engulfing me from this side, that side, all sides. (*R.V.* 1.179)

The non-Vedic and nonanalytical tradition of Samkhya, founded by
Kapila (c. 7 B.C.E.), offered a synthetic system that recognized spirit *(purusa)*
and matter *(prakrti)* as the two constituent principles of nature. The association
of the two generated the beginning of the world. Matter was personified as
the active cosmic female principle by means of which the spirit, the inactive
cosmic male principle, manifested itself in the evolutionary process. Although
power and energy in the patriarchal *Rig Veda* were principally male attributes,
local cults in which female energies were associated with Nature grew in
importance and evidently counteracted the void created by a male-oriented
philosophy. Members of the Tantric cult (Hindu, Buddhist, Jain), for example, were convinced that an individual's salvation, potency, and strength
could be increased by the esoteric and magico-religious ceremonial rituals
implicit in Sakti worship, as elaborated in the Tantras (c. 300–630 C.E.) (de
Bary 1958, 189ff.).

Although inroads had been made into the extremes of androcentrism,
women were valued for the most part as chattel and as objects. Female deities in Vedic society were important *only* in terms of the male, not as identities unto themselves. The polygamous society permitted the husband to own
wives and children, to sell them, and/or to cast them out as he saw fit. The
well-known hymn, "The Gambler's Lament," tells the story of a man who,
having lost his money in gambling, drove "away a devoted wife" (*R.V.*
10.34). Nevertheless—and this is one of the anomalies in Hindu culture—
women enjoyed greater freedom in Vedic times than in later centuries. Seemingly the woman had a voice in the choice of a husband, could choose to
attend feasts and dances, could join with men in religious sacrifices and, most
importantly, could engage in study and in philosophical discussions. If widowed, she was not prevented from remarrying, although it was considered
nobler to remain single (Altekar 1963, 3).

Nevertheless, because a girl could not perpetuate the family name, nor
help her nation in time of war, the birth of a daughter, with rare exceptions,
was considered a handicap. That a dowry was required for marriage made
her a financial burden as well. Not infrequently, therefore, did fathers either
kill or abandon their female offspring at birth. Charms and rituals described
in the *Atharva Veda* (c. 900 B.C.E.) were offered to guarantee the birth of a
son (Altekar 1963, 3).

In aristocratic and wealthy circles, however, the situation was somewhat different. Rituals were offered to parents to ensure the birth of a scholarly daughter (ibid.). Because girls were not required, until the third century B.C.E., to marry prior to the age of sixteen, they could devote their time, as did boys, to the ceremonies initiating them into Vedic studies *(upanayana)*, particular emphasis being placed on those involving sacrifices to the gods. In the *Ramayana*, for example, Sita is depicted performing her daily Vedic prayers (Altekar 1983, 10).

Philosophical pursuits were deemed important for girls inasmuch as a marriage, it was thought, could be successful only if a bride had been trained in them during her years of studentship *(brahmacharya)*. Not infrequently did female students of upper classes devote their entire lives—or their lives until their marriage *(sadyodvahas)*—to the study of theology and philosophy *(brahma-vadinis)*.

So popular were philosophical studies among upper-class women that ladies speculated on such important matters as Vedic sacrifices. Indeed, Gargi Vacaknavi, known for her extraordinary learning, participated in a debate under the patronage of Janaka, king of Videha. During the interchange she impressed her listeners by the finesse of her thinking and by the rather aggressive tone she used in questioning the renowned sage Yajnavalkya (Stutley 1984, 94).

Admission to the Buddhist Order encouraged women to develop their minds. Some were so enthusiastic about pursuing spiritually oriented truths that despite the fact that rich men had asked for their hand, they preferred to remain celibate. A case in point was Sanghamitra, who went to Ceylon, where she became a famous teacher. The daughter of the Jain king Sahasranika of Kausambi chose to remain celibate and received her ordination at the hand of Mahavira (d. 486 B.C.E.), an ascetic who had glimpsed enlightenment and died at the age of seventy-two of self-imposed starvation (Altekar 1983, 12–13).

In stark contrast to the relative freedom and intellectual incentives offered to women prior to 300 B.C.E., after that date not only were they prevented from studying Vedic literature but they were strongly dissuaded from learning how to read. The deleterious practice of child marriages instituted at approximately this time also preluded future generations of illiterate women. Unable to read Vedic prayers, utterly ignorant in almost all other domains, women deferred to their husbands, who henceforth took complete charge in the home. The system of purdah, which kept women in seclusion in their home was apparently unknown until 100 B.C.E. It gained credence and popularity with the advent of Muslim rule in India (ibid., 166f.).

As women grew increasingly helpless, so the custom of suttee (a widow's willful cremation on her husband's funeral pyre) gained ground. Although the origin of this practice is subject to controversy—it was practiced among the Gauls, the Goths, the Celts, etc.—some scholars consider that reference is made to the custom in the "Burial Hymn" in the *Rig Veda*:

> These women who are not widows, who have good husbands—let them take their places, using butter to anoint their eyes. Without tears, without sickness, well dressed let them first climb into the marriage bed.
>
> Rise up, woman, into the world of the living. Come here; you are lying beside a man whose life's breath has gone. You were the wife of this man who took your hand and desired to have you. (*R.V.* 10.18.7–8)

Other Vedic scholars suggest that these lines evoke a mimetic ceremony in which a widow climbed onto her husband's funeral pyre, lay next to him, then was led away by a friend or relative.

During the Vedic age suttee was considered barbaric and widows were encouraged to remarry by levirate or otherwise. There are no indications that the custom had been practiced after the Aryans came to India (Altekar 1983, 118). A few references to suttee are made, however, in the *Mahabharata* and in the *Ramayana*. (For further information on these and the subject in general, see Altekar 1983, 120). Mention is made of suttee in the Puranas (350 C.E.), an indication, it is believed, that the practice was gaining in popularity.

Valmiki, the alleged author of the *Ramayana*, was looked upon by some as a saint who had lived with his followers in isolation in an ashram in the Tamasa valley. Others claim that he was a thief turned ascetic; and still others, that he never existed at all (Vyas 1967, 3ff.). It is said that after receiving the bare outline of the tale from the sage Narada, Valmiki, while bathing in the Tamasa, spied by chance a pair of lovebirds. Seconds later, a hunter shot the male. The female's intense "grief" *(soka)* impacted so forcefully on Valmiki that he cursed the murderer. Upon his return to his ashram, bemoaning the event that had brought such "grief" to the lovebird, he became "lost in inner thought." Suddenly, as if divinely inspired, he began singing verses in *sloka* meter before Brahma (the lord of creation) who manifested himself at this moment. It was then that Brahma ordered him to write the entire history of Rama known as the *Ramayana*. Because the epic had been given him by the Divinity, Valmiki in turn presented it as an offering to the gods; and because the gods forever watched over and participated in the earthly happenings depicted in the *Ramayana*, it was considered sacred.

Archetypal Analysis

The protagonists in the *Ramayana* are not, as has been mentioned, mere mortals. Rather, they are divinities who have descended onto earth in human or theriomorphic (animal-form) avatars. Thus they cannot be conceived solely in terms of gods or of mortals, but rather as a fusion of both, with unlimited and limited understanding. Because of the sacred nature of the *Ramayana*, notions such as heroism and/or love, particularly as determinants of action, must not be interpreted in their specificity alone, but rather in universal and transpersonal terms. As manifestations of the All or of the divine realm, they encompass the unknowable, but are revealed in the world of phenomena as understandable conceptualizations.

In Valmiki's time it was believed—and the belief is still current—that the higher one's position in society, the more self-restraint is required. Adhesion to rigorous discipline was a sine qua non to avoid the slow erosion of one's power. A king and his successors, therefore, were required to uphold the laws of dharma—a code of ethics fundamental to all moral law (see below). Among other obligations devolving upon the ruler was the protection of mortals and immortals against violence by ridding the world of the *rakshasas* (demons).

According to Hindu belief, temporal existence, particularly for the higher echelons of society, must conform to the "Four Ends of Man" *(purushartha)*. These consist of *dharma* (duty), requiring righteousness and virtue in accordance with ethical works and standards; *artha* (wealth), encouraging an active life and material gain through heroic and chivalrous means, but always in harmony with the social welfare of the state and the family unit; *kama* (desire), the enjoyment of love and pleasure, but avoidance of enslavement by them; and *moksa* (deliverance), inviting withdrawal at the proper time from active participation in worldly matters and devotion thereafter to ascetic and spiritual practices (de Bary 1958, 206ff.).

As a philosophically oriented text, the *Ramayana* is characterized by certain mystical and tonal formulae capable of arousing specific states of being, or levels of consciousness, in the reader and/or hearer. The emotion elicited by certain intervals in the epic is called *rasa* (aesthetic emotion), resulting from an ability on the part of the reader to disconnect or abstract the painful event or ambiance from its personal cast, even while imbuing it with supramundane or archetypal qualities. The universalization and impersonalization of feeling conveys "a unique category of experience unlike anything that is known to result from ordinary worldly pleasure" (de Bary 1958, 259).

The Ramayana

The City: A Mandala

The impregnable fortress town of Ayodhya (Unconquerable), capital of the kingdom of Kosala, is the locus of the events occurring at the outset of the *Ramayana*. According to legend, this *ideal* city was founded by Manu, who was also responsible for endowing humankind with the thinking faculty and for setting down the second- or first-century B.C.E. Laws of Manu: a code of conduct governing the individual and society. Like other Indo-Aryan cities, Ayodhya was surrounded by high walls and a moat, deterrents against enemy attack. According to descriptions in the *Ramayana*, it was beautiful and elegant, and offered its inhabitants and visitors unlimited aesthetic delight.

Meticulously planned by architects, as were most ancient cities, Ayodhya, laid out according to specific geomantic laws, resembled an "octagonal chessboard." Not only did precise points in its eight-sided spatial construction correspond to the four castes in India, but the plan of its streets took on the form of a mandala (a meditative device), which may be taken as a metaphor for wholeness or psychic integration. Each move made by the protagonists to or away from the center of Ayodhya, or from the palace, may be said to represent a transfer of energy and indicate greater or diminished spiritual and/or psychological balance within the protagonist and/or his entourage.

Radiating from the palace were avenues graced by the homes of nobles and wealthy merchants, and shop-lined streets and alleys leading to the city gates. At night, lanterns supported on lamp-posts lit the well-swept and well-watered thoroughfares, which on ceremonial occasions were garnished with flowers. Exquisite gardens, groves, lawns, lotus ponds, orchards, and temples enhanced Ayodhya's beauty still further. Outside the city walls lay the jungle, retreats for hermits, and large tracts of land devoted to farming and the training of elephants and horses (Vyas 1967, 259).

Harmony reigned in Ayodhya; everyone derived benefit in this model patrilocal society. Its ruler, King Dasaratha, had three chief wives who differed in personality, age, and function, and each exerted her individual moral and emotional influence over the monarch. He also kept 350 concubines, and he would have known complete joy and satisfaction if only he had a male heir. After consultation with a sage, who advised him to perform certain sacrifices for one year, his three chief wives gave birth to four male heirs: Kausalya bore Rama; Kaikeyi,[2] Bharata; and Smithra, the twins, Lakshmana and Sathrugna.

Sita, the Divine Lakshmi, and Mother Earth

In time Rama married Sita, an avatar of the goddess Lakshmi ("chance" in the *Rig Veda;* and "misfortune" in the *Atharva Veda*). Lakshmi's early association with several male gods (Soma, Dharma, Indra, Bali, Kubera) suggests an element of inconstancy in her makeup. When she became Vishnu's consort, however, she apparently found the perfect mate. Unlike Lakshmi, Sita was always faithful to Rama (an avatar of Vishnu), although in some instances he may have suspected otherwise. But ambivalence also inhered in Sita: she played out her role as Sakti, but at the same time, at least on the surface, was the traditional Hindu wife, devoted and submissive to her husband, anticipating his needs.

As the director of events behind one of the most important Hindu myths, the "churning of the milk ocean," Vishnu understood that to agitate primordial waters was to lead to their distillation and to the revelation of their potential—"the nectar of immortality" and/or "the essence of creative power" (Kinsley 1988, 26–27). Unlike Vishnu, Rama, self-effacing and withdrawn, was not a catalytic force; while Sita, as Sakti, was the instigator who aroused his dynamism.

Rama, the future ruler of Ayodhya, was, like Vishnu, the prototype of the divine king dedicated to maintaining dharmic order in both social and domestic affairs. Generally slow to anger and disinterested in material gain, Rama's heroic qualities endeared him to the Indian people. But the control he demonstrated in his transcendence of empirical matters could perhaps not have been accomplished without Sita's complicity.

As an avatar of Lakshmi, Sita reflected this goddess's beauty, grace, and charm. Associated with both terrestrial and spiritual matters, Lakshmi held in one hand the lotus flower: its roots lie in the mud; its petals are purified as they rise and point toward celestial spheres. The same may said of Sita. She was referred to as "lotus-eyed"; her face was compared to "the hundred-petaled lotus"; "her feet [were] radiant as lotus cups"; and she bathed in water "fragrant with the scent of lotuses" (*R.* 2.54.15; *R.* 3.7.2). Flowers of all types bloomed and clustered around Sita in the *Ramayana*, their forms, colorations, and textures mirroring her joyous and tragic moods as well as her spiritual and earthly inclinations.

As the daughter of the Mother Earth goddess, a personification of the cosmos as a living, breathing, and forever mobile entity, Sita revered the sacred nature of both visible and invisible worlds. Through her divine mother she was connected to matter and nature; and as goddess, to spirit.

Sita's Miraculous Birth

Because Sita was both an avatar of Lakshmi and the daughter of the Mother Earth goddess, her birth was miraculous. Myth tells us that King Janaka of Mithila found a newborn in a furrow *(sita)* while ploughing a field, probably during a religious festival. He adopted her and raised her with the same love and kindness he had shown his own daughters.

Sita's nonhuman, "immaculate" birth may be viewed archetypally: rather than emerging from the womb of an individual woman, she was plucked out of a collective or universal womb. The plough had "split" the earth, as does a penis the vaginal lips; similarly Janaka had penetrated a mysteriously rich chthonic realm. It is in darkness that beings, thoughts, and feelings are begotten (Jung 1956, par. 180). This sexual imagery, approached psychologically, represents the phallus (plough) as libido (psychic energy), and thus as a creative and procreative force. Picking up the fruit of the womb, given to him by Mother Earth, Janaka had also symbolically opened up a world *in potentia: prakrti* (primal material nature)—that is, active female power.

As Sita grew into maidenhood, her beauty became renowned. Suitors flocked to Janaka's palace hoping to win her hand. Sita was not unaware of her attributes; she considered herself well-proportioned, endowed with fine features, smooth black hair, closely set teeth, and brows running together. She also used cosmetics, particularly red sandalwood cream. "She was a woman whom even creatures of the sky have never had a glimpse of before" (*R.* 2.30.8). The daughter of Mother Earth lived up to the terrestrial prototype of the ideal maiden: she remained unwooed, chaste, graceful, and as perfect in body as in mind.

Having been taught to read and write, Sita was not considered uneducated. She had received instruction in spiritual matters and had learned as well the rules and regulations of marriage and wifely obligations. Scholars surmise that in anticipation of fulfilling her role as future queen, she would have been indoctrinated into the lower levels of Vedic *mantras*. Indeed, because of the breadth of her knowledge and high tone of speech, she was referred to as *pandida* (Vyas 1967, 170–71). Nevertheless, her real education began after her subsequent marriage and exile.

Conquest of the Bride

Since, as was customary, fathers chose their children's mates, Janaka stipulated that Sita would be given in marriage to the young warrior who would prove his dexterity in contest by lifting, bending, and stringing Lord Shiva's enormous bow, which he had left in trust with one of Janaka's ancestors. To bring the bow in "its eight-wheeled chest" to the palace grounds required "five thousand tall and brawny men" (*R.* 1.66.4).

The *bow*, symbolizing the strength and power of the warrior, was also identified with Shiva's *lingam* (sacred phallus). Associated with generative and military power, it also had spiritual and philosophical dimensions. Any young man attempting to meet the challenge set by Janaka had to be possessed of great energy, strength, dexterity, and wisdom. Innumerable suitors thus far had failed in the endeavor, and the king was concerned.

Rama was considered by his mentor, the sage Visvamithra, sufficiently wise, righteous, and controlled to enter into marriage. His successful completion of specific trials—the killing of some forest demons that had prevented ascetics from performing their rituals—had already won him praise from his master.

Marriage, viewed as a sacrament in India, was also a duty, betrothal being the basis of family structure. Because the religious ceremony bound husband and wife to each other during their earthly existence as well as beyond it, a firm understanding of dharma was expected prior to marriage. Rama's training was arduous. It included the development of inner sight: deeper *awareness*, that is, the perception and/or recognition of good and evil forces, visible or invisible, and human, animal, or vegetal. Such development enables an individual to be conscious of his or her acts, as well of their ramifications. According to Hindu belief, each deed perpetrated not only affects the here and now, but also determines the person's karma, or cycle of births, deaths, and rebirths (de Bary 1958, 39).

Rama would try his luck at winning his bride. As to be expected, he had no trouble picking up the bow, nor bending, nor stringing it. After fitting an arrow to the bowstring, he drew it, whereupon "There was a tremendous noise loud as a thunder-clap, and a mighty trembling shook the earth, as if a mountain had been torn asunder" (R. 66.17–18). Rama's achievement may be likened to other important sacred events that were accompanied by cosmic cataclysms, such as Moses' ascent of Mt. Sinai and Christ's Crucifixion.

So delighted were Janaka and all the onlookers by the positive outcome of his efforts that a mood of festivity spread throughout the land: people embraced, anointed each other with perfumes, and sprinkled sandalwood powder in the air.

Janaka invited Dasaratha, his entourage, and the citizenry of Ayodhya to attend the wedding ceremony. Dasaratha was very pleased and arrived with a retinue in his train. The exodus from Ayodhya to Mithila offered a visual feast: elephants bore pennants and flags; horses, ox-drawn carriages, and chariots were adorned with glittering accouterments; and women wore gossamer garments draped about them in gentle folds.

The wedding ceremony proceeded as planned. Sita took her place opposite the groom. Janaka's words rang out clearly:

> This daughter of mine, Sita, shall be your lawful companion in life's duties. Accept her, bless you. Take her hand in yours. (R. 1.72.17)

Not only was Sita betrothed to Rama, but his three brothers, at the behest of Janaka, also married her three sisters.

That Rama married Sita was philosophically in order since a future king was symbolically wedded to his land, that is, to the feminine principle: Sita, as "furrow." Rama's marriage signified perpetual cohabitation and/or sexual interpenetration with the woman. Accordingly, after the couple's return to Ayodhya, they lived as *One*.

> And so Rama passed many seasons with Sita, devoted to her and absorbed in her. And she kept him ever in her heart. Sita was naturally dear to Rama, for she was the wife his father gave him. Yet because of her virtue and beauty, his love grew greater still. And yet in her heart she cherished her husband twice as much. Even their innermost hearts spoke clearly one to the other. . . . But even so . . . Janaka's daughter, lovely as a goddess and beautiful even as Sri [Lakshmi], goddess of beauty, knew his innermost heart especially well.
>
> In the company of that lovely and noble princess who loved him so dearly, Rama, son of a royal seer, was as well adorned as is lord Vishnu, lord of the immortal gods, by Sri, goddess of beauty. (R. 1.76.14–18)

Although deeply in love with Sita, Rama exhibited no outward sign of emotion. So disciplined was he, so profoundly embedded was his sense of propriety, that he concealed all feelings.

Wives: Kausalya and Kaikeyi

The now aging Dasaratha realized that he could no longer guide his people with the vigor, strength, and dynamism of former days. It was time, he felt, to name a successor from among his grown sons. No contest existed in his mind, his choice having fallen on his favorite son, the virtuous Rama. Upon being informed of the king's decision, Kausalya, Rama's mother, knew great happiness. That she had been essentially abandoned by Dasaratha in favor of the young and seductive Kaikeyi in no way diminished her nobility of character nor altered her wifely devotion to the king. She thanked the gods for his decision and fasted in expression of profound gratitude.

The passionate, beautiful, and generous but also naive Kaikeyi, mother of Bharata, was informed by her faithful but evil, hunchbacked female servant of Dasaratha's plan to install Rama as king. The servant predicted that the new monarch's first move would be to banish Bharata from Ayodhya, and advised her mistress to insist that Bharata be named heir to the throne and that Rama be banished to the forest for fourteen years.

Kaikeyi's servant fits into the plethora of evil and ugly nurses and step-mothers, along with beautiful and good fairy godmothers, who appear in myths, legends, and fairy tales. The evil figures very frequently represent women who, having been denied love, fill their relational void with hate and/or anger, which they try in devious ways to dissimulate. The servant's libido, bent in this case on destruction, was a catalytic force that precipitated a new orientation but at the same time brought about hardship and suffering.

The King Must Die! Long Live the King!

King Dasaratha, seeing Kaikeyi lying in tears on the floor of her private chamber, bereft of her jewels and beautiful garments, tried to console her: "[H]e caressed his lotus-eyed wife with his hands, sick with worry and desire. . . ." (R. 2.10.5). He swore to grant her any wish to restore her happiness. Her response: exile Rama, force him to lead a hermit's life for fourteen years in Dandaka Forest, and award the kingship to their son, Bharata.

Malicious, wicked woman, bent on destroying this House! Evil woman, what evil did Rama or I ever do to you? (*R.* 2.10.33)

So overcome with grief was Dasaratha at the thought of separation from his son that he collapsed unconscious on the floor, as if in death. That Dasaratha was already in his dotage was evident in the highly emotional and unthinking manner in which he reacted to Kaikeyi's state of disarray. His lack of insight into his own timorous nature is revealed by his heaping of blame on his wife, rather than shouldering the burden for his own rash promise. Because a promise was the equivalent of an oath in Hindu patriarchal society, it was binding. Were the king to have broken his word, he would have alienated not only his family but the entire population of Ayodhya as well.

Fearing unconsciously that his pusillanimous comportment might tarnish his son's image of him, Dasaratha fell into virtual incoherence. Was it also shame that accounted for his momentary lapse into speechlessness? The king had turned inward, regressing psychologically into his own underworld or primordial depths, apparently deadened to a situation he could not consciously face. As a result, Kaikeyi was the one to inform Rama of his future exile and Bharata's installation as king.

Kausalya was angered by the injustice meted out by her husband to her son: "You have destroyed this kingship and this kingdom, and all the people of the city; you have destroyed your counselors and yourself, destroyed me and my son!" (*R.* 2.55.20)

Moments later, however, upon looking at the pathetic old king, she shed tears and her usual compassion reasserted itself. She remained with the senile old man as he withdrew increasingly into his own world.

Rama's reaction was not anger but sorrow at his father's grief, and regret that he had not shared his pain. Unlike his father, Rama, conducting himself in accordance with dharma, would not allow an urge to power to interfere with domestic harmony or diminish his love for his family. His mother was so disconsolate that she insisted on following her son into exile, but perception and wisdom dictating his direction, he asked her to remain with the king. "So long as she lives," he told Kausalya, "a woman's one deity and master is her husband" (*R.* 2.21.17).

The citizens of Ayodhya, unlike Rama who was trained in spiritual disciplines, reacted negatively and overtly to his exile. In keeping with their androcentric point of view, they angrily looked upon the woman, Kaikeyi, and never the king, as the natural agent of the country's perdition. She was the temptress who had triggered the king's lust; she was the seductress, the infamous woman who used her flesh to bait an old man, to the detriment of the country. That Kaikeyi was a catalyst is a truism. As Sakti, she succeeded in altering her nation's destiny, but only because Dasaratha had already become ineffectual and spiritually impotent. He had already abandoned the kingship, at least symbolically, in favor of his physical obsession with the young Kaikeyi. That he had thoughtlessly yielded to her will was indicative of his faltering mental capacities, but the blame for the tragic aftermath was placed on the woman only—perfectly natural in a society that allowed polygamy and concubinage to prevail.[3]

Lakshmana, not so controlled as his brother Rama, did not temper his rage upon learning of Bharata's future installation as king. But Rama explained to him that his desire to accept his father's offer to rule the polity had been rash and unthinking. He was as yet unprepared for the task. His withdrawal into the forest would further, he believed, his initiation into manhood. He would follow the path of renunciation and asceticism and his fourteen-year stay in Dadanka Forest would privilege him to associate with enlightened hermits. Rama's words thus increased his brother's insight and awareness: what at first seemed a deprivation and punishment might turn out to be the beginning of a spiritual evolution.

The Exile

Although the notion of exile is implicit in myths of many nations and faiths, it is a basic concept in Hindu philosophy. As previously mentioned, the creation of the universe and its constellations, human procreation, and the birth of all else, including the arts, resulted from the primeval sacrifice or exile from the world of Purusha, the cosmic primal being. The exile or self-sacrifice of mythological or legendary heroes and heroines is considered by Hindus to be a reenactment of Purusha's primordial dismemberment and self-immolation.

Rama's exile—his relinquishing of the kingship and the comfortable way of life it implies—would cut him off from both family and society and force him to depend exclusively on his own resources for survival. Thus it represented, psychologically, a renunciation of all links to adolescence and a paving of the way for the birth or creation of a new, mature, and conscious being. With the help of a guru or single-handedly, Rama, like many Hindu initiates, would be compelled to expend energy and show courage and endurance in order to make his way through the maze of obstacles that would beset him. Only then could he acquire the wisdom needed to plot his life's future course—or perish.

Already Rama was beginning to understand human frailties through a father whom he could not venerate as a paternal deity. Rama was in essence confessing his own fear, one that would return to haunt him years later: "I fear the danger of unrighteousness . . . I fear what other people might say" (R. 2.47.26.).

Lakshmana having asked and been granted permission to accompany his brother, the two donned their ascetic garb and matted their hair, thus preparing at least outwardly for their rite of passage. What Rama and his brother Lakshmana had not counted on was Sita's reaction to their departure into exile. Rama was surprised and dismayed to see her, too, wearing clothes of bark skin rather than her finery when he went to bid her good-bye.

Most adamantly did "dark-eyed" Sita inform her husband that she was joining him in exile (R. 2.14.17). But, Rama answered equally firmly, Dasaratha had never meant that she should live a life of deprivation. Moreover, she had obligations at court. The forest, he said, is dangerous; it is not a place of pleasure, but rather one of pain. But in a show of strength and thoughtfulness, the usually subservient Sita countered her husband's statement with valid arguments.

> It is not her father or mother, not her son or friends or herself, but her husband, and he alone, who gives a woman permanent refuge in this world and after death. (R. 2.24.4)

> I shall live as happily in the forest as if it were my father's house, caring for nothing in the three worlds but to be faithful to my husband. (R. 2.24.9)

Despite the urgency of her words and the imperious tone of her voice, Rama tried to dissuade her from joining him and Lakshmana. She could remain at the court and look forward to his future return. Fourteen years of her life without her husband by her side, she retorted flatly, would be a living death for her. Realizing now that stronger measures were required, she resorted to threat:

> If you refuse to take me to the forest despite the sorrow that I feel, I shall have no recourse but to end my life by poison, fire, or water. (R. 2.26.19)

Unrelentingly, she then had recourse to irony, belittlement, and denigration, aiming cleverly at a man's most vulnerable area:

> What could my father Vaideha, the lord of Mithila, have had in mind when he took you for a son-in-law, Rama, a woman with the body of a man? (R. 2.27.3)

> But like a procurer, Rama, you are willing of your own accord to hand me over to others—your wife, who came to you a virgin and who has been a good woman all the long while she has lived with you. (R. 2.27.8)

Only when Rama's manhood was called into question did he recant. He took his wife's wishes seriously and acquiesced to her demand.

Sita's arguments in favor of sharing her husband's exile were based neither on a desire to prove her independence, nor her power over him; nor was she seeking to have her own way. On the contrary, with tact and rationality, she conceived arguments that would demonstrate, she felt, the extent of her loyalty to her husband. Life without her "master" and her "lord," she made it known to Kausalya, would be worthless, unlivable.

> I fully understand how to behave toward my husband; I have learned well. (R. 2.34.23)

> I am a high-born woman who has learned right from wrong. My lady [Kausalya], how could I be disdainful? A husband is a woman's deity. (R. 2.34.23, 27)

Thus did Sita comport herself not only with dignity and finesse, but with love. No longer the submissive wife, she was suddenly transformed into Rama's equal and, more importantly, she would function in an advisory capacity. Sita would set the law, while Rama would become the passive partner.

Although Sita's insistence on accompanying her husband into exile may seem at first glance to be a divergence from tradition, such contradictions, as previously indicated, lay at the heart of Indian society. The reaffirmation of the pre-Aryan cultures and their Great Mother cults, as opposed to the Vedic and post-Vedic patriarchal society that kept a woman in a state of servile dependency, had prevailed in this instance.

The "fair-hipped" Sita sat unveiled in an open carriage as she departed from Ayodhya with Rama and Lakshmana. Thus did she allow her face to be visible to the crowd (*R.* 2.35.12). (Although the wearing of the veil in India was virtually unknown prior to Muslim rule, exceptions do occur, as in the *Ramayana*, when Sita became the object of public gaze; see Altekar 1983, 166f.) In some versions of the *Ramayana*, it is suggested that Sita ruled the kingdom during Rama's absence: "[F]or of all those that wed, the wife is a second self. . . . Let Sita rule the earth in Rama's stead, being Rama's self, for be sure that Bharata will refuse to take the throne that should be Rama's" (Coomaraswamy 1967, 43).

Dasaratha died shortly after Rama's departure. Thus, once again, "the earth had been widowed" (*R.* 2.70.9). In accordance with custom, Bharata presided at his father's funeral rite; then, after a period of meditation, he went out into the forest in a vain attempt to convince Rama to return. A modus vivendi was reached: Bharata would rule for fourteen years and no longer; if Rama did not reappear at the conclusion of this time period, Bharata would immolate himself. Thereupon he asked Rama for his sandals, which he would place on the throne as symbols of his presence, while Bharata would live outside of the city, ruling the land as regent.

Sita's Initiation

Determined to follow Rama into exile, Sita was prepared to undergo her initiation ("to go within") into womanhood and cut her ties with adolescence. Psychologically, the process amounts to a descent into Self or the passage from one level of consciousness to another until the deepest spheres within the psyche are reached. Such a *katabasis* allows the initiate to reconnect with his or her own past and concomitantly with humanity's primordial existence. For Hindus, it implies rejoining one's previous incarnations.

So as not to diminish the value of their renunciation, Sita, Rama, and Lakshmana walked ever more deeply into the heart of Dadanka Forest or, psychologically, into themselves.

The Forest: The Domain of the Great Mother. As an animist, Sita considered everything about her—a blade of grass, a petal, a branch, or a pebble—to be a living, breathing, and growing entity. Coming upon any unfamiliar tree, flower, or fruit, she would stop and *question* Rama as to its name and virtue. The word "quest" (from the Latin *quaestus*) may be considered paradigmatic of the search for greater knowledge—a search, perhaps unconscious, for a new inner orientation and a right course in life. Sita's yearning to gain knowledge during the exile process is comparable in some respects to the search for one's *center* with the aid of a mandala, culminating in a sense of balance and harmony in place of uncertainty and perhaps even chaos.

Nature seemed to burgeon in the presence of Sita, the daughter of the earth goddess, and she reciprocally felt *awakened to* and *reborn in* another dimension of cosmic life.

> Sita takes the same delight in the desolate forests that she used to have when going out to the city gardens. (*R.* 2.54.9)

> The delightful Sita with her full-moon face is enjoying herself like a young girl, delighting in Rama and not at all despondent, in the desolate forest though she may be. (*R.* 2.54.10)

> On the road Vaidehi [Sita] asks about the villages and cities she sees, the courses of rivers and the different kinds of trees. (*R.* 2.54.12)

> No journey or gusting wind, no distress or scorching heat can dim Vaidehi's moonbeam radiance. (*R.* 2.54.13)

Herds of elephants or deer, flocks of lapwings or cuckoos, to mention but a few of the living creatures she observed, impassioned her by their beauty, strength, and song. Forests in flower, "ponds and lakes with clumps of blooming lotuses and sparkling clear water . . . stretches of wilderness echoing with the cries of peacocks"—all was wonderment for Sita (*R.* 3.7.13–15). The deep forest, the domain of the Great Mother or Mother Earth, contrasted sharply with the cultivated, orderly gardens of Ayodhya.

The world of the "green" mother being identified with the most primitive levels of the psyche, it may be considered a metaphor for Sita's return to her earth origins—the furrow. The daughter of the Earth Mother had chosen to immerse herself in nature, which, however, is destructive as well as protective. Nourisher and sustainer of life, nature also destroys weaker plants and animals. In it may lurk healthful or poisonous flora or fauna, harmless or dangerous animals, reptiles, and insects, or even *rakshasas*.

The forest, considered a symbol of the unconscious, may be awesome and fear-inspiring. A journey into its dark depths parallels a plunge into an unknown, disorienting world. Treacherous, yet infinitely yielding, the forest may be regarded as the container of repressed or unsuspected fears as well as the storehouse of extraordinary treasures.

Living close to Mother Nature's great mysteries afforded Sita the possibility of indwelling—that is, of communicating with the Absolute—beyond time and space as we know them. The phenomenological world for the Hindu—

the forest in this case—was not merely a locus, but rather a manifestation of Sita's emotional and spiritual condition.

Sita's body as well as her mind benefited from her new orientation. Walking from one ashram to another, up hills and down dales, bathing in lakes and ponds, resting in the open, and eating sparsely strengthened her both physically and philosophically. Not one without the other, for the two are *one*.

The Ashram, or Temenos. Whenever Sita, Rama, and Lakshmana chose another place in the forest to locate, Lakshmana, an engineer and architect, built a suitable ashram out of clay, thatch, leaves, and wood, with partitions to assure privacy to both himself and to the married couple (R. 3.14.20–24). Each ashram that they inhabited became a *temenos* (sacred space). Each may be considered metaphorically as a step in Sita's, Rama's, and Lakshmana's spiritual/psychological evolution.

During her forest experience, Sita's learning was garnered not only in association and dialogue with the wise men and students whom the three-some met in their various retreats, but also in their day-to-day life experiences. Interestingly enough, the male ascetics they encountered, such as the austere sages Bharadvaja and his pupils, showed no distinction in their behavior toward Sita and Rama. She was readily accepted in their intellectual milieu and, no longer the timid and delicate maiden she had once been, she now approached men as equals. The interchanging of ideas with young and old helped Sita to evolve psychologically. And as the years passed and her learning deepened, her confidence in herself increased, with even greater qualities of strength and self-reliance coming to the fore.

Instrumental in her growth process was Sita's meeting with the aged and revered ascetic Atri and his honored wife, Anasuya. From her she learned the secrets of the forest, rectitude, and obeisance to her husband. Nor did Anasuya neglect to stress the body as an important factor in maintaining balance and harmony of being. To Sita she gave a "heavenly garland, raiment and jewelry, and a cream . . . a precious salve" that would forever keep her beautiful (R. 2. 110.17).

Sita: Rama's Teacher. Never dogmatic, speaking always with an affectionate tone of voice, Sita amplified Rama's own thoughts by defining what she perceived to be that ever-elusive, complex, and ambiguous notion of dharma:

> Acquiring great righteousness requires the greatest care, and only he who avoids deliberate misdeeds can gain it in this world. (R. 3.8.2)

As for deliberate misdeeds, there are just three. Telling lies is bad enough, but the other two, sexual intercourse with another man's wife and unprovoked violence, are even worse. (R. 3.8.3)

You have never been, nor will you ever be, guilty of telling lies. . . . And how could you possibly lust after the wife of another man, an act that destroys righteousness. (R. 3.8.4) . . .

Both of these misdeeds can be avoided by those who have mastered their senses, and I know you control your senses, my handsome husband.

But the third one, violence—the taking of life without provocation, and recklessly—to this you may be prone. (R. 3.8.5–6)

Her preaching of nonviolence may to some extent have been influenced by the Jain Mahavira. A hylozoist, Mahavira believed that all matter has life. He preached that the killing of the tiniest insect or the hurting of a stone influenced one's karma. "If a man kills living things, or slays by the hand of another, or consents to another slaying, his sin goes on increasing" (*Sutrakrtanga*, 1.1.1, quoted in de Bary 1958, 53).

Sita's sharp perception of Rama's character and his proneness to killing reveals what strides she had made in her spiritual and emotional evolution. Killing the *rakshasas* who disturbed the forest monks' rituals might seem reasonable, but she pursues her point with finesse:

You and your brother are going to the forest bow and arrow in hand, and I fear the sight of any forest-dweller might cause you to shoot your arrows.

For in this world a bow to a kshatriya is kindling to a fire: If it comes too close, his blazing power flares up wildly.

Only because I love and respect you am I reminding you—not teaching you—that on no account should you take up your bow and unprovoked, turn your thoughts to killing the rakshasas of Dandaka. My mighty husband, I disapprove of your killing creatures that have done no wrong. (R. 3.8.11–12, 20-21)

The modernity of her thought is remarkable, as is her awareness of the dichotomies of behavioral patterns in the city and in the country:

How incongruous they are, weapons and the forest, the kshatriya order and the practice of asceticism—it is all so at odds. We must respect the customs of the place. (R. 3.8.22)

Wicked thoughts, my noble husband, can come from handling weapons. When you are back in Ayhodya, you may follow the kshatriya code. (R. 3.8.24)

Asking Rama to give "careful thought" to what she has said, she admonishes him to follow the paths of righteousness, control, and self-restraint. But the choice, she maintains, is his.

Rama parries Sita's arguments cleverly and purposefully, in a discussion reminiscent of Lord Krishna's with Arjuna in *The Bhagavad Gita* (The song of the Lord): Arjuna refuses to fight because relatives and friends are battling each other, while Krishna maintains that failure to fight for his side would be failure to perform his duty (dharma) as a warrior, and thus would constitute a sin. One must act impersonally, Krishna asserts—"acting and yet not acting" (de Bary 1958, 276).

> Do you do your allotted work, for action is superior to nonaction. Even the normal functioning of your body cannot be accomplished through actionlessness. (Ibid., 281)

Rama would continue to destroy the *rakshasas* in order to help the forest ascetics:

> And having once promised I could never, so long as I live, violate my pledge to the sages. For truthfulness has always been the one thing I cherish. (R. 3.9.17)

He conveys his impersonal approach to earthly existence and his own scale of values.

> I would sooner give up my life, Sita, or even you and Laksmana, than break a promise I have made, especially to brahmans. (R. 3.9.18)

Before long, Rama would have the opportunity of carrying out his promise, but perhaps not in the way he expected to.

The Senex Figure. Meanwhile, Sita and Rama encountered various theriomorphic creatures in the forest. Jatayu, the great eagle or vulture that had been a cherished friend of King Dasaratha during his warrior years, imparted love and affection to Sita, Rama, and Lakshmana. As a surrogate father, Jatayu watched over his protégés from the sky, shading them or protecting them from danger with his enormous wings. As psychopomp as well, he led them on their course. For the three wanderers, and particularly Sita, he took on the function of a senex figure, a role Dasaratha had once held in their lives.

Bird figures are quite common in myths. Looked upon frequently as spiritualizing forces or soul images, they inject a supernal and otherworldly feeling into earthly happenings. The ancient Egyptians, for example, identified birds with what they called the *Ba* (soul), because it flew upward after the death of the body. Such soul or bird forces frequently were associated with humans in life or in death, accompanying those who, like Sita and Rama, sought light, health, and awakening.

Love as Linga and Yoni. As they made their way ever more deeply into the forest, there were moments when Rama could not help but feel great gentleness and love for Sita. He embraced this daughter of Mother Earth not only as a woman but also as a manifestation of the virtually infinite beauties of nature. He saw her reflected in the forms, textures, tonalities, and inner rhythms of every flower, bud, creeper, or bush.

That Rama's thoughts during the forest experience should turn to love is not surprising. For Hindus, earthly love—viewed archetypally—is a mimetic replay of the divine union between Shiva (Creator and Destroyer), as symbolized in the *linga* (sacred phallus), and *sakti* (female energy), as symbolized in the *yoni* (sacred womb). Love, then, is a paradigm of the blending and fusing of all that is disparate in the world of contingencies, the multiple becoming *One*. Animists such as the Hindus believe not only in the existence of a sympathetic relationship between everything in the visible and invisible world but in the interlocking and interchangeability of everything in the cosmos.

The opening of a flower, the burgeoning of a plant, the first fruits, the livingness of a leaf, the glow of a stone, and the river's inviting waters are manifestations of love in the domain of nature. The human love experience, heightening and universalizing what Westerners consider to be personal emotional states, permit the couple to glimpse cosmic wholeness.

Demons. Bathing in the ecstasy and rapture of love, Rama was distracted from his task of ridding the forest of evil powers, even though the ascetics constantly reminded him of the torments of these evil creatures who deflected them from their spiritual aims.

A demon, psychologically speaking, may be considered as an archetypal power or a malevolent force that can beguile and lead one astray at any time during one's life (Franz 1980, 116). A person or a group (as in the case of the forest ascetics) to whom a demon figure becomes manifest may be said to be "contaminated with unconscious impulses" that seek to become conscious but cannot. Until the demon figure (or what it represents) is consciously faced, it may impact on the person's (or the group's) emotional side. Particularly in the case of vulnerable persons, mood swings may follow. If a person (or group) identifies with or is possessed by demons, these powers must, to use a biblical word, be exorcised (see Matt. 12:22–28) (Franz 1974, 69).

Hindus believe in the ever dynamic truth of Maya, the goddess of illusion, also referred to by psychologists as "the great entangler" who is able to lure people into good and/or evil. As a transitory power, Maya may take on a multitude of male, female, animal, or other forms. Her apparition as a celestial vision, an idealized phantasmagoria, or a gorgeous woman poses a danger to the vulnerable layman or to the sexually starved hermit or monk. Women are likewise duped by Maya: she may appear in the form of a venerable father figure, an ascetic or deity, or a great lover.

As a creation of the mind, Maya may take on the countenance of a demon, the Maya/demon power being considered by some as the personification of the darker side of humankind. The projection of one's fears or needs onto an outer subject or object—demon or other—implies remaining *unaware* or *unenlightened* about one's basic, or base, nature. Negative Maya figures in the guise of what men feared most in their wives—the carnal, lascivious female—yet lusted for outside of marriage make frequent appearances in the arts. On a positive note, however, since the Maya/demon power had the power to personify or become actualized, she enabled positive forces, such as deities or protective figures, to become manifest in human affairs, thus empowering a mortal to redress an evil.

The most feared power among all demons took the form of the ten-headed and twenty-armed Ravana, king of Lanka and chief of the demons. It was he who had to be destroyed. Only a mortal—Rama—so the gods said, could accomplish this heroic deed.

The Hierodule. In order to proceed in his worldly work—the eradication of demons—Rama had to face a harrowing ordeal. Sita was to be the victim and it was she who would have to deal with the continuity and extremes of adversity.

A *hierodule* (servant of the god)—the temptress of patriarchal societies—happened to cross Rama's path. Hierodules in Babylon, Cyprus, Greece, and other ancient societies were usually associated with religious worship, including the performance of sexual rites (Kluger 1991, 32). The popularity of the hierodule figure in myths gives evidence of the male's fixated fear of women. Such a psychological condition may lead to the male's obsessive need of *complete and continuous proof and assurance of female chastity.* So extreme is the emphasis on virginity in the *Ramayana* that wives had forever to be prepared to prove their "purity" at any time and under all circumstances.

The *rakshasa*/hierodule, Surpanakha, Ravana's sister, happened upon Rama, Sita, and Lakshmana seated in front of their ashram. Casting her eyes on what she saw as a divinely handsome Rama, she longed for him. Although like other hierodules she had the power "to take on any form at all," she chose to remain as she was: ugliness personified. As for her speech, "her words were sinister and her voice struck terror" in those around (*R.* 3.16.8–10). Rama, the monogamous husband—unusual for his day and for centuries to come in India—maintained his dignified manner, but could not refrain from conversing, albeit ironically and humorously, with this creature. He went so far as to tell her his life story.

The more she gazed at Rama, the more her passion for him grew, to the point that she proposed marriage to him. Her hatred for her rival, Sita, increased concomitantly: "I will devour this misshapen slut, this hideous human female with her pinched waist" (*R.* 3.17.23). As Surpanaka readied to pounce on her enemy, Rama ordered Lakshmana to "mutilate this misshapen slut, this pot-bellied, lustful raksasa woman." Lakshmana "drew his sword and in a rage cut off the creature's ears and nose" (*R.* 3.17.21).

Such mutilation would not go unpunished, the bloodied hierodule vowed. Rushing to her *rakshasa* brother, Khara, she obtained his help in the form of fourteen powerful demons to fight the enemy—a challenge incisively met by Rama, who killed them all. Terrified by the turn of events, Surpanakha, returning to her brother, persuaded him to pursue the battle himself at the head of his army of fourteen thousand demons. Single-handedly Rama annihilated them all, including Khara. At her wit's end, Surpanakha fled to the palace of Ravana, the lecherous and formidable king of Lanka.

Sita's Abduction

Upon her arrival, Surpanakha found Ravana luxuriously ensconced amidst a bevy of gorgeously appareled females. Skilled in the art of cunning, she deprecated Ravana's unbridled licentiousness, accusing the ruler of failing to recognize his real enemy, Rama, and thus attacking his pride. But Surpanakha saved her most exquisite verbal lure for the last—a panegyric of Sita:

> And what a glorious woman she is, with her large eyes, slender
> waist, and full hips.

No mortal woman so beautiful have I ever seen before on the
  face of this earth.
How broad her hips, how full and high her breasts, how lovely
  her face.

(R. 3.32.14, 15, 18)

Such a rapturous description could not fail to activate an intense illusion (Maya) in Ravana's mind. Igniting an all-consuming flame in him, it prompted an instantaneous decision to pursue this woman. He hopped into his chariot and flew through the air "like a thunder-cloud in the sky" to seek the help of his friend, Marica (R. 3.33.9). "I fear the daughter of Janaka was born to take your life," Marica warned him. "I fear some awful doom will strike because of Sita" (R. 3.35.5). But his words fell on deaf ears. Forced to help Ravana, Marica yielded to the request that he assume the shape of a heavenly looking golden deer that would bewitch Sita.

The Golden Deer. Predictably, Sita was tantalized and mystified by this divine apparition. He had stolen her heart away, she told Rama, beseeching him to capture this unique golden beauty for her.

Rama, equally dazzled by the glitter of this fabulous visitation so antipodal to the darkness of his forest experience, acquiesced. Although he sought to please his wife, he might also have longed unconsciously for the facile world of artifice, luxury, and physical pleasures he had once known and that this animal called to mind.

Allowing themselves to be led astray by the glittering visitation of Maya, the protagonists may have been attempting unconsciously to balance their own one-sidedness. The rigors of forest life—renunciation, austerity, penitence—contrasted dramatically with the glitter and luxury of palace life. Victims of one or the other polarity, both Sita and Rama lost sight of the complete personality and, by extension, of the breadth of life's potential. Religious texts of all faiths are replete with figures whose extreme postures produced fantasies. Suffice it to name such saints as Anthony, Christopher, Teresa, and Cosmas and Damian.

The ungovernable power that had taken hold of Sita and Rama overwhelmed their psyches by bringing the opposite polarity into play. Illusion had depotentiated empirical reality, thus activating a "daemonic compulsion" or the domination of the irrational (Jung 1990, par. 346).

A golden deer fascinates by its beauty, grace, and glitter. When identified with the sun, as in Cambodian and Chinese myths, it may dazzle the onlooker, blinding him or her to the realities of the object beheld. Earthly gold, representing the highest and purest of values, is considered a mediator between heaven and earth and may, like the Westerner's Lucifer *(lux + fer)*, be the harbinger of enlightenment.

Sita and Rama, not sufficiently evolved either spiritually or psychologically, were ensnared. "If rulers of men are not their own masters and fail to protect their realm, their grandeur disappears, like mountains sunk beneath the sea" (R. 3.31.6).

Lakshmana, on the other hand, known for his wisdom and not deluded by Maya's lure, warned Rama to keep entirely away from the elusive and illusory golden deer, which might be a product of a *rakshasa's* magic powers. But Lakshmana's warnings went unheeded and Rama, after asking him to remain with Sita at all times during his absence, left for the hunt.

The excitement of the hunt—the search, the capture, the kill—was an added enticement for Rama. Swept up by what may be called his "undomesticated libido" or "daemonic possession," the usually highly disciplined Rama suddenly lost his self-control. But then, had not Sita already understood the gaping schism in his psyche: self-denial and deprivation on the one hand, and the attraction of the beguiling pleasures of the hunt on the other?

Rama's defeat was predictable. To arrest an illusion or to possess an abstraction—the golden deer—is as readily accomplished as arresting time in the differentiated world. Whenever Rama approached the animal, it darted off farther away. The more duplicitous the animal's behavior, the greater was Rama's determination to overcome its resistance. Thus was Rama led on an endless chase, separating himself further and further from his wife.

At last Rama realized the folly and the vanity of his would-be heroic act. Incited by Maya, he had succumbed to pride and self-delusion. That he had been duped by an animal, albeit a demon, triggered his irrational anger and an onslaught of libido, or increased energy and purpose. He shot his arrows. Before succumbing to them, the golden deer had one more ruse in store: it imitated Rama's voice and called to Sita and Lakshmana for help. Predictably the latter would rush to his brother's defense, thereby leaving the woman unprotected.

Sita's asceticism had dredged up repressed contents from her subliminal sphere and had made her, too, vulnerable to the lure of the pleasure principle. Her affective reaction to the golden deer represented a descent or straying from the higher levels of consciousness that she had attempted to reach during her initiatory process. Because impulses of such strength may interrupt a person's (or society's) established order and custom, the influx of such "untamed libido" has frequently been looked upon by religious people as sent by god(s) or demon(s) (Jung 1990, par. 347). In Sita's case, paradoxically, her irrational behavior would act as a catalyst for the fulfillment of her earthly trajectory.

Sita the Deceiver. Stricken with panic when she heard what she thought was Rama's cry for help, Sita acted impulsively once again, ordering Lakshmana to save her husband. Although he argued that no one could kill or overcome Rama, and that "the magic of that rakshasa [was as] unreal as a mirage," Sita's anguish was undiminished. Her eyes blazing, she talked wildly, deprecating Lakshmana: "Ignoble, cruel man, disgrace to your House!" (R. 3.43.15, 3.43.20). She went so far as to accuse him of wanting her for himself, to which with sagelike reverence he replied that he looked upon her as a goddess and not a human. Since Rama's plight seemed not to affect him, she retorted, she had but one course to follow: to build a pyre and throw herself onto it. Thereupon, Lakshmana launched into a misogynist tirade:

> Women care nothing for righteousness, they are flighty, sharp-tongued, and divisive. . . .
>   Curse you and be damned, that you could so suspect me, when I am only following the orders of my guru. How like a woman to be so perverse! (R. 3.43.29)

Nonetheless, pained by Sita's suffering, he left in search of Rama.

Ravana, who had been observing the two from a distance, emerged from hiding. He appeared to Sita dressed in hermit's garb: a saffron robe, with topknot, parasol, and sandals, complete with staff, begging bowl, and water pitcher hanging over his left shoulder. In the most courteous of terms he addressed her, comparing her to the loveliest of goddesses, Sri-Laksmi (*sri* suggests "capability, power, good fortune").

As required by etiquette, Sita invited the mendicant into her ashram, and with great respect offered him a cushion to sit on, food, and water for his feet (R. 3.44.32–34).

So overwhelmed was Ravana by Sita's beauty that he quickly made his intentions clear: he offered to make her chief queen and give her five thousand slave women to wait on her. The usually soft-spoken and mild Sita repulsed his advances. Unaccustomed to contravention, particularly by a woman, Ravana's "yellow-rimmed eyes turned fiery red" (R. 3.47.5). He dropped his disguise, returning to his colossal size. "With his left hand he seized lotus-eyed Sita by her hair and with his right hand by her thighs" and carried her off in his airborne chariot.

Rivers, mountains, clouds, flocks of birds, herds of beasts, flowers, trees—all of Nature heard Sita's cries. As soon as Jatayu, the great eagle, spied them, he reminded Ravana that he had violated the social code of his day, which forbade the kidnapping and seduction of married women. His voice was threatening.

The two locked in battle. Ravana's missiles tore into Jatayu; with whatever strength he could muster the aged bird clawed his enemy's body and feet, destroying Ravana's splendid chariot and bow in the process. Finally forced to earth, the exhausted bird hurled himself onto the ten-headed Ravana. Undaunted, Jatayu continued the fight until Ravana, drawing his sword, severed his wings, feet, and flanks. Blood splattered every place; the "moon-faced Sita...took him in her arms and wept" (R. 3.49.40). And Lord Brahma, who had witnessed the outrage, said: "What had to be done has been done" (R. 3.50.10).

Ravana took Sita to the island of Lanka, where she was placed in an asoka grove under the guard of horrific *rakshasa* women. Although grieving and wretched, she was "resplendent with a radiance which now shone but simply so that she seemed like a flame wreathed in smoke" (Kinsley 1988, 72).

The Quest for Sita Imprisoned. Rama, having encountered Lakshmana in the forest, now returned gloomily to the empty ashram. "Without the golden daughter of Janaka, I would spurn lordship over the whole earth . . . over the deathless gods themselves" (R. 3.56.5–6).

The two brothers set out in search of Sita. They happened upon the fallen Jatayu, whose insurmountable will had kept him alive until he could apprise Rama of events. Then the noble bird expired. Other theriomorphic helpers joined in the search for Sita. One of the most outstanding, courageous, and learned of these was Hanuman (monkey-chief).

Dispatched to Lanka to ascertain Sita's whereabouts, Hanuman from a treetop spied her sitting silently and motionless in her yellow dust-covered sari. Neither Ravana's unctuous words, nor his proposal to make her his favorite wife, nor his threats to cut her up and eat her if, within the space of two months, she had not yielded to his advances, had altered Sita's feelings of repulsion for him.

Hanuman, bounding down from the tree, suggested he might carry her on his back to Rama. She refused. According to tradition, a married woman must not allow her body to come into contact with that of any other man, be he anthropomorphic or theriomorphic. Moreover, to allow another to rescue her would deprive Rama of committing his "heroic act." Here again, Sita's thoughtfulness conformed to the image of the ideal Indian wife: she generously considered her husband's prerogatives over her own welfare.

Once Hanuman had returned to the mainland and apprised Rama of the situation, it was decided that he, Rama, and Lakshmana, together with an army of apes, would attack Lanka. In the course of the furious battle, Ravana was killed.

Sita's Ordeal

Rama, unwilling to brave the populace in its demand for punishment of a wayward wife's unchastity—albeit forced on her—pandered to tradition. Instead of receiving Sita with open arms and in joy, he stated flatly that he had not rescued her out of love or for any personal reasons, but rather to vindicate the honor, code, and values of his family and ancestors. Nor was it customary for a man, he continued, to readmit a wife into his household after she had resided alone and for so long in a stranger's home. The very thought of living together again as man and wife, he informed her, was out of the question. She was free to live as she liked, to reside wherever she pleased, and associate herself with one of his brothers or a demon if she so desired.

Sita was confounded by Rama's words. His coldness and utter insensitivity to her suffering filled her with a sense of humiliation and degradation. Far more vicious than Ravana's violence was Rama's seeming determination to hurt her. A demon such as Ravana behaves according to his evil nature and in keeping with his character, resorting to deception, lies, cruelty, and rage. That Rama had become her torturer, however, was not predictable. He was acting out of character. Or was he?

Although shocked by her husband's announcements, Sita nevertheless retrieved her senses. Friendless, thrust on her own once again, but this time cut off from what she thought had been her husband's sustaining love, the formerly obedient and subservient wife revealed unexpected resiliency by refusing to accept her fate passively. Nor would she yield to torment or anger. Acting with vigor, judgment, and resolve, she requested that Lakshmana prepare a funeral pyre for her. He hesitated, then looked at Rama for guidance. But Rama did not countermand her order.

Once the pyre was lit, the flames blazed, reaching high and wide. The shocked crowd watched Sita approach the fire, prostrate herself before its incandescence, and utter a prayer to Agni, the god of fire, the regenerator of life, asking him to be a witness to her chastity and to grant her protection.

As the fire principle, Agni, one of the most important Hindu gods, burned away the mounds of detritus obstructing human enlightenment. The sacred flame emanating from Him rose heavenward funneling heat and energy throughout the cosmos. Transformed into a connecting agent linking humankind to divinity—or the world of multiplicity to cosmic spheres—he created Oneness.

The fact that Sita's prayer to Agni was verbal associated him, in keeping with Vedic texts, with the fire and heat generated by speech. In the *Aitareya Upanishad* 1.1.4 we read: "From the mouth speech, from speech fire" (Radhakrishnan 1978, 516). The reverse—fire becomes speech—is defined in the *Brihadaranyaka Upanishad,* further indicating the fluidity of energetic or fiery matter.

In that both fire and speech are identified with psychic energy (libido or mana), its canalization suggests an intensifying of ardor, strength, and passion, as well as sharpness of thought. So *ardent* and *flammable* had been Sita's prayer to Agni that the words themselves, as if by magic, had ignited her entire being into participation. Thus did she succeed through the mediation of language in carrying her message to Agni (God) or the Self (the total psyche). As a bridge between celestial and earthly realms, Agni's presence underscored the numinosity of the entire experience. The authenticity of Sita's renunciation of the life experience and the purity of her *words* revealed a *truth* beyond human dimension.

A miracle occurred. As Sita entered the flames, Agni rose from within them bearing her with him, after which he handed her unscathed to Rama.[4] Unbeknownst to Rama, it was not the former Sita whom he now welcomed into his arms, but rather one reborn following the sacrifice. Her ordeal marked a turning point in her life: the death of the formerly subservient wife and the birth of a new woman, increasingly conscious of her identity and self-worth. The vital energy streaming from the flames had released the powerful anxieties that had built up in her since her abduction and especially after her release.

Rama had revealed himself to be a timorous man. His feigned indifference to Sita's lot in consideration of popular opinion masked the truth of his feelings. He had pandered to social norms, custom, and the collective's expectations of kingship. Whereas the heat of the flames had liberated Sita from a searing sense of bondage, the intensity of Rama's passion to seek the collectivity's approval had devoured his sense of justice, righteousness, and purpose—dharma—as king and ruling consciousness of the land.

But, on the other hand, he may have reasoned that had he not respected tradition, he, as future ruler—as the Divinity's earthly representative, the highest authority of the land, the purveyor of justice, balance, and harmony—might not have merited the trust of kingship. On a more personal level, it may also be suggested that Rama could not endure the shame that Sita's "blemished" presence cast on him vis-à-vis his people. Or was he simply jealous of the physical rapture Sita had aroused in another man? Whatever his motivations, Rama sought to save face.

Other explanations have been offered to elucidate Rama's unexpected behavior toward Sita. Could his love for his wife have been powerfully aroused during their separation, only to diminish upon her return? For the wife—and Sita is no exception—"love in separation" *(viraha)* was no different from love in togetherness: complete preoccupation with the husband, his welfare and reputation, constituted her only focus in life (O'Flaherty 1980, 122).

A man's reaction to love, although powerful, is diversified. Despite Rama's intermittent moods of melancholia and some moving laments of Sita's disappearance, he had other commitments to occupy his thoughts—most importantly, those involving kingship. Thus he judged that placating the populace was central to his position; secondary was his love for his beautiful and loyal wife.[5]

The *Ramayana*, reflecting a culture's flagrant demeaning of womankind, required a deus ex machina to readmit Sita into Rama's household. Had the epiphany not occurred, Sita would have been consumed by Agni's flames, which would have released her, according to Hindu belief, from the great illusion that is life.

Sita's Return to Mother Earth

The coronation ceremony marking the couple's return to Ayodhya was unparalleled in its magnificence. Rama ascended the throne at the age of forty-four. As described by the patriarchal Valmiki, Rama was the ideal ruler, his reign reflecting *his* understanding of dharma. R. K. Narayan's adaptation of *The Ramayana*, based on Kamban's eleventh-century C.E. version of the epic, concludes on this happy note. But in editions of Valmiki's epic allegedly of a later date, Sita is required to go through yet another ordeal.

After the failure of the harvest, the suffering people of Ayodhya, in need of a scapegoat, blamed Rama's acceptance of his unchaste wife back into the household, in total disregard of moral law. Informed of the public's discontent, once again Rama permitted himself to be swayed by public opinion rather than allow his own sense of righteousness—dharma—to dictate his acts. That he resorted to deception rather than courageously confronting his wife with alternatives was not surprising in light of his previous behavior. Since the now-pregnant Sita had expressed a desire to visit Dadanka Forest again in order to recall her youth and better times, he decided to grant her wish. He ordered Lakshmana to accompany Sita into the forest and then—in an act of *adharma*—to abandon her there.

The mystery and ambiguity revolving around the Hindu concept of dharma must once again be scrutinized, particularly with respect to the moral and religious obligations of kingship. Ideologically and psychologically, dharma is a process that requires continuous reevaluation by an individual or a society in terms of specific or collective acts committed in the fluid and dynamic world of contingencies. Vigilant, periodic reviews of a person's reactions to his or her thoughts and feelings are required during life, viewed as an ever altering course. The code of ethics that sustains the well-being of a society rests on the strength and vision of its ruler. Dharma, in this context, represents a continuous challenge.

As previously mentioned, dharma is included in the "Four Ends of Man," the other three being, *artha* (wealth), *kama* (desire), and *moksa* (deliverance). The last requires withdrawal from active participation in worldly matters and devotion thereafter to contemplation in order to gain release from the spirit's perpetual transmigration and allow its reabsorption in Brahman.

After Sita's reentry into the forest, it was she, interestingly, and not Rama, who would experience the noble truth of *moksa*. Deserted by Lakshmana, Sita was left to wander alone and unprotected. Valmiki found her and took her to an ashram where she later gave birth to twin sons—Kusa and Lava. During their growing years, Valmiki not only initiated the boys into the world of higher learning but also taught them the poem, the *Ramayana*, which he had composed in celebration of Rama's heroic exploits. In time, the two lads were invited to court and sang the epic. Their father not only recognized them, but accepted them as his sons and invited Sita to return to Ayodhya.

Sita Redeemed

Redemption for the Hindu, as previously noted, implied freedom from the pull of opposites, liberation from torment and conflict within soul and psyche, and indifference to the polarities implicit in the world of contingencies. To experience a state of detachment is to know transcendence. Upon Sita's return to Ayodhya, her acceptance as the king's wife was contingent on public reaffirmation of her chastity and integrity before the populace. Her emotions might have been aroused by such a demand had she not become a woman transformed. Her renunciation of the world during her second forest experience had gained her access to a truth beyond that of human understanding. Dignity and restraint, bitterness and torment, had been replaced by protracted tranquility. Having given birth in the forest and having raised her sons with love and wisdom, and having carried on her meditations and studies under the tutelage of Valmiki, Sita had reached a higher sphere of learning/understanding—in *moksa*.

Moving toward transcendence, a nonrational condition in which opposites neutralize each other, Sita called upon the single power that would accept her for the spotless being that she was: her mother, the goddess Earth.

As Sita spoke, the sound of her words went into the air in a universal embrace. Neither a code, a tool, or a system, but an aspect of cosmic reality itself, her invocations had become a mantra. She beseeched her mother to end the tragedy of her mortality and, as her words resounded, a throne borne by serpents rose from the ground. Mother Earth, embracing her long-suffering daughter, took her back into a domain beyond cognition and comprehension. Sita now reposed in Brahman alone—"The Imperishable Source of Things Unperceivable," that all-pervading, self-existent power.

Rama clamored for his wife's return, but silence was Mother Earth's only reply.

Unlike Sita, Rama was insufficiently prepared for *moksa*. The priority he gave to his role as king, his need of adulation by his people, and his dependency on the external world of objects and sense-perception caused him to be overly preoccupied with personal and material matters. Rama lacked the detachment necessary to enter impersonal, abstract spheres. Only after Sita's disappearance did he begin to understand the consequences of his misguided efforts. Yielding to public opinion rather than allowing the truth of his inner convictions and the dictates of his heart to prevail relegated him to the lowest common denominator in society—that of the uninitiated. Too late did Rama realize that the earthly years allotted to him without Sita no longer had meaning for him.

Sita, the real heroine of the *Ramayana*, courageously and knowingly had taken the giant leap beyond mortal comprehension into the Absolute where the Multiple is One.

> The eye cannot see it; mind cannot grasp it.
> The deathless Self has neither caste nor race,
> Neither eyes nor ears nor hands nor feet.
> Sages say this Self is infinite in the great
> And in the small, everlasting and changeless,
> The source of life.
>
> As the web issues out of the spider
> And is withdrawn, as plants sprout from the earth,
> As hair grows from the body, even so,
> The sages say, this universe springs from
> The deathless Self, the source of life.
>
> The deathless Self meditated upon
> Himself and projected the universe
> As evolutionary energy.
> From this energy developed life, mind,
> The elements, and the world of karma,
> Which is enchained by cause and effect.
>
> The deathless Self sees all, knows all. From him
> Springs Brahma, who embodies the process
> Of evolution into name and form
> By which the One appears to the many.
>
> (*Mundaka Upanishad* 1.1.6–9,
> quoted in Easwaran 1987, 672)

CONCLUSION

We have come to the end of our hermeneutical trajectory through time and space. The divine and human archetypal figures analyzed in *Women in Myth*, simultaneously time-ridden and time-transcendent, live on, albeit diversely, in the minds and psyches of today's women and men. Their impact on the reader depends largely on the depth of her or his projection onto the specific character(s).

The ectypal and archetypal explorations are designed to reveal the conditions that provoked these extraordinary mythical women into fighting, loving, despising, agonizing, and accepting or remedying the wrongs perpetrated against them. It is up to readers to make the connections and to draw the parallels that will trigger new insights and different ways of fulfilling their own potential or, at least, of avoiding some of life's pitfalls.

Since mythical time is reversible, even today lessons may be learned from the goddesses and legendary figures of ancient times. Whenever Isis, a thinking and strong-willed woman who was balanced in mind and body, allowed awareness to wane, she experienced periods of excoriating evil. But instead of succumbing to morosity, she *quested* for ways to rectify her plight, thereby *renewing* what had grown worn and strengthening what had become vulnerable. Forever evolving as a wife and mother and independent in her own right, she has become the prototype of today's self-reliant woman, sensitive to her own needs as well as to those of others.

Tiamat, less sophisticated, was and remained *prima materia*. Although undifferentiated and impulsive, the motivation of love steered her into the safeguarding of her rambunctious children against her husband's uncompromising wrath and killing instinct. When overcome by rage, she was destroyed/

239

transformed. The Tiamat type lives on today as *prima materia*, the spawner of life—as *cosmic womb*.

The delightfully naive Iphigenia was and is the model of the fiancée who gleefully anticipates a joyous future as wife and mother. Upon learning that she was to be sacrificed for the well-being of the collective, she came to understand the complex notion involved in martyrdom: the death of stasis and/or traditional systems and the birth of new ones. Envisioning herself as a savior figure, she offered herself up for immolation, experiencing *ekstasis* in the process. Nevertheless, hidden within the subtle leitmotif of martyrdom was the equally subtle presence of pride.

Deborah—the visionary, the thinking/feeling type—was unique. Open to earthly and divine worlds, she was pragmatic in her evaluation of political, judicial, military, and psychological matters. In touch with her inner voice—emerging as it does from the Self or the god within—she, like the biblical prophets, was *conscious* of her course in life. As a poet, Deborah verbalized her emotions, sensations, and thoughts—musically, rhythmically, and visually.

So traumatized was Dido by the demise of her husband that she remained unable to function and was driven into the depths of her subliminal world. She had heeded the emerging dream images that encouraged her to leave her native land. Once in Carthage, she had worked to transform the barren land into a magnificent cultural center, and in the process discovered her creative and organizational abilities. A victim of passion, however, she lost touch with reality. Camilla the Amazon, a lover of life, sports, and battle, stepping out of her usual behavioral pattern focused but for a second on a distracting object, and was killed. Decentered and destabilized, both Dido and Camilla faltered and failed.

How many mothers identify with their daughters? And daughters with their mothers? Neither lives out her individual destiny; neither may be called a *whole* being. Herodias and Salome were appendages of each other—the daughter, a nonperson, remaining a one-sided mirror image of the unfulfilled mother. Spawned in conflictual times, these incomplete women succumbed to the pull and tug of the patriarchal asceticism that opposed so-called feminine license.

Amaterasu the sun goddess—an oblique and highly complex figure for Westerners—underscores the inability of contemporary societies to relate to nature. The product of an earth-oriented philosophy of life, this ecological goddess not only spread her light throughout the world but also revealed intriguing personality traits: patience, generosity, strength, sensitivity, and explosive anger when justifiable.

The fragmented nature of Chinese goddesses encouraged me to focus on the accomplishments of several divinities: Nü-Kua, the creatrix of humankind and savior of her creatures from cosmic catastrophe; Hsi Wang Mu, the purveyor of the elixir of immortality; Ch'ang-O, the beautiful goddess of the moon; Pi-hia Yuan-kun, or holy mother; Kuan Yin, the goddess of compassion. Each, endowed with a personality of her own, not only fulfilled a function in the society that called her into existence but spoke to diverse communities as well.

Sita and Rama are ideals of the prototypal married couple. Rama is the paradigm of the hero-king; Sita, of the perfect wife, whose destiny was tragic but whose self-abnegation and loyalty to her husband for generations set the hearts and minds of the Indian population aglow—and still do. Unlike other Hindu wives of that era and ours, Sita was not her husband's appendage. An anomaly, she stood *her* ground, courageously championing her own values. Authentic, dauntless, and great-heartedly, she is for me the *real* heroine/hero of the *Ramayana*. And she remains an inspiration for many in our contemporary world!

NOTES

Chapter 1. Isis: Harmony of Flesh/Spirit/Logos

1. According to the Pyramid Texts, Osiris had been murdered; in keeping with "Memphite Theology," he had drowned.

2. Parallels have been made between the raising of the *djed* pillar within which Osiris's body rested, the chaining of Prometheus to a pillar in the Caucasus, and Christ's crucifixion on the wooden cross (Neumann 1954, 250).

3. For others, Horus's birth was the result of parthenogenesis.

4. In the western church Mary was replaced by the institution of the Church, as is evidenced by the priest celebrating his first Mass: "for it takes the form of a wedding in which he is the bridegroom, and instead of a human girl he marries the Church. He is the bride of God; he is feminine and the bride of Christ. . . . If he understands what he is doing, it is a great experience of totality, reached by the painful and terrible sacrifice of sexual life" (Franz 1970, 11:13ff.).

5. Secret—even personal—names in ancient times represented both the living person and his or her soul. Of such extreme importance were cognomens that one of the two names given Egyptians remained secret: to reveal a name empowered strangers to take possession of that person. When names were pronounced it was believed that the rhythms and sounds emitted took on creative or representational powers: after the Egyptian sun god Ra had uttered his secret name, he brought forth the world. Because God's name for the Hebrews was charged with infinite energy, it remains unknown. In Islamic tradition, the Great Name *al-ismu'l-a'zam* represents divinity's hidden essence.

Chapter 2. Enuma Elish: *The Feminine Maligned*

1. These are exactly the words Savonarola used in his attacks from the pulpit against the city of Florence, personified as an abominable woman.

2. The translation is from O'Flaherty 1981.

3. In references to the *Enuma Elish,* abbreviated in the text as *E.E.,* the first number is the tablet number, the second number is that of the verse, and the third that of the page. The translation is taken from Heidel 1951.

4. Henceforth, all shrines devoted to the cult of Ea and those of other gods were likewise called Apsu.

Chapter 3. Deborah: *Judge/Prophet/Poet/Military Leader*

1. Some scholars, including Pfeiffer, claim that Deborah was not the author of the ode.

2. Quotations from the Bible use the Jewish Publication Society version, 5708–1948.

3. The actual fighting occurred on the plain of Megiddo and Jezreel, near the river Kishon to the north of Carmel. Prior to the outbreak of hostilities, such fortresses as Taanach and Megiddo had impeded communication among the Israelite tribes. Looked upon as barriers, they accounted significantly for the lack of cohesion among the Israelite communities, which only rarely, during extreme emergencies, achieved a semblance of unity.

Chapter 4. Euripides' Iphigenia: *Marriage or Sacrificial Altar?*

1. The translations of *Iphigenia in Aulis,* abbreviated as *I.* in the text are from Euripides 1977. The numbers following *I.* are the line numbers.

2. The translations of the *Iliad* quoted in this chapter are taken from Homer 1961.

3. Frequently related to Persephone's rape/marriage by Pluto.

Chapter 5. Herodias/Salome: *Mother/Daughter Identification*

1. Translations of Josephus's *Jewish Antiquities* used in the text are from Josephus 1965.

2. John's notion of baptism "in the wilderness," and of "baptism of repentance for the remission of sins" is reminiscent of Essenian and Judaic (Isaiah) rituals.

> Wash you, make you clean; put away the evil of your doings from before mine eyes; cease to do evil;
> Learn to do well; seek judgment, relieve the oppressed, judge the fatherless, plead for the widow. (Isa.1:16–17)

3. Whether John was an Essene or a dissident Essene is not known. What he preached, however, was militant asceticism, resembling in many instances the Essenian *Manual of Discipline,* which called for reward for the righteous ("Sons of Light") and punishment for the wicked ("Sons of Darkness"). Such a credo allowed believers to bear the pain of this earth while anticipating some future beatitude.

4. Antipas's disordered mental condition (his father, it is thought, had become insane at the end of his days), which was given as the reason for his heinous deed, also served to elicit pity from the reader.

Chapter 6. Virgil's Aeneid: *Let Us Sing of Arms and Women*

1. The Aeneas myth was also treated by the Greek historian Timaeus (365–260 B.C.E.), the Latin playwright Naevius (270–204 B.C.E.), who fought in the First Punic War, and Pompeius Trogus, who wrote during the Augustan era. Translatons of passages from the *Aeneid* quoted in this chapter are from Virgil 1981.

2. Carthage, a colony of Phoenician Tyre, was founded in 814 B.C.E. After the downfall of Tyre (seventh century B.C.E.), the Carthaginians subdued North Africa's native tribes, including the Libyans and the Numidians. They increased their power on land and commercially on the seas. Extending their rule to include southern Sardinia and southern Spain, as well as the western part of Sicily, they clashed with the Greeks and finally, with Rome, after Rome consented to help liberate Messene from Carthaginian domination. Carthaginian heroes, such as Hamilcar and Hannibal, were known for their deeds of valor. Carthage became a Roman province; Caesar colonized the territory; and Augustus encouraged the settlement there of new inhabitants.

3. The horse sacrifice practiced in ancient Rome, identified as the "October-Horse," required that the animal be sacrificed following a chariot race on the Campus Martius. Not only does this practice identify the animal with fertility rites but, more importantly for our purposes, the circling of the horse during the ritual suggests the circularity of both the course of the year and the nature of an all-powerful fate (Herzog 1967, 69).

4. The translation, by Philip Vellacott, is from Aeschylus 1989.

Chapter 7. Japan's Sun Goddess: The Divine Amaterasu

1. Translations of quotations from the *Nihongi* are taken from Aston 1984.

2. The word Shinto comes from *shin* (in Chinese, *shen:* unfathomable spiritual power, superhuman or godlike nature or being) and *do* or *to* (in Chinese, *tao:* way, path, or teaching). Kitagawa 1987, 139.

3. Such activity is reminiscent of the Hindu myth of the churning of the ocean myth of milk (see chapter 9).

4. Translations of passages of the *Kojiki* are taken from Chamberlain 1993.

5. The Fire God was deeply feared during windy seasons in Japan, since most houses were built of highly flammable wood. Complex ceremonies enacted at shrines required that a pure fire—the embodiment of the god—be made by a priest through friction (by rubbing two pieces of wood, hard stone, or steel together). On New Year's Day, the faithful make their way to the shrine, receive the pure fire directly from the priest, which they then take home and use to light carefully the fire in their hearths, believing it will protect them throughout the year. The emperor's food must also be cooked in this pure flame (*New Larousse Encyclopedia of Mythology*, 8th ed., s.v. "Japanese Mythology").

6. In time, Izanagi, having completed his divine task, constructed an abode for himself "of gloom in the island of Ahaji, where he dwelt forever in silence and concealment" (*N*. 1.34).

7. A fertility ceremony known as the Shinto Homan Matsuri is celebrated each spring (15 March) to this day by priests (Tagata Shrine in Komaki City near Nagoya). Its origins date back approximately twelve hundred years, when prayers in this rice-farming area were offered for a good rice crop at the outset of the planting season. While the Tagata Jinja section of the shrine, identified with the male, is dedicated to fertility, the Ogata Jinja, another part of the shrine, celebrates female fertility. On the morning of the festival, a labial-shaped tree trunk, enshrined in a sacred palanquin, is paraded through the streets near the sanctuary and its environs. In the afternoon procession, the giant phallus, borne by eight men dressed in the white robes of Shinto priests, is carried through the rice fields behind the shrine. The senior priest leading the procession throws handfuls of rice, like holy water, to purify the way. Each of the several Shinto maidens following the procession hugs a two-foot-long wooden phallus. After walking about twenty yards, the priests put the phallus down, then it is blessed by the owner of the field, who in turn pours sake for the members of the group. Once the procession is over, the sacred phallus is brought to rest inside the shrine until it is bought by a bidder acceptable to the Shinto clergy. The new owner must treat this sacred object with proper care, continuously purifying and paying it homage. Never again must it be put on public display. *Week Ender*, 15 February 1974, i, quoted in Knapp 1992b, 194.

8. Japanese theater is said to have originated from this event. Amaterasu's withdrawal into her cave may be identified with an eclipse of the sun.

9. A rope, symbolizing the one used to prevent Amaterasu from withdrawing into her cave again, is tied around trees at Shinto shrines. At Ise "it stretches across a ravine, through which the sun is seen and adored at dawn. The straw is pulled about by the roots." Mackenzie 1994, 369.

Chapter 8. China's Fragmented Goddess Images

1. The translation, by Lau, is from Lao Tzu 1963.
2. The translation, also by Lau, is from Confucius 1979.
3. Quotations of the *Shan Hai Ching* are taken from Cheng, Pai Cheng, and Them 1985.
4. In pre-Chou times (1122–255 B.C.E.), red, identified with the female, represented creative and sexual power; white, weakness and death.

Chapter 9. *The* Ramayana: *Sita Sanctified*

1. The following abbreviations are used in this chapter: *R. V.* = *The Rig Veda; R.* = *The Ramayana of Valmiki.* The number sequences refer to book, chapter, and verse. Translations are from O'Flaherty 1981 and Valmiki 1984, 1986, 1991, respectively.
2. That Kaikeyi had been on the battlefield suggests that she, and most probably other women of her class, had not only been educated in the military arts but had had the strength and intelligence to take her husband to safety during the fighting.
3. In the *Mahabharata*, polyandry was practiced by Draupadi, the wife of five Pandava brothers. It was practiced also in some communities in Kerala, in the foothills of the Himalayas, as well as among non-Aryan tribes in South India.
4. Some scholars suggest that Sita established the custom of suttee.
5. Nor has Rama's attitude toward Sita ceased to trouble even modern-day readers of the *Ramayana*. Why, for example, had Rama, while allowing Sita to undergo her horrendous ordeal by fire, overlooked the moral lapses of other wives toward their husbands as depicted in the *Ramayana*? Even the gods found it difficult to explain his actions. Had Rama lost sight of his divine origins, some asked, and reacted with the limited vision of a mortal?

BIBLIOGRAPHY

Aeschylus. 1989. *The Oresteian Trilogy.* Translated by Philip Vellacott. Harmondsworth, U.K.: Penguin Books.

Albright, William F. 1963. *The Archaeology of Palestine.* Baltimore: Penguin.

Allan, Sarah. 1981. "Sons of Suns: Myth and Totemism in Early China." *Bulletin of the School of Oriental and African Studies* 44:290–326.

Altekar, A. S. 1983. *The Position of Women in Hindu Civilization: From Prehistoric Times to the Present Day.* Delhi: Motilal Banarsidass.

Archer, Léonie J. 1983. "The Role of Jewish Women in the Religion, Ritual and Cult of Graeco-Roman Palestine." In *Images of Women in Antiquity,* edited by Averil Cameron and Amélie Kuhrt. Detroit, Mich.: Wayne State University Press.

Aschkenasy, Nehama. 1986. *Eve's Journey.* Philadelphia: University of Pennsylvania Press.

Aston, W. G. 1977. *A History of Japanese Literature.* Tokyo: Charles E. Tuttle.

———. 1984a. Foreword to *Nihongi,* translated by W. G. Aston. Tokyo: Charles E. Tuttle.

———, trans. 1984b. *Nihongi.* Tokyo: Charles E. Tuttle.

Bachofen, J. J. 1973. *Myth, Religion, and Mother Right.* Translated by Ralph Manheim. Princeton: Princeton University Press.

Bal, Mieke. 1988. *Murder and Difference: Gender, Genre, and Scholarship on Sisera's Death.* Translated by Matthew Gumpert. Bloomington: Indiana University Press.

Ballou, Robert O. 1945. *Shinto.* New York: Viking.

Balsdon, J. P. V. D. 1962. *Roman Women: Their History and Habits.* London: The Bodley Head.

Baron, Salo W. 1952. *A Social and Religious History of the Jews.* Philadelphia: The Jewish Publication Society of America.

Barrett, William. 1962. *Irrational Man.* Garden City, N.Y.: Doubleday Anchor.

249

Baurain, Claude, and Corinne Bonnet. 1992. *Les Phéniciens: Marins des trois continents*. Paris: Armand Colin.

Birrell, Anne. 1994. *Chinese Mythology*. Baltimore: The Johns Hopkins University Press.

Bloomfield, Maurice, trans. 1967. *Hymns of the Atharva-Veda*. Vol. 42 of *Sacred Books of the East*, edited by F. Max Müller. Delhi: Motilal Banarsidass.

Bodde, Derk. 1981. *Essays on Chinese Civilization*. Edited and introduced by Charles Le Blanc and Dorothy Borei. Princeton: Princeton University Press.

Bodkin, Maud. 1965. *Archetypal Patterns in Poetry*. London: Oxford University Press.

Brazell, Karen, trans. 1973. *The Confessions of Lady Nijo*. Stanford, Calif.: Stanford University Press.

Buber, Martin. 1967. *Kingship of God*. Translated by Richard Scheimann. Atlantic Highlands, N.J.: Humanities Press International.

———. 1970. "Symbolic and Sacramental Existence in Judaism." In *Eranos Yearbooks*, 4:168–85. Reprint, Princeton: Princeton University Press. Originally published in 1931.

Budge, E. A. Wallis. 1967. *The Egyptian Book of the Dead*. Reprint, New York: Dover Publications. Originally published in 1895.

———. 1973. *Osiris and the Egyptian Resurrection*. Vols. 1 and 2. Reprint, New York: Dover Publications. Originally published in 1911.

Buhler, Georg, trans. 1967. *The Laws of Manu*. Vol. 25 in *Sacred Books of the East*, edited by F. Max Müller. Delhi: Motilal Banarsidass.

Buitenen, J. A. B. van. 1978. *"The Indian Epic," in the Literatures of India*. Chicago: University of Chicago Press.

Bunce, William K. 1970. *Religions in Japan*. Tokyo: Charles E. Tuttle.

Buonaiuti, Ernesto. 1970. "Christ and St. Paul." In *Eranos Yearbooks*, vol. 6, translated by Ralph Manheim. Princeton: Princeton University Press.

Burkert, Walter. 1983. *Homo Necans. The Anthropology of Ancient Greek Sacrificial Ritual and Myth*. Translated by Peter Bing. Berkeley: University of California Press.

———. 1985. *Greek Religion*. Translated by John Raffan. Cambridge: Harvard University Press.

Cairns, Francis. 1989. *Virgil's Augustan Epic*. Cambridge: Cambridge University Press.

Cesare, Mario A. 1974. *The Altar and the City*. New York: Columbia University Press.

Chamberlain, Basil Hall, trans. 1993. *Kojiki*. Tokyo: Charles E. Tuttle.

Cheng Hsiao-Chieh; Pai Cheng Hui-Chen; and Kenneth L. Thern, trans. 1985. *Shan Hai Ching*. Taipei: National Institute for Compilation and Translation.

Chernin, Kim. 1987. *Reinventing Eve: Modern Woman in Search of Herself*. New York: Times Books.

Christie, Anthony. 1985. *Chinese Mythology*. New York: Peter Bedrick Books.

Chuang Tzu. 1964. *Chuang Tzu.* Translated by Burton Watson. New York: Columbia University Press.

Clark, Rundle T. R. 1991. *Myth and Symbol in Ancient Egypt.* London: Thames and Hudson.

Confucius. 1979. *The Analects.* Translated by D. C. Lau. Harmondsworth, U.K.: Penguin Books.

Cohn-Sherbok, Dan. 1988. *The Jewish Heritage.* London: Basil Blackwell.

Coomaraswamy, Ananda, and Sister Nivedita. 1967. *Myths of the Hindus and Buddhists.* New York: Dover Publications.

Corbier, Mireille. 1991. "Family Behavior of the Roman Aristocracy, Second Century B.C.–Third Century A.D." Translated by Ann Cremin. In *Women's History and Ancient History,* edited by Sarah B. Pomeroy. Chapel Hill: The University of North Carolina Press.

Cowan, Lyn. 1982. *Masochism: A Jungian View.* Dallas, Texas: Spring Publications.

Craigie, P. C. 1977. "Three Ugaritic Notes on the Song of Deborah." *Journal for the Study of the Old Testament* 2:33–49.

Craven, Roy C. 1976. *Indian Art.* New York: Praeger.

Czaja, Michael. 1974. *Gods of Myth: Stone Phallicism in Japanese Folk Religion.* Tokyo: Weatherhill.

Davis, Hadland F. 1989. *Myths and Legends of Japan.* Singapore: Graham Brash.

de Bary, Wm. Theodore, ed. 1958. *Sources of Indian Tradition.* Vol. 1. New York: Columbia University Press.

———. 1960. *Sources of Chinese Tradition.* New York: Columbia University Press.

———. 1964. *Sources of Japanese Tradition.* Vol. 1. Compiled by Ryusaka Tsunoda, Theodore de Bary, and Donald Keene. New York: Columbia University Press.

Dhruvarajan, Vanaja. 1989. *Hindu Women and the Power of Ideology.* Granby, Mass: Bergin and Garvey.

Dimmitt, Cornelia. 1986. "Sita: Fertility Goddess and *Sakti.*" In *The Divine Consort: Rhada and the Goddesses of India,* edited by John Stratton Hawley and Donna Marie Wulff, 211–22. Boston: Beacon Press.

Donovan, Josephine. 1991. *Feminist Theory.* New York: Continuum.

Downing, Christine. 1981. *The Goddess: Mythological Images of the Feminine.* New York: Crossroad.

Dubois, Claude-Gilbert. 1986. *Une Mythologie de l'inceste. Les transgressions familiales et leurs métamorphoses mythiques dans la famille des Hérodes.* Bordeaux: Eidolon.

Dumézil, Georges. 1970. *The Destiny of the Warrior.* Translated by Alf Hiltebeitel. Chicago: University of Chicago Press.

Dupont-Sommer, A. 1973. *The Essene Writings from Qumran.* Translated by G. Vermes. Gloucester, Mass.: Peter Smith.

Earhart, Byron H. 1969. *Japanese Religion: Unity and Diversity.* Belmont, Calif.: Dickenson.

Easwaran, Eknath, trans. 1987. *The Upanishads.* Berkeley, Calif.: The Nigiri Press.

Eberhard, Wolfram. 1987. *A History of China.* Berkeley: University of California Press.

———. 1989. *A Dictionary of Chinese Symbols.* London: Routledge.

Edinger, Edward. 1978. *Melville's Moby-Dick.* New York: New Directions.

———. n.d. "Outline of Analytical Psychology." Unpublished paper.

———. 1988. *Anatomy of the Psyche.* La Salle, Ill.: Open Court.

Eliade, Mircea. 1958. *Rites and Symbols of Initiation.* Translated by Willard R. Trask. New York: Harper and Row.

———. 1960. *Myths, Dreams, and Mysteries.* New York: Harper and Row.

———. 1971. *The Forge and the Crucible.* Translated by Stephen Corrin. New York: Harper and Row.

———. 1974a. *The Myth of the Eternal Return.* Translated by Willard R. Trask. Princeton: Princeton University Press.

———. 1974b. *Patterns in Comparative Religion.* Translated by Rosemary Sheed. New York: New American Library.

———. 1979. *Histoires des croyances et des idées religieuses.* Vol. 1. Paris: Payot.

———. 1980. *Histoires des croyances et des idées religieuses.* Vols. 2 and 3. Paris: Payot.

Euripides. 1977. *Ten Plays.* Translated by Moses Hadas and John McClean. New York: Bantam Books.

Evans, George E., and David Thomson. 1972. *The Leaping Hare.* London: Faber.

Faber, Phillip A., and Graham S. Saayman. 1984. "On the Relation of the Doctrines of Yoga to Jung's Psychology." In *Jung in Modern Perspective,* edited by Renos K. Papadopoulos and Graham S. Saayman, 165–81. Middlesex, England: Wildwood House.

Fantar, Muhamed. 1970. *Carthage. La prestigieuse cité d'Elissa.* Tunis: Maison Tunisienne de l'Edition.

Fau, Guy. 1978. *L'Emancipation féminine dans la Rome antique.* Paris: Société d'édition "Les Belles Lettres."

Field, Stephen. 1986. *Tian Wen.* New York: New Directions.

Finley, M. I. 1972. *The Ancient Greeks.* New York: Viking.

Flusser, David. 1988. *Judaism and the Origins of Christianity.* Jerusalem: Magnes Press.

Foley, Helen P. *1985. Ritual and Irony: Poetry and Sacrifice in Euripides.* Ithaca: Cornell University Press.

Franz, Marie-Louise von. 1970. *Apuleius' Golden Ass.* New York: Spring Publications.

———. 1972. *Creation Myths.* Zurich: Spring Publications.

———. 1974. *Shadow and Evil in Fairytales.* Zurich: Spring Publications.

———. 1980. *Projection and Re-Collection in Jungian Psychology.* Translated by William H. Kennedy. London: Open Court.

———. 1986. *On Dreams and Death.* Translated by Emmanuel X. Kennedy and Vernon Brooks. Boston: Shambhala.

Fritsch, Charles T. 1956. *The Qumran Community*. New York: Macmillan.

Gardiner, Sir Alan. 1972. *Egypt of the Pharaohs*. Oxford: Oxford University Press.

Gaster, Theodor H., ed. and trans. 1957. *The Dead Sea Scriptures*. Garden City, N.Y.: Doubleday Anchor.

Ginzberg, Louis. 1956. *Legends of the Bible*. Philadelphia: Jewish Publication Society.

Girardot, N. J. 1983. *Myth and Meaning in Early Taoism*. Berkeley: University of California Press.

Gordis, Robert. 1971. *Poets, Prophets, and Sages*. Bloomington: Indiana University Press.

Gordon, R. L. 1981. *Myth, Religion and Society*. Cambridge: Cambridge University Press.

Granet, Marcel. 1975. *The Religion of the Chinese People*. Translated by Maurice Freedman. New York: Harper and Row.

Graves, Robert. 1966. *The White Goddess*. New York: Farrar, Straus, and Giroux.

Grayzel, Solomon. 1970. *A History of the Jews*. Philadelphia: Jewish Publication Society.

Hall, John W. 1970. *Japan from Prehistory to Modern Times*. New York: Delacorte Press.

Hani, J. 1976. *La religion égyptienne dans la pensée de Plutarque*. Paris: Société d'Edition "Les belles lettres."

Harding, Esther. 1965. *The Parental Image*. New York: G. P. Putnam's Sons.

————. 1971. *Woman's Mysteries*. New York: G. P. Putnam's Sons.

Harrison, Jane. 1966. *Epilegomena to the Study of Greek Religion and Themis*. New Hyde Park, N.Y.: University Books.

Hart, George. 1990. *Egyptian Myths*. Austin: University of Texas Press.

Heidel, Alexander. 1951. *The Babylonian Genesis*. Chicago: University of Chicago Press.

Henry, Elisabeth. 1989. *The Vigour of Prophecy*. Carbondale: Southern Illinois University Press.

Herbert, Jean. 1967. *Shinto: At the Fountainhead of Japan*. New York: Stein and Day.

Herodotus. 1972. *The Histories*. Translated by Aubrey de Sélincourt. Harmondsworth, U.K.: Penguin.

Herrmann, Siegfried. 1981. *A History of Israel in Old Testament Times*. Philadelphia: Fortress Press.

Hervouet, Yves. 1964. *Un poète de cour sous les Han: Sseu-ma Siang-jou*. Paris.

Herzog, Edgar. 1967. *Psyche and Death*. Translated by David Coxe and Eugene Rolfe. New York: Putnam's Sons.

Hillman, James. 1980. *Facing the Gods*. Irving, Texas: Spring Publications.

Hoehner, Harold W. 1980. *Herod Antipas*. Grand Rapids, Mich.: Zondervan.

Holtom, D. C. 1965. *The National Faith of Japan*. New York: Paragon Book Reprint Corp.

Homer. 1961. *The Iliad*. Translated by Richmond Lattimore. Chicago: Phoenix
    Books.

Hopkins, Thomas J. 1971. *The Hindu Religious Tradition*. Encino, Calif.:
    Dickenson.

Hori, Ichiro. 1969. *Folk Religion in Japan*. Chicago: University of Chicago Press.

Hugues, Dennis D. 1991. *Human Sacrifice in Ancient Greece*. London: Routledge.

Hunt, William H. 1973. *Forms of Glory*. Carbondale: Southern Illinois University
    Press.

Irigaray, Luce. 1985. *This Sex Which Is Not One*. Translated by Catherine Porter.
    Ithaca: Cornell University Press.

Jacobi, Mario. 1985. *Longing for Paradise*. Translated by Myron B. Gubitz. Boston:
    Sigo Press.

Jacobi, Yolande. 1959. *Complex Archetype Symbol in the Psychology of C. G. Jung*.
    Translated by Ralph Manheim. Princeton: Princeton University Press.

Josephus. *Jewish Antiquities*. 1965. Translated by Louis H. Feldman. Edited by G.
    P. Goold. Cambridge: Harvard University Press.

———. 1959. *The Jewish War*. Translated by G. A. Williamson. Harmondsworth,
    U.K.: Penguin.

Jung, C. G. 1953. *Collected Works*. Vol. 7. Translated by R. F. C. Hull. New
    York: Pantheon Books.

———. 1956. *Collected Works*. Vol. 5. New York: Pantheon Books.

———. 1963a. *Collected Works*. Vol. 11. Translated by R. F. C. Hull. New York:
    Pantheon Books.

———. 1963b. *Collected Works*. Vol. 14. Translated by R. F. C. Hull. New York:
    Pantheon Books.

———. 1967. *Collected Works*. Vol. 13. Translated by R. F. C. Hull. Princeton:
    Princeton University Press.

———. 1969. *Collected Works*. Vol. 8. Translated by R. F. C. Hull. Princeton:
    Princeton University Press.

———. 1988. *Nietzsche's Zarathustra*. Edited by James L. Jarrett. Princeton:
    Princeton University Press.

———. 1990. *Collected Works*. Vol. 6. Translated by H. G. Baynes. Revised by
    R. F. C. Hull. Princeton: Princeton University Press.

Jung, C. G., and C. Kerényi. 1969. *Essays on a Science of Mythology*. Princeton:
    Princeton University Press.

Kaufmann, Walter. 1976. *Religions in Four Dimensions*. New York: Reader's Digest
    Press.

Kawai, Hayao. 1988. *The Japanese Psyche*. Translated by Hayao Kawai and Sachiko
    Reece. Dallas, Texas: Spring Publications.

Kerényi, Carl. 1980. "A Mythological Image of Girlhood: Artemis." In *Facing the
    Gods*, edited by James Hillman, 39–46. Irving, Texas: Spring Publications.

———. 1963. *Prometheus: Archetypal Image of Human Existence*. Princeton:
    Princeton University Press.

Kinsley, David. 1988. *Hindu Goddesses*. Berkeley: University of California Press.

Kitagawa, Joseph M. 1987. *On Understanding Japanese Religion*. Princeton: Princeton University Press.

Kitto, H. D. F. 1958. *The Greeks*. London: Penguin Books.

Kluger, Rivkah Scharf. 1991. *The Archetypal Significance of Gilgamesh*. Einsiedeln, Switzerland: Daimon Verlag.

Knapp, Bettina L. 1992a. *Images of Chinese Women*. Troy, N.Y.: The Whitston Press.

———. 1992b. *Images of Japanese Women*. Troy, N.Y.: The Whitston Press.

———. 1995. *Manna and Mystery*. Chicago: Chiron Press.

Kraemer, Ross. 1988. *Maenads Martyrs Matrons Monastics*. Philadelphia: Fortress Press.

———. 1992. *Her Share of the Blessings*. New York: Oxford University Press.

Kramer, Samuel Noah. 1969. *The Sacred Marriage Rite*. Bloomington: Indiana University Press.

———. 1972. *Sumerian Mythology*. Philadelphia: University of Pennsylvania Press.

———. 1975. *Sumerian Culture and Society*. Philippines: Cummings Publishing Co.

———. 1981. *History Begins at Sumer*. Philadelphia: University of Pennsylvania Press.

Kramrisch, Stella. 1975. "The Indian Great Goddess." *History of Religions* 14, no. 4:235–65.

Kuan Yin: The Legends of the Eight Immortals. 1944. Los Angeles: Quon-Quon Company.

Kuryluk, Ewa. 1987. *Salome and Judas in the Cave of Sex*. Evanston, Ill.: Northwestern University Press.

Labat, René. 1939. *Le caractère religieux de la royauté Assyro-Babylonienne*. Paris: Adrien-Maisonneuve.

Lagerwey, John. 1987. *Taoist Ritual in Chinese Society and History*. New York: Macmillan.

Lamy, Lucie. 1991. *Egyptian Mysteries*. London: Thames and Hudson.

Lao Tzu. 1963. *Tao Te Ching*. Translated by D. C. Lau. London: Penguin.

Larrington, Carolyne, ed. 1992. *The Feminist Companion to Mythology*. New York: Harper Collins.

Lauter, Estella, and Carol S. Rupprecht, eds. 1985. *Feminist Archetypal Theory*. Knoxville: University of Tennessee Press.

Lefèvre, Gustave. 1976. *Romans et contes égyptiens*. Paris: Librairie d'Amérique et d'Orient.

Lefkowitz, Mary R. 1986. *Women in Greek Myth*. Baltimore: The Johns Hopkins University Press.

Lefkowitz, Mary R., and Maureen B. Fant. 1992. *Women's Life in Greece and Rome*. Baltimore: The Johns Hopkins University Press.

Legge, James, trans. 1967. *The Book of Poetry (Shih ching)*. New York: Paragon Book Reprint Corporation.

————. 1962. *The Texts of Taoism: The Tao Te Ching of Lao Tzu; The Writings of Chuang Tzu.* Vol. 1. New York: Dover Publications.

Lehmann, W. P. 1988. "The Quality of Presence." *World Literature Today* 62, no. 4 (autumn): 578–81.

Lévi-Strauss, Claude. 1969. *The Raw and the Cooked.* Translated by John Weightman and Doreen Weightman. New York: Harper and Row.

Lichtheim, Miriam. 1975. *Ancient Egyptian Literature.* Vol. 1. Berkeley: University of California Press.

————. 1976. *Ancient Egyptian Literature.* Vol. 2. Berkeley: University of California Press.

Lieh-tzu. 1990. *The Book of Lieh-tzu.* Translated by A. C. Graham. New York: Columbia University Press.

Loewe, Michael. 1979. *Ways to Paradise: The Chinese Quest for Immortality.* London: George Allen & Unwin.

Mackenzie, Donald A. 1994. *Myths of China and Japan.* New York: Gramercy Books.

Major, John S. 1993. *Heaven and Earth in Early Han Thought.* Albany: State University of New York Press.

Malamud, René. 1980. "The Amazon Problem." In *Facing the Gods,* edited by James Hillman. Irving, Texas: Spring Publications.

Malinowski, Bronislaw. 1954. *Magic, Science and Religion.* Garden City, N.Y.: Doubleday Anchor.

Margolis, Max L., and Alexander Marx. 1980. *A History of the Jewish People.* New York: Atheneum.

Maspero, Henri. 1924. "Légendes mythologiques dans le *Chou King.*" *Journal asiatique* 204 (January–March): 1–100.

————. 1963. "The Mythology of Modern China." In *Asiatic Mythology.* New York: Thomas Y. Crowell.

————. 1981. *Taoism and Chinese Religion.* Translated by Frank A. Kierman Jr. Amherst: University of Massachusetts Press.

Mathieu, Rémi. 1983. *Etude sur la mythologie et l'ethnologie de la Chine ancienne.* Paris: Institut des Hautes Etudes Chinoises.

————. 1989. *Anthologie des mythes et légendes de la Chine ancienne.* Paris: Gallimard.

McCullough, W. S., ed. 1963. *Essays in Honor of T. J. Meek.* Toronto: University of Toronto Press.

Mercatante, Anthony S. 1978. *Who's Who in Egyptian Mythology.* New York: Clarkson N. Potter.

Mies, Maria. 1980. *Indian Women and Patriarchy.* New Delhi: Concept Publishing Company.

Moore, Rev. George F. 1895. *A Critical and Exegetical Commentary on Judges.* Edinburgh: T. & T. Clark.

Morris, Ivan, trans. 1971. *As I Crossed a Bridge of Dreams (The Diary of Sarashina)*. New York: The Dial Press.

Murray, D. F. 1979. "Narrative Structure and Technique in the Deborah-Barak Story." In *Studies in the Historical Books of the Old Testament,* edited by J. A. Emerton. Leiden: E. J. Brill.

Murray, Gilbert. 1913. *Euripides and his Age*. New York: Henry Holt.

Nanda, B. R., ed. 1976. *Indian Women From Purdah to Modernity*. Bombay: Vikas Publishing House.

Needham, Joseph. 1969. *Science and Civilisation in China*. Vol. 2. Cambridge: Cambridge University Press.

————. 1983. *Science and Civilisation in China*. Vol. 5. Cambridge: Cambridge University Press.

Neumann, Erich. 1954. *The Origins and History of Consciousness*. Translated by R. F. C. Hull. New York: Pantheon Books.

————. 1956. "The Moon and Matriarchal Consciousness." *Spring*.

————. 1963. *The Great Mother*. Translated by Ralph Manheim. New York: Pantheon Books.

Niditch, Susan. 1989. "Eroticism and Death in the Tale of Jael." In *Gender and Difference in Ancient Israel,* edited by Peggy L. Day. Minneapolis, Minn.: Fortress Press.

Nietzsche, Friedrich. 1937. *The Philosophy of Nietzsche*. New York: The Modern Library.

Oates, Joan. 1986. *Babylon*. London: Thames and Hudson.

O'Flaherty, Wendy Doniger. 1980. *Women, Androgynes, and Other Mythical Beasts*. Chicago: University of Chicago Press.

————, trans. 1978. *Hindu Myths*. New York: Penguin.

————. 1981. *The Rig Veda*. Edited by Wendy Doniger O'Flaherty. New York: Penguin.

O'Hara, James J. 1990. *Death and the Optimistic Prophecy in Vergil's Aeneid*. Princeton: Princeton University Press.

Orenstein, Gloria Feman. 1990. *The Reflowering of the Goddess*. New York: Pergamon Press.

Otto, Walter F. 1979. *The Homeric Gods*. Translated by Moses Hadas. London: Thames and Hudson.

Paglia, Camille. 1991. *Sexual Personae*. New York: Vintage Books.

Parrinder, Geoffrey. 1980. *Sex in the World's Religions*. New York: Oxford University Press.

Parthasarathy, R. 1988. "*The Chessmaster and His Moves:* The Novel as Metaphysics." *World Literature Today* 62, no. 4 (autumn): 561–66.

Patai, Raphael. 1967. *The Hebrew Goddess*. New York: Ktav Publishing House.

Paul, Diana, Y. 1985. *Women in Buddhism*. Berkeley: University of California Press.

Perera, Sylvia Brinton. 1981. *Descent to the Goddess.* Toronto: Inner City Books.

Perret, Jacques. 1942. *Les Origines de la légende troyenne de Rome.* Paris: Société d'édition "Les belles lettres."

Perry, John Weir. 1989. *The Far Side of Madness.* Dallas, Texas: Spring Publications.

Pfeiffer, Robert H. 1948. *Introduction to the Old Testament.* New York: Harper and Row.

Piankoff, Alexander, trans. 1964. *The Litany of Re* . With a commentary by Alexander Piankoff. New York: Pantheon Books.

Plutarch. 1879. *Lives of Illustrious Men.* Vol. 1. Translated by John Langhorne and William Langhorne. London: Chatto and Windus.

————. 1924. *Isis et Osiris.* Traduction Mario Meunier. Paris: L'Artisan du livre.

Pomeroy, Sarah. 1975. *Goddesses, Whores, Wives, and Slaves: Women in Classical Antiquity.* New York: Schocken Books.

Pratt, Annis. 1981. *Archetypal Patterns in Women's Fiction.* Bloomington: Indiana University Press.

Pritchard, James B. 1955. *Ancient Near Eastern Texts.* Princeton: Princeton University Press.

Psichari, Jean. 1915. "Salomé et la décollation de Saint Jean-Baptiste." *Revue de l'histoire des religions* 72:131–58.

Radhakrishnan, S., ed. and trans. 1978. *The Principal Upanisads.* New York: Humanities Press.

Reis, Patricia. 1991.*Through the Goddess.* New York: Continuum.

Reischauer, Edwin O. 1946. *Japan Past and Present.* New York: Alfred A. Knopf.

————. 1974. *Japan: The Story of a Nation.* Rev. ed. Tokyo: Charles E. Tuttle.

————. 1979. *The Japanese.* Tokyo: Charles E. Tuttle.

Rexroth, Kenneth, and Ling Chung. 1972. *The Orchid Boat.* New York: Continuum.

Roth, Cecil. 1961. *History of the Jews.* New York: Schocken Books.

Roux, Georges. 1972. *Ancient Iraq.* London: Penguin.

Rowland, Benjamin. 1981. *The Pelican History of Art: The Art and Architecture of India.* New York: Penguin.

Ruether, Rosemary Radford. 1983. *Sexism and God-Talk: Toward a Feminist Theology.* Boston: Beacon Press.

Saggs, H. W. 1962. *The Greatness That Was Babylon.* New York: New American Library.

Sandars, N. K. 1971. *Poems of Heaven and Hell from Ancient Mesopotamia.* Translated and by N. K. Sandars. London: Penguin.

Schiffeler, John W. 1978. *The Legendary Creatures of the Shan Hai Ching.* Taipei: Hwa Kang Press.

Schurer, Emil. 1961. *A History of the Jewish People in the Time of Jesus.* Edited by Nahum Glatzer. New York: Schocken Books.

Sievers, Joseph. 1989. "The Role of Women in the Hasmonean Dynasty." In *Josephus, the Bible, and History*, edited by Louis H. Feldman and Gohei Hata. Detroit, Mich.: Wayne State University Press.

Singer, June. 1976. *Androgyny: Toward a New Theory of Sexuality*. Garden City, N.Y.: Doubleday Anchor.

Sokyo Ono. 1969. *Shinto the Kami Way*. Tokyo: Charles E. Tuttle.

Soren, David, Aicha ben Abed ben Khader, and Hedi Slim. 1990. *Carthage: Uncovering the Mysteries and Splendors of Ancient Tunisia*. New York: Simon and Schuster.

Soulié, Pierre. 1976. *Médecines initiatiques aux sources des psycho-thérapies*. Paris: Editeurs Epi.

Ssu-ma Ch'ien. 1969. *Shi chi (Records of the Historian)*. Translated by Burton Watson. New York: Columbia University Press.

———. 1971. *Shu Ching. (Book of History)*. A modernized edition of the translations of James Legge by Clae Waltham. Chicago: Henry Regnery.

———. 1979. *Selections from Records of the Historian*. Translated by Yang Hsien-yi and Gladys Yang. Peking: Foreign Language Press.

Stein, Murray. 1995. Foreword to *Manna and Mystery*, by Bettina L. Knapp. Chicago: Chiron Press.

Steindorff, George, and Keith C. Seele. 1971. *When Egypt Ruled the East*. Chicago: University of Chicago Press.

Stone, Merlin. 1976. *When God Was a Woman*. New York: Harcourt Brace Jovanovich.

———. 1979. *Ancient Mirrors of Womanhood*. Vol. 2. New York: Sibylline Books.

Stutley, Margaret, and James Stutley. 1984. *Harper's Dictionary of Hinduism*. New York: Harper and Row.

Suetonius. 1967. *History of Twelve Caesars*. Translated by Philemon Holland. Vol. 2. Reprint, New York: AMS Press. Originally published in 1606.

Taylor, Glen J. 1982. "The Song of Deborah and Two Canaanite Goddesses." *Journal for the Study of the Old Testament*, no. 23 (July): 374–81.

Tharu, Susie, and K. Lalita. 1991. *Women Writing in India*. Vol. 1. New York: The Feminist Press.

Thomas, Joel. 1981. *Structures de l'imaginaire dans l'Eneide*. Paris: Société d'Edition "Les belles lettres."

Thompson Laurence G. 1969. *Chinese Religion: An Introduction*. Belmont, Calif.: Dickenson.

Ulanov, A. B. 1981. *Receiving Woman*. Philadelphia: Westminster Press.

Valmiki. 1984. *The Ramayana of Valmiki*. Translated by Robert P. Goldman. Vol. 1. Princeton: Princeton University Press.

———. 1986. *The Ramayana of Valmiki*. Edited by Robert P. Goldman. Translated by Sheldon I. Pollock. Vol. 2. Princeton: Princeton University Press.

————. 1991. *The Ramayana of Valmiki.* Edited by Robert P. Goldman. Translated by Sheldon I. Pollock. Vol. 3. Princeton: Princeton University Press.

Vellacott, Phillip. 1975. *Ironic Drama: A Study of Euripides' Method and Meaning.* London: Cambridge University Press.

Vernant, Jean-Pierre. 1991. *Mortals and Immortals.* Edited by Froma I. Zeitlin, Princeton: Princeton University Press.

Vidal-Naquet, P. 1981. "Recipes for Greek Adolescence." In *Myth, Religion, and Society,* edited by R. L. Gordon. Cambridge: Cambridge University Press.

Virgil. 1981. *The Aeneid of Virgil.* Translated by Allen Mandelbaum. New York: Bantam Books.

Vyas, S. N. 1967. *India in the Ramayana Age.* Delhi: Atma Ram and Sons.

Waley, Arthur, trans. 1960. *The Book of Songs (Shih ching).* New York: Grove Press.

We Japanese. 1950. Hakone: Fujiya Hotel.

Weigle, Marta. 1982. *Spiders and Spinsters.* Albuquerque: University of New Mexico Press.

————. 1989. *Creation and Procreation.* Philadelphia: University of Pennsylvania Press.

Werner, Edward T. C. 1961. *A Dictionary of Chinese Mythology.* New York: The Julian Press.

Whitmont, Edward C. 1980. "Reassessing Femininity and Masculinity: A Critique of some Traditional Assumptions." *Quadrant* 13, no. 2 (fall): 108–21.

Wilkins, W. J. 1981. *Hindu Mythology.* Calcutta: Rupa and Co.

Williams, C. A. S. 1976. *Outlines of Chinese Symbolism and Art Motives.* New York: Dover Publications.

Williams, R. D. 1987. *The Aeneid.* London: Allen & Unwin.

Wiltshire, Susan Ford. 1989. *Public and Private in Vergil's "Aeneid."* Amherst: University of Massachusetts Press.

Wolkstein, Diane, and Samuel Noah Kramer. 1983. *Inanna Queen of Heaven and Earth.* New York: Harper and Row.

Wulff, David M. 1986. "Prolegomenon to a Psychology of the Goddess." In *The Divine Consort Radha and the Goddesses of India,* edited by John Stratton Hawley and Donna Marie Wulff, 283–97. Boston: Beacon Press.

Yacoub, Mohamed. 1982. *Le Musée du Bardo.* Tunis: Ministère des Affaires Culturelles.

Zaehner, R. C., ed. 1966. *Hindu Scriptures.* London: Everyman's Library.

INDEX

Abdon, 51

Abraham: Isaac and, 72

Achilles, 81; Clytemnestra and, 79

Actaeon, 74

Adam and Eve legend, 48–50; clay and, 150; John the Baptist and, 94–95; Nü Kwa and, 182; Salome and, 99. *See also* Eve

Aditi, 205

Aeneas, 111; *ekstasis* of, 126; in Hades, 130–31; Mercury and, 126–27; son of, 111, 112

Aeschylus, 70; *Eumenides,* 133

Agamemnon, 69, 78

Agave, 122

Agni, 233

Agrippa, 95

Akitu, 22

Alcestis, 85

Alexander the Great: Indian campaign of, 204; as Pharaoh, 3; rulers after, 88

Allah, xvii, 41

Allegory, myth vs., xii

Amaterasu, xxi, 141–67, 240–41; Artemis and, 155; birth of, 153; Brunhild and, 155; characteristics of, 141; cult of, 165–67; as fructifier, 158–61; harvest prayer to, 166–67; Persephone and, 163; as solar heroine, xvii; as stallion, 155; Susano-wo vs., 153–58; as weaver, 161–64

Amazons, xxi; mythology of, 132; Oriental, 199

Ame-waka-hiko, 164–65

Anahita, 27

Anath, 47

Androgyny: of Isis, 5; of Kuan Yin, 197; scorpion-man and, 37

Anima image: Eve as, 49; Iphigenia as, 83

Anshar, birth of, 28

Anthony, Saint, 107, 228

Antigone, 85

Antiochus IV, 89

Antipas. *See* Herod Antipas

Antipater, 89

Antony, Mark: Cleopatra and, 112; as leader, 112; Octavian and, 89–90; wife of, 114

Anu, 41; birth of, 28; god of the skies, 38

Aphrodite, 27

Apollo: Artemis and, 73, 74

Apophis, the serpent, 18

Apsu, 26; creation myth and, 28; inertia of, 29; murder of, 34; revolt against, 31–32

Archetype(s): defined, xiii–xiv; female, xx; impact of, xv

Aretas IV, 91, 101

Aristobulus, 96

Aristotle, 71

Arjuna, 224

Arkteuin, 75

Artabanus, xii

Artemis: Amaterasu and, 155; appeasement of, 69–70; Brauronia of, 75, 77; cult of, 73–76; as virgin, 73. *See also* Diana

Ascanius, 111, 112, 122

Aschkenasy, Nehama, 54

Asherah, 47

Ashtoreth, 47

Ashur, 56

Ashurbanipal, 25
Asoka, 204
Aspasia: Pericles and, 71
Astarte, 47
Atalanta, 132
Athaliah, 99
Athena, 74
Atum, 3; creation of, 5; Horus and, 13; sacred eye of, 12
Augustus. *See* Octavian.
Ayodhya, 210, 211, 236

Baal, 47; Zeus and, 89
Babylon: history of, 23; as sacred space, 42; as woman, 21–22
Babylonian captivity, 48
Bacchus, xvii
Barak: Deborah and, 45–46, 50, 52–56
Barrett, William, 110
Bear, act of, 75
Bee, 51
Bel. *See* Marduk
Belus, 117
Bhagavad Gita, 224
Bharata, 215–17, 220
Birth, miraculous, 5–7
Bodhi: defined, 143
Brauronia, of Artemis, 75, 77
Britomartis, 132
Brunhild: Amaterasu and, 155
Brutus, 112
Buber, Martin: on Deborah, 55–56; on prophecy, 58
Buddha, xvii, 204; as messianic myth, xvii; wheel of, 36
Buddhism, women in, 143–44, 172
Byblos, 8

Caesar, Julius: lineage of, 112; murder of, 112; Pompey and, 89
Calchas: Agamemnon and, 70, 79; Iphigenia and, 84
Caligula, 95–96; Suetonius on, 105
Callimachus, 74
Camilla, xxi, 132–39, 240; *ekstasis* of, 138; Mars and, 135; Metabus and, 133–35; Penthesilea and, 137; as solar heroine, xvii; Turnus and, 133, 136
Canaan, 45

Cassius, 112
Caste system, Hindu, 204
Castration: Great Mother and, 87; of Osiris, 10–11, 16; of Uranus, 30
Cato the Elder, 130
Chandragupta, 204
Chang Hua: *Po-wu-chih,* 189
Ch'ang-O, xxi, 169, 193–95, 241
Chaos, in Chinese myth, 177
Chiang T'ai-kung, 198
Chiang Yuan, 179–80
Ch'ih Yu, 173
Child, divine, xvi–xvii
Childbirth, protectress of, 169
Ch'in dynasty, 175
Chinese deities, xxi–xxii, 169–200; of creation, 41, 177–78
Chou dynasty, 174, 179
Christ. *See* Jesus
Christianity: creation myth in, 41; sacrifice in, 72
Christopher, Saint, 228
Chrysanthemum, as symbol, 142
Chuang-tzu, 179
Chuan-hsü, 183
Chung Ho Tzu: *Yü Fang Pi,* 188
Ch'u-tz'u, 184
City, as mandala, 210–11
Cleopatra, 3; Antony and, 112
Clytemnestra, 76, 79; Electra and, 99
Collective unconscious: defined, xiii; Jung on, xviii–xix; personal vs., xiv
Confessions of Lady Nijo, 142
Confucianism: phallocentric, 170, 185; teachings of, 171; women in, 143, 144, 172
Confucius, 144, 171, 179, 204
Coriolanus, 113
Cornelia, 114
Cosmas, Saint, 228
Cow: Isis as, 1, 16; Ra and, 19
Creation myth(s): Apsu and, 28; Chinese, 41, 177–78; Christian, 41; *Enuma Elish* as, 21–22; Hindu, 41; Islamic, 41; Judaic, 41; Nü Kua and, 181–85; Tiamat and, 28; water in, 26–28
Cronus, 30
Crucifixion: Pilate and, 91; Rama and, 214
Crusades: John the Baptist cult and, 88

Cult(s): of Amaterasu, 165–67; of Artemis, 73–76; fish, 11; Hindu, 204; John the Baptist, 88; of Susano-wo, 167; Tantric, 206
Cybele, 27
Cyclone, creation of, 38
Cyrus the Great, 25

Damian, Saint, 228
Damkina, Ea and, 35
Dance, of Salome, 87–88, 95, 97
Daniel, Book of, 24
Dasaratha, King, 210–11, 214–16, 224
Daughter/mother identity, 99–100, 240
Da Vinci, Leonardo, 49
Deborah, xx, 45–68, 240; archetypal analysis of, 50–52; Barak and, 45–46, 50, 52–56; as "bee," 51–52; characteristics of, 45; as cultural symbol, xvi; ectypal analysis of, 47–50; as Joan of Arc, 46, 68; as judge, 51, 56–58; as military advisor, 45–46, 50, 52–56; as poet, 59–63; as prophet, 58–59; as solar heroine, xvii; Song of, 46, 50, 51, 59–62, 68
Deer: golden, 228–30; Iphigenia and, 85
Demeter, Persephone and, 99
Deus Faber: Marduk as, 21
Dharma, 235
Diana, 115, 132. *See also* Artemis
Dido, 118–32, 240; as Carthage's founder, 119; as cultural symbol, xvi; *ekstasis* of, 126; in Hades, 130–31; Jung on, 131; as solar heroine, xvii; stallion of, 125; suicide of, 129; Venus and, 122; in Virgil, xxi, 111–12
Differentiation, psychic, xv
Diodorus, 2, 7, 10
Dionysus, xvi–xvii
Divine child myths, xvi–xvii
Djed pillar, 8–9
Dragon: as female personification, 36; Tiamat and, 21, 26, 36; Vritra, 30
Dreams: Artabanus on, xii; myth and, xii
Duat, 10

Ea, 41; Damkina and, 35; as earth deity, 28–29; powers of, 33–34; as wisdom deity, 33
Earth deity: Chinese, 173; Ea as, 28–29; Isis as, 1; Sita as, 211–12, 234–35
Ectypal: defined, xiii

Eden. *See* Garden; Adam and Eve legend
Egg, cosmic, 177–78
Ego: defined, xiv
Egyptian Book of the Dead, 2, 3
Ehud, 51
Einstein, Albert, 49
Ekstasis: of Camilla and Turnus, 138; defined, 84; of Dido and Aeneas, 126; Salome and, 100
El, 47
Electra: Clytemnestra and, 99
Eliade, Mircea, xii–xiii
Elon, 51
Enantiodromia: defined, 123
Enheduanna, 23–24
Enlil, Lord of Wind, 41
Ennead, defined, 4
Enuma Elish, xx, 21–43; archetypal analysis of, 26–43; as creation myth, 21–22; early copies of, 25; ectypal analysis of, 23–26; as New Year's celebration, 22
Esagila, 22, 25; as *imago mundi,* 41
Essenes, 91–93
Esther, 50
Euhemerism, in Chinese mythology, 169
Euripides: life of, 70–71; sacrifice in, 71–73. Works of: *Bacchantes,* 62, 70; *Iphigenia in Aulis,* 69–85; *Medea,* 70
Eurydice, Izanami as, 151
Eve: accomplishments of, 49–50; birth of, 48–49. *See also* Adam and Eve legend
Excrement, as symbol, 159–60
Eye: of Horus, 16; Sacred, 12, 15
Ezekiel, 58, 68

Fable: defined, xvi
Fall of humanity, 49–50
Fate: *genius* and, 116; Juno and, 116
Faust, 17; Herod and, 104
Feces, as symbol, 159–60
Fertility: Hou Ch'i myth and, 179; Indian symbols of, 203; Isis and, 6; Osiris and, 6–7
Fish: cult of, 11; as symbol, 11
Flaubert, Gustave, xxi, 88
Flesh: Isis and, xx; spirit and, 1–20
Floating Bridge, 149–50
Forest, of Great Mother, 220–22
Fu Hsi, 173, 181, 184

Fulvia, 114
Fumiko Enchi, *Masks,* 142

Gaea, 30
Galileo, 49
Garden: of Eden, 49–50; of Hesperides, 36.
    See also Adam and Eve legend
Geb, 5
Gemmio, Empress, 147
Generational revolt, of deities, 29–32
Genmei, 147
Gensho, 147
Ghirlandaio, Domenico, xxi, 88
Gideon, 51
Gnosticism: Ouroboros in, 36; tree of
    knowledge and, 49
Gold: feces and, 160; as symbol, 118
Golden Fleece, 36
Grass, as symbol, 8
Great Mother. *See also* Mother.; forest of, 220–
    22; of Indus Valley, 203; Isis as, 10; Taoist
    notion of, 170, 178–79

Hadd, 47
Hadrian, 114
Hair, as symbol, 8
Hammurabi, 24
Han dynasty, 175, 180
Hannah, barrenness of, 50
Han P'in, 175
Hanuman, 231–32
Han Wu ti, 189
Harpalyke, 132
Harvest prayer, 166–67
Hathor, 148
Hatshepsut, 3
Head, as symbol, 8
Heaven; Mother of, 1; Rock-Cave of, 162
Heber, 63–66
Heine, Heinrich: *Atta Troll,* 88
Helen of Troy, 81
Heliopolis, 3
Hellenization, of Middle East, 88–89
Heng-O, xxi, 169, 193–95, 241
Heraclitus, 109; *enantiodromia* in, 123
Hermaphroditism. *See* Androgyny
Hermeneutics, xviii
Hermopolis, 3
Herod Antipas, 87–88, 90–91; as antihero,

101; Faust myth and, 104; John the Baptist
    and, 100–101; voyeurism of, 103
Herodias, 87–110, 240; archetypal analysis of,
    93–110; ectypal analysis of, 88–93; John
    the Baptist and, 93–94; marriage of, 991; as
    mother figure, xxi; *Walpurgisnacht* and, 88
Herodotus, xii, 25
Herod Philip, 91, 94
Herod the Great, 89–90
Hesperides, Garden of, 36
Hierodule, 226–27
Hinduism: caste system of, 204; creation myth
    of, 41; cults of, 204; sacrifice in, 72
Hippolytus, Artemis and, 74
Hippopotami, battling of, 15
Ho, Lady, 175
Holy Eye, 12, 15
Holy Ghost: *Ka-mutef* and, 14
Homer, 27; *Iliad,* 69
Horace, 113
Horse, as symbol, 120. *See also* Stallion
Horus: Atum and, 13; birth of, 5, 12; as divine
    child, xvii; Female, 1; Isis and, 12–13, 16;
    myth of, 2; nursing of, 6; as Ptah, 4;
    punishment of, 1; restoration of, 14–15;
    role of, 12–13; Seth and, 14–17; Trinity
    and, 14
Hou Ch'i myth, 173, 179–80
Hsia dynasty, 173
Hsi Wang Mu, xxi, 169, 185–93, 241
Hu: Shu and, 177
Hubris: Agamemnon's, 69, 78; John the
    Baptist and, 107; sacrifice as, 69
Huldah, as prophet, 50
Humanity, creation of, 41–42
Hun, as symbol, 124–25
Hun-tun, 177
Hurricane, creation of, 38
Huysmans, Joris-Karl, xxi, 88
Hypsipyle, Queen, 132
Hyrcanus, 89

Ibzzan, 51
Incest, among Egyptian royalty, 2
Individuation, defined, xv
Indra, as atmospheric god, 30
Initiation rite: Brauronian, 75, 77; Iphigenia's,
    82
In (male) principle, 149

Iphigenia, xx, 240; as *parthenos,* 76–82; sacrifice of, 69, 82–85; wedding of, 82
Iris: Dido and, 130
Isaac: Abraham and, 72
Isaiah, as prophet, 58
Ishtar, Gate of, 23
Isis, xx, 1–20, 239; androgyny of, 5; archetypal analysis of, 5–20; birth of, 5–6; characteristics of, 1; as cow, 1, 16; as cultural symbol, xvi, 1; decapitation of, 14–17; Diodorus on, 2; drama of, 20; ectypal analysis of, 2–5; as Egyptian monarch, 7; fertility and, 6; as Great Mother, 10; headdress of, 1; Horus and, 12–13; as kite, 11; miracles of, 5; moon and, 6; names of, 1–2; Nile floods and, 6; nursing and, 6, 9; Plutarch on, 2; power principle and, 17–20; Ra's poisoning and, 18–19; as scorpion, 1, 37; as swallow, 9; Tiamat vs., 42–43; totemism and, 9; Virgin Mary and, 14; worship of, 1
Islam, xvii, 41
Iusas, 4
Izanagi/Izanami, 149–52; Orpheus/Eurydice as, 151

Jade, significance of, 173–74
Jael, as heroine, 63–66
Jainism, 204
Jair, 51
Janaka, King, 212–14, 231
Jatayu, 224, 231
Jephthah, 51
Jeremiah (prophet), 58
Jericho, 47
Jesus: as divine child, xvi; as messianic myth, xvii; on Pharisaism, 92; sacrifice by, 62, 72. *See also* Christianity
Jezebel, 99
Jimmu Tenno, 165
Jito Tenno, 147
Joan of Arc, Deborah as, 46, 68
John the Baptist, 87, 105–10; as archetype, 106; beheading of, 105, 109; cult of, 88; Herod Antipas and, 100–101; Herodias and, 93–94; hubris and, 107
Josephus, Flavius, 93, 95, 105; *Jewish Antiquities,* 90, 91, 101, 106; *The Jewish War,* 87

Joshua: as charismatic leader, 56; as military ruler, 45, 47
Judaism: creation myth in, 41; hellenization movement in, 88–89; matriarchal aspects of, 48, 50; patriarchal aspects of, 48; sacrifice in, 72
Judas Iscariot, 105
Judas Maccabaeus, 89
Judge: Deborah as, 51, 56–58; defined, 51
Judith, 50
Julian Laws, 115
Jung, C. G.: amplication method of, xviii; on collective unconscious, xiii, xviii–xix; on Dido, 131; four psychic functions of, xv; on God's need for humanity, 52–53; on myths, xii; transcending gender and, xix
Juno, 115; Aeneas and, 116; characteristics of, 116; Dido's temple to, 121
Jupiter: Aeneas and, 116

Ka: defined, 3; origin of, 4
Kaikeyi, 215–17
Kali, 203
Kami, 143; domain of, 149, 151
Kami Yamato Ihare-biko, 165
Ka-mutef, 13–14; Holy Ghost and, 14
Kao-Tsu, 175, 180, 181
Kataribe: defined, 147
Kausalya, 215, 219
Khu: defined, 9
Kingu, 37; punishment of, 41–42
Kish, 23
Kishar, birth of, 28
Kite: Isis as, 11
Kogyoku Tenno, 147
Krishna, 224
Kuan shih yin tzu tsai. *See* Kuan Yin.
Kuan Yin, xxii, 169–70, 196–98, 241
Kung-kung, 182–83
K'un Lun, 187
Kusa, 235
Kyrene, 132

Lahamu, 28
Lahmu, 28
Lakshmana, 217–18, 222
Lakshmi, 202, 211
Lao Tzu, 179, 204; *Tao Te Ching,* 40, 170, 200

Lappidoth, 46
Latinus, King, 133
Lava, 235
Lavinia: Turnus and, 133
Leto: Artemis and, 73
Lévi-Strauss, Claude, xiii
Li Chi, 174
Lieh-Tzu, Book of, 190
Life: elixir of, 188; Lady of, 1; Vase of, 20;
    waters of, 30
Lingam: as phallus, 213; yoni and, 225
Lion, as symbol, 36, 37
Liu An, *Huai-nan Tzu*, 182–84
Liu Chi, 180
Livia, 114, 115
Logos: creation myths and, 41; doctrine of, 4;
    Isis and, xx; spirit and, 1–20
Lotus, Horus's eyes as, 16
Love: Lady of, 1; lingam/yoni and, 225
Lü, Empress, 175
Lucifer, 229
Luini, Bernardino, 88

Maat, 14
Maccabaeus, Judas, 89
Maecena: Augustus and, 113
Magpies, Song of, 175
Mahabharata, 208
Mahavira, 207, 223
Malinowski, Bronislaw, xii
Mallarmé, Stéphane, xxi
Mandala, city as, 210–11
Manu, Laws of, 210
Marduk, xx; as *Deus Faber,* 21; king worship
    of, 22–23; Temple of, 22, 25, 41; against
    Tiamat, 37–40
Margins, Mistress of, 76
Mariamme II, 91
Marica, 228
Marlowe, Christopher, 112
Mars: Camilla and, 135
Mary. *See* Virgin Mary.
Massenet, Jules, xxi, 88
Mater dolorosa: Tiamat as, 32–38. *See also*
    Mother
Matriarchy: patriarchy vs., 38–43
Mauryan dynasty, 204
Maya, 226–29
Medea, 122, 128

Memphis, 3, 4
Menelaus, 78
Menes, 4
Mercury: Aeneas and, 126–27
Mer-Neith, 3
Metabus, King, 133–35
Miao-Chuang Wang, 196
Miao-shan, 196–97
Miraculous birth: Isis and, 5–7
Miriam, 50
Mirrors, in Shinto, 164
Moksa, 235
Moon deity: Artemis as, 74; Ch'ang-O as,
    193–95; Isis as, 6; Thoth and, 11; Tsuki-
    yomi-no-mikoto as, 153
Moreau, Gustave, xxi, 88
Moses: as charismatic leader, 56; as divine
    child, xvi; as messianic myth, xvii; Philo
    Judaeus on, 89; Rama and, 214; Sargon
    and, 23
Mother: as castrator, 87; of Heaven, 1;
    Herodias as, xxi; Hsi Wang Mu as, 185;
    Isis as, 10; Sheng Mu as, 198; of Sisera, 66–
    68; Tethys as, 27; Tiamat as, 21, 23, 26–
    29. See also *Mater dolorosa;* Great Mother
Mother/daughter identity, 99–100, 240
Mount Ephraim, 57
Mount Meru, 30
Mount Tabor, 53, 55
Mu, King, 190–91
Mummu, 27; as Apsu's adivsor, 31; creation
    myth and, 28; imprisonment of, 34
Myrine, 132
Mythology: defined, xv–xvi; Lévi-Strauss on,
    xiii
Myths: allegories vs., xii; cosmogonic, Eliade
    on, xii–xiii; as cultural symbols, xvi;
    defined, xii; dreams and, xii; experience of,
    xvi; functions of, xvii; modern relevance
    of, xix–xx; psychic projections on, xviii;
    reality factor in, xii; religion and, xii–xiii;
    structures of, xv; time in, xv

Nabi: defined, 58, 68
Nabopolassar, 24
Name: secret, of Ra, 18–19; unknown, of
    power, 17
Nanna, 148
Naomi, 50

Narada, 208
Nash, Thomas, 112
Nebuchadnezzar, 24
Nefertari, 3
Nefertiti, 3
Nephthys, birth of, 5
Net: as symbol, 38, 40; in *Tao Te Ching*, 40
New Year's celebration, xvi; *Enuma Elish* as, 22
Nietzsche, Friedrich: *Thus Spake Zarathustra*, 109
Nihongi, 147–49
Nile floods, 6–7
Nose, as symbol, 154
Nu Gua. *See* Nü-Kua.
Nü-Kua, xxi, 169, 241; as creator/savior, 181–85
Numinosum: defined, xiv
Nun, 3
Nut, birth of, 5
Nü Wa. *See* Nü-Kua

Oceanus, 27
Octavian, 111; after Caesar's death, 112; Herod the Great and, 90; Julian Laws and, 115; wife of, 114
Omohi-kane, 164–65
Orpheus, Izanagi as, 151
Osiris: birth of, 5; Diodorus on, 2; dismemberment of, xvi, 10–11, 16; as Egyptian monarch, 7; fertility and, 6–7; murder of, 7–8; Plutarch on, 2; Ra and, 11; resurrection of, 11–14; Tree of Life and, 8–9; Trinity and, 14
Othniel, 51
Ouroboros, 36
Ovid: *Art of Love*, 115

Pan Gu, 178
Paris (Trojan prince), 120
Parshvanatha, 204
Parthenos, Iphigenia as, 76–82
Parzival, 64
Patriarchy: in Chinese society, 177; matriarchy vs., 38–43
Paul, Saint, 59
Peaches: Feast of, 188–89; of immortality, 196
Peer Gynt, 159
Penthesilea, 137

Pericles, 71
Persephone: Amaterasu and, 163; Demeter and, 99
Personal unconscious. *See* Unconscious, personal
Phaedra, 122, 128
Phallus: in Confucianism, 170, 185; as jeweled spear, 150; lingam as, 213, 225; Osiris's, 10; tree as, 8–10
Pharisees, 91–92
Philo Judaeus of Alexandria, 89; *Apology for the Jews*, 93
Pigs, as sacrifice, 89
Pi-hia yüan-kün, 169, 241
Pilate, Pontius, 90–91
Pillar, *djed*, 8–9
Pimiko (shaman), 146
Plato, 204; on dance, 77–78; *Phaedrus*, 109; *Symposium*, 71
Pliny, 93
Plutarch: on Isis and Osiris myth, 2, 6, 7, 12, 20; *Lives of Illustrious Men*, 105
Pneuma: Amaterasu and, 158; Aneas and, 130
Polyxena, 85
Pompey: Caesar and, 89
Power principle: Isis and, 17–20
Prajapati, 27
Pratt, Annis, xix
Projections, psychic, xviii
Prometheus, 17; hubris of, 37
Propertius, 113
Prophet, 204; Deborah as, 58–59
Psyche, crime of, 152
Psychic differentiation, xv
Ptah: Horus as, 4; worship of, 4
Ptolemies, 88, 89
Puella, Salome as, 99, 104
Punic Wars, 111, 116
Purcell, Henry, 112
Pure Land Sutra, 143–44, 172
Purification ritual: Izanagi's, 153
Purusha, 27, 72, 204
Pygmalion, 117

Ra, 148; as Atum avatar, 3; as creator, 17–18; Female, 1; litany of, 18; Osiris and, 11; sacred eye of, 12; secret name of, 18–19; worship of, 18
Rachel, 50

Rakshasa, 227–30

Rama: as hero-king, xxii; Moses and, 214; Sita and, 201, 211, 241; teacher of, 222–24

Ramayana, xxii, 201–37; virginity in, 227

Ramses, 2, 15

Ravana, 227–31

Rebeka, 50

Religion: myths and, xii–xiii

Religious: defined, xvi

Revelation, Book of, 21–22

Rhea, 30

Ruh, as wind/spirit, 38

Rupprecht, Carol S., xv

Ruth, 50

Sacred Eye, 12, 15

Sacrifice: in Christianity, 72; in Euripides, 71–73; Greek, 85; in Hinduism, 72; as hubris, 69, 78; human, 174; of Iphigenia, 82–85; in Judaism, 72; pigs as, 89

Sadducees, 91, 92

Saharanika, 207

Sakaki tree, 162

Sakti worship, 203, 206, 211

Salome, xxi, 87–110, 240; archetypal analysis of, 93–110; as archetype, 98; dance of, 87–88, 95, 97; ectypal analysis of, 88–93; as *puella,* 99, 104; *Walpurgisnacht* and, 88

Samsara: defined, 143; Wheel of, 36

Samson, 51

Sanghamitra, 207

Sarah, 50

Sarashina, Diary of, 141

Sargon the Great, 23–24; Moses and, 23

Sarpanit, 42

Scintillae, 49

Scipio Africanus, 114

Scorpion: Horus and, 14–15; Isis and, 1, 37; poison of, 19; as symbol, 37

Scorpion-man, 36, 37

Seleucid kings, 88, 89

Sempronia, 114

Serpent, 36; Apophis, 18; in Garden of Eden, 49; Isis as, 1; as symbol, 36

Serqet, 37

Seth: birth of, 5; characteristics of, 7; Horus and, 14–17; Osiris and, 7–8, 10; as thunder, 17

Seti I, 13

Shadow: defined, xiv

Shakespeare, William, 49

Shaman, 146

Shamash, 148

Shamgar, 51

Shamshu, 148

Shang dynasty, 173–74, 180

Shang ti, 17, 174

Shan Hai Ching, 199

Sheng Mu, 198

Shen Nung, 173

Shi chi, 173

Shih ching, 179

Shinto: mirrors in, 164; women in, 143

Shiva, 203, 204

Shotoku, Prince, 148

Shu: Hu and, 177; origin of, 4–5

Shu Ching, 173

Siegfried's treasure, 36

Sisera, 46, 53–54, 54, 55; Jael and, 63–65; mother of, 66–68; as Parzival, 64

Sita, 201–37, 241; abduction of, 227–32; birth of, 212–13; initiation of, 220–27; marriage of, 213–15; ordeal of, 232–34; as perfect wife, xxii; quest for, 231–32; as Rama's teacher, 222–24; redemption of, 235–36; return of, 234–35

Snake. *See* Serpent

Socrates, 204

Sokar, 13

Sol, 148

Song of Roland, 126

Sophocles, 70

Sparagmos, 83

Spirit: flesh and, 1–20; Isis and, xx; wind as, 38, 158

Ssu-ma Ch'ien, 173, 174

Ssu-ma Hsiang-ju, 187–88

Stallion: Amaterasu as, 155; Dido's, 125; as omen, 121; as symbol, 120. *See also* Horse

Strauss, Richard: *Salome,* xxi, 88

Suetonius, 105

Suiko, Empress, 147–48

Sujin, Emperor, 165

Sulis, 148

Sun goddess. *See* Amaterasu

Sunna, 148

Surpanakha, 227
Susano-wo: Amaterasu vs., 153–58; birth of, 153; cult of, 167; role of, 154
Suttee, 207–8
Swallow, Isis as, 9
Sword: Susano-wo's, 156, 158
Sychaeus, 117–19
Symbols: cultural, xvi. *See also specific types*

Tablet of Destinies, 40
T'ang dynasty, 182
Tantric cult, 206
Tao-hsüan, 196
Taoism, Great Mother in, 170, 178–79
Tao Te Ching, 170, 200; nets in, 40
Tefnut, 3; origin of, 4–5
Temenos, 222
Temmu, 146–47
Tengu, 154
Teresa, Saint, 228
Thales, 27
Thebes, 3, 5
Thet, 1
Thethys, 27
Thoth: characteristics of, 11; as Ptah, 4
Thunder: Hadd as, 47; Seth as, 17
Tiamat, xx, 239–40; as archetype, 43; as avenger, 36; as destroyer, 21–22; dismemberment of, 40–41; as dragon, 21, 26; inertia of, 29; Isis vs., 42–43; as life force, 32; Marduk against, 37–40; as *mater dolorosa,* 32–38; as primordial mother, 21, 23, 26–29; revolt against, 31–32; son of, 27; transformation of, 21–22
Tian Wen, 184, 187
Ti K'u, 173, 179
Time, in myths, xv
Titian: Herodias/Salome myth and, xxi, 88
Tiy, 3
Toad, three-legged, 194–95
Tola, 51
Toneri, Prince, 147
Totemism: Isis and, 9
Tou-mu, 196
Transformation rituals, weaving as, 161
Tree: cassia, 194; of knowledge, 49; peach, 188–89; as phallus, 8–10; Sakaki, 162
Tree of Life: Osiris myth and, 8–9

Trinity: Mary and, 14
Trojan War, 70
T'sai Yen, 176
Ts'ai Yung, 176
Tsuki-yomi, 153
Turnus: Camilla and, 133, 136; *ekstasis* of, 138

Unconscious: personal, xiv. *See also* Collective unconscious
Unknown Name of Power, 17
Untouchables, women as, xx
Upanayana, 207
Upanishads, 38, 204, 233, 237
Uranus, 30
Utu, 148

Vaideha, 219
Valmiki: *Ramayana,* 201–37
Vardhamana Mahavira, 204
Varuna, 27, 30
Vase of Life, 20
Vedas, 203–4; study of, 206–7; water in, 27–28
Venus, 115; Aeneas and, 111, 112; Dido and, 122
Virgil: death of, 113; *Aeneid,* xvi, xxi, 111–39
Virginity: in *Ramayana,* 227; Ti K'u and, 179–81
Virgin Mary: Isis and, 14; nursing by, 6; Trinity and, 14
Vishnu, 202, 204, 211
Visvamithra, 213
Volsunga Saga, 138
Voyeurism: Herod and, 103
Vritra, the dragon, 30
Vulture, Isis as, 1

Walpurgisnacht, 88
Water: Apsu and, 26; creation myths and, 26–28; of life, 30; Tiamat and, 26
Weaver, Amerterasu as, 161–64
Wheel of Samsara, 36
Whirlwind, creation of, 38
Whitehead, A. N., 109
Wilde, Oscar, xxi, 88
Wind: Artemis and, 76; evil, 40; Lord of, 41; as symbol, 38

Wisdom: Ea and, 33; tree of knowledge and, 49

Womb, as symbol, 43

Women: in ancient Egypt, 2–3; in ancient Greece, 70–71; archetypes of, xx; in Asian religions, 143–44, 172; Chinese kingdom of, 199–200; divine child myth and, xvii; in Judaism, 48, 50; as untouchables, xx; worship of, xix–xx

Wu, King, 198

Xenophon, 71

Xerxes' dream, xii

Yahweh: as patriarchal abstract, 48; as protector-god, 56

Yajnavalkya, 207

Yasumaro Futo no Ason, 147

Yi, Divine Archer, 193

Yin dynasty, 173

Yin/yang, 149, 170, 171, 176; creation of, 178

Yoga, 204

Yomi, Land of, 151–52

Yo (female) principle, 149

Yü the Great, 173, 199–200

Zacharias, 109

Zadok, 92

Zarathustra, 204

Zeus, 30; Artemis and, 73; Baal and, 89

Ziggurat, 24